D1828487

Kohlhammer

Maike Maria Domsel/Maurice Steffens (Hrsg.)

Compassion als Schlüssel für eine zukunftsfähige Bildung nachhaltiger Entwicklung?!

Auftrag und Weiterentwicklung eines theologischen Prinzips

Verlag W. Kohlhammer

Die Publikation wurde mit finanzieller Unterstützung des Stiftungszentrums des Erzbistums Köln gedruckt.

1. Auflage 2024

Alle Rechte vorbehalten
© W. Kohlhammer GmbH, Stuttgart
Gesamtherstellung: W. Kohlhammer GmbH, Stuttgart

Print:
ISBN 978-3-17-043138-6

E-Book-Format:
pdf: 978-3-17-043139-3

Für den Inhalt abgedruckter oder verlinkter Websites ist ausschließlich der jeweilige Betreiber verantwortlich. Die W. Kohlhammer GmbH hat keinen Einfluss auf die verknüpften Seiten und übernimmt hierfür keinerlei Haftung.

Dieses Werk einschließlich aller seiner Teile ist urheberrechtlich geschützt. Jede Verwendung außerhalb der engen Grenzen des Urheberrechts ist ohne Zustimmung des Verlags unzulässig und strafbar. Das gilt insbesondere für Vervielfältigungen, Übersetzungen, Mikroverfilmungen und für die Einspeicherung und Verarbeitung in elektronischen Systemen.

Inhaltsverzeichnis

Vorwort

Liebe Leser*innen,

mit diesem Sammelband wird das Ziel verfolgt, zwei theologisch-gesellschaftliche Strömungen miteinander zu verbinden. Insbesondere in Zeiten des sozialen Wandels, der Vielfalt an Weltanschauungen und der zunehmenden Notwendigkeit erhöhter Ambiguitätskompetenz ist es von größerer Bedeutung als je zuvor, sich selbst und seine Handlungen auf persönlich validierte und gesellschaftlich akzeptierte Wertvorstellungen zu stützen. Hierbei lassen sich zwei gesellschaftliche Anliegen in Besonderem herausfiltern, die einen genuin theologischen Ursprung haben und gleichsam als vortheologische und vorspirituelle Dimensionen das gegenwartsgesellschaftliche Leben prägen: soziale Verhaltensbereitschaften und nachhaltiges Leben. Beides wurde durch die Corona-Pandemie und ihre Nachwirkungen zum gesellschaftlichen Brennglas, welches die Notwendigkeit einer konsensfähigen Grundlage compathischer und nachhaltiger Werte akzentuiert. Insbesondere in schulischen Kontexten wird dies deutlich, wo einerseits die Forderungen der heutigen Schüler*innen-Generation nach einer nachhaltigen Gestaltung des Alltags- und Schullebens immer lauter werden, andererseits jedoch wenig Kompromissbereitschaft und Aushandlungskompetenz vorhanden sind.

Die vorliegende Ausgangslage lenkte unsere Aufmerksamkeit auf die theologischen Paradigmen der Compassion und der Verantwortung für die Schöpfung, welche längst über das genuin Christliche hinausgehen und zu einer multikulturellen und interkonfessionellen Grundlage des postmodernen Zusammenlebens geworden sind. Infolgedessen stellt sich für die Religionspädagogik die bedeutende Frage, welchen Beitrag der (Religions-)Unterricht sowie das schulische Leadership von (Religions-)Lehrkräften leisten können, um den Schüler*innen bei der Ausbildung einer ethisch fundierten Grundhaltung inmitten dieser vielfältigen Paradigmen zu unterstützen.

Bonn und Tönisvorst im Winter 2023

Maike Maria Domsel und Maurice Steffens

Nachhaltigkeit als vortheologisch-compathisches Paradigma? – Auftrag und Weiterentwicklung eines theologischen Prinzips

Maike Maria Domsel & Maurice Steffens (geb. Andree)

> „Wir brauchen engagierte Menschen, die sich auf den Weg machen und die Debatten über neue, nachhaltige Formen des Wirtschaftens und des Lebens führen, damit wir den kommenden Generationen eine bessere Welt hinterlassen.“[1]

Nachhaltiges Leben, verbunden mit den Ausdrücken der *Zeitenwende* oder des *kein Weiter-so* entwickeln sich in den letzten Jahrzehnten immer stärker zu einer neuen konsensfähigen Wertegrundlage. Während genuin christliche Wertevorstellungen schon lange keine Selbstverständlichkeit postmoderner Gesellschaften mehr darstellen, wird der Ruf nach einer tragfähigen und konsensfähigen Wertebasis im Hinblick auf eine gelingende und sichere Zukunftsgestaltung immer lauter. Die immer größer werdende Diversität an Weltanschauungen und die hiermit einhergehenden Ungewissheiten sowie Ambivalenzen, das Dasein betreffend, lassen das Individuum verstärkt nach dem suchen, was tragfähig ist und Sicherheit für eine gelingende Zukunft darbietet. Gerade diese Suche hinsichtlich der Zukunft verbindet die verschiedenen gesellschaftlichen Strömungen und Kulturen scheinbar als kleinsten gemeinsamen Nenner. Es vermittelt den Anschein, dass diese Suchbewegung zu einer Form postmoderner-gemeinschaftsstiftender Ethik[2] wird, welche in ihrer kollektiven Erscheinungsform dazu beitragen kann, Krisen zu bewältigen.[3]

Nachhaltigkeit scheint hierbei das Leitbild dieser Suchbewegung zu sein. Trotz anhaltender Diffusität des Begriffs sowie der in diesem enthaltenen Kanon von Werten und Normen erfährt die Nachhaltigkeit als normatives Leitbild eine hohe gesellschaftliche Akzeptanz.[4] Wenn Greta Thunberg in ihrer Rede auf dem

---

1 Bundesministerium für Umwelt, Naturschutz, Bau und Reaktorsicherheit (BMUV) / Umweltbundesamt (UBA): Umweltbewusstsein in Deutschland, Berlin: Publikationsversand der Bundesregierung 2017, 7.

2 Ethik wird in diesem Kontext als Theorie der menschlichen Lebensführung und des menschlichen Umgangs mit Ereignissen verstanden.

3 Vgl. Andree, Maurice / Domsel, Maike Maria: Die Paradigmen der Compassion und Freiheit als Bindeglieder zwischen Theologie und Ethik? Möglichkeiten spirituell-reflexiver Praxis im schulischen Kontext, in: ÖRF 30 (1/2022), 110–127, 113 und 117. DOI: 10.25364/10.30:2022.1.7

4 Vgl. Birkel, Simone: Warum wir dran sind. Lernen für ein zukunftsfähiges Leben, in: KATBL 144 (3/2019), 177–181, 178.

Weltwirtschaftsforum in Davos die führenden Wirtschafts- und Politikexpert*innen mit den Worten „I want you to act as you would in a crisis. I want you to act as if the house was on fire. Because it is."[5] zum Handeln auffordert, stellt kaum einer die Tatsache infrage, dass der Umwelt- und Klimaschutz zu den grundlegenden Bedingungen nachhaltigen Lebens und damit zu einer der zentralen Zukunftsaufgaben gehört. Wenn der Papst in seiner Sozialenzyklika *Laudato si' - Über die Sorge für das gemeinsame Haus* aus einem sozialökologischen und katastrophentheoretischen Ansatz heraus zur Reflexion des Menschen-, Welt-Schöpfungs- und Gottesverständnis und damit einhergehend zur Umkehr aufruft, einen ökotheologischen Zukunftsansatz formuliert[6] und von den Grünen sogar als Öko-Papst bezeichnet wird,[7] muss zwangsläufig der Zusammenhang zwischen Nachhaltigkeit und Religion genauer hinterfragt werden. Handelt es sich bei den beschriebenen Suchbewegungen doch um solche spiritueller Art,[8] insbesondere im Sinne einer vortheologischen und unideologischen Größe? Bedarf der Mensch gerade in Krisenzeiten, in denen er gezwungen ist, Altes und Vertrautes loszulassen und sich mit einer bedrohlich gewordenen Realität abzufinden,[9] nicht gerade spiritueller Deutungsangebote von Welt und Mensch? An dieser Stelle soll das Forschungsfeld des vorliegenden Sammelbandes präziser umrissen werden. Wir sehen die Aufgabe des vorliegenden Werkes darin, der Frage nachzugehen, ob das Paradigma der Compassion in seiner Weiterentwicklung, angepasst an die Herausforderungen der Zeit, als Schlüssel für eine zukunftsfähige, nachhaltige Lebensgestaltung und Bildung dienen kann. Dabei orientieren wir uns an christlichen Suchbewegungen, die ein gerechtes, mitfühlendes, solidarisches, friedliches und verantwortungsbewusstes Leben anstreben.

Compassion von Metz bis zu den neueren Entwicklungen

Das Paradigma der Compassion hat die Theologie der Gegenwart maßgeblich beeinflusst und betont die Bedeutung von Mitgefühl und Solidarität in Theologie

---

5 THUNBERG, Greta: Rede in Davos vom 25. Januar 2019.

6 Vgl. VOGT, Markus: ein neues Kapitel der katholischen Soziallehre, in: KATBL 144 (3/2019), 173.

7 Vgl. ALTMEYER, Stefan / STOCKINGER, Helena: Ökologisches Lernen IST religiöses Lernen, in: KATBL 144 (3/2019), 167.

8 Als spirituelle Suchbewegungen werden in diesem Kontext Formen der Selbsttranzendenz und Sinnsuche, welche transzendentale Bezüge aufweisen, verstanden. Vgl. HELLER, Birgit: Spiritualität versus Religion / Religiosität?, in: HELLER, Birgit / HELLER, Andreas (Hg.): Spiritualität und Spiritual Care. Orientierungen und Impulse, Bern: Hogrefe 2014, 47–49.

9 Vgl. ROEBBEN, Bert: Volharden in de broosheid. Spiritualiteit in tijden van corona, Antwerpen: Halewijn 2020, 28 und 71–73.

und Gesellschaft. Es hat die Art und Weise verändert, wie Theolog*innen über die Rolle der Kirche in der Gesellschaft denken und trägt zur wissenschaftstheologischen Diskussion bei, indem es nahelegt, dass das Leiden der Unterdrückten und Marginalisierten die Stimme Gottes in der Welt bezeichnet.

Der Begriff „Compassion" wurde primär von dem Fundamentaltheologen Johann-Baptist Metz vor dem Hintergrund eines empathischen Monotheismus und einer leidempfindlichen Gottesrede geprägt und kann aus dem Englischen oder auch dem Französischen am ehesten als „Mitleidenschaft" übersetzt werden. Metz möchte daran erinnern, dass Jesu Blick nicht der Sünde, sondern vor allem dem Leid der Menschen galt, insbesondere jenen, die kaum wahrgenommen oder gesellschaftlich benachteiligt wurden (vgl. Lev 19). Metz betrachtet Compassion nicht als bloß passives Mitgefühl, sondern als aktive Solidarität und tätige Mitleidenschaft mit den Armen und Schwachen. Seine Betonung der Bedeutung von Leid und Schmerz als Quellen des Verständnisses und des Mitgefühls hat zu einer Neubewertung dieser Aspekte in der christlichen Theologie geführt und die Bedeutung von Mitgefühl und Solidarität hervorgehoben. In diesem Kontext ist beachtenswert, dass Compassion nicht nur Christ*innen anspricht: Als vortheologische und unideologische Größe ist eine empathische und compathische Spiritualität richtungsweisend für die Zukunft des Menschen, denn sie kann gläubige, spirituelle und areligiöse Menschen vereinen.[10] Compassion schickt uns – so Metz – „an die Front der politischen, der sozialen und kulturellen Konflikte in der heutigen Welt. Fremdes Leid wahrzunehmen und zur Sprache zu bringen, ist die unbedingte Voraussetzung aller zukünftigen Friedenspolitik, aller neuen Formen sozialer Solidarität."[11] Hier geht es um den Abbau von Vorurteilen und falschen Bildern vom anderen und auch um das Bemühen, in Bildungsprozessen aufzuklären, um „engagierte[...] Mitmenschlichkeit,

---

10 In diesem Kontext ist beachtenswert, dass Regina Polak den Einsatz für Gleichheit und Gerechtigkeit als Kernthemen der drei monotheistischen Weltreligionen ansieht. Hierzu gehört die Gleichheit aller Menschen in ihrer Würde, der Einsatz für eine gerechtere Gesellschaft, vor allem für Arme und Marginalisierte sowie der verantwortungsvolle Umgang mit Macht; vgl. POLAK, Regina: „(...) die unendliche Vielzahl, die das Gesetz der Erde ist" (Hannah Arendt). Warum die Auseinandersetzung mit religiöser Vielfalt (über)lebensnotwendig ist. Interdisziplinäre Perspektiven auf eine globale Herausforderung, in: KROBATH, Thomas / LINDNER, Doris / PETSCHNIGG, Edith (Hg.): ‚Nun sag, wie hast du's mit der religiösen Vielfalt?'. Zwischen Konflikt und Kompetenz in Kindergärten, Schulen und Jugendarbeit, Wien: Schriften der Kirchlich Pädagogischen Hochschule Wien/Krems, 2019, 11–37, 37.

11 METZ, Johann Baptist: Compassion. Zu einem Weltprogramm des Christentums im Zeitalter des Pluralismus der Religionen und Kulturen, in: DERS. / KULD, Lothar / WEISBROD, Adolf (Hg.): Compassion. Weltprogramm des Christentums. Soziale Verantwortung lernen, Freiburg – Basel – Wien: Herder, 2000, 9–20, 13–14.

die Leiden, welcher Art und aus welchem Grund auch immer, nicht einfach indifferent hinnimmt.“[12] In Einklang mit einem solchen Compassion-Verständnis im Sinne von Mitleidenschaft, unterscheidet sich dieses dezidiert von dem problematischen Begriff des Mitleids, welcher eher eine asymmetrische Beziehung beschreibt, eine „Haltung von Starken gegenüber Schwachen.“[13] Compassion hingegen meint das Streben nach Gleichberechtigung und einer Kommunikation, welche möglichst auf Augenhöhe stattfinden sollte.

Das Paradigma der Compassion hat zahlreiche Fortführungen und Anwendungen in der Gegenwart gefunden und zu neuen (theologischen) Ansätzen geführt, die sich auf soziale Gerechtigkeit, Umweltethik und interreligiöse Zusammenarbeit konzentrieren. Initiativen, die auf dieser Leitidee basierten, widmeten sich anfangs jedoch mitnichten den Herausforderungen der Erderwärmung und der Klimakrise. Vielmehr bestand das allgemeine Ziel darin, eine Kultur des Mitgefühls in der Gesellschaft zu etablieren und positive soziale Beziehungen zu fördern, um zu einem harmonischen und friedlichen Zusammenleben beizutragen. Dabei sollten Mitgefühl und Empathie als zentrale gesellschaftliche Werte gestärkt werden, sowohl in Bezug auf das eigene Selbst als auch auf andere.[14] Zu den Zielgruppen gehören sowohl Jugendliche als auch Erwachsene in unterschiedlichen Bereichen wie Bildung, Medizin und Pflege. Entsprechend geht es bei der Umsetzung des von Lothar Kuld in den 90er Jahren des Letzten Jahrhunderts ins Leben gerufene „Compassion-Projekt“ für den schulischen Bereich, welches hier meist als „Sozialpraktikum“ bezeichnet wird, nicht lediglich um die Möglichkeit eines Berufspraktikums, sondern auch und vor allem um die Entwicklung von Mitgefühl und Empathie gegenüber den betreuten Personen in Einrichtungen wie Krankenhäusern, Alten- und Pflegeheimen. Hierdurch kann diese Erfahrung auch für die Schüler*innen selbst zu einer bereichernden emotionalen, sozialen und möglicherweise auch spirituellen Erfahrung werden.[15]

---

12 Kuld, Lothar: Art. Compassion (2016), in: Das wissenschaftlich-religionspädagogische Lexikon im Internet, online im Internet: https://www.bibelwissenschaft.de/fileadmin/buh_bibelmodul/media/wirelex/pdf/Compassion__2020-04-29_14_56.pdf, [abgerufen am 27.11.2021, 23.33 Uhr].

13 *Kuld* 2016 [Anm. 12], 2.

14 Metz, Johann Baptist: Compassion. Weltprogramm des Christentums, Freiburg – Basel – Wien: Herder, 2000.

15 Vgl. Weisbrod, Adolf / Kuhn, Franz / Hirsch, Friedrich: Compassion – Ein Praxis- und Unterrichtsprojekt sozialen Lernens. Menschsein für andere, in: Engagement. Zeitschrift für Erziehung und Schule 1994 (H. 2–3), 268–307.

Nachhaltigkeit als Zeichen der (Post)-Moderne

Das Konzept der Nachhaltigkeit hat sich in den letzten Jahrzehnten zu einem zentralen Thema in Politik, Wirtschaft und Gesellschaft entwickelt. Es beruht auf der Idee, dass unsere Handlungen heute so gestaltet sein sollten, dass sie auch künftigen Generationen eine lebenswerte Zukunft ermöglichen. Im heutigen Verständnis umfasst Nachhaltigkeit nicht nur ökologische, sondern auch soziale und ökonomische Aspekte.[16] Ausgangspunkt für das gegenwärtige Verständnis von Nachhaltigkeit ist die Brundtland-Kommission, die 1987 den Bericht „Our Common Future" veröffentlichte. Hierin wurde Nachhaltigkeit als „eine Entwicklung, die die Bedürfnisse der Gegenwart befriedigt, ohne zu riskieren, dass künftige Generationen ihre eigenen Bedürfnisse nicht befriedigen können"[17] definiert. Diese Definition umfasst somit sowohl ökologische als auch soziale und ökonomische Aspekte und betont die Bedeutung langfristiger Perspektiven. In der Folgezeit wurde Nachhaltigkeit vor allem als ökologisches Konzept verstanden, das sich auf den Schutz natürlicher Ressourcen und die Bewahrung der Umwelt konzentriert. Dies änderte sich jedoch in den 1990er Jahren, als die sozialen und ökonomischen Aspekte von Nachhaltigkeit stärker in den Fokus rückten. So wurden beispielsweise im Rahmen der Agenda 21, die auf der Rio-Konferenz 1992 beschlossen wurde, Ziele für eine nachhaltige Entwicklung formuliert, die ökologische, soziale und ökonomische Aspekte gleichermaßen berücksichtigen.[18]

Gegenwärtig umfasst das Verständnis von Nachhaltigkeit vor allem die zuletzt genannten drei Dimensionen, wobei jedoch weiterhin Diskussionen darüber bestehen, wie diese in der Praxis umzusetzen sind. In der ökologischen Dimension geht es vor allem um den Schutz und die Bewahrung der natürlichen Ressourcen, um langfristig eine lebenswerte Umwelt für alle zu gewährleisten. In der sozialen Dimension stehen Themen wie Gerechtigkeit, Chancengleichheit und Armutsbekämpfung im Vordergrund, mit dem Ziel eine nachhaltige Gesellschaft zu schaffen, in der möglichst alle Menschen ein gutes Leben führen können. In der ökonomischen Dimension geht es darum, ein nachhaltiges Wirtschaftssystem zu entwickeln, das nicht nur auf kurzfristige Gewinnmaximierung, sondern auch auf langfristiger Stabilität und Ressourcenschonung ausgerichtet ist.[19]

---

16 Vgl. Leal Filho, Walter / Azul, Anabela Marisa (Hg.): Handbook of sustainability science and research. Cham: Springer, 2021.

17 World Commission on Environment and Development (WCED): Our Common Future. Oxford: Oxford University Press 1987, 8.

18 Vgl. WCED Agenda 21: Programme of Action for Sustainable Development. United Nations 1992.

19 Vgl. UN General Assembly: Transforming our world. The 2030 Agenda for Sustainable Development. Resolution adopted by the General Assembly on 25 September 2015. A/RES/

Im Rahmen von Natur- und Gesellschaftswissenschaften wird Nachhaltigkeit als interdisziplinäres Konzept verstanden, das sich mit der Bewahrung der natürlichen Ressourcen, dem Schutz der Biodiversität, dem Klimaschutz, der sozialen Gerechtigkeit sowie der wirtschaftlichen Stabilität beschäftigt. Um Nachhaltigkeit zu erreichen, müssen alle Aspekte des menschlichen Handelns berücksichtigt werden. Ein diesbezüglich zentrales Konzept für die Umsetzung von Nachhaltigkeit stellt das Prinzip der „nachhaltigen Entwicklung" dar. Hierbei geht es darum, ökologische, soziale und ökonomische Aspekte miteinander in Einklang zu bringen und langfristig zu etablieren. Herausforderungen ergeben sich jedoch dadurch, dass oft unterschiedliche Interessen und Ziele miteinander vereinbart werden müssen, was nicht selten zu Konflikten und Schwierigkeiten führt.

In der politischen Diskussion wird Nachhaltigkeit oft als Leitprinzip für die Entwicklung von Gesellschaft und Wirtschaft genannt. So hat die UNO im Jahr 2015 mit der Agenda 2030 für Nachhaltige Entwicklung einen umfassenden Plan angelegt, in dem 17 Nachhaltigkeits- bzw. Entwicklungsziele herausgearbeitet wurden, zu denen unter anderem der Schutz der Umwelt, die Bekämpfung von Armut und Hunger sowie die Verbesserung der Bildungschancen gehören.[20]

Der Beitrag der rBNE in Verbindung mit dem Compassion-Gedanken

Religiöse Bildung vermag einen wichtigen Beitrag zur Förderung einer nachhaltigen Entwicklung zu leisten, da sie dazu beitragen kann, das Bewusstsein für Umweltprobleme und soziale Gerechtigkeit zu schärfen und moralische Werte wie Verantwortung, Mitgefühl und Nachhaltigkeit zu fördern. Als vortheologische und nicht-ideologische Größe kann eine empathische und compathische Spiritualität richtungsweisend für die Zukunft des Menschen sein, weil sie gläubige, spirituelle und sogar nicht-religiöse Menschen vereinen kann. Dieses verbindende und kommunikationsfördernde Potenzial könnte zudem im Kontext des schulischen Leaderships zum Tragen kommen. Dort, wo klassische Leistungsprinzipien eingetauscht werden gegen einen subjektorientierten Blick auf den Menschen mit dem Ziel einer guten Zukunft, ist sowohl der Compassion-Gedanke verwirklicht wie auch eine nachhaltige Entwicklung am Menschen selbst. Hierbei kommt dem Religionsunterricht und den (Religions-)Lehrkräften eine besondere Vorbildfunktion zu, weil sie sich auf professionelle Weise mit

---

70/1.https://www.un.org/ga/search/view_doc.asp?symbol=A/RES/70/1&Lang=E, [abgerufen am 27.11.2021, 23.33 Uhr].

20 Vgl. UNITED NATIONS: Transforming our world: The 2030 Agenda for Sustainable Development. New York: United Nations 2015.

existenziellen Fragen, mit spirituell-religiösen Deutungsmustern und Reflexionen bezüglich einer guten Zukunft von Welt und Mensch befassen. So kann der theologische Compassion-Gedanke beispielsweise wesentlich zum sozialen Lernen beitragen und dessen spirituell-religiöse Dimensionen vor dem Hintergrund einer christlichen Liebesethik beleuchten. Wenn diesbezügliche Reflexionen über den genuin religiösen bzw. religionspädagogischen Kontext hinaus fortentwickelt werden, ist es möglich, eine denkerische Verbindung zu den Sustainable Development Goals der Unesco herzustellen.[21]

Mithin kommt dem Ethik- und Religionsunterricht und der dort eingelagerten rBNE die essenzielle Aufgabe zu, Schüler*innen darin zu unterstützen, sich mit der vorgefundenen Diversität auf verantwortungsvolle und profunde Weise auseinander zu setzen und sich in dieser individuell verorten zu können.[22] Gleichzeitig muss betont werden, dass der Ethik- und Religionsunterricht dies nicht alleine leisten können, sondern ein nachhaltiges und zukunftsfähiges Lernen nur in interdisziplinären, partizipativen und generationsübergreifenden Lernkontexten erfolgen kann. Dennoch weist gerade der Religionsunterricht Schlüsselkompetenzen auf, die sowohl als religiöse Kompetenzen, wie auch als Nachhaltigkeitskompetenzen verstanden werden können und ermöglicht somit einen vereinfachten Zugang zum Perspektivwechsel und somit zum Umdenken, weg von einer Moralisierung hin zu einer Motivation und Verinnerlichung.[23] Compassion und rBNE weisen somit die gleiche Zielperspektive auf: Den Graben zwischen Wissen und Handeln zu überbrücken und die Scheu – vor dem Versuchen den Graben zu überbrücken – zu nehmen.

Resüme: Nachhaltigkeit und Compassion

Der Zusammenhang zwischen dem Paradigma der Compassion und Nachhaltigkeit liegt in der gemeinsamen Zielsetzung einer positiven Veränderung und nachhaltigen Entwicklung: Compassion bezieht sich auf die Etablierung einer mitfühlenden und empathischen Haltung, die dazu beitragen kann, gesellschaftliche Probleme zu lösen und positive Veränderungen herbeizuführen. Nachhaltigkeit zielt darauf ab, eine lebenswerte Zukunft für alle Menschen zu schaffen, indem ökologische, ökonomische und soziale Aspekte berücksichtigt werden.

Das Paradigma der Compassion kann dazu beitragen, dass Menschen eine stärkere Sensibilität für soziale und ökologische Herausforderungen entwickeln und bereit sind, sich aktiv für Nachhaltigkeit einzusetzen. Eine mitfühlende und empathische Haltung kann dazu führen, dass Menschen ein tieferes Verständnis

---

21 Vgl. ANDREE / DOMSEL 2022 [Anm. 3], 113–114.

22 Vgl. Ebd.

23 Vgl. BIRKEL 2019 [Anm. 4], 178–180.

für die Bedürfnisse und Interessen anderer haben und bereit sind, auf deren Bedürfnisse Rücksicht zu nehmen. Eine solche Kompetenz umfasst einen wesentlichen Aspekt der Nachhaltigkeit, da eine wirklich nachhaltige Entwicklung nur dann möglich ist, wenn die Interessen aller Beteiligten compathische Berücksichtigung finden.

Insgesamt erfordert die Postmoderne eine Neuorientierung unseres Verständnisses von Nachhaltigkeit, die sich auf eine ganzheitliche Sichtweise und alternative Wissensformen einlässt, sowie auf eine Veränderung unserer Lebensweisen und gesellschaftlichen Strukturen abzielt und eine Verbindung mit spirituellen und ethischen Werten herstellt. Um eine solche modifizierte bzw. erweiterte Perspektive auf Nachhaltigkeit zu entwickeln, sind Sichtweisen vonnöten, welche die Komplexität und Verwobenheit von Mensch und Natur berücksichtigen. Dieser Sammelband möchte mögliche modifizierte und erweiterte Sichtweisen aufzeigen, indem die nachfolgenden Beiträge ihren je spezifischen Zugang zu dem Verhältnis von Compassion und (r)BNE aufzeigen. In dem ersten Teil des Sammelbandes soll das Verhältnis fachtheoretisch ergründet werden, indem *Willem Marie Speelmann* im Kontext der Bildung eine zweideutige Natur des Mitgefühls zwischen immanent-menschlichem Mitleid und transzendent-göttlichem Erbarmen am Beispiel franziskanischer Spiritualität diskutiert; *Lothar Kuld* der Frage nachgeht, was der spezifische Beitrag des Christentums zu BNE sein kann; *Bert Roebben* den moralpädagogischen Diskurs der letzten 50 Jahre hinsichtlich der Notwendigkeit moralischer Bildungsprozesse rekonstruiert; *Maike Maria Domsel* Compassion als Untersuchungsperspektive postkolonialer Strukturen anwendet, um einen Perspektivwechsel und Transformationsprozesse zu evozieren und *Christian Feichtinger* potenzielle Probleme eines zu optimistischen Empathieansatzes aus moralpsychologischer Perspektive betont.

Im zweite Teil des vorliegenden Sammelbandes wird der Fokus auf Beispiele transformatorischen Handelns gelegt, indem *Peter Ramers* aufzeigt inwieweit compathisch-soziale Seiten Bestandteil buddhistischer Lebensweisen sein können; *Asfa Widiyanto* die Herausforderungen indonesisch-islamischer Bildung im Hinblick auf die Vermittlung von Mitgefühl und religiöser Mäßigung untersucht; *Lukas Wiesenhütter* die Rolle von Narrativen im interreligiösen Gespräch und im Hinblick auf die Komparative Theologie der Compassion analysiert; *Kathleen Clark und Alexander Rödlach* die Anleitung amerikanischer Studierender der Gesundheitsberufe mithilfe des Metz'schen Compassionskonzepts zur Entwicklung eines mitfühlenden beruflichen Habitus erläutert und *Janieta Bartz* Compassion als Schlüssel zu einem neuen Verständnis von Behinderung betont.

Der dritte Teil will abschließend der Anwendung des untersuchten Verhältnisses auf die schulische Praxis Rechnung tragen, indem *Annika Krahn* die Symbiose (religions-)unterrichtlicher Verbindung von Compassion und dem Capability-Approach nach Nussbaum zur Ausbildung emotional-sozialer Kompetenzen untersucht; *Maurice Steffens (geb. Andree)* das sinnstiftende und gesellschaftliche

Potenzial des gemeinsamen Erzählens im Kontext des Religionsunterrichts untersucht; *Daniela Zahneisen* im Kontext des ethischen Lernens an Dilemmata das Potenzial von Compassion und rBNE im Hinblick auf den konstruktiven Umgang mit Mehrdeutigkeit aufzeigt; *Nina Frenzel* in einem Werkstattbericht über die aktuellen Bestrebungen des Erzbistums Köln zur Verknüpfung von rBNE und Verbraucherbildung in der Religionslehrer*innenbildung berichtet; *Christina Steffens* am Beispiel des Schulgartens aufzeigt, wie Ansätze der Montessoripädagogik die intrinsische Motivation der Schüler*innen für Naturschutz mit der Ausbildung einer compathisch-ethischen Wertegrundlage verbinden kann; *Jennifer Jakob und Martin Rothgangel* die Wahrnehmung von Compassion als religionspädagogische Schlüsselkategorie bei österreichischen Religionslehrkräften untersuchen und *Mevlida Mešanović* die Auseinandersetzung muslimischer Schüler*innen mit dem Compassion-Gedanken im islamischen Religionsunterricht skizziert.

Literatur

Altmeyer, Stefan / Stockinger, Helena: Ökologisches Lernen IST religiöses Lernen, in: KATBL 144 (3/2019), 165–167.

Andree, Steffens / Domsel, Maike Maria: Die Paradigmen der Compassion und Freiheit als Bindeglieder zwischen Theologie und Ethik? Möglichkeiten spirituell-reflexiver Praxis im schulischen Kontext, in: ÖRF 30 (2022) 1, 110–127. DOI: 10.25364/10.30:2022.1.7

Birkel, Simone: Warum wir dran sind. Lernen für ein zukunftsfähiges Leben, in: Katechetische Blätter (2019) 3, 177–181.

Heller, Birgit: Spiritualität versus Religion / Religiosität?, in: Heller, Birgit / Heller, Andreas (Hg.): Spiritualität und Spiritual Care. Orientierungen und Impulse, Bern: Hogrefe, 2014, 45–68.

Kuld, Lothar: Art. Compassion (2016), in: Das wissenschaftlich-religionspädagogische Lexikon im Internet, online im Internet: https://www.bibelwissenschaft.de/fileadmin/buh_bibelmodul/media/wirelex/pdf/Compassion__2020-04-29_14_56.pdf, [abgerufen am 27.11.2021, 23.33 Uhr].

Leal Filho, Walter / Azul, Anabela Marisa (Hg.): Handbook of sustainability science and research. Cham: Springer, 2021.

Metz, Johann Baptist: Compassion. Weltprogramm des Christentums, Freiburg: Herder 2000.

Metz, Johann Baptist: Compassion. Zu einem Weltprogramm des Christentums im Zeitalter des Pluralismus der Religionen und Kulturen, in: *Ders.*: Compassion. Weltprogramm des Christentums. Soziale Verantwortung lernen, Freiburg/Basel/Wien: Herder, 2000, 13–14.

Polak, Regina: „(...) die unendliche Vielzahl, die das Gesetz der Erde ist" (Hannah Arendt). Warum die Auseinandersetzung mit religiöser Vielfalt (über)lebensnotwendig ist. Interdisziplinäre Perspektiven auf eine globale Herausforderung, in: Krobath, Thomas / Lindner, Doris / Petschnigg, Edith (Hg.): ‚Nun sag, wie hast du's mit der religiösen Vielfalt?'. Zwischen Konflikt und Kompetenz in Kindergärten, Schulen und Jugendarbeit, Wien: Schriften der Kirchlich Pädagogischen Hochschule Wien/Krems, 2019, 11–37.

United Nations: Transforming our world: The 2030 Agenda for Sustainable Development. New York: United Nations, 2015.

UN General Assembly: Transforming our world: The 2030 Agenda for Sustainable Development. Resolution adopted by the General Assembly on 25 September 2015. A/RES/70/1. https://www.un.org/ga/search/view_doc.asp?symbol=A/RES/70/1&Lang=E.

ROEBBEN, Bert: Volharden in de broosheid. Spiritualiteit in tijden van corona, Antwerpen: Halewijn, 2020.
VOGT, Markus: ein neues Kapitel der katholischen Soziallehre, in: KATBL 144 (3/2019), 172–176.
WCED. Agenda 21: Programme of Action for Sustainable Development. New York: United Nations, 1992.
WEISBROD, Adolf / KUHN, Franz / HIRSCH, Friedrich: Compassion – Ein Praxis- und Unterrichtsprojekt sozialen Lernens. Menschsein für andere, in: Engagement. Zeitschrift für Erziehung und Schule 1994 (H. 2-3), 268–307.
WORLD COMMISSION ON ENVIRONMENT AND DEVELOPMENT (WCED): Our Common Future, Oxford: Oxford University Press, 1987.

Sonstige Quellen

THUNBERG, Greta: Rede in Davos vom 25. Januar 2019.

Teil I

Compathisch-empathische Spiritualität und ihre fachtheoretische Begründung

Pity and Mercy – The Human and Divine Poles of Compassion

Willem Marie Speelman

Auf der Suche nach einer Kultur des Mitgefühls im Kontext der Bildung wird die zweideutige Natur des Mitgefühls diskutiert. Es gibt nicht nur falsches und wahres Mitgefühl, sondern auch einen Unterschied zwischen einer immanent-menschlichen und einer transzendent-göttlichen Seite, zwischen Mitleid und Erbarmen.

Das Wort Compassion drückt die geheimnisvolle Fähigkeit unseres immanentesten Wesens aus: dass unser Fleisch das, was geschieht, genauso spürt wie das Fleisch eines anderen. Als vollkommener Mensch fühlte Jesus die Leiden und Freuden der anderen. Wenn jemand von uns ganz Mensch werden will, wird er oder sie dies tun, indem er oder sie sich auf Beziehungen des Mitgefühls einlässt. In der Erinnerung an diese Beziehungen wird das Selbst geweckt. Aber Jesus war auch ganz Gott und hat die Leiden und Freuden in der Perspektive des göttlichen Reiches überwunden. Er löste nicht die Probleme, wie wir es in unserer heutigen Kultur versuchen, sondern öffnete den Menschen die Augen für dieses andere Geheimnis, die göttliche Barmherzigkeit. Und obwohl Jesus seine Nachfolger ausgesandt hat, um dasselbe zu tun, können wir ihm darin nur folgen, wenn wir die göttliche Natur der Barmherzigkeit respektieren.

Wahre Barmherzigkeit ist ein göttliches Werk, das von Menschen ausgeführt wird, die wissen, dass dieses Werk ihre Fähigkeiten übersteigt. Wahre Hilfe ist nicht der Versuch, Probleme zu lösen, sondern im Dienst präsent zu sein, wo Leid und Freude im Licht des menschlichen und göttlichen Geheimnisses transzendiert werden. Als Beispiel für diese Praxis werden mehrere Geschichten von Franz von Assisi erörtert, die mit seinem berühmten Sonnengesang schließen.

Spiritualität; Franz von Assisi; Barmherzigkeit; Werke der Barmherzigkeit; Bildung

In search of a culture of compassion in the context of education, the ambiguous nature of compassion is discussed. Not only does false versus true compassion exist, but there is also a difference between an immanent-human and transcendent-godly side, pity and mercy.

The word compassio expresses the mysterious capacity of our most immanent being: that our flesh senses that what happens just like someone else's flesh does. As fully human, Jesus felt the sufferings an joys of others. If anyone of us wants to become fully human, he and she will do this by engaging in relations of compassion. In the remembrance of these relations the self is awakened. But Jesus was also fully God, and transcended the sufferings and joys in the perspective of the divine Kingdom. He did not solve the problems, as we try to do in our present culture, but opened people's eyes for this other mystery, the divine mercy. And although Jesus sent His followers to do the same thing, we can only follow Him in this by respecting the divine nature of mercy.

True mercy is a divine work, carried out by humans who know that this work transcends their abilities. True aid is not an attempt to solve problems, but to be present in the service where suffering and joy are transcended in the light of human and divine mystery. As an example of this practice, several stories of Francis of Assisi are discussed, closing with his famous Canticle of the Creatures.

Spirituality; Francis of Assisi; Compassion; Works of Mercy; Education

A theology of compassion

A ninety-five-year-old sister told me that in the year in which she was to start her training to become a nurse she became seriously ill and was hospitalized for six months: "In those six months I learned more about nursing than from any book or training program." If you know where it hurts, and how that feels, you know where and when your nourishment is needed. That is how true compassion works. I learned this because the sister told me her story, and she learned it because something had happened to her. But people tend to forget things easily, do not listen to the stories of old sisters, or have other ways of numbing their natural bodily sensitivity to the suffering and the welfare of others. Therefore, it would be good to develop a culture in which stories such as these are shared and appropriated as valuable memories. Any human culture must remember that the 'passive activity' of empathy for the suffering and welfare of others is an essential human capability. In search for such an "anamnetic-culture" – from the Greek *anamnesis*, remembrance – the German theologian Johann Baptist Metz developed a theology of compassion.[1]

A theology of compassion would enhance the development of this anamnetic or remembering culture, not only by prohibiting the waning of attention for the suffering of others, but by leading a sustained attention to God, or the ultimate Mystery of our shared life here on earth. The background question of Metz, the so-called theodicy – "Why, if there is an almighty and good God, is there suffering in the world?" – is not an issue here. The issue here is how Jesus encountered the "negative Mysterium" of suffering as fully human and fully God,[2] and why it is so important to remember Him when we consider the value of compassion. I will try to explain this.

---

1 METZ, Johann Baptist: Memoria passionis. Ein provozierendes Gedächtnis in pluralistischer Gesellschaft, Freiburg: Herder, 2006. For some reason, theologians and philosophers tend to focus only on the negative side of empathy with suffering, but it is also important to be capable of sharing the happiness of the human you are communicating with. Is not this sharing of enjoyment what squares up the beauty of music?

2 For suffering as a "negative Mysterium," see METZ 2006, 21. For a Christological approach Metz refers to RAHNER, Karl: Jesus Christus – Sinn des Lebens (Schriften zur Theologie XV.),

In the Christian story, God became flesh in Jesus,[3] and as human flesh He shared the human propensity to joy and suffering. Jesus knew how it felt to be thirsty, or ignored, but also how it felt to be caressed. And, as Metz writes, He first felt these sensations in His flesh when confronted with the sufferings and enjoyments of others and responded to it with mercy; only then would He possibly warn against sins.[4] Is this not the natural order of perception? The sensations of the flesh precede any judgment; the flesh senses directly, and responds directly, and only then – after the signals have been processed by the brain – judgments may follow. Common judgment helps us avoid suffering and seek enjoyment. This usually means that people immediately search for the 'sins' that led to suffering and gather the 'virtues' that result in enjoyment. However, being not only human but also the Son of God – which I believe Jesus Christ to be – Jesus was able to respond in a different, merciful way. He perceived all the sensations of human life in the perspective of the coming Kingdom of God. He could feel the pain and the joy and at the same time the reality in which pain and enjoyment could be transcended. Instead of solving all people's problems, He was near to them in their joys and sufferings, showing mercy and asking others to continue to do so (Mt 25:31–46). This clarifies why there is a need for a theology of compassion. The memory of the story of Jesus – Metz calls this *memoria passionis* – not only urges us to pay sustained attention to the suffering in the world but also shows us ways of responding differently. Instead of immediately attacking all troublesome situations with our coping mechanisms – which often make matters worse – the remembrance of His story helps us to respond with our active presence and with a perspective of the good life within every situation.

I will argue that in the *memoria passionis,* we need to distinguish between human and divine cooperation. A true *memoria passionis* is fulfilled in prayer, for whereas humans know where it hurts, only God knows how to heal the wounds. This is not to say that humans cannot help, or that problems should not be solved. But ultimately, human solutions will fail or will be mere gestures to *show* mercy; for only God, the Merciful One can turn passion into the good life. I will exemplify this distinction as a different approach to reality, in which the "negative Mysterium" of suffering is indeed approached as a mystery instead of a

---

Zürich u. a.: Benziger, 1983, 206–216. who proposes that the role of Christ can start from His experiences as a human being, "realizing classical Christology in an existential way."

3 With flesh, 'chair' in French, I refer to the German 'Leib', which is the body as a living being. The body, French 'corps', German 'Körper', is the physical reality, but the flesh refers to its living, seeing, hearing, touching capabilities, et cetera. HENRY, Michael, Incarnation: Une philosophie de la chair, Paris: Seuil, 2000, 29: "Ainsi s'énonce une définition d'un homme invisible en même temps que charnel – invisible en tant que charnel." ["Thus, a definition is expressed of a human, invisible at the same time as carnal – invisible as carnal," trans. WMS].

4 METZ: 2006 [note 1], 163: "Jesu erster Blick galt nicht der Sünde der Anderen, sondern dem Leid der Anderen."

problem. A problem demands to be solved, a mystery asks for your presence. But first I will investigate the *memoria passionis* as a way of awakening the self of the human individual and of learning about life from and with others. Finally, I will present the *memoria passionis* as practiced by Francis of Assisi, and where it brought him. Remembering Jesus at all moments in his life, "following in His footprints" (1Pet 2:21), Francis discovered along the road that this memory opened him up to the brotherhood of all creatures. When he went out wishing peace to all, not only humans but also other creatures returned this peace and showed themselves as compassionate beings. Francis recognized all men and women, animals, enemies (Muslims), and finally all creatures as brothers and sisters. I will explore some stories in which compassion opened the road for Francis to endless brotherhood. In his *Canticle of Brother Sun,* also known as *Canticle of the Creatures,* we can follow how the human capacity of *Einfühlung* with all creatures allows us to resonate with their lives.

Memoria passionis as an awakening of the self to life

The remembrance of Jesus's suffering is, according to Metz, a dangerous memory.[5] Not because His suffering could also happen to you, but because the active remembrance opens your "buffered self" to the suffering of others.[6] When someone gets to you, you feel danger. Your body will react defensively, your flesh will try to recover from the impressions of the encounter (even if it was a nice one), and your 'self' will be awakened, for it is the 'I' who senses the impressions.

To explain this first reaction, I refer to the philosopher Michel Henry, who developed a phenomenology of the flesh, in which any encounter with the other will leave impressions in the flesh.[7] An impression is not yet an experience, and only later becomes a thought or a word; initially, it is the simple sensation of what happens. As a natural reaction, the flesh tries to heal any 'wound' that seems to threaten its innocent existence. The flesh is inexplicably capable of healing most of its wounds. However, the first response to an impression will be a feeling of danger. Secondly, the impression will become a meaningful experience that connects one with other people and with life. This is a natural response

5 METZ, Johann Baptist: Facing the World. A Theological and Biographical Inquiry, in: *Theological Studies* 75:1 (2014), 29.

6 The Canadian philosopher Charles Taylor speaks of the modern self as a "buffered self", a self that assures itself that nothing really needs to touch him or her. The modern self can do this by disengaging from reality, so to speak, just as a problem can be placed before us as if it were not our reality and someone else should solve it for us. TAYLOR, Charles: *A Secular Age*, Cambridge and London: Harvard University Press, 2007, 38.

7 HENRY 2000 [note 3].

to a confrontation with suffering, or with enjoyment. It is, however, important that this remembrance is engaged and active and that the one who remembers actually participates in the feeling of the other and is touched by it.

The second reaction, the awakening of the self, is described by Antonio Damasio.[8] This neuroscientist describes the self as a double identity, comprising a nuclear consciousness and an extended consciousness. The nuclear consciousness is summed up by the answer to the question: "Who is feeling what is happening right now?" – "I". It is a self without a past, a future, or a story, for it is only the recipient of the sensations of what touches the flesh now. The extended or autobiographical consciousness grows out of all these sensations of the flesh, by weaving them actively into a story, and eventually into a life story in which "I" is the hero: this is "me", with my past, my future, my successes, and my sins. It may be expected that especially the autobiographical self will feel danger when something happens that might threaten its reputation or even its life. But this double identity shows that there is always a relation, a communion between an individual's forgetting and forgiving soul and a public person with a story.

It is worrying that so many scientists treat the human being as an isolated self and that the awakened soul has so far been ignored. The isolated self experiences reality as an 'outside' otherness, which is initially approached as a danger, and thus as a problem that needs to be removed (until it has been appropriated and adapted to the flesh: *my* land, *my* people). The memory of the suffering of others, however, begins with the growth of the self in encounters. It is the memory that awakens me, not only as a self and an autobiographical self, but also in communion. When the first human – the Hebrew word '*adam*', connected with *dam* (blood) and *adamah* (soil) signifies human – met the first woman, he shouted: "Flesh from my flesh!" It was like saying: "I am not alone, for you are another, and yet if you hurt your toe, I know how that feels. We are kin." Remembering the suffering of the other is dangerous, but at the same time it is how one learns to know the other and via the other learns to know him- or herself. And this other may be a human, or God or any creature.

The awakening of the self: facing the other

Someone becomes a human because things happen to him or her and because he or she meets others. The philosopher Martin Buber describes this encounter as the effect of approaching the other a "you." Buber distinguishes two primary words, which are actually word pairs: the one is "I–You" and the other is "I–It".[9]

---

8 DAMASIO, Antonio: The Feeling of What Happens. Body and Emotion in the Making of Consciousness, New York: Vintage, 2000.

9 BUBER, Martin: Ich und Du, Heidelberg: Lambert Schneider, [11]1983.

Most of the time, people live in a world of things, many things, different things; even humans (including me) are considered as things, characteristics, identities. This thing-world, however, is the effect of speaking the other primary word pair: "I–It". The "I" in relation to "you" is different from the "I" in relation to (other) things. An I–You relation is like looking directly into each other's eyes; everything vanishes, it is just you and me in each other's sight. This encounter is an encounter of love and brings forth life. But this direct encounter can only last for a short moment before it turns into an "I–It" reality.[10]

Buber begins his description with a human-to-human encounter, but also includes possible encounters with other creatures and with God. According to Pope Francis, the human being lives in three fundamental or vital relations: with other humans, with the divine, and with the environment.[11] And indeed, the human can approach God as You (by speaking the primary word pair I–You) or as It or He (by speaking the other primary word pair: I–It). When we discuss whether God exists, we speak the primary word pair I–It: we question the existence of God and the answer is 'yes' or 'no.' But when we pray, the existence of God is not a question, but a dialogue or an invocation: "Are you there? Will you answer me?"[12] People can pray to God without believing that He exists (as a being, as an "It"). This is also true of human relationships with their fellow humans and their environment. We can talk with people and plants, speaking the primary word pair "I–You", or talk about them ("I–It").

All three relations are mutual: even without a language, the dog or the tree communicates with us, *as* dog and *as* tree, and in response, the human gives them names corresponding to their self-communication (cf. Gen 2:19). The same is true of our relationship with God, who communicates with us, and in response, we name Him in correspondence with His self-communication: "the Light", "the Eternal", "the Merciful".[13] Yet, in all three relations, if we approach the other in an encounter, we can never be sure whether or not we will get the desired response.

Discussing the double identity (Damasio), the I–You relationship (Buber), and the three fundamental or vital relationships (Pope Francis), it may be clear

---

10 Buber does not explain this. But after reading Michel Henry, one might understand this short moment as a natural reaction of the body, which cannot stand the intensity of the impressions of the encounter and withdraws (cf. Buber 1983 [note 9], 17.). Then it becomes a lonely 'I' and speaks the primary word I–It.

11 Pope Francis: Second Encyclical Laudato Si', 2015,66. https://www.vatican.va/content/frances-co/en/encyclicals/documents/papa-francesco_20150524_enciclica-laudato-si.html [accessed February 28, 2023].

12 Close to the thoughts of Buber are those of the French philosopher and playwright Gabriel Marcel, for example in his Journal métaphysique, Paris: Gallimard, 1927. Translated by Katharine Farrer in Gabriel, Marcel: *A Metaphysical Diary*, in: idem, Being and Having, Glasgow: University of Glasgow, 1949.

13 Only when Moses asks God His name, he receives as an answer that God is not all those things, but "I am who I am: an I in relation to you." (Ex 3:13–14).

that humans are *not* individuals, but relationships. I become 'I' because of you, I cannot be separated from nature for my flesh *is* nature, and I am related to the divine Mystery. Ultimately, there is a shared self in everything, a "we", a communion in which life, as well as vulnerability and brotherhood are shared. This means that an encounter is a return to an original memory: *memoria* is a remembrance of what was never lost.

Learning in encounters

The basic life act in encounters is turning towards the other[14] and tuning in with each other. After the encounter, impressions are left in my flesh. These impressions awaken my consciousness and become experiences, good or bad, and eventually evolve into strategies for new practices and stories. Through encounters I learn, and my autobiographical self grows and weaves a life story. The tuning-in is described by the theologian Kees Waaijman, who defines spirituality as a human-divine interaction in which both the human and the divine become (trans)formed.[15] His explicit description of the transforming process of the encounter provides insight into the comprehensive nature of the formation process: a whole life can change because of an encounter. At the same time, is this not true for the structure of any formation? If I approach the things that happen to me as an encounter, that is, interpreting the impressions of these events as messages, teaching me about 'you' as well as myself, we will work a process of formation in mutual interaction.

When Bert Roebben describes his "pedagogy of otherness," he mentions the Latin word from which education derives: *e-ducere*, to lead out. He explains that the formation of the (moral) self is an emancipation, which can be considered as a leading out from diffuse options to a clear, justifiable, and sustainable position.[16] In the context of his proposed practice of learning by encounters, or, as he often quotes Mary C. Boys: "learning in the presence of the other," education may also mean that the individual is momentarily led away from his or her 'buffered self' towards the otherness of the other. This encounter transforms him or her, consciously and unconsciously, and the otherness is appropriated *as* other-

14 BUBER, Martin: Between Man and Man. Translated by Ronald Gregor-Smith, London, New York: Routledge 2004, 26.

15 WAAIJMAN, Kees: Spirituality: Forms, Foundations, Methods. Translated by John Vriend, Leuven: Peeters, 2002, 426.

16 ROEBBEN, Bert: Living and learning in the presence of the other. Defining religious education inclusively, in: International Journal of Inclusive Education (2011), 5. DOI: 10.1080/13603116.2011.552648.

ness. The appropriation of the otherness *as* otherness means growth and learning.[17] But as it is appropriated, this otherness is shared and the individual can sense the other resounding in himself or herself. Encounters lead to the formation of the self-in-communion.

In his description of a child's natural learning process the philosopher Maurice Merleau-Ponty shows that the formation of the responsible self presupposes an encounter with the other on an equal level. Merleau-Ponty accurately describes how a child develops bodily relations with others, and through them, relations with himself or herself. The face is important in this process. It begins with an undifferentiated union between mother and child, with the child not even yet counting its feet as its own. Ultimately, the child naturally follows its mother by bodily imitation and thus starts making movements. Gradually it learns that the maker of those movements is a self. But there is yet no other to respond to. Later, a transition takes place in which the bodily self of the child mirrors itself in the face of another child and discovers in that mirror the space of the "I" as its "double". The child learns to recognize that the other is an "I," and that, by virtue of their mutual relationship, the self is also an "I" to the other. At this stage it is enough to realize that the formation of a responsible self presupposes the encounter on equal ground with the other in terms of a realization that I could have been you, but I am not.

Learning about life, a mystery-based approach

I realize that this is only one way of learning. When someone must learn how to solve problems, another strategy might be more effective. Learning through encounters with otherness is more appropriate when the learning is related to the mysteries of life. A mystery is not a problem, as Gabriel Marcel wrote in his *Metaphysical Diary*.[18] A problem – from the Greek *problema*: thrown forward (in defense) – is something blocking my passage and needs to be resolved so that I can continue my path without any adaptation from my side. A mystery is not before me, but all around me; it does not need to be resolved but asks for my presence and attention. A mystery *can* present itself as a problem, such as, for example, a poor man standing on 'my' path. In such a case, we will call the police to get rid

---

17 Buber 2004 [note 14], 24 – "Certainly in order to be able to go out to the other you must have the starting place, you must have been, you must be, with yourself. Dialogue between mere individuals is only a sketch, only in dialogue between persons is the sketch filled in. But by what could a man from being an individual so really become a person as by the strict and sweet experiences of dialogue which teach him the boundless contents of the boundary?"

18 Marcel 1949 [note 12], 100–121.

of him: "That is in my path, solve my problem!" In this problem-solving approach, we turn this man into an object – from the Latin *objectum*: thrown forward – and this object may be studied in detail. Studying this object, I keep at a distance – things do not get to me, Charles Taylor would say – which allows me to think clearly and act in a controlled manner: to solve the problem, that is, to get rid of it. And what is more, in a problem-solving approach I can ask others to solve it: the government, the industry, and my daddy, always to get rid of my problems.

In a mystery-based approach, this man may have a message for me and ask me to change my life. He needs my attention, and I will get the chance to learn to know him, not only *about* him. This encounter may even change my life. A mystery does not want me at a distance but wants me to be involved. Although I cannot solve your or my shortcomings, a mystery approach allows me to sense them, relate to them, and eventually show mercy. This mercy is not only for the other but comes back to me, for I share the shortcomings in which I am involved. I too am in this situation. The mystery teaches us something about our life, about being human and living with shortcomings.

Learning about life is what Jesus did. Therefore, from the way Jesus taught His disciples, we may learn some elements of the mystery approach in teaching. Jesus did not teach His disciples by telling them what to believe, but by forming a community with them in which they would follow their Lord "in His footsteps" (1 Pet 2:21). This is similar to the example of Merleau-Ponty in which the mother does not tell the child what to do, but offers a *living example,* while the child closely follows her in every movement. Keith Ferdinando mentions two typical features of Jesus's teaching, to which I would add a third in terms of a bodily learning model.[19] First, Jesus taught on occasion. Walking through His environment, He met people with needs and questions to which He responded. His teaching was rooted in the bodily reality of everyday life. In doing so, He always pointed to the coming of the kingdom of God. Thus, He opened the minds of His hearers every time an opportunity arose. Second, Jesus taught with stories. He invited His hearers to engage with the narrative, unlocking a deeper meaning and a new perspective. He urged the hearer to determine his or her own position: "What would I do in such a situation?" Third, and this is the feature that I would like to add, Jesus taught in gestures. By bringing in the outcast, healing the sick, freeing the possessed, and raising the dead, He taught that God's kingdom is a gift of grace to all who open themselves to it. These were gestures and examples of behavior that unlocked a deeper meaning and brought it closer while doing so. But because the meaning of the gesture is a communicative one, his actions were not aimed at solving the problems of exclusion, disease, possession, and death. The message of the gesture is that fulfillment comes from another source. The philosopher Giorgio Agamben writes that the gesture – from

19 FERDINANDO, Keith: Jesus, the Theological Educator, Themelios 38:3 (2013), 360, 74.

the Latin *gerere*, meaning to bear, carry out, demonstrate – is an act done on behalf of someone else.[20] As gestures, the works of mercy can be performed by human hands, but the effect of their actions is in the hands of God. Through bodily imitation of their Lord and Teacher, His disciples learned to become new people and continue his mission, in real-life events, in stories, and in gestures.[21] I shall next focus on the gesture of compassion, and on how man and God cooperate in it, as if it were a sacrament.

The mystery of compassion: a human-divine cooperation

That a human is capable of compassion is in itself a mystery, the mystery of empathy, *Einfühlung*. Because we share the same flesh, I can feel as you feel and thus can come very close to your feeling. When you say: "I feel the sun on my face," I replicate the same sensation as if the sun were shining on my own face. I use my own feelings to get to know your unique and unattainable feeling. It takes imagination to enjoy and suffer with each other, but that imagination is based on our most immanent reality: our feeling body, which we share with every other human. Our immanent flesh is also our ability to transcend ourselves and open up to the suffering and joy of others. True compassion is a sharing of joys and sufferings with others. One senses that the other is hungry, and subsequently one feeds the hungry one.[22]

In the work *Rhetoric*, traditionally attributed to Aristotle, compassion is indeed considered a shared feeling. As compassion is related to the pain that might happen to you, it is connected with fear. Moreover, the degree of pity is proportional to one's sense of connection with the other, whether he or she is of the same sex, age, or status. The suffering of a rich Dutch woman affects a rich Dutch

---

20 *KARMAN*, Giorgio Agamben: A Brief Treatise on Action, Guilt, and Gesture. Translated by Adam Kotsko, Stanford: Standford University Press, 2018.

21 SPEELMAN, Willem Marie, Franciscus van Assisi. Leraar op de wijze van een leerling, in: VAN WIERINGEN, Archibald / KOET, Bart (Hg.): Modellen van Leraarschap: van Jesaja tot Bioshock (Utrechtse Studies XIX), Almere: Parthenon, 2017, 167–188.

22 SAINT AUGUSTINE, De Civitate Dei IX, 5: Quid est autem misericordia nisi alienae miseriae quaedam in nostro corde compassio, qua utique si possumus subvenire compellimur? – Was aber ist Mitleid anderes als das Mitempfinden fremden Elends in unserem Herzen, durch das wir jedenfalls angetrieben werden zu helfen, so weit wir können? Quoted in Historisches Wörterbuch der Philosophie Bd. 5, Darmstadt: WBG, 1980, 1411.

woman more than a poor Senegalese boy, who cannot imagine why she is suffering from these minor things.[23] In his *Poetics*, Aristotle adds another, estheticized, form of compassion. In tragedy, the act is imitated, and the emotion aroused does not incite the spectator to act, but to purge his own emotions.[24] We can recognize this estheticized compassion in the professionalized compassion of an aid worker. A homeless man said that aid workers take good care of his weaknesses, but will never become friends, because they do not share their own.

Compassion, therefore, has a positive and a negative side. It can be a humiliation of the other or a negation of their suffering if one focuses completely on one's own suffering. Compassion can relegate the other person to being pitiful ("Oh poor one, come and be with Mommy!"); it can refer to someone who cannot keep a distance ("I can't stand this, I must intervene immediately! Action! Action!"); it may be a form of self-exaltation ("It's always something with Africa, they can't organize as we do?"); or even a negation of the other (when politicians say "Our thoughts and prayers are with...," while only thinking of their re-election.) These are all examples of false compassion. At best, it tries to solve the suffering of the other as if it were only a problem for the individual or society. But the suffering and the joys of the other are not only a problem, they are also a mystery that bears a message to us: we can be touched by the joys and sufferings of the other. In all its inadequacy, compassion brings to light that all creatures in their humblest, bodily state are intimately connected. True compassion reveals my own weakness in the recognition of the other: "flesh from my flesh".

The true response to this *compassio* – literally 'shared suffering' – is to show mercy. In doing works of mercy, we transcend ourselves. The first transcendence, as we have seen, is not a way up, but down, by feeling the joys and sufferings of the other. Isaiah 53:11 says that the suffering servant will bear the shortcomings of many. We can read this as the figure of the scapegoat. But the suffering servant can also be the one who senses the joys and sufferings of the other in his or her own flesh. He or she is like a doctor who knows what it is like to be sick and therefore has a knowledge that goes beyond the medical literature. A human, sensing his or her own shortcomings, can relate to the shortcomings of someone else; therefore he or she can become a servant of God, for he or she senses where the mercy of God is needed. The human communicates his or her deficiencies to God, and God responds to the deficiencies with mercy. In doing mercy – *facere misericordiam* – which follows the sensing of the other's shortcomings – *compassio* – the human is a servant doing the work of God. The works of mercy in Matthew 25 show why human is needed to sense where mercy must be done: the hungry do not need clothes, but food; the thirsty do not need freedom,

---

23 PSEUDO-ARISTOTLE: Rhetoric, book 2, part 8. See: http://classics.mit.edu/Aristotle/rhetoric.2.ii.html [accessed February 28, 2023].

24 ARISTOTLE, Poetics: section 1, part VI. See: http://classics.mit.edu/Aristotle/poetics.1.1.html [accessed February 28, 2023].

but water. This is active remembrance, to let the suffering get to you and respond to that suffering.

But, again, there is also false mercy. Mercy presupposes superiority. A servant is not merciful toward his master, a child not to his mother. This means that one who dares to call himself merciful considers himself superior to others. Here false mercy can come in, namely, when someone, out of a sense of superiority to another, believes he can overcome the other's deficiencies. A famous businessman said: "Give the people what they want." But the effect of, for example, buying a new iPhone is only that the shortage grows, as soon as another new version comes on the market. A famous writer said: "Forgive, but do not forget." But the effect of this mercy is only that one's superiority over the other grows, and the guilt shall be written on his face. But in a television interview Lilian Gonçalves-Ho Kang You, who was asked if she could ever forgive the people who had killed her husband, said: "Perhaps, forgiveness is too big a word for people."[25]

The works of mercy mentioned in Matthew 25 suppose that we can alleviate the sufferings of other people. But when Jesus commands us to do something, it is often way beyond our capacities: "Love thy enemies" (Lk 6:27); "Love one another as I have loved you" (John 13:34); "And forgive us our debts, as we also have forgiven our debtors" (Mt 6:12); "Heal the sick, raise the dead, cleanse those who have leprosy, drive out demons" (Mt 10:8). And when, in Luke 18, the disciples tell Him that His commandments are impossible to fulfill, He replies: "What is impossible with man is possible with God." And this is the clue. True mercy is a divine work, carried out in gestures by human servants, but gestures always refer back to the Merciful One who initiated the work. True compassion is like a liturgy: it is performed by living human beings, who are considered the body of Christ, and therefore at the same time such acts are performed by the One Christ, Son of God.[26] In the story of the works of mercy, not only the performer, but also the recipient of mercy is Christ: "Whatever you did for one of the least of these brothers and sisters of mine, you did for me" (Mt 25:40). In works of mercy, vital relations are restored, and good life is restored for the earth, the humans, and God.

25 She was interviewed by Hugo Brandt Corstius in the Dutch television program Zomergasten in August 2011.

26 The Constitution of the Sacred Liturgy Sacrosanctum Concilium, no. 7, confirms that it is actually Christ who celebrates the liturgy in and through the bodies of the faithful.

Francis of Assisi: a life of encounters

We have seen that it is important to remember the unique passion of Jesus Christ, who is recognized as fully human and fully God.[27] As a human being, He was capable of feeling how other human beings suffered pain and enjoyed pleasure, and as God, He was capable of forgiving people's sins, healing the sick, and accomplishing the divine works of mercy. Sensing all human shortcomings and at the same time transcending them towards divine perfection, His compassion was not a program aimed at solving all people's problems, but a way of opening up the perspective of the divine mystery, even at the deepest level of life. It is especially the human side of this compassion, which is the mystery of our ability to feel with the feelings of another, that can open up people's "buffered selves" and prepare them for encounters with others, that is, with the otherness of others. In such encounters, we become who we are, and who we are is therefore always a being-in-relations, a communion. Learning from encounters with otherness is an approach to life as a mystery. This learning practice can be recognized in the way Jesus taught His disciples about the advent of the divine mystery in daily life: by seizing the opportunity when it comes, by telling stories, and by making gestures of compassion. Francis of Assisi did exactly this after he decided to follow Jesus in His footprints: he seized the occasions, told stories, and enacted gestures to open up the perspective of the divine mystery. I will choose a few stories to exemplify this and to show how Francis came to expand the *memoria passionis* to all creatures and the Creation in its deepest materiality.

Francis's vocation

The story of Francis's vocation is found in *The Legend of the Three Companions,* a bundle of stories gathered by three of his closest companions and published in 1246. Considering it from the perspective of education, I have rewritten it as a story that I would tell to young people.[28]

> *A gentile count summoned young men to join him in the battle against Apulia. Fame and riches were promised. Young Francis was eager for this. He measured himself in extravagant armor, with money from his father, and set out.*

---

27 Council of Chalcedon (451).

28 For the source see: https://franciscantradition.org/francis-of-assisi-early-documents/the-founder/the-legend-of-the-three-companions/1161-fa-ed-2-page-70 [Accessed, 28 February 2023].

> *One night he had a dream. Someone called him by name and led him to a magnificent palace filled with knightly arms and glittering shields on the walls. Francis asked: "To whom does all this belong?"; The man said, "This belongs to you and your knights."*
>
> *The next morning Francis woke up delighted: "Now I know for sure! One day I will be a great prince!" He continued on his way to join the count. But when he arrived in Spoleto, he felt a little ill. He laid down on his bed, and while half asleep he heard someone speak to him: "Francis, where are you going and what do you hope to find there?" Francis told him of his plans, whereupon the man asked, "Who can do more good for you, the Lord or the servant?"; Francis replied: "The Lord, of course," to which the man said: "Then why do you forsake the Lord for the servant, and the King for the subject?" Then Francis asked: "What do You want me to do, Lord?"; The man said: "Go back to the place where you belong. There you will be told what to do. You must understand the dream you have had differently."*
>
> *Francis returned to Assisi. Henceforth he only wanted to know what the Lord had in mind for him.*

As any young person, Francis followed his dreams, and those dreams were aimed at a better life. But he fell ill and became perhaps a little more sensitive to messages. In the story, the identity of the voice remains unclear. It is Francis who recognizes the Lord in it. The voice asks: "What are you doing?" And when Francis realizes that the Lord is pointing him in a different direction, he asks: "What do You want me to do, Lord?" The voice gives another unclear answer: "Go back to where you belong, and there you will be told what to do." It is worth noting that the voice does *not* say: *I* will tell you what to do; the message can come from any encounter. Francis returns home and decides to do only what the Lord wants of him. It is mostly in one's vital relationships that one learns what is to be done: this is learned in encounters, in stories, and practice. These vital connections include a close relationship with God. This means that there is a mystery and a message in every encounter.

Do not ignore yourself

In the next story, which is from the *Assisi Compilation*,[29] Francis meets a brother who has no compassion for himself, and this is again in my own re-telling of the narrative:

---

29 https://franciscantradition.org/francis-of-assisi-early-documents/the-founder/the-assisi-compilation/1240-fa-ed-2-page-149 [Accessed, 28 February 2023].

In the very beginning, when Francis received his first brothers, they stayed in a shed at Rivo Torto. One night, around midnight, when they were all asleep, one of the brothers cried out: "I'm dying! I'm dying!" Startled and frightened, the brothers woke up. Francis said: "What's the matter, brother? Why are you dying?" The brother said: "I'm dying of hunger." Immediately, Francis told the brothers to set the table, so that they would all eat together. The hungry brother had just entered the brotherhood and afflicted his body excessively. After the meal, Francis said: "My brothers, each of you must consider his own condition. One can live on less food than the other. And I do not want the one who needs more food to try to imitate the other. Rather he should provide his body with what he needs. As we must beware of excessive eating, we must be even more beware of excessive abstinence. The Lord desires mercy and not sacrifice."

Had Francis said, "You must pray and do better," or "You must eat and be quiet," he would have solved the friar's problem and the problem of the brotherhood. The friar's weakness was a problem to be overcome, a challenge, or just a lost battle, but the order of his religious life was intact. However, Francis was touched by the shame felt by the brother who had come up against his limits. And that is not a problem to be solved. The crisis of the brother brought Francis closer to his own limits and the limits of the other brothers. Therefore, he approached the problem as a mystery: the mystery of the shared weakness of the human body. During the shared meal, the hungry brother was welcomed into the circle of brothers who all had their own weaknesses. Then Francis said: "the Lord desires mercy and not sacrifice." Francis showed that there is mercy, but did not do anything. He fulfilled the brother's lack by being sensitive to his hunger and his shame, and by teaching his brothers to be sensitive to one another. But to satisfy his hunger, Francis needed his brothers, the fruits of the earth, and the grace of God. He could only share what he received, for he had nothing. In other words, the person who shows mercy shares the mercy that he or she, through others and Mother Earth, has received from God. The Lord asks that we should be merciful, ultimately, to Him. The weak and hungry brother allowed Francis and his brothers to give back what they had received from the Lord, the Merciful One.

That leper – Christ Himself?

The presence of the Lord in the play of compassion is concealed in the story of Francis and the leper. I read the version of *The Legend of the Three Companions*, no. 11, and again, I am telling it as my own story for present-day young listeners.[30]

> *Mounted on his horse, Francis trekked around the San Damiano area. As he was absorbed in prayer he heard a voice: "If you want to know what I want from you, go and despise as of no value everything to which you have attached yourself and what you have pursued. Everything that you thought you tasted as sweetness until now will be bitter to you."*
>
> *Francis was still under the spell of these words, which he perceived as a beckoning from God when he encountered a leper near Assisi. The mere sight of lepers made him shudder, and usually, he fled from them in disgust. But the beckoning words made him dismount from his horse. He walked up to the leper, gave him a coin, and kissed his hand. Thereupon the leper embraced him and gave him the kiss of peace. Francis then mounted his horse again and continued his ride.*

Thinking about true dialogue, Martin Buber wrote: "For where unreserve has ruled, even wordlessly, between men, the word of dialogue has happened sacramentally."[31] I wonder if he knew this story, for this is exactly what is happening here. The two do not speak a word. The only words spoken are from an unidentified voice that Francis heard during his prayer; again, it was he who identified that voice as the voice of God. It seems as if the encounter was an explanation, or perhaps better, an exemplification of those words: stop dreaming of a high position in this world – Francis was riding a horse, as knights do – and return to the earth where you will learn what to do. The encounter is described in a flow of gestures, performed without hesitation. But if you read with attention (and some knowledge), you may be reminded of the Catholic liturgy. If the faithful approach the Eucharist, they offer their gifts, usually a coin. If the faithful approach the Pope, the vicar of Christ, they kiss his hand. Before the faithful have communion they embrace each other and give the kiss of peace. The leper that Francis met was not just a leper. It is worth noting that both partners in this encounter crossed borders that were forbidden. A leper is excluded from the world, and it is forbidden to approach one, let alone touch one, let alone be kissed by one. The most exciting thing in the story is that Francis mounted his horse and continued his ride as if nothing had happened. Only years later did he remember this as the moment of his conversion.

---

[30] https://franciscantradition.org/francis-of-assisi-early-documents/the-founder/the-legend-of-the-three-companions/1165-fa-ed-2-page-74 [Accessed, 28 February 2023].

[31] Buber 2004 [note 14], 5.

The fierce wolf of Gubbio

On several occasions, Francis learned that animals can also be approached as brothers and sisters. I will tell the story of the Wolf of Gubbio as it appeared in the *Fioretti*, again in my own words.[32]

> *Francis was once staying in the town of Gubbio, when a large, ferocious, and bloodthirsty wolf appeared in the area, devouring not only animals but also people. Everyone was afraid. No one dared to leave the town.*
>
> *Francis had compassion for the people of the town. He decided to go out to the wolf. As soon as the wolf caught sight of him, it ran at Francis with its maw open, growling dangerously. Francis made a sign of the cross over him and said, "Come here, brother wolf, and do me and others no harm." The wolf stopped, let its mouth fall shut, and, tame as a lamb, came to lie at Francis' feet.*
>
> *Francis said, "Brother wolf, you are causing much misery in this area, and you have misbehaved abominably by maiming and killing creatures of God without His permission. Everyone hates you, everyone is afraid of you. But, brother wolf, I want you to make peace with the people. If you promise not to harm them anymore, I promise that they will always feed you. For I do know that you were driven by hunger." The wolf agreed to Francis' words by moving his body and nodding his head. He was ready to obey. Then Francis said, "Brother wolf, do you promise never again to harm any human or animal?" The wolf lifted his right paw and placed it in Francis' outstretched hand. To everyone's dismay, Francis and the wolf walked into town to the marketplace. There Francis addressed the citizens of Gubbio: "Brothers and sisters, it is because of your sins that God allows trials like this. For the voraciousness of this wolf is nothing compared to the hell you deserve! Therefore, return to God and repent. Then God will deliver you from the wolf and hell." The citizens repented of their sins and they promised to take care of the wolf.*
>
> *For two more years, the wolf lived in peace in Gubbio. He went around the houses like a tame animal, going from door to door, without bothering anyone or being harassed by people. Everyone gave him food and shelter. Then he died of old age. And people mourned his death because he reminded them of Francis.*

Everybody knows a 'ferocious wolf' in his or her environment. But let us stick to the story and talk about the animal that does not act like the animal he or she is.

---

32 https://franciscantradition.org/francis-of-assisi-early-documents/the-prophet/the-little-flowers-of-saint-francis/2502-fa-ed-3-page-601 [Accessed, 28 February 2023].

The people of Gubbio only felt their own fear and only saw their own problems. The best solution seemed to be that the wolf must be eliminated. The story tells us that Francis felt two things at the same time to the wolf and the people: anger, because they did not act as God wanted them to, and compassion, because they were clearly out of control. He left his safe space and went out to the dangerous wolf. When the wolf attacked him, he made the sign of the cross. The sign of the cross is a liturgical gesture: it indicates a different approach to reality. If you approach someone from the holy order of the liturgy, there is a chance that the other will conform to that order, because he or she too longs for the peace established in that liturgical order. When there was peace between the wolf and Francis, the latter told him or her the truth: "Your conduct is bad, so everyone hates you; but I feel that you suffer from great hunger. Let us try to restore relations." Francis was even more angry with the people of Gubbio because they did not have a reason for acting so badly, locking themselves up, feeling no compassion for the hungry animal. The people agreed to his peace proposal, incorporating the wolf into their community. But the story tells us more, for the words "placed his right paw in Francis's hand" and "going from door to door" are used to express how a new brother enters into the order and how the friar goes out asking for alms: the ferocious wolf became a friar! The Franciscan brotherhood turns out to be bigger than Francis would have expected.

This story exemplifies what Buber wrote on true dialogue, meaning "... events which open into a genuine change from communication to communion, that is, in an embodiment of the word of dialogue."[33] Wolves and humans do not share the same language, and yet there is an original form of communication possible, namely the exchange of what we have in common as living creatures. From that what is exchanged in our shared vital relationships, in our being-in-communion, people may find words. And that is what Francis did in his *Canticle of the Creatures.*

Sonnengesang or the Canticle of the Creatures

Francis decided to "follow in the footsteps of his Lord". The quotation is from 1 Peter 2:21, which in the Vulgate is referred to as *sequamini vestigia eius.* The Latin word for footsteps, *vestigia,* means 'impressions'. Consequently, we could read this as following the impressions left on Francis's flesh after his encounter with the Lord. After some years his first brothers came. Clare of Assisi then added young women to the brotherhood by founding a small monastery at the Church of San Damiano. Men and women wanted to join him, and Francis wrote a kind of life form for worldly Franciscan life. In addition, he recognized brothers and sisters in all kinds of animals, birds, a wolf, a hare, et cetera. During the fifth

---

33 BUBER 2004 [NOTE 14], 6.

Crusade on the threshold of a battle, he engaged in an encounter with Sultan Malik al Kamil and recognized that the so-called 'infidels' could be brothers and sisters in faith. Finally, at the end of his life, Francis discovered that not only creatures, but the elements from which the Creation is formed, are brothers and sisters as well. Let us read his famous *Canticle of Brother Sun.*[34]

1 Most High, all-powerful, good Lord, Yours are the praises, the glory, and the honour, and all blessing.

2 To You alone, Most High, do they belong, and no human is worthy to mention Your name.

3 Praised be You, my Lord, with all Your creatures, especially Sir Brother Sun, Who is the day and through whom You give us light.

4 And he is beautiful and radiant with great splendour; and bears a likeness of You, Most High One.

5 Praised be You, my Lord, through Sister Moon and the stars, in heaven You formed them clear and precious and beautiful.

6 Praised be You, my Lord, through Brother Wind, and through the air, cloudy and serene, and every kind of weather, through whom You give sustenance to Your creatures.

7 Praised be You, my Lord, through Sister Water, who is very useful and humble and precious and chaste.

8 Praised be You, my Lord, through Brother Fire, through whom You light the night, and he is beautiful and playful and robust and strong.

9 Praised be You, my Lord, through our Sister Mother Earth, who sustains and governs us, and who produces various fruit with coloured flowers and herbs.

10 Praised be You, my Lord, through those who give pardon for Your love, and bear infirmity and tribulation.

11 Blessed are those who endure in peace for by You, Most High, shall they be crowned.

12 Praised be You, my Lord, through our Sister Bodily Death, from whom no one living can escape.

34 https://franciscantradition.org/francis-of-assisi-early-documents/the-saint/writings-of-francis/the-canticle-of-the-creatures/129-fa-ed-1-page-113 [Accessed, 28 February 2023].

[13] Woe to those who die in mortal sin. Blessed are those whom death will find in Your most holy will, for the second death shall do them no harm.

[14] Praise and bless my Lord and give Him thanks and serve Him with great humility.

In this famous song by Francis, the first chapter in the history of Italian literature, the creatures are addressed as brothers and sisters. This is a new way of approaching living creatures. But if we look more closely, the creatures addressed are brother sun, sister moon and stars, brother wind (air), sister water, brother fire, and sister mother earth: they are the celestial bodies and the elements of creation. These are followed by the penitents who pardon and endure. The last creature is *sister bodily death.* In short, the praise resounds with an appreciation of the bodies of creation.

Another remarkable thing is that Francis adds adjectives as he appraises these bodies, which are all positive. This is not so much because he likes them as such, but because he is touched by their good qualities as they return the goodness to their Creator by their very being. The philosopher Paul Ricoeur wrote that the human psyche expresses itself by exploring the world and by deciphering the sacrality of the world. Ricoeur calls this poetic imagination.[35] And I think this is what Francis is doing here. When he calls sister water "very useful and humble and precious and chaste," he is also referring to the virtues of his own soul. Just as a human can share feelings with another human's feelings, which we have described as true compassion, a human can also feel his own soul resonate with the creatures. And just as we described the growth of one's identity by encountering the other in true compassion, Francis became who he truly was through his encounter with the creatures. True compassion is not only feeling the sufferings of others, it is a much more encompassing virtue: it is an involvement of the human being with all the vital relations in which he or she lives. This is the meaning of "going back to the place where he belongs; there he will be told what to do." And what he hears is only praises.

A third remarkable thing is that after confessing that no human is worthy of mentioning[36] God's name, Francis continued the song in the passive form: "Praised be to You." One may ask: praised by whom? An answer might be: by the creatures. But the *Canticle* does not say that: it says "through" (*per*) the creatures. In theology, the term *passivum theologicum*, for example in "Let God be praised," "Hallowed be Thy Name," and "Blessed be the Lord," expresses that God is the One who praises, hallows, blesses, *and* the One who is being praised, hallowed, and blessed. To exemplify what I mean, I would like to picture the praises of the

35 Ricoeur, Paul: The Symbolism of Evil. Translated by Emerson Buchanan, Boston: Beacon Press, 1969, 13.

36 In the original *mentovare,* which comes from the Latin *mente habere:* to imagine something before giving it a name. God is too great to imagine, so do not even try to give Him or Her a name.

creatures as the playing of a cello: the music comes from above, but the strings and the soundboard of the cello resound it and make it audible by vibrating in the air. Francis is tuned into the creation to such an extent that he hears the sound of the divine praises through the creatures, in their utter material state, namely from the elements from which they are made. He is only giving words to his impressions.

A final reflection is from Eric Mascall, who asked the question: "What happens when we taste the perfect life?"[37] His answer is that all forms of activity and of being that could help man to attain the perfect life suddenly become useless. I need to acknowledge what is good and bad rather than love for a space protecting me, a power directing me, or a supplication to put my needs before God. All that remains is praise. When I taste the perfect life, I want nothing more than to give myself completely: not my knowledge, love, power, or prayer, but only my praise – myself offering pure praise agreeing with that pure praise of the perfect life.

References Cited

AGAMBEN, Giorgio: The Kingdom and the Glory, in: The Omnibus Homo Sacer II,4, 363–641. Stanford: Stanford University Press, 2017.

AGAMBEN, Giorgio: Karman. A Brief Treatise on Action, Guilt, and Gesture. Translated by Adam Kotsko, Stanford: Standford University Press, 2018.

BUBER, Martin: Ich und Du, Heidelberg: Lambert Schneider, [11]1983.

BUBER, Martin: Between Man and Man. Translated by Ronald Gregor-Smith, London/New York: Routledge 2004.

DAMASIO, Antonio: The Feeling of What Happens. Body and Emotion in the Making of Consciousness, New York: Vintage, 2000.

FERDINANCO, Keith: Jesus. the Theological Educator, in: Themelios 38:3 (2013), 360–74.

POPE FRANCIS: Encyclical Letter Laudato si'. On care for our common home, May 24, 2015.

FRANCIS OF ASSISI: Early Documents. Vol. I–III, Ed. by Regis J. Armstrong, J.A. Wayne Hellmann, William J. Short. New York: New City Press, 1999, 2000, 2001.

HENRY, Michel: Incarnation. Une philosophie de la chair, Paris: Seuil, 2000.

HISTORISCHES WÖRTERBUCH DER PHILOSOPHIE Bd. 5, Darmstadt: WBG, 1980.

MARCEL, Gabriel: A Metaphysical Diary, in: Idem, Being and Having. Transl. by Katharine Farrer, Glasgow: Univ. of Glasgow, 1949.

METZ, Johann Baptist: Memoria passionis. Ein provozierendes Gedächtnis in pluralistischer Gesellschaft, Freiburg: Herder, 2006.

METZ, Johann Baptist: Facing the World: A Theological and Biographical Inquiry, in: Theological Studies 75:1 (2014), 23–33.

---

37 MASCALL, Eric, Primauté de la louange, in: *Dieu Vivant*, Quoted in Giorgio Agamben, The Kingdom and the Glory, in: The Omnibus Homo Sacer II,4, 363–641, Stanford: Stanford University Press, 2017, 571–572.

RAHNER, Karl: Jesus Christus – Sinn des Lebens, in: Schriften zur Theologie XV, Zürich u. a.: Benziger, 1983, 206–216.

RICOEUR, Paul: The Symbolism of Evil. Translated by Emerson Buchanan, Boston: Beacon Press, 1969.

ROEBBEN, Bert: Living and learning in the presence of the other. Defining religious education inclusively, International Journal of Inclusive Education (2011), 1–13, 5. DOI: 10.1080/13603116.2011.552648.

SPEELMAN, Willem Marie: Franciscus van Assisi: Leraar op de wijze van een leerling, in: VAN WIERINGEN, Archibald / KOET, Bart (Hg.): Modellen van Leraarschap. van Jesaja tot Bioshock. (Utrechtse Studies XIX), Almere: Parthenon, 2017.

TAYLOR, Charles: A Secular Age, Cambridge and London: Harvard University Press, 2007.

WAAIJMAN, Kees: Spirituality. Forms, Foundations, Methods. Translated by John Vriend, Leuven: Peeters, 2002.

„Menschsein für andere“ – Compassion in Zeiten der Klimakrise

Lothar Kuld

Die Klimakrise aufgrund der Erderwärmung bedroht die Freiheit und Lebenschancen künftiger Generationen. Die große Transformation von Wirtschaft und Gesellschaft ist unumgänglich. Die Haltung der Compassion, frei übersetzt „Mitleidenschaft“ mit jenen, die leiden, übersehen und vergessen werden, ist nach Johann Baptist Metz die Mitgift des Christentums für die entstehende Weltgesellschaft. Im Sozialprojekt Compassion wird diese Option praktisch. Im Zeichen der Klimakrise müssen die Theologie und Praxis der Compassion auf die kommenden Generationen hin ausgerichtet werden.

Compassion; Klimakrise; große Transformation; Bildung

The climate crisis caused by global warming threatens the freedom and life chances of future generations. The great transformation of economy and society is inevitable. The attitude of compassion, loosely translated “sympathy” with those who suffer, are overlooked and forgotten, is, according to Johann Baptist Metz, the dowry of Christianity for the emerging world society. In the social project compassion, this option becomes practical. In the light of the climate crisis, the theology and practice of compassion must be directed towards the coming generations.

Compassion; climate crisis; great transformation; education

Der Theologe Johann Baptist Metz bezeichnete die Haltung der *Compassion* als „das Schlüsselwort“ und „Programm des Christentums.“[1] Compassion oder frei übersetzt *Mitleidenschaft* führe das Christentum an die Front gegenwärtiger Konflikte und fordere die Fähigkeit von Christ*innen heraus, das Leid der anderen, auch das der Feind*innen zu sehen und eingedenk auch fremden Leids zu handeln. Solche Haltung sei freilich eine Herausforderung und Zumutung, fordere sie doch die Solidarität mit fremdem Leid und Hilfeleistungen an andere und fremde Menschen heraus, die man nicht kennt und von denen man nicht von vornherein schon weiß, was man von ihnen selbst zu erwarten hat. Wem aber könne man dies zumuten, fragt Metz, wenn nicht jungen Menschen?[2]

---

1 METZ, Johann Baptist: Compassion. Weltprogramm des Christentums, Freiburg: Herder 2000.

2 Vgl. METZ, Johann Baptist: Die Autorität der Leidenden. Compassion – Vorschlag zu einem Weltprogramm des Christentums, in: Süddeutsche Zeitung 14./25./26. Dezember 1997, Nr. 296, 57.

Das Sozialprojekt Compassion ist angetreten, genau diese Verhaltensbereitschaft im Sozialen unter Jugendlichen zu stärken.[3] Als dieses Projekt in den neunziger Jahren des letzten Jahrhunderts begonnen und theologisch mit Hilfe der Theologie der Compassion[4] reflektiert wurde, war nicht die Erderwärmung und Klimakrise im Blick, sondern die Beobachtung eines gesellschaftlichen Wandels, in dem Menschen, die aus welchen Gründen auch immer nicht mitkommen und auf Hilfe und Unterstützung angewiesen waren, an den Rand gedrückt werden und die ersten sind, die man übersieht und sitzen lässt, sobald Stress entsteht. Die Politik während der Corona-Pandemie (2020 und 2021) hat diesen Reflex bestätigt. Schulen wurden geschlossen, Kinderspielplätze gesperrt und zu den alten und sterbenden Menschen kamen die Angehörigen und Helfer*innen von außen nicht mehr durch. Aus Fairness sei gesagt, dass man sich damals nicht besser zu helfen wusste und man im Wissen um das eigene Nichtwissen, was effektiv gegen das Corona-Virus hilft, und durchaus aus Rücksicht auf die am meisten gefährdeten Gruppen in der Gesellschaft diese Maßnahmen ergriffen hat. Heute meinen Expert*innen, Schulschließungen seien gar nicht notwendig gewesen. Sie haben in der Tat vielen Kindern eher geschadet. Handeln aus Compassion kann also auch falsch sein und naheliegend wäre, sich überhaupt nicht mehr zu engagieren, um dieser Ambivalenz des Engagements zu entgehen. Aber das wäre das Ende des gesellschaftlichen Zusammenhalts, also auch kein Weg.

Nun zeigt sich angesichts der Klimakrise, dass dieser Blick auf die anderen auch gebraucht wird, wenn es um Maßnahmen für künftige Generationen geht, die wir nicht kennen und nie kennen lernen werden und deren Lebensqualität und Überleben davon abhängt, wie wir ihnen die Erde hinterlassen. Die *Große Transformation* von Wirtschaft und Gesellschaft, welche die Vereinten Nationen 2015 ausgerufen haben, wird man politisch mit Gesetzen durchzusetzen versuchen. Sie wird gelingen, wenn sie auch von Menschen mitgetragen wird, die sich vorstellen können, wie künftige Generationen unter der fortlaufenden Erderhitzung leiden und bereit sind, auf Wachstum in Produktion, Konsum und Kapital und damit wirtschaftlichen Wohlstand zu verzichten und die diesen Umbau aus Solidarität mit künftigen Generationen heraus auch richtig finden.

Im Folgenden analysieren wir zuerst einige Annahmen über die Klimakrise und die Notwendigkeit einer *Großen Transformation*. Danach ist zu fragen, was religiöse Bildung in Zeiten der Klimakrise vermag, warum der Aufruf zur *Bewahrung der Schöpfung* etwas anderes ist als die Feststellung einer Klimakrise und warum Aktionen wie die der *Letzten Generation* nichts anderes sind als ein einziger Schrei nach *Mitleidenschaft* (Compassion) mit den kommenden Generationen.

---

[3] Vgl. WEISBROD, Adolf u. a.: Compassion – Ein Praxis- und Unterrichtsprojekt sozialen Lernens. Menschsein für andere, in: Engagement. Zeitschrift für Erziehung und Schule 1994 2–3, 268–307.

[4] Vgl. METZ [Anm.1]; HAKER, Hille: „Compassion als Weltprogramm des Christentums" – Eine ethische Auseinandersetzung mit Johann Baptist Metz, in: Concilium 4 (2001), 436–450.

Klimakrise und große Transformation

Im Prozess gegen die Klimaaktivistin Clara Hinrichs vor dem Berliner Amtsgericht Tiergarten (am 16. Februar 2023) ließ „der zuständige Richter das Argument nicht gelten, mit ihren Aktionen [Sitzblockaden auf Straßen] wolle die *Letzte Generation* das Leben auf der Erde retten." „Kakerlaken auch?" habe er gefragt und weiter ausgeführt: „Und die Dinos sind schließlich auch ausgestorben. Der Mensch wird sowieso aussterben, davon bin ich fest überzeugt. Das lässt sich nicht verhindern, dafür ist er zu dumm."[5] Nun kann man zu Straßenblockaden als Mittel des Protests, die hier zur Anklage geführt haben, verschiedener Meinung sein und die Aussicht, dass die Menschheit eines Tages von der Erde verschwindet, ist denkbar, aber darum geht es nicht. Was der Richter zu verstehen gibt, ist schlicht, dass ihn, der über eine mögliche Ordnungswidrigkeit oder einen möglichen Straftatbestand zu entscheiden hat, die Lebenschancen künftiger Generationen als rechtlich relevantes Argument herzlich wenig interessieren. Rechtsprechung ist schwierig und für einen Laien wie den Verfasser dieses Textes nicht immer zu verstehen. Zudem ist Rechtsprechung in Bewegung. Am 24. März 2021 hat das Bundesverfassungsgericht nämlich ganz anders gesprochen. Es hat auf die grundgesetzliche Verpflichtung des Staates hingewiesen, die Freiheit, das Leben und die körperliche Unversehrtheit seiner Bürgerinnen und Bürger zu sichern (Art. 2 Abs. 2 Satz 1 GG), und diese Verpflichtung schließe künftige Generationen mit ein. Das Gericht forderte den Gesetzgeber auf, seine Klimapolitik daraufhin neu auszurichten und nachzubessern. Die Bewahrung der Freiheit künftiger Generationen schließe „die Notwendigkeit ein, mit den natürlichen Lebensgrundlagen so sorgsam umzugehen und sie der Nachwelt in solchem Zustand zu hinterlassen, dass nachfolgende Generationen diese nicht nur um den Preis radikaler eigener Enthaltsamkeit weiter bewahren könnten."[6] Dieses Urteil weckte bei Klimaschützer*innen Hoffnung. Wie wir wissen, hat es sich in der nachfolgenden Rechtsprechung (noch) nicht so richtig durchgesetzt. Gerichte sind nun mal keine Klimaaktivist*innen. Sie können nur urteilen, wo Rechte formuliert sind. Rechte zu formulieren, ist Aufgabe des Gesetzgebers. Er ist gefordert. Einschränkend sagt das Gericht, dass Art. 20 a GG zwar zum Klimaschutz verpflichte, dieses Recht aber „keinen unbedingten Vorrang gegenüber anderen Belangen" genieße[7] Klimaschutz sei im Konfliktfall in Abwägung mit anderen Rechtsgütern und Verfassungsprinzipien zu bringen. Dabei nehme „das

---

5 TAZ lab, abgerufen 21.02.2023.

6 BVERFG, Beschluss des Ersten Senats vom 24. März 2021, - 1 BvR 2656/18 -, Rn. 1–270.

7 Ebd.

relative Gewicht des Klimaschutzgebotes“ mit dem fortschreitenden Klimawandel allerdings zu.[8] Klimaschutz muss also in der Sicht des Gerichts um der nachfolgenden Generationen willen eine erheblich größere Rolle spielen. Das ist unbequem, aber unumgänglich.

Die fortschreitende Erderwärmung scheint sich einem kritischen Kipppunkt zu nähern. Wird sie nicht gestoppt, ist die Zukunft der Menschheit bedroht und jener biblische Glaube an das göttliche Versprechen nach der Sintflut, dass die Menschheit ewig bleibt, solange die Erde besteht (Gen 8,21), ist dann Makulatur, so die fast einhellige Erkenntnis der Klimaforschung. Dazu unten mehr. In den Debatten der Gegenwart überragt die Klimakrise zu Recht inzwischen alle anderen Themen: weltweite Fluchtbewegungen, globale wirtschaftliche und gesellschaftliche Ungleichheit, Armut, die Bildungsgerechtigkeit, Pandemien, Krieg und Frieden. All diese Themen erscheinen nahezu zweitrangig im Verhältnis zur drohenden Klimakatastrophe, obwohl sie zum Teil unmittelbar mit der Erderwärmung und dem Klimawandel verbunden sind, etwa die Fluchtbewegungen, und deshalb macht ja die junge Generation, die um ihre Zukunft bangt, zu Recht Druck.

Man könnte noch einwenden, dass es in der Erdgeschichte schon immer Hitze- und Kälteperioden gab.[9] Im Unterschied zu diesen Schwankungen ist die heutige Erderwärmung aber menschengemacht, wenn die Daten aus den vorliegenden Klimastudien stimmen.[10] Das ist der große Unterschied. Nicht die Natur, auch kein Gott oder das Schicksal haben die Erderwärmung geschickt. Es ist der Mensch, der sie verursacht hat. Und wenn das stimmt, müssen Menschen die Verantwortung für das Ende der Erderwärmung übernehmen.[11] *Der Mensch* ist näher gesehen natürlich auch falsch, weil es nicht alle Menschen sind, die die Klimakrise verursacht haben. Es sind nicht die Menschen in Afrika und nicht die auf den Inseln im Pazifik. Ursache der Erderwärmung ist nach heutigem Wissen die im 19. Jahrhundert einsetzende industrielle Produktions- und kapitalistische Wirtschaftsweise der Länder der nördlichen Hemisphäre. Sie muss zurückgenommen werden, das geht aber nicht einfach so, weil das abrupte Ende von Wirtschaftswachstum unweigerlich mit Wohlstandsverlusten zu bezahlen und kaum jemand dazu bereit wäre. Deshalb spricht man lieber von Transformation als

---

8 Ebd.

9 Vgl. zum Folgenden KULD, Lothar: Klimawandel und Schöpfungsglaube. Religionspädagogik in Zeiten der Großen Transformation, in: LANG-WOJTASIK, Gregor / KÖNIG, Stefan (Hg.): Bildung 2050. Interdisziplinäre Perspektiven, Ulm: Klemm und Oelschläger, 2022, 35–41.

10 Vgl. MEADOWS, Dennis u. a.: Die Grenzen des Wachstums, München: Deutsche Verlags-Anstalt: 1972; RANDERS, Jorgen: 2052. Der neue Bericht an den Club of Rome: Eine globale Prognose für die nächsten 40 Jahre, München: oekom Verlag 2016.; MEADOWS, Donella u. a.: Grenzen des Wachstums – Das 30-Jahre-Update: Signal zum Kurswechsel. Leipzig: S. Hirzel [8]2023.

11 Vgl. JONAS, Hans: Das Prinzip Verantwortung, Frankfurt: Suhrkamp [10]2020; WEIZSÄCKER, Ernst Ulrich von / WIJKMAN, Anders: Wir sind dran: Was wir ändern müssen, wenn wir bleiben wollen, München: Pantheon Verlag. [3]2019.

dem Königsweg hin zu klimaneutralen postfossilen Produktionsformen und nachhaltiger Wirtschaft. Das ist denn auch das erklärte Ziel der von den Vereinten Nationen 2015 ausgerufenen *Großen Transformation.*[12]

Ohne Frage steckt in der globalen Produktion und Wirtschaft, die nur Wachstum kennt und Wachstum braucht, um zu funktionieren,[13] viel Hybris. Sie stößt jetzt an Grenzen. Ob sich mit ihrer Technik und ihrem Bewusstsein die weitere Erderwärmung überhaupt auf die angestrebten 1,5 Grad begrenzen lässt, ist fraglich, wahrscheinlich gelingt das nicht. Aber nehmen wir an, das sei möglich, dann muss man erklären, wie das zustande gebracht werden kann. Vor allem Vertreter*innen der Wirtschaft und des Kapitals sagen, man könne dem Klimawandel durch bessere Technik und umweltbewusstes Handeln der Individuen begegnen, und Wirtschaft und Industrie setzen alles daran, diese Position als richtig zu beweisen. Dann bliebe Wachstum erhalten. Die Gegenposition besagt, dass man schwerlich mit eben diesem Denken, das in die Klimakrise geführt hat, aus der Krise auch wieder herauskommt. Adorno und Horkheimer haben schon in den vierziger Jahren des letzten Jahrhunderts die Ambivalenz dieses Denkens in der *Dialektik der Aufklärung* beschrieben.[14] Die Emanzipation des Menschen vom Naturzwang und der Siegeszug der *instrumentellen Vernunft* (Horkheimer) über die Natur habe sich in den Katastrophen des 20. Jahrhunderts in ihr Gegenteil verkehrt. Die Barbarei des 20. Jahrhunderts sei nicht denkbar ohne die Dominanz einer Vernunft und eines Denkens, das vernichtet, was seinen Interessen im Weg steht, sei es die Natur oder Menschen.

Langsam dämmert die Einsicht, dass es für das Überleben der Menschheit mehr braucht als Mülltrennung, die Vermeidung von Plastik und veganes Essen, also mehr als nur individuelle Verhaltensänderungen,[15] und mit der *großen Transformation* ein weitreichender globaler Umbau von Wirtschaft und Gesellschaft in Gang gesetzt ist, der alle Akteur*innen und Konsument*innen sehr viel kosten wird. Diese Einsicht dämmert langsam und nicht alle sind bereit sie zu akzeptieren, wie der Blick in den Gerichtssaal von Berlin gezeigt hat.

---

12 VEREINTE NATIONEN: Transformation unserer Welt: die Agenda 2030 für nachhaltige Entwicklung. Resolution der Generalversammlung, New York 2015. https://www.un.org › depts › german › band1 (abgerufen 26.10.2021).

13 Vgl. HERRMANN, Ulrike: Das Ende des Kapitalismus, Köln: Kippenheuer & Witsch 2022.

14 Vgl. HORKHEIMER, Max / ADORNO, Theodor W.: Dialektik der Aufklärung. Philosophische Fragmente. Frankfurt a. M.: Fischer 1969.

15 Vgl. FOER, Jonathan S.: Wir sind das Klima! Köln: Kiepenheuer&Witsch 2019.

Bewahrung der Schöpfung – Was religiöse Bildung vermag

Man braucht keine Religion, um die Klimakrise zu verstehen. Viele Klimaaktivist*innen sind nicht religiös, aber aus den Religionen und Kirchen erwächst ihnen viel Zuspruch und Unterstützung. So plädierten schon 1983 die europäischen und nordamerikanischen Kirchen auf der Vollversammlung des ökumenischen Rates der Kirchen in Vancouver (Kanada) für eine Kampagne zur *Bewahrung der Schöpfung*, ein Thema, das damals noch ganz am Anfang des öffentlichen Bewusstseins stand und von den Kirchen aus anderen Weltregionen zunächst nicht unterstützt wurde. Die Kirchen der ehemaligen DDR waren mit Blick auf das damalige Wettrüsten zwischen Ost und West auf die Friedensfrage fokussiert. Die Kirchen der sog. Dritten Welt machten das Thema *Gerechtigkeit* als Voraussetzung für Frieden stark. Das war aus der Situation dieser Kirchen heraus verständlich. Man stand also vor global und regional unterschiedlichen Notwendigkeiten und Bedürfnissen, die schließlich in der Formel *Gerechtigkeit, Frieden und Bewahrung der Schöpfung* zusammengefasst wurden, nicht ohne Spannung. Klar war aber: Ohne Gerechtigkeit gibt es keinen Frieden und ohne Frieden keine Zukunft und nachhaltige Entwicklung. Mit dieser dreifachen Themensetzung gewannen die Kirchen in den 80er Jahren eindeutig an Profil.

Andreas Feige u. a. haben in ihren empirischen Studien zum Selbstverständnis von Religionslehrkräften gezeigt, dass die Stichworte *Gerechtigkeit, Frieden und Bewahrung der Schöpfung* das religionspädagogische Selbstverständnis der in den 80ger und 90ger Jahren des letzten Jahrhunderts sozialisierten Religionslehrerschaft geprägt haben.[16] Unverkennbar kommt dieses religionsprofessionelle Profil mit der Pensionierung dieser Alterskohorte heute an sein Ende. In der Religionspädagogik der Gegenwart ist zum Thema Frieden kaum etwas zu lesen. Der Krieg in der Ukraine brachte jetzt ein böses Erwachen. Und man wird warten müssen, bis religionspädagogisch etwas kommt. Politische Themen sind einstweilen ästhetischen Fragestellungen und Spurensuchen religiösen Selbstausdrucks gewichen. Der Eindruck eines biedermeierlichen Rückzugs ist nicht verkehrt. Plädoyers für die (Wieder-) Gewinnung der politischen Dimension des Religionsunterrichts sind singulär.[17] Dabei hätte die Religionspädagogik in den Papieren zum gerechten Frieden[18] genug Material und bei der Klimafrage kann sie

[16] Vgl. FEIGE Andreas u. a.: Religionsunterricht im religionsneutralen Staat? Ostfildern/Stuttgart: Schwabenverlag/Kohlhammer 2005.

[17] Vgl. GRÜMME, Bernhard: Religionsunterricht und Politik, Stuttgart: Kohlhammer 2009; THEO WEB Zeitschrift für Religionspädagogik, 18. Jahrgang 2019, Heft 2: Politische Dimensionen religiöser Bildung (Themenheft), https://www.theo-web.de/ausgaben/2019/18-jahrgang-2019-heft-2; DRESSLER, Bernhard: Kann religiöse Bildung einen Beitrag zur Demokratie leisten?, in: DERS., Religion verstehen, Stuttgart: Kohlhammer 2020, 195–215.

[18] Vgl. SCHOCKENHOFF, Eberhard: Die Bergpredigt. Aufruf zum Christsein, Freiburg i. Br.: Herder 2014.

auf Initiativen und öffentlich viel beachtete Beiträge der Kirchen zur Klimapolitik zugreifen: auf evangelischer Seite die Denkschrift des Rates der EKD „Umkehr zum Leben. Nachhaltige Entwicklung im Zeichen des Klimawandels" (2009) und auf katholischer Seite das sozialökologische Lehrschreiben *Laudato si'* von Papst Franziskus (2015).[19] Gemeinsam ist diesen Schreiben die Priorisierung des Klimawandels als absolut zentrales Problem der Gegenwart und sie erinnern daran, dass der Klimawandel, genauer: die Erderhitzung die Menschen in den armen Ländern der Erde am härtesten trifft. Er berühre die Agenda globaler Gerechtigkeit. Die Religionspädagogik steht also beim Thema Klimawandel und große Transformation nicht mit leeren Händen da. Aber sie hat wie die Pädagogik die Aporie des Sprungs vom Wissen zum Handeln. In der Unterrichtspraxis geht es, wie an religionspädagogischen Lehrmaterialien abzulesen ist, in der Regel um ein verändertes Umweltverhalten, um Müllsammeln, um die Vermeidung von Plastik und die Sympathie mit Fridays for Future.[20] Das ist naheliegend. Was aber hat das mit der Domäne des Religionsunterrichts, dem Glauben an Gott und Theologie zu tun?

Gewiss ist der Schöpfungsglaube, aus dem heraus die Kirchen zur *Bewahrung der Schöpfung* aufrufen, ein großer Motivator der christlichen Initiativen, aber man sollte bedenken, dass der Glaube an Schöpfung und Klimawandel verschiedene Dinge sind[21] und genau diese Unterscheidung für religiöse Bildung wichtig ist. Die Feststellung des Klimawandels beruht auf Faktenwissen, das umstritten sein mag und entsprechend diskutiert werden muss, aber es geht um messbare Fakten. Der Aufruf zur *Bewahrung der Schöpfung* beruht auf dem Glauben an einen Gott mit Compassion, der die Erde für den Menschen *gut* (Gen 1,31) eingerichtet hat und der nach den Worten der Bibel „solange die Erde besteht, [...] nicht mehr aufhören [lässt] Saat und Ernte, Kälte und Hitze, Sommer und Winter, Tag und Nacht." (Gen 8,22). Wie prekär diese Zusage Gottes ist, illustriert vor dieser Zusage die schon erwähnte sog. Sintfluterzählung. Aber noch in der Katastrophe der vollständigen Vernichtung – hier zeigt sich die Parallele von Sintfluterzählung und dem Ende Israels in der Zeit des Babylonischen Exils – zeichnet die Bibel das Bild eines Gottes, der sich um den Menschen kümmert und dafür sorgen wird, dass die Katastrophe der Sintflut *fortan* (Gen 8,22) *um des Menschen willen* (Gen 8,21) nicht mehr über die Erde kommen wird.

Wie wir aus der Erdgeschichte wissen, haben Klimakatastrophen nie aufgehört. Klimawandel gab es schon einige. Die Dinosaurier verschwanden vermutlich aufgrund einer Klimakatastrophe und es ist in manchen Projektionen der

---

19 Vgl. EKD: Umkehr zum Leben. Denkschrift des Rates der EKD, Gütersloher Verlagshaus, Gütersloh 2009; FRANZISKUS, Papst: Enzyklika Laudato si'. Über die Sorge für das gemeinsame Haus 2015, https://www.vatican.va/content/francesco/de/encyclicals/documents/papa-francesco_20150524_enciclica-laudato-si.html (abgerufen 26.10.2021).

20 Vgl. BEDERNA, Kathrin: Every day for future, Ostfildern: Grünewald 2019.

21 Vgl. DRESSLER, Bernhard: Überlegungen zur Didaktik der Schöpfungstheologie, ZPT 61, 2009, 391–401.

Klimaforschung denkbar, dass auch die Menschen eines Tages von der Erde verschwinden. Damit hat der Berliner Richter in seiner Belehrung ja vielleicht recht. Im Licht solcher Belehrung erscheint nun der Glaube an die göttliche Zusage, dass die Menschheit bestehen bleibt, solange die Erde besteht, wohl schlicht als naiver Irrtum, vorausgesetzt, man liest diese Zusage als empirisch überprüfbaren Sachverhalt. Das geht natürlich nicht. Und auch die Aussage, dass alles *sehr gut* (Gen 1,31) sei, macht nur im Glauben an einen unbedingt guten Gott Sinn, der als der Unbedingte und Unverfügbare den Menschen *gemacht* hat und, weil er der allmächtige Schöpfer ist, letztlich auch des Menschen zur Rettung seiner Welt nicht bedürfte. Dieser Satz wiederum wäre verheerend und auch ein wenig komisch, wenn man mit ihm die Aktivist*innen der *Letzten Generation* von ihrem Tun würde abhalten wollen. Er würde auch gar nicht stimmen, weil die Klimakrise ein Faktum ist. Ein Faktum ist nicht zu leugnen und durch Glauben nicht zu ändern. Religion will das auch gar nicht. Religion ist Deutung. Am Glauben an Gottes gute Schöpfung könnte man auch als gläubiger Mensch angesichts der drohenden faktischen Unbewohnbarkeit der Erde zweifeln, aber man darf eben auch getrost daran festhalten, wenn man diesen Glauben nicht als eine Behauptung alternativer Fakten missversteht, sondern eben als das, was Glauben ist: eine Sinnstiftung und Sinndeutung. Dann kann man z. B. mit dem Theologen Andreas Benk sagen: Die Schöpfungserzählungen beschreiben eine Utopie, wie die Welt nach Gottes Willen sein sollte und nie war.[22] Diese Vision einer heilen Welt, wie Gott sie wollte, ist nicht folgenlos. Sie motiviert Christ*innen zur Aktion. Religion kann also ein starker Motivator sein, sich für Klimapolitik zu engagieren. Sie tritt jedoch nicht an ihre Stelle. Religiöse Bildung arbeitet auf diese Unterscheidung hin.

Compassion im Kontext der Klimakrise

Soziales, pazifistisches und ökologisches Engagement führt Christ*innen unweigerlich an die Front gegenwärtiger Konflikte. Es verändert ihren Blick auf die Welt und auch ihre Theologie. Das ist der Kern der politischen Theologie von Johann Baptist Metz, die er auch *Theologie mit dem Gesicht zur Welt* genannt hat. Menschheitsgeschichte sei Leidensgeschichte. In ihr gebe es viel unabgegoltenes Leid. Die Frage, die Metz beschäftigt, lautet: Was ist mit denen, die ungerecht leiden mussten, die verloren gingen, die übersehen und an den Rand gedrängt wurden. Theologie, die so fragt, sei Theologie eingedenk fremden Leids. Sie sei *memoria passionis* und *gefährliche Erinnerung* (Metz), welche die Mentalität einer Siegergesesellschaft, die Opfer einfach vergisst, durchkreuzt. Die Solidarität mit

22 Vgl. BENK, Andreas: Schöpfung – eine Vision von Gerechtigkeit. Was niemals war, doch möglich ist, Ostfildern: Grünewald, 2016.

den Verlorenen, Übersehenen und an den Rand Gedrängten lehre, primär das Leid und nicht die Verfehlungen von Menschen zu sehen. In der Tat: Religiöse Menschen und Kirchenleute werden ja gern moralisch und sie urteilen wie Priester und Levit in der Samariterparabel (Lk 10,25–37) nach *rein* und *unrein* und vergessen darüber wie Priester und Levit in der Samariterparabel einfach jene elementare Mitmenschlichkeit und Leidempfindlichkeit, die von ihnen in der Begegnung mit Menschen, hier: dem Überfallenen, gefordert gewesen wäre. Religion, kann man daran sehen, ist kein Garant für Mitmenschlichkeit. Mitmenschlich agiert in dieser Geschichte der Samariter, der religiöse Bedenken (Tote galten als *unrein*) nicht kennt und sich anrühren lässt von dem, was er sieht. Jesus wurde nicht müde, Frömmigkeit ohne Compassion als Tor zur Heuchelei anzuklagen. „Die Sünde war ihm nicht zuletzt Verweigerung der Teilnahme am Leid der Anderen, war ihm Weigerung, über den dunklen Horizont der eigenen Leidensgeschichte hinauszudenken."[23] Diese elementare Empfindlichkeit für das Leid der anderen – bis hin zum Leid der Feinde – sei die Botschaft des Christentums. Die christliche Gottesrede sei „im Kern eine leidempfindliche Gottesrede."[24] Sie führe „die Christen an die Front der politischen, der sozialen und kulturellen Konflikte in der heutigen Welt."[25] Was wäre, fragt Metz, wenn in den politischen Konflikten unserer Zeit die Parteien jeweils auch das Leid der Feinde sähen und in ihrem Handeln in Betracht zögen? Was wäre eine Globalisierung, die nicht auf Kosten der von den globalen Märkten marginalisierten und ausgegrenzten Menschen und Kontinente voranschritte? Was wäre die Parole von der Gleichheit aller Menschen für ein Gewinn, wenn sie nicht auch die heute schon unter den Folgen der Klimakrise Leidenden und die kommenden Generationen, muss man ergänzen, einschließen würde?[26] Die Leidempfindlichkeit christlicher Gottesrede dränge zu diesen Fragen. Sie dränge zu einer „Mystik der offenen Augen."[27] Ihr Imperativ laute: „Aufwachen. Die Augen öffnen!" Und weiter schreibt Metz: „Das Christentum ist kein blinder Seelenzauber. Es lehrt nicht eine Mystik der geschlossenen, sondern eine Mystik der offenen Augen. Im Entdecken, im Sehen von Menschen, die im alltäglichen Gesichtskreis unsichtbar bleiben, beginnt die Sichtbarkeit Gottes, öffnet sich seine Spur."[28] Diese elementare Empfindlichkeit für das Leid der anderen sei „das Schlüsselwort" des Christentums und seine „Mitgift für ein sittliches Weltprogramm in diesem Zeitalter der Globalisierung."[29]

---

23 METZ, Johann Baptist: Memoria Passionis, Freiburg: Herder 2006, 163.
24 Ebd., 162.
25 Ebd., 168.
26 Vgl. Ebd., 171.
27 Ebd., 164.
28 METZ 1997 [Anm.2], 57; METZ 2000 [Anm.1], 17; METZ 2006 [Anm. 23], 177.
29 METZ 2000 [Anm.1], 15.

Ob man so viel Empathie von Politik erwarten kann? Metz weiß es nicht. Aber er hat die biblische Botschaft einer „gerechtigkeitssuchende[n] Compassion“[30] auf seiner Seite. In der Gerichtsparabel Matthäus 25, 35–45 stellte „Jesus die gesamte Menschheitsgeschichte [...] unter die Autorität der Leidenden“[31] und mit der Parabel vom barmherzigen Samariter habe er sich gleichsam ins Menschheitsgedächtnis hineinerzählt.[32]

Exkurs: Biblische Referenztexte einer Theologie der Compassion

Die Gerichtsparabel in Matthäus 25 ist in den Versen 35–45 in der Tat ein einziger Aufruf zur Solidarität mit den Leidenden. Die Parabel vom barmherzigen Samariter (Lk 10,25–37) hat eine lange Auslegungsgeschichte.[33] Gerd Theißen[34] hat sie einmal im Blick auf die Krise des Helfens interpretiert, die in der Gegenwart von drei Einwänden bestimmt sei: 1. Hilfe ist Selbstausbeutung. Der Helfer könne sich nicht richtig vom Hilfsbedürftigen abgrenzen, er habe eine Art Helfersyndrom. 2. Mitleid und Barmherzigkeit haben mit Macht zu tun. Der Helfer helfe nur sich selbst. 3. Hilfsbereitschaft ist letztlich egoistisch. Sie diene nur den eigenen Nachkommen oder soziobiologisch formuliert: dem Fortbestand der eigenen Gene.

Es lohnt sich, mit diesen Argumenten die Parabel vom barmherzigen Samariter zu lesen. Dann zeigt sich ein Modell mitleidigen Handelns, das vom Samariter zu tun verlangt, was er leisten kann, nicht mehr, nicht weniger. Er hat ganz offensichtlich kein Helfersyndrom und er beutet sich nicht aus. Er verabschiedet sich nämlich von dem Überfallenen, sobald er den zweiten Helfer, der den Verletzten übernimmt, gefunden hat. Die Zuwendung des Samariters bleibt also zeitlich begrenzt. Er kann sich offenbar gut lösen. Er bleibt nicht, bis er selbst nichts mehr hat, sondern setzt seinen Weg alsbald fort.

Vielleicht aber genießt er die Macht, einen so hilflosen Menschen vor sich zu haben? Er ist der Starke und dort ist der Schwache?

---

30 Ebd., 12.

31 Ebd., 16.

32 Vgl. Metz 2006 [Anm. 23], 164.

33 Vgl. zum Folgenden Kuld, Lothar: Compassion – Raus aus der Ego-Falle, Münsterschwarzach: Vier-Türme-Verlag 2003, 57–67; Kuld, Lothar: Compassion. solidarisch handeln lernen, in: Sauter-Meister, Jochen / Zwick, Elisabeth (Hg.): Religion und Bildung – Antipoden oder Weggefährten?, Paderborn: Schöningh 2019, 321–335.

34 Vgl. Theißen, Gerd: Die Bibel diakonisch lesen. Die Legitimitätskrise des Helfens und der barmherzige Samariter. In: von Schäfer, Gerhard K. / Strohm, Theodor (Hg.): Diakonie – biblische Grundlagen und Orientierungen, Heidelberg: Heidelberger Verlagsanstalt, [3]1998, 376–393.

Um hier weiterzukommen, muss man den Unterschied zwischen Barmherzigkeit und Nächstenliebe im antiken Umfeld beachten. In der orientalischen Antike war Barmherzigkeit in der Tat ein Gnadenerweis der Mächtigen. So denkt auch die Bibel die Barmherzigkeit Gottes. Barmherzigkeit war ein Geschehen unter grundsätzlich Ungleichen. Die Mächtigen und Reichen, die auf gesellschaftliches Ansehen Wert legten, rühmten sich ihrer Barmherzigkeit. Barmherzigkeit war eine Statusfrage und hatte ihren Platz in einer autoritären Gesellschaft mit ausgeprägten Standesunterschieden. Dagegen war die Nächstenliebe ein Konzept der Beziehung unter Gleichen. Es taucht ebenfalls in der (römischen) Antike schon auf und ist wie Freundschaft nur unter Gleichgestellten und Gleichberechtigten denkbar. Nächstenliebe in dieser Bedeutung einer Beziehung zwischen Menschen, die sich als gleich und ebenbürtig erachten, ist symmetrisch. Nächstenliebe gibt es nur zwischen Menschen, die sich gegenseitig als gleichwertig akzeptieren. Der *Nächste* ist immer nur der, der mir gleich ist und den ich als mir gleich akzeptiere. Der Nächste ist der mir gleiche Mensch. Wenn es am Ende der Zehn Gebote heißt: „Du sollst nicht begehren das Haus deines Nächsten. Du sollst nicht begehren das Weib deines Nächsten, noch seinen Knecht, noch seine Magd, noch sein Rind, noch seinen Esel, noch irgendetwas, was deinem Nächsten gehört." (Ex 20,17), dann ist mit dem *Nächsten* der vermögende Nachbar gemeint, nicht irgendein mittelloser und hilfsbedürftiger Mensch, Tagelöhner oder Sklave. Die Liebe zum Nächsten gibt es in der Antike nur unter Gleichen. Jedes Machtgefälle muss ausgeschlossen sein.

In der Parabel vom barmherzigen Samariter treffen zwei aus der Gesellschaft ausgeschlossene Menschen aufeinander. Der Überfallene ist ausgeschlossen aufgrund seines bösen Geschicks, der Samariter aufgrund seiner Außenseiterrolle auf jüdischem Gebiet. Zwischen beiden Menschen besteht in dieser Hinsicht Symmetrie, und sie begegnen sich auf dieser Ebene als gleiche. Ein Machtgefälle besteht kaum. Und einen Vorteil kann der Samariter aus seiner Hilfsbereitschaft auch nicht ziehen. Es ist sehr unwahrscheinlich, dass der Überfallene die gleichen Gene hat. Es ist unklar, ob der *halbtot* daliegende Mann tatsächlich überlebt. Nicht abzusehen ist, ob der Überfallene dem Samariter mit gleichem vergelten kann. Das würde z. B. auch voraussetzen, dass zwischen beiden nun eine lange Beziehung entsteht. Der Samariter aber geht weiter, nachdem er erste Hilfe geleistet hat.

Alle Erwägungen, ob der Samariter nicht doch nur an sich gedacht haben könnte, greifen bei dieser Geschichte also nicht. Und es kommt noch eine Schwierigkeit hinzu, die sich erst am Ende der Geschichte auflöst: Der Samariter ist nicht von vornherein *der Nächste*. Das wird er erst durch die Frage und den Kommentar, den Jesus seiner Geschichte anfügt. „Welcher von diesen dreien [Priester, Levit, Samariter] scheint dir der Nächste geworden zu sein, dem, welcher unter die Räuber fiel?" (Lk 10,36) Die Fragestellung ist entscheidend. Jesus fragt nicht: *Wer ist der Nächste gewesen?*, sondern: *Wer ist der Nächste geworden*? Darum geht es: Wie wird ein Mensch zum Nächsten? Im griechischen Text liegt hier ein kleines Wortspiel vor. Frei übersetzt fragt Jesus nämlich: „Welcher von diesen dreien scheint dir dem, welcher unter die Räuber fiel, nahe gekommen zu sein?“ Das ist offensichtlich und ganz handfest der Samariter. Der *Nächste* ist der, der sich auf das Opfer zubewegt und ihm dadurch *der Nächste* wird. Das erscheint banal, ist aber für das Verständnis, wer im christlichen Verständnis einem Menschen der Nächste ist, entscheidend. Der Nächste ist nicht jener, der aufgrund seines Status als Familienmitglied oder aufgrund der Rechtslage Anspruch auf Hilfe hat. Das macht ihn noch nicht zum Nächsten. Der Nächste ist der, den und dem wir uns zum Nächsten machen, dem wir uns nähern, um Hilfe leisten zu können. Dabei kommen wir ihm unwillkürlich *nahe*. In christlichem Verständnis ist *Bruder* und *Schwester* dann nicht nur der Mensch, mit dem man genetisch oder aufgrund eines Rechtsstatus verwandt ist, sondern prinzipiell jeder Mensch.

Von hier aus erschließt sich das Streitgespräch am Anfang der Geschichte. Für Priester, Levit und Samariter war der Überfallene *halbtot*. Die Frage, ob es sich lohnt, noch zu helfen, musste sich allen drei stellen. Nimmt man an, dass der Überfallene Jude war (das wird nicht ausdrücklich gesagt), müssten Priester und Levit ihm als einem Volksgenossen am nächsten stehen und am ehesten helfen. Sie geben ihn jedoch auf. Er ist aus ihrem Leben herausgefallen. Diesem Verlorenen, Aufgegebenen und Aussortierten wendet sich der Samariter zu. Der Verlorene, Aufgegebene, Aussortierte ist sein *Bruder* und gehört zu jenen *Geringsten*, mit denen sich der Weltenrichter in der großen Gerichtsrede des Matthäusevangeliums selbst identifiziert (Mt 25,31–46). Am Schluss der Samariterparabel hat man fast vergessen, dass sie im Anschluss an die theologische Frage nach dem *ewigen Leben* erzählt wird. Das *ewige Leben* erlangt, wer das Doppelgebot der Liebe erfüllt, sagt der Gesetzeslehrer, und Jesus stimmt ihm ausdrücklich zu. Er sagt ihm: „Tu das, und du wirst leben.“ (Lk 10,28) Was heißt hier *leben*?

Die christliche Rede vom Jüngsten Gericht, vom Weltenrichter und ewigen Leben ist ein wenig aus der Mode gekommen. Man kann dieser Mythologie in der Regel wenig abgewinnen. Dennoch sollte man den Impuls, der in diesen Bildern vom Endgericht und in der Sehnsucht nach *ewigem Leben* steckt, nicht vergessen. Endgericht meint, dass jedes Leben wichtig ist, keines verloren geht und gerade das übergangene, aufgegebene, aussortierte und weggeworfene Leben von Gott angeschaut wird und vor Gott Wert hat. Ewiges Leben in diesem Sinne ist mehr als biologisches Leben. In biologischer Sicht unterliegt das Leben des Menschen der Selektion. Mit der modernen Reproduktionsmedizin und Biopolitik beginnt der Mensch, die Selektion selbst in die Hand zu nehmen. Das beschädigte Leben, in das zu investieren unendliche Mühe kostet, wird immer früher erkannt und kann aussortiert werden. Um der biologisch und evolutionär notwendigen Auslese willen nimmt der Mensch den Tod in Kauf. Das ist das Leben. *Ewiges Leben* beginnt, wenn die Selektion des verloren gegebenen Lebens aufhört. Der Imperativ der Samariterparabel lautet: Rette das Verlorene! Der christlichen Nächstenliebe, schreibt Theißen, werden die Argumente für das Helfen schnell ausgehen, „solange man nur von einem Leben im biologischen Sinne spricht und Hilfe dadurch begründen will, was biologisch (und evolutionär) funktional ist"; und zwar „gerade dort, wo christliche Nächstenliebe immer ihre besondere Aufgabe gesehen hat: bei den zerstörten, zerrütteten, hilflosen Menschen, die oft nur noch ein Schatten ihrer selbst sind."[35]

Das Compassionprojekt im Kontext der Klimakrise

Die Klimakrise ist per se keine pädagogische, auch keine religionspädagogische Fragestellung. Die Forschungsergebnisse von Meteorologen zur Klimakrise sind noch keine Pädagogik. Sie ändern per se nichts. Würden sie es tun, müsste man Kindern nur die Prognosen der Erderwärmung für die nächsten Jahre vorlegen, um sie zu klimabewussten Akteur*innen zu machen. Offensichtlich reicht das nicht. Es muss schon die Übersetzung in eine pädagogische Fragestellung hinzukommen, die erklärt, was und warum ein Kind etwas von der Klimakrise verstehen soll und wie der Gegenstand aufbereitet sein muss, damit ein Kind bzw. Jugendlicher etwas davon versteht und mit guten Gründen ins Handeln kommt oder begründet auch nicht.

Das Compassion-Projekt ist ein Projekt sozialen Lernens an Schulen. Schüler*innen gehen während des Schuljahrs für kurze Zeit statt in die Schule in soziale Einrichtungen und begegnen dort Menschen, die sonst für die meisten in ihrem Alltag unsichtbar sind: alte Menschen, behinderte Menschen, Kranke, Kinder, Obdachlose, Flüchtlinge. Die Praktika werden unterrichtlich begleitet und reflektiert. Die Annahme des Projekts ist die Überzeugung, dass Sozialpraktika in Verbindung mit Reflexion langfristig zu veränderten Verhaltensbereitschaften im Bereich des Sozialen führen.[36] Die Evaluationen des Projekts haben diese Annahme bestätigt.[37] Das Compassionprojekt ist kein ökologisches Projekt und kein Friedenscamp, auch kein Berufspraktikum. Diese Projekte haben unterschiedliche Zielsetzungen. Ihre Zielsetzungen sind nicht beliebig und auch

---

35 Theißen 1998 [Anm. 34], 393.

36 Vgl. Rekus, Jürgen: Compassion – ein erlebnisbezogenes Bildungskonzept, in: Metz 2000 [Anm.1], 75–88.

37 Vgl. Kuld, Lothar / Gönnheimer, Stephan: Compassion – Sozialverpflichtetes Lernen und Handeln, Stuttgart: Kohlhammer 2000; Kuld, Lothar: „Früher wäre ich wohl kaum dazu gekommen, mich mit einem Obdachlosen zu unterhalten", in: Frech, Siegfried / Juchler, Ingo (Hg.): Dialoge wagen, Schwalbach Ts.: Wochenschauverlag, 2009, 252–265; Weber-Jung, Alexandra: Soziales Engagement und Geschlecht, Berlin: Lit 2011; Hensinger, Juliane: Soziales Lernen aus der Lehrerperspektive. Masterarbeit – Master of Arts (MA) Pädagogische Hochschule Weingarten 2011; Angele, Claudia u. a. (Hg.): Lernchance Sozialpraktikum, Freiburg: Lambertus 2012; Kuld, Lothar: Was bewirkt Compassion?, in: Fricke, Michael u. a. (Hg.): Konzepte sozialer Bildung an der Schule, Münster: Waxmann 2018, 123–137.

nicht austauschbar. So wurde das Compassionprojekt in den neunziger Jahren des letzten Jahrhunderts von den Katholischen Freien Schulen als Beitrag von Schulen zu bürgerschaftlichem Engagement entwickelt und es hat diesen Schulen nicht zuletzt auch als Instrument der Profilbildung gedient.[38] Wenn andere Schulen, wogegen nichts zu sagen ist, ökonomische Kompetenzen, Wirtschaftsaffinität und neue Medien favorisieren, wie es in den neunziger Jahren tatsächlich der Fall war, dann ist soziales Lernen ein Alleinstellungsmerkmal. „Menschsein für andere", so der Zusatz zum Titel des Compassionprojekts, war, so merkwürdig das heute klingt, in den Augen vieler Jugendlicher und ihrer Eltern zum Zeitpunkt der Einführung des Projekts keine Aufgabe der Schule. Projektentwicklungen und Schulentwicklung stehen immer in einem Kontext. Dreißig Jahre später ist die Klimakrise das alles andere überragende Thema. Die Zukunft der Menschheit steht auf dem Spiel. Wenn wir diesen Befund der Klimaforschung wirklich ernst nehmen, haben wir eine neue Lage und vieles, was die Schulen heute machen, erscheint obsolet. Wenn die Zukunft der Erde und das Leben künftiger Generationen auf dem Spiel steht, wendet sich leidempfindliche Theologie und Pädagogik von der Gegenwart nicht ab, sie rückt jedoch mit Emphase das Lebensrecht kommender Generationen ins Bild. Die Zuwendung zu den Kindern von heute und zu jenen, die noch nicht geboren sind und mit den Bedingungen der Erde zurechtkommen müssen, wie wir sie ihnen hinterlassen werden, zwingt zu einer Ausweitung der Compassion-Initiative unter dem Vorzeichen der Klimakrise.

Literatur

ANGELE, Claudia / BRÜLL, Hans-Martin / DINTER, Astrid / KULD, Lothar (Hg.): Lernchance Sozialpraktikum - Wirkungen sozialen Engagements Jugendlicher in sozialen Einrichtungen, Freiburg: Lambertus, 2012.

BEDERNA, Katrin: Every day for future. Theologie und religiöse Bildung für nachhaltige Entwicklung, Ostfildern: Grünewald, 2019.

BENK, Andreas: Schöpfung – eine Vision von Gerechtigkeit. Was niemals war, doch möglich ist, Ostfildern: Grünewald, 2016.

BVERFG [BUNDESVERFASSUNGSGERICHT], Beschluss des Ersten Senats vom 24. März 2021, – 1 BvR 2656/18 -, Rn. 1–270, http://www.bverfg.de/e/rs20210324_1bvr265618.html (abgerufen am 21.02.2023).

DRESSLER, Bernhard: Überlegungen zur Didaktik der Schöpfungstheologie, ZPT 61, 2009, 391–401.

DRESSLER, Bernhard: Kann religiöse Bildung einen Beitrag zur Demokratie leisten? Zum Verhältnis von Religion und Politik in Bildungsprozessen, in: DERS. (Hg.): Religion verstehen.

[38] Vgl. WEISBROD 1994 [Anm. 3]; WEISBROD: Ein Pilotprojekt, in: METZ 2000[Anm. 1], 97–100.

Beiträge zur Religionshermeneutik und zu religiöser Bildung, Stuttgart: Kohlhammer, 2020, 195–215.

EKD: Umkehr zum Leben. Nachhaltige Entwicklung im Zeichen des Klimawandels", Denkschrift des Rates der EKD, Gütersloher Verlagshaus, Gütersloh, 2009.

FEIGE, Andres u. a.: Religionsunterricht im religionsneutralen Staat? Unterrichtliche Zielvorstellungen und religiöses Selbstverständnis von ev. und kath. Religionslehrerinnen und -lehrern in Baden-Württemberg. Eine empirisch repräsentative Befragung, Ostfildern/Stuttgart: Schwabenverlag/Kohlhammer, 2005.

FOER, Jonathan Safran: Wir sind das Klima! Wie wir unseren Planeten schon beim Frühstück retten können, Köln: Kiepenheuer&Witsch, 2019.

PAPST FRANZISKUS: Enzyklika „Laudato si'. Über die Sorge für das gemeinsame Haus", Vatikan 2015. https://www.vatican.va/content/francesco/de/encyclicals/documents/papa-francesco_20150524_enciclica-laudato-si.html (abgerufen 26.10.2021).

GRÜMME, Bernhard: Religionsunterricht und Politik. Bestandsaufnahme – Grundsatzüberlegungen – Perspektiven für eine politische Dimension des Religionsunterrichts, Stuttgart: Kohlhammer, 2009.

HAKER, Hille: „Compassion als Weltprogramm des Christentums" – Eine ethische Auseinandersetzung mit Johann Baptist Metz, in: Concilium 4 (2001), 436–450.

HENSINGER, Juliane: Soziales Lernen aus der Lehrerperspektive. Eine Untersuchung zur Implementierung und Akzeptanz des Sozialprojekts Compassion. Masterarbeit – Master of Arts (MA), Weingarten: Pädagogische Hochschule Weingarten 2011.

HERRMANN, Ulrike: Das Ende des Kapitalismus: Warum Wachstum und Klimaschutz nicht vereinbar sind – und wie wir in Zukunft leben werden, Köln: Kippenheuer & Witsch, 2022.

HORKHEIMER, Max / ADORNO, Theodor W.: Dialektik der Aufklärung. Philosophische Fragmente. Frankfurt a. M.: Fischer, 1969, (Nachdruck als Taschenbuch 1988).

JONAS, Hans: Das Prinzip Verantwortung. Versuch einer Ethik für die technologische Zivilisation. Mit einem Nachwort von Robert Habeck, Frankfurt: Suhrkamp, 2020 (Erste Auflage 1979).

KULD, Lothar / GÖNNHEIMER, Stefan: Compassion – Sozialverpflichtetes Lernen und Handeln, Stuttgart: Kohlhammer, 2000.

KULD, Lothar: Compassion – Raus aus der Ego-Falle, Münsterschwarzach: Vier-Türme-Verlag, 2003.

KULD, Lothar: „Früher wäre ich wohl kaum dazu gekommen, mich mit einem Obdachlosen zu unterhalten" – Wirkungen des Sozialprojekts „Compassion", in: FRECH, Siegfried / JUCHLER, Ingo (Hg.), Dialoge wagen. Zum Verhältnis von politischer Bildung und Religion, Schwalbach Ts.: Wochenschauverlag, 2009, 252–265.

KULD, Lothar: Was bewirkt Compassion?, in: Fricke, Michael / Kuld, Lothar / Sliwka, Anne (Hg.): Konzepte sozialer Bildung an der Schule. Compassion – Diakonisches Lernen – Service Learning, Münster: Waxmann 2018, 123–137.

KULD, Lothar: Compassion: solidarisch handeln lernen, in: SAUTERMEISTER, Jochen / ZWICK, Elisabeth (Hg.): Religion und Bildung – Antipoden oder Weggefährten? Diskurse aus historischer, systematischer und praktischer Sicht, Paderborn: Schöningh, 2019, 321–335.

KULD, Lothar: Klimawandel und Schöpfungsglaube. Religionspädagogik in Zeiten der Großen Transformation, in: LANG-WOJTASIK, Gregor / KÖNIG, Stefan (Hg.): Bildung 2050. Interdisziplinäre Perspektiven (Weingartner Dialog über Forschung 5), Ulm: Klemm und Oelschläger, 2022, 35–41.

MEADOWS, Dennis u. a.: Die Grenzen des Wachstums. Bericht des Club of Rome zur Lage der Menschheit, Stuttgart: Deutsche Verlags-Anstalt, 1972.

MEADOWS, Donella u. a.: Grenzen des Wachstums - Das 30-Jahre-Update. Signal zum Kurswechsel, Leipzig: S. Hirzel, [8]2023.

METZ, Johann Baptist: Die Autorität der Leidenden. Compassion – Vorschlag zu einem Weltprogramm des Christentums, in: Süddeutsche Zeitung 14./25./26. Dezember 1997, Nr. 296, 57.

METZ, Johann Baptist: Compassion. Zu einem Weltprogramm des Christentums im Zeitalter des Pluralismus der Religionen und Kulturen, in: METZ, Johann Baptist u. a. (Hg.): Compassion. Weltprogramm des Christentums. Soziale Verantwortung lernen, Freiburg: Herder, 2000, 9–18.

METZ, Johann Baptist, Memoria Passionis. Ein provozierendes Gedächtnis in pluralistischer Gesellschaft, Freiburg: Herder, 2006.

RANDERS, Jorgen: 2052. Der neue Bericht an den Club of Rome: Eine globale Prognose für die nächsten 40 Jahre, München: oekom Verlag, 2016.

REKUS, Jürgen: Compassion – ein erlebnisbezogenes Bildungskonzept, in: METZ, Johann Baptist u. a. (Hg.): Compassion. Weltprogramm des Christentums. Soziale Verantwortung lernen, Freiburg: Herder, 2000, 75–88.

SCHOCKENHOFF, Eberhard: Die Bergpredigt. Aufruf zum Christsein, Freiburg i. Br.: Herder, 2014.

THEIẞEN, Gerd: Die Bibel diakonisch lesen. Die Legitimitätskrise des Helfens und der barmherzige Samariter, in: SCHÄFER, Gerhard K. / STROHM, Theodor (Hg.): Diakonie – biblische Grundlagen und Orientierungen. Ein Arbeitsbuch zur theologischen Verständigung über den diakonischen Auftrag, Heidelberg: Heidelberger Verlagsanstalt, [3]1998, 376–393.

THEO WEB Zeitschrift für Religionspädagogik, 18. Jahrgang 2019, Heft 2: Politische Dimensionen religiöser Bildung (Themaheft), https://www.theo-web.de/ausgaben/2019/18-jahrgang-2019-heft-2.

VEREINTE NATIONEN: Transformation unserer Welt: die Agenda 2030 für nachhaltige Entwicklung. Resolution der Generalversammlung, New York 2015. https://www.un.org › depts › german › band1 (abgerufen 26.10.2021).

WEBER-JUNG, Alexandra: Soziales Engagement und Geschlecht. Untersuchung zu genderspezifischen Wirkungen des Compassion-Projekts, Berlin: Lit, 2011.

WEISBROD, Adolf / KUHN, Franz / HIRSCH, Friedrich: Compassion – Ein Praxis- und Unterrichtsprojekt sozialen Lernens. Menschsein für andere, in: Engagement. Zeitschrift für Erziehung und Schule 1994 (2–3), 268–307.

WEISBROD, Adolf: Ein Pilotprojekt: Genese, Besonderheiten, Ziele, in: METZ, Johann Baptist u. a. (Hg.): Compassion. Weltprogramm des Christentums. Soziale Verantwortung lernen, Freiburg: Herder, 2000, 97–100.

WEIZSÄCKER, Ernst Ulrich von / WIJKMAN, Andreas: Wir sind dran. Was wir ändern müssen, wenn wir bleiben wollen - Club of Rome: Der große Bericht, München: Pantheon Verlag, [3]2019.

Compassion als lebensspendende Unterströmung in der Bildung – Moralpädagogische Perspektiven

Bert Roebben

Dieser Beitrag stellt zunächst eine Rekonstruktion des moralpädagogischen Diskurses der letzten 50 Jahre vor. Der Schwerpunkt lag vor allem auf der Entwicklung einer persönlichen moralischen Kompetenz auf der Grundlage eines wertekommunikativen Handelns in der Gemeinschaft. Der Aspekt der moralischen Emotion drohte in diesem stark kognitiven Rahmen unterzugehen. Die ethischen Herausforderungen in einer globalen Gesellschaft erfordern jedoch mehr als argumentativ-ethische Kompetenz. In diesem Zusammenhang wird im zweiten Teil die Aufmerksamkeit auf Compassion als Unterströmung in Lernprozessen gelenkt. Emotionales Engagement für das Wohlergehen anderer wird als lebensspendende Querschnittsaufgabe in jedem moralischen Bildungsprozess verstanden, und zwar in seinen drei konstitutiven Momenten: im Sehen, Urteilen und Handeln (Joseph Cardijn). Im dritten Teil dieses Beitrags werden Handlungsimpulse vorgeschlagen, die diese Unterströmung konkretisieren. Zum Schluss wird die Frage aufgeworfen, ob und inwieweit eine religiöse Einstellung für die moralische Begründung der Compassion notwendig ist.

Moralische Bildung; Wertekommunikation; moralische Emotionen; Compassion; Verletzlichkeit; Joseph Cardijn

This contribution first proposes a reconstruction of the moral pedagogical discourse of the last fifty years. The emphasis was mainly on the development of personal moral competence based on values-communicative action in the community. The "moral emotion" dimension was in danger of being snowed under in this highly cognitive framework. However, the ethical challenges in a global society require more than argumentative-ethical competence. It is in this context that attention is called to compassion as an undercurrent in ethical learning processes. Emotional involvement in the well-being of others is taken as a life-giving undercurrent in any educational process and this in its three constitutive moments: in the seeing, judging and acting of the moral person (Joseph Cardijn). The third part of this contribution proposes action impulses that concretize this undercurrent. At the end, the question is raised whether and to what extent a religious disposition is necessary for the moral grounding of compassion.

Moral education; values communication; moral emotions; compassion; vulnerability; Joseph Cardijn

Ein doppelter autobiografischer Impuls

Erster Impuls: Wozu bilden?

Vor fast 30 Jahren, am 21. Juni 1994, verteidigte ich meine Dissertation über moralische Bildung an der KU Leuven. Genau ein Jahr später erschien mein Buch mit dem Titel „Een tijd van opvoeden. Moraalpedagogiek in christelijk perspectief."[1] Das Thema schien gut auf dem Markt anzukommen, wovon die vielen Einladungen zeugten, die ich in Flandern und weit darüber hinaus erhielt, um Vorträge zu halten und Artikel über meine Forschung zu schreiben. Offensichtlich hatte ich mit meiner These, dass am Ende des zweiten Jahrtausends die Frage nach dem *Wozu* in der moralischen Bildung viel wichtiger ist als die Frage nach dem *Wie*, einen Nerv in der Welt der Erziehung, Bildung und Ausbildung getroffen. Im Spannungsfeld von Heteronomie und Autonomie, von autoritärer und antiautoritärer Erziehung, von *Anpassung und Widerstand* im Leben des Heranwachsenden geht es nicht um die Anwendung der richtigen Erziehungsmethoden, sondern um die pädagogische Kernfrage selbst: Haben Eltern überhaupt noch einen Sinn in der Erziehung, sind Lehrer*innen in einer Zeit der pädagogischen Unsicherheit noch bereit, Farbe zu bekennen, und ist die Gesellschaft noch in der Lage, ein Bildungsprojekt für die kommenden Generationen zu konzipieren und zu verwirklichen?[2] Der deutsche Religionspädagoge Karl Ernst Nipkow brachte das Thema in seinem Lemma über „Bildung" mit einem Satz auf den Punkt: „Die Pädagogik steht heute vor der Erziehungsfrage, weil die Gesellschaft vor der Sinnfrage steht."[3]

In den Jahren zuvor hatte sich die Moralpädagogik als vollwertige akademische Disziplin herausgebildet und einen konzeptionellen Rahmen entwickelt, um die komplexe Realität der moralischen Bildung empirisch zu beschreiben und normativ zu begründen. Auffallend war dabei das Engagement vor allem deutschsprachiger katholischer Theolog*innen, die in den 1970er und 1980er Jahren an der Schnittstelle von Moraltheologie und Religionspädagogik tätig waren und konziliare Vorstellungen von Gewissensfreiheit und Gewissensbildung für die (Moral-)Pädagogik umsetzten, wie Alfons Auer, Albert Biesinger, Adolf Exeler, Konrad Hilpert, Johannes Hoffmann, Wolfgang Langer, Norbert Mette,

---

1 Vgl. Roebben, Bert: Een tijd van opvoeden. Moraalpedagogiek in christelijk perspectief, Leuven/Amersfoort: Acco, 1995.

2 Vgl. Ebd., 111–115.

3 Nipkow, Karl Ernst: Art. Erziehung, in: Theologische Realenzyklopädie (Band 10), Berlin/New York: De Gruyter, 1982, 232–254, hier 252.

Dietmar Mieth, Helmut Peukert und Günter Stachel.[4] Beim erneuten lesen meiner Doktorarbeit ist mir aufgefallen, wie viele deutsche Quellen ich damals konsultiert habe. Aber auch in der niederländischsprachigen Welt mit Jozef Bulckens, Chris Hermans, Louis Janssens, Johannes A. van der Ven und später Hans-Georg Ziebertz war das Thema *en vogue*, teilweise befeuert durch die deutsche Moraltheologie (mit vielen Übersetzungen ins Niederländische), aber auch durch neue Erkenntnisse, die auf anderen moralphilosophischen Quellen beruhten.

Eine wichtige zusätzliche Dimension in der Forschung boten die moralpsychologischen Erkenntnisse, die aus den Vereinigten Staaten kamen, mit Akteuren wie Louis E. Raths *(values clarification)* und Lawrence Kohlberg *(values development)*. Sie gipfelte in J. A. van der Vens Meisterwerk (Vorming in waarden en normen), das 1985 auf Niederländisch veröffentlicht wurde.[5] Vor dem Hintergrund des Modells der *values inculcation*, mehr spezifisch der *character education*[6] und der Modelle von Raths und Kohlberg entwarf Van der Ven ein eigenes Modell, das der Wertekommunikation *(values communication)*. In Anlehnung an die Sozialphilosophie von Jürgen Habermas ging Van der Ven von einer Situation aus, in der die Bildungsteilnehmer*innen mit einer gemeinsamen Problemdefinition, vernünftigen Argumenten, einem Perspektivwechsel und einer Diskussionskultur nach dem suchen, was für das Gemeinwohl aller erstrebenswert und nachhaltig ist. In diesem Modell wird das moralische Selbst der Person in der Interaktion mit anderen ausgefeilt und geformt. Der Einfluss dieses Modells auf Lernprozesse in Erziehung, Bildung und Ausbildung war enorm und spielt bis heute eine diskursprägende Rolle.[7]

---

4 Auf den Tagungen des Deutschen Katechetenvereins (DKV) im Jahr 1975 und der Arbeitsgemeinschaft Katholischer Katechetik-Dozenten (AKK) im Jahr 1976 wurde das Thema explizit aufgegriffen, vgl. ROEBBEN 1995 [Anm. 1], 51–53. Vgl. in diesem Zeitraum die Veröffentlichungen von AUER, Alfons / BIESINGER, Albert / GUTSCHERA, Herbert (Hg.): Moralerziehung im Religionsunterricht, Freiburg im Breisgau: Herder, 1975; STACHEL, Günter / MIETH, Dietmar: Ethisch handeln lernen. Zu Konzeption und Inhalt ethischer Erziehung, Zürich: Benziger, 1978; NIPKOW, Karl Ernst: Moralerziehung. Pädagogische und theologische Antworten, Gütersloh: Mohn, 1981.

5 VAN DER VEN, Johannes: Vorming in waarden en normen, Kampen: Kok-Agora, 1985.

6 LICKONA, Thomas: Educating for character. How our schools can teach respect and responsibility, New York:Bantam Books, 1991.

7 Zur Beschreibung der vier Modelle Übertragung (oder Vermittlung), Erhellung, Entwicklung und Kommunikation, vgl. ZIEBERTZ, Hans-Georg / ROEBBEN, Bert: Art. Moralpädagogik, in: Lexikon für Theologie und Kirche (Band 7), Freiburg im Breisgau: Herder, ³1998, 455–458. Später erschien die Vierteilung als Organisationsprinzip z. B. in der Jugendpastoral [vgl. TZSCHEETZSCH, Werner: Identität durch Kommunikation. Kirchliche Jugendarbeit als Ort interkultureller Wertekommunikation, in: SCHREIJÄCK, Thomas (Hg.): Religion im Dialog der Kulturen, Münster: Lit Verlag, 251–259.] und in der Religionsdidaktik [ZIEBERTZ, Hans-Georg: Art. Ethisches Lernen, in: HILGER, Georg / LEIMGRUBER, Stephan / ZIEBERTZ, Hans-Georg (Hg.): Religionsdidaktik. Ein Leitfaden für Studium, Ausbildung und Beruf, München: Kösel, 2010, 434–452.]. Dass die Verbindung zu der

In meiner eigenen Postdoc-Forschung habe ich damals verstanden, dass die moralische Identität der Person nicht nur durch die Entwicklung einer argumentativ-rationalen Kompetenz wie in der Wertekommunikation von J. A. van der Ven bestimmt wird, sondern dass neben kognitiven auch emotionale und konative Elemente eine Rolle spielen.[8] Moralische Persönlichkeitsbildung impliziert Denken, aber auch Fühlen und Handeln. Moralisch gebildet sind jene die die moralische Aufladung einer Situation wahrnehmen, die klar unterscheiden können, um welche Werte und Normen es geht, und die in Übereinstimmung mit Emotion und Kognition angemessen handeln können. Sehen, Urteilen, Handeln: Da klingelt es bei jedem vernünftigen praktischen Theolog*innen. Ich werde später darauf zurückkommen.

Moralische Emotionen, wie z. B. Mitgefühl, und moralische Handlungs-optionen, wie z. B. tugendhafte Praktiken, sind eine notwendige Voraussetzung für die Entwicklung moralischer Ko mpetenz. In den englischen[9] und deutschen[10] Übersetzungen seines grundlegenden Werkes – mehr als ein Jahrzehnt später – hat Van der Ven seine Erkenntnisse auch aus der Perspektive der Ausprägung der Emotionen und Gestaltung des Charakters neu formuliert, und zwar ausgehend von Paul *Ricœurs* Ansatz der narrativen Identität. Was als Problemstellung in meiner eigenen Dissertation theoretisch im Keim angelegt wurde, die ganzheitliche Betrachtung der moralischen Person als Ziel der moralischen Bildung (eine Person, die moralisch angemessen fühlen, urteilen und handeln kann),[11] wurde im Laufe der Jahre immer deutlicher. Die *Wozu*-Frage bzw. die Frage nach dem gesellschaftlichen Zweck der moralischen Bildung erwies sich als die richtige Frage. In den Worten evangelischer Kolleg*innen klingt diese *Bestimmungsfrage* seither so: „Subjekt muss der Mensch im Prozess seiner Bildung erst werden, Person ist er immer schon."[12] Aufgabe einer Bildungs-theorie (und -Praxis!)

---

ursprünglichen Forschung von J. A. van der Ven inzwischen verschwunden ist, geht u. a. hervor aus NAURATH, Elisabeth: Übertragung, Erhellung, Entwicklung, Kommunikation, Erfahrung. Strategien ethischer Bildung im Religionsunterricht, in: LINDNER, Konstantin / ZIMMERMANN, Mirjam (Hg.): Handbuch Ethische Bildung. Religionspädagogische Fokussierungen, Tübingen: Mohr Siebeck, 2021, 224.

8 Diese Elemente waren bereits in meiner Dissertation angelegt, wurden aber ausführlicher behandelt in ROEBBEN, Bert: Moralpädagogik und moralische Sensibilität, in: Jugendwohl. Zeitschrift für Kinder- und Jugendhilfe 79 (1998) 11, 510–519 und in DERS.: Religionspädagogik der Hoffnung. Grundlinien religiöser Bildung in der Spätmoderne, Berlin: Lit-Verlag, 2011 (= Forum Theologie und Pädagogik 19), 19–41 (ursprünglich ein 1999 veröffentlichter Beitrag, der auf einem 1997 auf Niederländisch erschienenen Beitrag basierte).

9 Vgl. VAN DER VEN, Johannes: Formation of the Moral Self, Grand Rapids: W.B. Eerdmans 1998.

10 Vgl. VAN DER VEN, Johannes: Das moralische Selbst. Gestaltung und Bildung, Münster: Lit-Verlag, 1999 (= Empirische Theologie 1).

11 Vgl. ROEBBEN 1995 [Anm. 1], 123–206.

12 BIEHL, Peter: Erfahrung – Glaube – Bildung. Studien zu einer erfahrungsbezogenen Religionspädagogik, Gütersloh: Mohn, 1991, 156.

ist es, „dieses Person-Sein als (anthropologische) Grundlage, welche der menschlichen Verfügbarkeit entzogen ist und ihr vorausgeht, für den Bildungsprozess fruchtbar zu machen.“[13] Die *Wozu*-Frage kommt unausweichlich auf uns zu, insofern wir uns intensiv mit Grenz- und Sinnfragen im konkreten Bildungsalltag beschäftigen: Wozu wollen wir Kinder und Jugendlichen erziehen? Was ist erstrebenswert, damit jede*r Einzelne und alle zusammen zu ihrem Recht kommen? Welche Art von Mensch in der Gemeinschaft haben wir vor Augen? Wie kann persönliche Integrität als „biographisch stabilisierte Verantwortlichkeit“[14] gestaltet werden? Es geht um „eine grundlegende Neuvergewisserung aller Betroffenen hinsichtlich der Ziele der gesellschaftlichen (und damit auch der jeweils eigenen) Entwicklung.“[15]

In den Niederlanden wird dies inzwischen als „neues Wir“ bezeichnet: ein Versuch, über die partikularen Unterschiede der Gemeinschaften hinweg eine universelle Bestimmung für die Gesellschaft zu finden, zu der jede*r mit seinen / ihren singulären Talenten beiträgt.[16] Bei alledem ist zu erwähnen, dass für mich persönlich diese Grundeinsicht in meiner eigenen Bildungspraxis immer mehr Gestalt annahm – in den Jahren, in denen ich als Vater meine Kinder erzog, in der Jugendpastoral tätig war und junge Erwachsene an der Universität unterrichtete.

Zweiter Impuls: Fliehen ist nicht mehr möglich!

Die großen Krisenerfahrungen zu Beginn des neuen Jahrtausends haben diesen vagen kulturellen Optimismus in Gesellschaft und Bildung jedoch konterkariert. Hier ist eine zweite autobiografische Notiz zu machen. Aus dem erhofften *neuen Wir*, das starke individuelle moralische Persönlichkeiten erfordert, ist ein *neues*

13 ROTHGANGEL, Martin / SCHELANDER, Robert: Art. Bildung, in: Wirelex 2015, 5.

14 SAUTERMEISTER, Jochen: Identität und Integrität, Verantwortliche Lebensführung und Orientierung in Zeiten der Instabilität, in: BERGHOLD, Ralph / SAUTERMEISTER, Jochen / SCHRÖDER, André (Hg.): Dem Wandel eine menschliche Gestalt geben. Sozialethische Perspektiven für die Gesellschaft von Morgen, Freiburg im Breisgau: Herder, 2017, 43–60, hier 51. – Für eine ähnliche Position siehe HILPERT, Konrad: Ethisches Lernen, in: Religionsunterricht an höheren Schulen 36 (1993) 2, 70–82, hier 80: „Vielzahl und Heterogenität stellen für das moralischen Lernen eine qualitativ neue Herausforderung dar, insofern der einzelne in seiner Entwicklung jetzt nicht mehr bloß über sich hinauswachsen und zu übergreifenden Grundsätzen vordringen muss, sondern auch eine Weise finden muss mit der Menge differierender Grundsätze zurechtzukommen“ – vgl. auch EID, Volker / ELSÄSSER, Antonellus / HUNOLD, Gerfried W. (Hg.): Moralische Kompetenz. Chancen der Moralpädagogik in einer pluralen Lebenswelt, Mainz: Grünewald, 1995.

15 METTE, Norbert: Bildung und verbindliches Handeln. Identität in universaler Solidarität, in: Stimmen der Zeit 119 (1994) 7, 453–464, hier 454.

16 Vgl. www.nieuwwij.nl (abgerufen 07.03.2023).

verletzliches Wir geworden.[17] Die Menschen scheinen seit 9/11, der Klimakrise, der Covid-19-Pandemie und dem Krieg in der Ukraine das Vertrauen in sich selbst und ineinander verloren zu haben. Das so klar formulierte Bildungsziel, nämlich „die Beziehung eines Subjekts zu sich selbst als eine *Praxis der Freiheit* angesichts von Kontingenzen und Machtdynamiken, in denen es sich selbst vorfindet“[18] hat sich für viele nicht nur als undurchführbar, sondern auch als bedrohlich erwiesen. Die für die moralische Persönlichkeitsentwicklung so notwendige Berührbarkeit wird zur Verletzlichkeit, wenn die Person handlungsunsicher wird. Zugänglichkeit wird als Bedrohung empfunden, wenn die Person zu viel Fremdheit erfährt und ihr mit einer Haltung der Gleichgültigkeit oder des Extremismus entgegentritt. Die großen globalen Fragen steigen über den Köpfen der Menschen auf, der Bezug zum Alltag verschwindet aus dem Blickfeld. Berührbarkeit und Zugänglichkeit als emotionale Dimensionen von Moral und moralischer Bildung werden unterlaufen, das Urteilsvermögen wird getrübt und die Aussicht auf Handeln aufgeschoben. Inzwischen übernehmen die sozialen Medien den moralischen Diskurs. Dort können moralisch relevante Erfahrungen (von Schmerz oder Lust, von Leid oder Freude) noch gelebt werden. Mehr noch: Dort kann der Mensch noch reagieren, wenn auch mit einem *Emoji*, aber ohne dafür haften und / oder handeln zu müssen.

Die moralischen Herausforderungen waren bereits global, sind aber erst jetzt in ihrer globalen Dringlichkeit in das Bewusstsein vieler Menschen gedrungen. Selbst die Bedrohung durch die „Pandemie der Gleichgültigkeit“ (Papst Franziskus) ist global geworden. Ich weiß noch genau, wann mir diese Einsicht während meiner Dissertation dämmerte. Als ich Anfang der 1990er Jahre nach einem Vortrag des Theologen und Pädagogen Helmut Peukert in Leuven seinen Text in den Frankfurter Heften las, blieb ich an diesem Satz hängen: „Das prinzipiell Neuartige an der Situation, in die wir hineinwachsen, besteht nun darin, dass die Menschheit, die die Rückwirkungen ihres Handelns aus der einen Biosphäre auf sich als ganzer immer unmittelbarer erfährt und damit zur Einheit wird, keinen Konkurrent mehr außerhalb ihrer selbst hat, sondern nur noch Konkurrent ihrer selbst ist.“[19] Fliehen ist nicht mehr möglich, habe ich damals

---

[17] Vgl. ROEBBEN, Bert: Volharden in de broosheid. Spiritualiteit in tijden van corona, Kapellen/Baarn: Halewijn/Adveniat, 2020.

[18] SAUTERMEISTER, Jochen: Achtsamkeit und Selbstbildung. Theologisch-ethische Anmerkungen zu Selbstkompetenz und Identität, in: SAUTERMEISTER, Jochen / ZWICK, Elisabeth (Hg): Religion und Bildung. Antipoden oder Weggefährten. Diskurse aus historischer, systematischer und praktischer Sicht, Paderborn: Schöningh, 2019, 217–232, hier 226 (Hervorhebung BR).

[19] PEUKERT, Helmut: Über die Zukunft von Bildung, in: Frankfurter Hefte-Extra 5 (1984) 129–137, hier 133. – „Meine These dabei ist, dass wir nur dann, wenn wir unser Wissen und Können schon im ersten Ansatz in eine Ethik intersubjektiver Kreativität in einem universalen Horizont einbinden, eine Chance haben werden, radikalen Gefährdungen zu entgehen, – und dies auch nur, wenn es uns gelingt, den umfassenden und differenzierten

gelernt. Diese Einsicht ist immer stärker geworden und hat sich viele Jahre später in ein Büchlein manifestiert, das ich als Reaktion auf die Pandemie geschrieben habe.[20] Werden wir in der Zerbrechlichkeit ausharren, werden wir lernen, mit der Verletzlichkeit zu leben, als neues moralisches Paradigma für Gesellschaft und Bildung? Und wie wird dies mit der Notwendigkeit einer nachhaltigen Handlungsfähigkeit der Menschen in Einklang zu bringen sein? Niemand weiß, wie es mit den globalen Herausforderungen für die Menschheit weitergeht. Niemand kann abschätzen, welche Auswirkungen das auf die Persönlichkeitsbildung künftiger Generationen haben wird. Eines ist jedoch sicher: Es muss anders werden. Wie dieses *anders* aussehen könnte, versuche ich im nächsten Abschnitt dieses Beitrags anhand des Konzepts der *Compassion* zu definieren.

Compassion als lebensspendende Unterströmung

Ich beginne diesen Abschnitt mit dem Gleichnis vom barmherzigen Samariter im Neuen Testament.[21] Die Geschichte ist bekannt: Ein Mann wird überfallen. Zweimal wird er absichtlich von einem Volksgenossen verletzt zurückgelassen. Eine dritte Person – ein Fremder wohlgemerkt – kümmert sich um ihn, bringt ihn in einer Herberge in Sicherheit und bezahlt die weitere Versorgung. Die Geschichte ist sprachlich sorgfältig aufgebaut. Zweimal heißt es, dass jemand vorbeigeht, das Opfer wahrnimmt und dann in einem weiten Bogen um es herumgeht (im Griechischen wird die Präposition *anti* verwendet). Die dritte Person kommt ebenfalls vorbei, sieht das Opfer und verspürt Mitleid (im Griechischen heißt es: Er ist bis in die Eingeweide gerührt). Die *Compassion* ist von der Größenordnung der *Gebärmütterlichkeit*, wie der Belgische Moraltheologe Roger Burggraeve es umschreiben würde.[22] Der Samariter ist bis in die Eingeweide berührt: Er kann nicht anders, als zu helfen. „Diesem Verlorenen, Aufgegebenen und Aussortierten wendet sich der Samariter zu."[23] Die Frage „Wer ist mein Nächster?" wird in der Geschichte also umgedreht: „Wessen Nächster kann ich werden? Von

Begriff von Bildung und Vernunft in den Bereichen der Politik und der Ökonomie zur Geltung zu bringen und Regressionen des Bewusstseins, auch des religiösen, zu vermeiden" (Ebd., 129–130).

20 Vgl. Roebben 2020 [Anm. 17].

21 Lukas 10, 25–37. sowie Vgl. Roebben, Bert: Religionspädagogische Kartographie, Münster: Lit-Verlag, 2023 (= Forum Theologie und Pädagogik 26), 66–67.

22 Vgl. Burggraeve, Roger: Baarmoederlijkheid van mens en God, Antwerpen: Halewijn, 2021.

23 Kuld, Lothar: Compassion: solidarisch handeln lernen, in: Sautermeister, Jochen / Zwick, Elisabeth (Hg): Religion und Bildung. Antipoden oder Weggefährten. Diskurse aus historischer, systematischer und praktischer Sicht, Paderborn: Schöningh, 2019, 321–335, hier 327.

wem werde ich berührt und wende ich mich zu, für wen kann ich konkret lebensdienlich werden?"[24]

In der Geschichte geht es um menschwürdiges Leben. Muss dieser Mann halbtot zurückbleiben oder ist die Rettung nah? Kann er auf einen Mitmenschen bauen der ihn aufrichtet, wieder in Bewegung bringt und ihm neues Leben schenkt, oder wird sein Leben unwiderruflich auf der Schattenseite der Gesellschaft scheitern? Und welches Leben wartet auf ihn nach der Erlösung: Leben in Fülle (Johannes 10,10) vielleicht? Jedenfalls nimmt ihn der Samariter mit in eine Herberge und bezahlt für Kost und Logie. So ist wenigstens sein Alltag nicht verloren. Er kann wieder weiterziehen. Dieses Recht auf ein erfülltes Leben als Unterströmung bildet die Rahmenerzählung dieses biblischen Textes. Es geht im Grunde um das, was wir als Menschen in „verletzlicher Differenz"[25] mit-einander teilen, nämlich das Leben selbst.

In der moralischen Bildung geht es darum, dieses *de facto* schon gegebene Leben auch *in actu* zu ermöglichen und im Sinne einer „Solidaritätsschöpfung"[26] weiterzuentwickeln. Sinnvolles und menschwürdiges Leben muss immer durch empathisches Einfühlungsvermögen, kluges Urteilsvermögen und solidarisches Handeln ermöglicht werden und kann nicht als selbstverständlich vorausgesetzt werden. Leben muss sich zu „gestaltetem Leben"[27] oder „gelingendem Leben"[28] entwickeln können. „Die Hinwendung zum anderen, die grundsätzliche Sorge um dessen Wohlergehen, Mitmenschlichkeit und Solidarität" muss „generiert", „verankert"[29] und als „Wertprimärerfahrung"[30] eingeübt werden, mit Blick auf das gute Leben für alle. Die Lehrperson ist diejenige, die glaubt, dass diese Grundhaltung erlernbar ist, weil sie selbst "in a profession of faith, faith in the nature of ultimate reality, in the matrix of mercy in which our lives are embedded"[31] verankert ist.

---

24 Vgl. JANS, Jan: Zichzelf als naaste, in: MERKS, Karl-Wilhelm / SCHREURS, Nico (Hg.): De passie van een grensganger. Theologie aan de vooravond van het derde millennium, Baarn: Ten Have, 1997, 227–236.

25 ROEBBEN, Bert: Schulen für das Leben. Eine kleine Didaktik der Hoffnung, Stuttgart: Calwer Verlag, 2016, 54–56.

26 KULD 2019 [Anm. 23], 333.

27 EXELER, Adolf: Gestaltetes Leben. Grundlinien einer Moralpädagogik, in: KatBl 102 (1977) 1, 6–23.

28 ENGLERT, Rudolf: Ethische Bildung im Horizont von Pluralität und Wahrheitsfragen, in: LINDNER, Konstantin / ZIMMERMANN, Mirjam (Hg.): Handbuch Ethische Bildung. Religionspädagogische Fokussierungen, Tübingen: Mohr Siebeck, 2021, 273–280, hier 279.

29 LENZ, Viktoria: Empathie lernen – Moralpsychologische Perspektiven, in: SAUTERMEISTER, Jochen / ZWICK, Elisabeth (Hg): Religion und Bildung. Antipoden oder Weggefährten. Diskurse aus historischer, systematischer und praktischer Sicht, Paderborn: Schöningh, 2019, 349–360, hier 356.

30 Konstantin Lindner, zitiert in NAURATH 2021 [Anm. 7], 227.

31 PALMER, Parker: Let your life speak. Listening for the voice of vocation, San Francisco: Jossey-Bass, 2000, 65.

Compassion kann also als eine warme, lebensspendende Unterströmung in der Moral und in der moralischen Bildung definiert werden. Es bedeutet buchstäblich, mit den Mitmenschen mitzufühlen, aber auch mit ihnen mitzudenken und mitzuhandeln. Wir sind alle auf der Suche nach einem sinnvollen und erfüllten Leben, einem Leben, das wir miteinander teilen, indem wir aus derselben Lebensquelle trinken. Die amerikanische Religionspädagogin Jennifer Ayres drückt es folgendermaßen aus: "Human life is rooted in what Judith Butler (...) calls 'primary vulnerability', a kind of bodily and emotional fragility that connects us with other human beings and with the more-than-human world (...)."[32] Leben ist das, was wir als verletzliche Menschen mit verletzlichen Mitmenschen und mit der gesamten verletzlichen Welt und Schöpfung teilen.

In einer integrierten Perspektive der moralischen Bildung (siehe Abschnitt 1, erster autobiographischer Impuls) und vor dem Hintergrund der großen globalen Herausforderungen (siehe Abschnitt 1, zweiter autobiographischer Impuls) erhält die Trias Sehen-Urteilen-Handeln dann eine neue Interpretation. Sie wird mit Leben gefüllt, mit der Verletzlichkeit, die den Menschen, den Gemeinschaften und dem Kosmos so eigen und vertraut ist, die aber immer wieder vergessen, verleugnet oder abgetan wird. Um diese Quelle des Lebens auszudrücken, bedarf es keiner gesonderten Kategorie in der Trias, wie es oft versucht wurde. Der deutsche Religionspädagoge Reinhold Boschki etwa sprach von einer vierten Kategorie, die dem Trias vorausgeht, nämlich „Orientierung"[33] als „Standort-bestimmung und Blickrichtung."[34] Der amerikanische Praktische Theologe David F. White fügte zwischen Urteilen und Handeln einen sogenannten „spiritual-imaginative Modus" hinzu, bei dem „remembering and dreaming" eine zentrale Rolle spielen.[35] Im Grundlagendokument der Christlichen Arbeiterjugend wiederum heißt es, dass nach dem dreigleisigen Vorgehen ein Moment des Feierns stattfinden soll.[36] Positionierung, Imagination und Feiern sind drei emotional geprägte Aktivitäten, die auch in den traditionellen Trias als Ganzes und / oder in jeden Schritt einzeln als lebensspendende Aktivitäten eingebaut werden können. Wer sich orientiert, wer sich vorstellt und wer feiert, lässt sich in seiner primären Verletzlichkeit (Judith Butler) von der lebendigen Gegenwart des anderen berühren.

Diese inhaltliche Füllung der Trias mit *Leben-in-Fülle* lässt sich auch historisch begründen. So hat der belgische Priester Joseph Cardijn (1882–1967), Gründer der Christlichen Arbeiterjugend (CAJ), diesen Dreiklang auf der Grundlage

---

32 AYRES, Jennifer: A Pedagogy for Precarious Times. Religious Education and Vulnerability, in: Religious Education 116 (2021) 4, 327–340, hier 328.

33 Vgl. BOSCHKI, Reinhold: Einführung in die Religionspädagogik, Darmstadt: WBG ³2017, 84–85.

34 Ebd., 117–144.

35 Vgl. WHITE, David F.: Practicing Discernment with Youth. A Transformative Youth Ministry Approach, Cleveland (OH): The Pilgrim Press, 2005, 74–77.

36 CHRISTLICHER ARBEITERJUGEND (CAJ): Sehen – Urteilen – Handeln. Einige Grundlagen, Essen, s. d., 12.

einer christlichen Dialektik[37] entworfen, in der übrigens das Urteilen an erster Stelle steht (als These: die religiöse Wahrheit und Sendung des Arbeiters), gefolgt vom Sehen (als Antithese: die entmenschlichende Lebenswirklichkeit des Arbeiters) und vom Handeln (als Synthese: die Gründung der CAJ als pastorale Antwort auf diese Situation).[38] Für Cardijn war die hermeneutische und pädagogische Wirkung dieses dreigliedrigen Ansatzes mit der moralisch qualifizierten Erfahrung der Empörung über das Schicksal der Arbeiter zu Beginn des 20. Jahrhunderts verbunden. Dies war „kein Leben mehr". Das musste geändert werden. Mit Cardijn entstand eine Perspektive der *Compassion*, die einfühlsam, kritisch und handlungsorientiert ist. Auch zu Beginn des 21. Jahrhunderts bleibt seine Einsicht lebenswichtig.[39]

Pädagogische Konkretisierung von Verletzlichkeit

Vor dem Hintergrund der Analyse, dass das Leben als Quelle moralischer Entscheidungsfindung und Sinngebung prekär[40] geworden ist und „der Mensch in seiner freien, verantwortlichen Existenz zu einem Anachronismus zu werden droht, zu einem Auslaufmodell",[41] schlagen Autoren wie Jennifer Ayres vor, an einer „pedagogy for precarity"[42] zu arbeiten, in der „embodiment, storytelling and community" die zentralen Ansatzpunkte sind. Diese drei Aspekte möchte ich hier kurz als Kraftquellen erläutern.

In menschlichen Beziehungen berührt zu werden, setzt Körperlichkeit voraus, die Fähigkeit, mit anderen körperlich zu interagieren. Interaktionsmöglichkeiten für Kinder und Jugendliche sind in zwei Bereichen vorhanden: mit Gleichaltrigen und mit Erwachsenen. In beiden Fällen geht es darum, Verantwortung zu übernehmen, persönlich auf die Frage oder das Bedürfnis des anderen einzugehen, zu lernen, sich in der eigenen moralischen Kraft und Präsenz zu positionieren. Mit den Worten des australischen praktischen Theologen Terry Veling in Anlehnung an Lévinas:

---

37 Vgl. BRIEDEN, Norbert / HEGER, Johannes: Art. Handlungswissenschaft, in: Wirelex 2018, 5–6.

38 Vgl. ANTONY, Bernhard: Art. Cardijn, Josef, in: METTE, Norbert / RICKERS, Folkert (Hg.): Lexikon der Religionspädagogik, Neukirchen-Vluyn: Neukirchener Verlag, 2001, 252–253; vgl. auch CHRISTLICHER ARBEITERJUGEND [Anm. 36], 3.

39 Vgl. die Analyse der amerikanischen Politik nach Trump aus dieser Sicht in DICK, John: See, Judge, Act, in: Today's American Catholic. A Journal of Enquiry, Reflection and Opinion 2021 – online: https://www.todaysamericancatholic.org/2021/11/see-judge-act/ (abgerufen am 07.03.2023).

40 Judith Butler spricht von "precarious life", vgl. AYRES 2021 [Anm. 32], 338.

41 GRÜMME, Bernhard: Menschen bilden? Eine religionspädagogische Anthropologie, Freiburg im Breisgau: Herder, 2012, 493.

42 AYRES 2021 [Anm. 32], 335–337.

> "I cannot ask someone else to answer for my life. I have no 'alibi' that can come to my defense. I cannot evade 'the answerable act or deed' of my own life – no one can answer for me or take my place. Only I can respond to another, and this is what constitutes the singularity of my unique place in existence, and the unique vocation or answerability of my life. In other words: I am required."[43]

Im Umgang mit Gleichaltrigen kann z. B. in der Schule an einer „just community" (Lawrence Kohlberg) gearbeitet werden, in der z. B. *Mobbing*, das heute nicht nur physisch, sondern auch digital stattfindet und Verletzungen verursacht, nicht ignoriert, sondern thematisiert und effektiv bearbeitet wird. Im Umgang mit Erwachsenen ist das Thema der Persönlichkeit des / der Erzieher*in oder des / der Lehrer*in von großer Bedeutung: wie er / sie die Kluft zwischen moralischem Fühlen, Denken und Handeln überbrückt, wie er / sie Kindern und Jugendlichen auf der Suche nach dem guten Leben ein Vorbild ist und dafür Zeugnis ablegt, auch wenn dies zu Reibungen führt. Reibung in der Erziehung ist auf den ersten Blick etwas Negatives, da es sich um einen Konflikt handelt. Aber dieser Konflikt kann auch heilsam sein: Reibung erzeugt Wärme, Engagement, Anwesenheit und Interesse.[44] Als Ansprechpartner ist der Erwachsene vor allem ein „Träger einer Begründungspraxis",[45] jemand, der tut, was er sagt und sagt, was er tut.

Storytelling ist ein zweiter Schwerpunkt in einer Pädagogik der Verletzlichkeit. Jennifer Ayres verbindet dies vor allem mit dem Ausdruck von Trauer zum Zweck der Traumaverarbeitung. Ich verbinde es vielmehr mit der „weltanschaulichen Deutungsoffenheit"[46] von Geschichten, Symbolen und Figuren,[47] die dafür sorgen, dass Menschen – über weltanschauliche Grenzen hinweg – eine Sprachebene finden, um sich interkontextuell aufeinander einzulassen und sich über

---

43 VELING, Terry: For You Alone. Emmanuel Levinas and the Answerable Life, Eugene: Cascade Books, 2014, 133.

44 Vgl. ROEBBEN, Bert: Erziehung als Gastfreundschaft. Über Normen, Werte und Sinngebung in der Erziehung in der Familie, in: Jugendwohl. Zeitschrift für Kinder- und Jugendhilfe 76 (1995), 480–489; vgl. ROEBBEN 2016 [Anm. 25]. Dieser Gedanke liegt mir auch nach all den Jahren noch am Herzen, siehe z. B. die Rolle der Lehrperson als Vermittler*in zwischen den aufeinanderprallenden Welten der Jugendkultur einerseits und der Schulkultur andererseits, vgl. ROEBBEN, Bert: Kollidierende Welten im Religionsunterricht? Religionspädagogische Perspektiven auf Ambiguität in Umbruchszeiten, in: SAUTERMEISTER, Jochen / BLUMENTHAL, Christian / HORNUNG, Christian / ROEBBEN, Bert (Hg.): Ambiguitäten – Identitäten – Sinnentwürfe. Theologische Perspektiven, Freiburg im Breisgau: Herder, 2023, 167–182.

45 SAUTERMEISTER 2017 [Anm. 14], 50.

46 TOASPERN, David: Lernen durch wertbasiertes Handeln, in: LINDNER, Konstantin / ZIMMERMANN, Mirjam (Hg.): Handbuch Ethische Bildung. Religionspädagogische Fokussierungen, Tübingen: Mohr Siebeck, 2021, 318–325, hier 323.

47 Vgl. ZIMMERMANN, Ruben: Narrative Ethik, in: LINDNER, Konstantin / ZIMMERMANN, Mirjam (Hg.): Handbuch Ethische Bildung. Religionspädagogische Fokussierungen, Tübingen: Mohr Siebeck, 2021, 77–83.

die Beweggründe und Triebkräfte ihres Engagements auszutauschen.[48] Solche Erzählungen können ausgetauscht werden, Menschen können von den Sinnentwürfen der anderen lernen, um das professionelle Handeln, das sie mit anderen teilen, in ihrer individuellen Profession oder Berufung, in ihrer eigenen Lebensgeschichte zu verankern.

Und schließlich gibt es die Bedeutung der Gemeinschaft als Nährboden für die Unterströmung des Lebens und damit für die moralische Bildung. Die großen Fragen des Lebens, die globalen Herausforderungen, vor denen wir als Menschheit stehen und die unausweichlich sind, müssen im Kleinen, im Alltag und im Zusammenleben mit konkreten Mitmenschen beantwortet werden, im Sinne von be-antwort-bar sein. Die *kleine Schwester* der Barmherzigkeit, die Höflichkeit, kann dies unterstützen. Sie ist verblüffend einfach: ein guter Morgen am Schultor, ein Kompliment im Unterricht, ein Moment der Rücksichtnahme auf den anderen in der Not, eine Meinungsverschiedenheit, die höflich ausgetragen wird, eine Grundhaltung des „Nach dir." Gelebt wird diese Kultur von Eltern, Erzieher*innen und Lehrer*innen, die glaubwürdig sind und die für diese Werte heute, aber auch morgen, verantwortlich sind. „Wer anderen Gutes tut, dem geht es selber gut" (Sprüche 11, 25). Die Superdiversität wird in unserer sich globalisierenden Gesellschaft noch komplexer werden, aber es ist die Herausforderung für die Gesellschaft und ihr Erziehungshandeln, die Unterschiede in der Weltanschauung und im Lebensgefühl zuzulassen und dennoch höflich miteinander umzugehen.

Eine theologische Schlussfolgerung?

Sollte dieser Beitrag mit einer theologischen Reflexion enden? Offensichtlich nicht. Moralische Bildung braucht keine Begründung aus einer transzendenten Perspektive. Ihr genügt das gleichzeitig in Freiheit und Verantwortung gelebte Leben: das Fühlen, Denken und Handeln zusammen mit konkreten Menschen. Aber moralische Bildung stößt an ihre Grenzen bei schwierigen (sprich: ambivalenten und komplexen) Entscheidungen. Dann stellen sich Fragen wie: Warum überhaupt moralisch sein? Warum sich nicht in Zynismus oder Extremismus verlieren und der Verantwortung entziehen? Was hält einen Menschen letztlich aufrecht, um frei und verantwortungsbewusst – sprich: integer – zu leben? Und wie weit darf man gehen, wenn man mit anderen mitfühlt, wenn man mit anderen mitleidet?

---

48 Vgl. das Projekt von Eboo Patel in den VSA und die Konkretisierung des „Lernens in der Gegenwart des Anderen", in: Roebben 2016 [Anm. 25], 96–99, sowie die Idee der spirituellen Kommunikation bei Mikhail Bakhtin, in: Ebd. 99–100.

Man kann die Geschichte des barmherzigen Samariter als eine moralische Beispielgeschichte lesen, „als ein Modell realistischer Mitleidenschaft", so der Neutestamentler Gerd Theissen.[49] „Der Samariter hilft, soweit die Situation es von ihm erfordert und soweit, wie er es kann. Er hilft nicht grenzenlos, aber der Situation angemessen. Die Frage, wem mein Mitgefühl und meine Hilfs-bereitschaft gelten, ergibt sich aus der Situation."[50] Man kann die Geschichte aber auch als ein Zeugnis der *Compassion* gegenüber einem konkreten Menschen lesen, der für die gesamte Menschheit steht. Die Geschichte erzählt dann von einer *Entgrenzung* der moralischen Verantwortung gegenüber all jenen, die potenziell zum Nächsten werden könnten, von einem Überschuss an Menschlichkeit, der sich gegenüber Fremden, ja sogar Feinden ausdrückt.[51] Die Geschichte ist also nicht nur eine schöne, nachahmenswerte Beispielgeschichte, sondern auch eine, die zum Nachdenken anregt über menschlichen Umgang und den Wunsch, wie mit einem umgegangen wird, über Leben geben und Leben nehmen, über Freiheit und Verantwortung.

> „Als vortheologische und unideologische Größe ist eine empathische und compathische Spiritualität richtungsweisend für die Zukunft und das Wohlergehen der Menschen, denn sie kann gläubige, spirituelle und areligiöse Menschen vereinen, weil sie aus dem christlichen Glauben und anderen glaubensbasierten Traditionen ebenso schöpft wie aus humanistischen Motiven."[52]

Diese Spiritualität ist zugleich in Traditionen verankert und geht über Traditionen hinaus. Für die Menschheit der Zukunft besteht die Aufgabe darin, neue Wege für diese Spiritualität des Gutes-tun-ohne-Worum-Willen (Meister Eckhart) zu entdecken und tatsächlich zu leben.

Literatur

ANDREE, Maurice / DOMSEL, Maike Maria: Die Paradigmen der Compassion und Freiheit als Bindeglieder zwischen Theologie und Ethik? Möglichkeiten spirituell-reflexiver Praxis im schulischen Kontext, in: ÖRF 30 (2022) 1, 110–127.

---

49 Zitiert in KULD, Lothar: Art. Compassion, in: METTE, Norbert / RICKERS, Folkert (Hg.): Lexikon der Religionspädagogik, Neukirchen-Vluyn: Neukirchener Verlag, 2001, 293–295, hier 295.

50 Ebd.

51 "The class of 'neighbour' has no bounds", so David Pailin, zitiert in REINDERS, Hans: Receiving the Gift of Friendship. Profound Disability, Theological Anthropology and Ethics, Grand Rapids: Eerdmans, 2008, 191 und 221.

52 ANDREE, Maurice / DOMSEL, Maike Maria: Die Paradigmen der Compassion und Freiheit als Bindeglieder zwischen Theologie und Ethik? Möglichkeiten spirituell-reflexiver Praxis im schulischen Kontext, in: ÖRF 30 (2022) 1, 110–127, hier 121–122.

AUER, Alfons / BIESINGER, Albert / GUTSCHERA, Herbert (Hg.): Moralerziehung im Religionsunterricht, Freiburg im Breisgau: Herder, 1975.

ANTONY, Bernhard: Art. Cardijn, Josef, in: METTE, Norbert / RICKERS, Folkert (Hg.): Lexikon der Religionspädagogik, Neukirchen-Vluyn: Neukirchener Verlag, 2001, 252–253.

AYRES, Jennifer: A Pedagogy for Precarious Times. Religious Education and Vulnerability, in: Religious Education 116 (2021) 4, 327–340.

BIEHL, Peter: Erfahrung – Glaube – Bildung. Studien zu einer erfahrungsbezogenen Religionspädagogik, Gütersloh: Mohn, 1991.

BOSCHKI, Reinhold: Einführung in die Religionspädagogik, Darmstadt: WBG, [3]2017.

BRIEDEN, Norbert / HEGER, Johannes: Art. Handlungswissenschaft, in: Wirelex, 2018.

BURGGRAEVE, Roger: Baarmoederlijkheid van mens en God, Antwerpen: Halewijn, 2021.

CHRISTLICHER ARBEITERJUGEND (CAJ): Sehen – Urteilen – Handeln. Einige Grundlagen, Essen, s.d.

DICK, John: See, Judge, Act, in: Today's American Catholic. A Journal of Enquiry, Reflection and Opinion 2021 – online: https://www.todaysamericancatholic.org/2021/11/see-judge-act (abgerufen am 07.03.2023).

EID, Volker / ELSÄSSER, Antonellus / HUNOLD, Gerfried W. (Hg.): Moralische Kompetenz. Chancen der Moralpädagogik in einer pluralen Lebenswelt, Mainz: Grünewald, 1995.

ENGLERT, Rudolf: Ethische Bildung im Horizont von Pluralität und Wahrheitsfragen, in: LINDNER, Konstantin / ZIMMERMANN, Mirjam (Hg.): Handbuch Ethische Bildung. Religionspädagogische Fokussierungen, Tübingen: Mohr Siebeck, 2021, 273–280.

EXELER, Adolf: Gestaltetes Leben. Grundlinien einer Moralpädagogik, in: KatBl 102 (1977) 1, 6–23.

GRÜMME, Bernhard: Menschen bilden? Eine religionspädagogische Anthropologie, Freiburg im Breisgau: Herder, 2012.

HILPERT, Konrad: Ethisches Lernen, in: Religionsunterricht an höheren Schulen 36 (1993) 2, 70–82.

JANS, Jan: Zichzelf als naaste, in: MERKS, Karl-Wilhelm / SCHREURS, Nico (Hg.): De passie van een grensganger. Theologie aan de vooravond van het derde millennium, Baarn: Ten Have, 1997, 227–236.

KULD, Lothar: Art. Compassion, in: METTE, Norbert / RICKERS, Folkert (Hg.): Lexikon der Religionspädagogik, Neukirchen-Vluyn: Neukirchener Verlag, 2001, 293–295.

KULD, Lothar: Compassion: solidarisch handeln lernen, in: SAUTERMEISTER, Jochen / ZWICK, Elisabeth (Hg): Religion und Bildung: Antipoden oder Weggefährten. Diskurse aus historischer, systematischer und praktischer Sicht, Paderborn: Schöningh, 2019, 321–335.

LENZ, Viktoria: Empathie lernen – Moralpsychologische Perspektiven, in: SAUTERMEISTER, Jochen / ZWICK, Elisabeth (Hg): Religion und Bildung. Antipoden oder Weggefährten. Diskurse aus historischer, systematischer und praktischer Sicht, Paderborn: Schöningh, 2019, 349–360.

LICKONA, Thomas: Educating for character. How our schools can teach respect and responsibility, New York: Bantam Books, 1991.

METTE, Norbert: Bildung und verbindliches Handeln. Identität in universaler Solidarität, in: Stimmen der Zeit 119 (1994) 7, 453–464.

NAURATH, Elisabeth: Übertragung, Erhellung, Entwicklung, Kommunikation, Erfahrung. Strategien ethischer Bildung im Religionsunterricht, in: LINDNER, Konstantin / ZIMMERMANN, Mirjam (Hg.): Handbuch Ethische Bildung. Religionspädagogische Fokussierungen, Tübingen: Mohr Siebeck, 2021, 222–229.

NIEUW, Wij – www.nieuwwij.nl (abgerufen am 07.03.2023).

NIPKOW, Karl Ernst: Moralerziehung. Pädagogische und theologische Antworten, Gütersloh: Mohn, 1981.

NIPKOW, Karl Ernst: Art. Erziehung, in: Theologische Realenzyklopädie (Band 10), Berlin/New York: De Gruyter, 1982, 232–254.

PALMER, Parker: Let your life speak. Listening for the voice of vocation, San Francisco: Jossey-Bass, 2000.

PEUKERT, Helmut: Über die Zukunft von Bildung, in: Frankfurter Hefte-Extra 5 (1984), 129–137.

REINDERS, Hans: Receiving the Gift of Friendship. Profound Disability, Theological Anthropology and Ethics, Grand Rapids: Eerdmans, 2008.

ROEBBEN, Bert: Een tijd van opvoeden. Moraalpedagogiek in christelijk perspectief, Leuven/Amersfoort: Acco, 1995.

ROEBBEN, Bert: Erziehung als Gastfreundschaft. Über Normen, Werte und Sinngebung in der Erziehung in der Familie, in: Jugendwohl. Zeitschrift für Kinder- und Jugendhilfe 76 (1995), 480–489.

ROEBBEN, Bert: Moralpädagogik und moralische Sensibilität, in: Jugendwohl. Zeitschrift für Kinder- und Jugendhilfe 79 (1998) 11, 510–519.

Roebben, Bert: Religionspädagogik der Hoffnung. Grundlinien religiöser Bildung in der Spätmoderne, Berlin: Lit-Verlag, 2011 (= Forum Theologie und Pädagogik 19).

ROEBBEN, Bert: Schulen für das Leben. Eine kleine Didaktik der Hoffnung, Stuttgart: Calwer Verlag, 2016.

ROEBBEN, Bert: Volharden in de broosheid. Spiritualiteit in tijden van corona, Kapellen/Baarn: Halewijn/Adveniat, 2020.

ROEBBEN, Bert: Kollidierende Welten im Religionsunterricht? Religionspädagogische Perspektiven auf Ambiguität in Umbruchszeiten, in: SAUTERMEISTER, Jochen / BLUMENTHAL, Christian / HORNUNG, Christian / ROEBBEN, Bert (Hg.): Ambiguitäten – Identitäten – Sinnentwürfe. Theologische Perspektiven, Freiburg im Breisgau: Herder, 2023, 167–182.

ROEBBEN, Bert: Religionspädagogische Kartographie, Münster: Lit-Verlag, 2023 (= Forum Theologie und Pädagogik 26).

ROTHGANGEL, Martin / SCHELANDER, Robert: Art. Bildung, in: Wirelex 2015.

SAUTERMEISTER, Jochen: Identität und Integrität. Verantwortliche Lebensführung und Orientierung in Zeiten der Instabilität, in: BERGHOLD, Ralph / SAUTERMEISTER, Jochen / SCHRÖDER, André (Hg.): Dem Wandel eine menschliche Gestalt geben. Sozialethische Perspektiven für die Gesellschaft von Morgen, Freiburg im Breisgau: Herder, 2017, S. 43–60.

SAUTERMEISTER, Jochen: Achtsamkeit und Selbstbildung. Theologisch-ethische Anmerkungen zu Selbstkompetenz und Identität, in: SAUTERMEISTER, Jochen / ZWICK, Elisabeth (Hg): Religion und Bildung: Antipoden oder Weggefährten. Diskurse aus historischer, systematischer und praktischer Sicht, Paderborn: Schöningh, 2019, 217–232.

STACHEL, Günter / MIETH, Dietmar: Ethisch handeln lernen. Zu Konzeption und Inhalt ethischer Erziehung, Zürich: Benziger, 1978.

TOASPERN, David: Lernen durch wertbasiertes Handeln, in: LINDNER, Konstantin / ZIMMERMANN, Mirjam (Hg.): Handbuch Ethische Bildung. Religionspädagogische Fokussierungen, Tübingen: Mohr Siebeck, 2021, 318–325.

TZSCHEETZSCH, Werner: Identität durch Kommunikation. Kirchliche Jugendarbeit als Ort interkultureller Wertekommunikation, in: SCHREIJÄCK, Thomas (Hg.): Religion im Dialog der Kulturen, Münster: Lit-Verlag, 251–259.

VAN DER VEN, Johannes: Vorming in waarden en normen, Kampen: Kok-Agora, 1985.

VAN DER VEN, Johannes: Formation of the Moral Self, Grand Rapids: W.B. Eerdmans, 1998.

VAN DER VEN, Johannes: Das moralische Selbst. Gestaltung und Bildung, Münster: Lit-Verlag, 1999 (= Empirische Theologie 1).

VELING, Terry: For You Alone. Emmanuel Levinas and the Answerable Life, Eugene: Cascade Books, 2014.

WHITE, David F.: Practicing Discernment with Youth. A Transformative Youth Ministry Approach, Cleveland (OH): The Pilgrim Press, 2005.

ZIEBERTZ, Hans-Georg / ROEBBEN, Bert: Art. Moralpädagogik, in: Lexikon für Theologie und Kirche (Band 7), Freiburg im Breisgau: Herder, [3]1998, 455–458.

ZIEBERTZ, Hans-Georg: Art. Ethisches Lernen, in: HILGER, Georg / LEIMGRUBER, Stephan / ZIEBERTZ, Hans-Georg (Hg.): Religionsdidaktik. Ein Leitfaden für Studium, Ausbildung und Beruf, München: Kösel, 2010, 434–452.

ZIMMERMANN, Ruben: Narrative Ethik, in: LINDNER, Konstantin / ZIMMERMANN, Mirjam (Hg.): Handbuch Ethische Bildung. Religionspädagogische Fokussierungen, Tübingen: Mohr Siebeck, 2021, 77–83.

Exploring Climate Justice and Compassion through the Lens of Theology – Thought-Provoking Impulses from a European and Filipino Perspective

Maike Maria Domsel

In diesem Artikel wird auf die Auswirkungen des Postkolonialismus auf heutige Gesellschaften eingegangen, wobei ein besonderer Schwerpunkt auf dem Verhältnis zwischen kolonialen Strukturen, Nachhaltigkeit und Umweltfragen auf den Philippinen liegt. Besondere Aufmerksamkeit wird der Ungleichheit zwischen ehemaligen Kolonisatoren und den Kolonisierten gewidmet, die durch die globale Klimakrise noch weiter verstärkt wird. Durch die Einbindung des Compassion-Paradigmas von Metz und des Fähigkeitsansatzes von Sen und Nussbaum wird dieser Zusammenhang genauer untersucht. Das Ziel besteht darin, vor dem Hintergrund philippinischer und europäischer Perspektiven ein Bewusstsein für diese Thematik zu schaffen, insbesondere durch die Auseinandersetzung mit einer Theologie der Schöpfung.

Dekoloniale Theologie; Klimagerechtigkeit; Compassion; Capabilities-Ansatz; Schöpfungstheologie

This article focuses on the impact of postcolonialism on contemporary societies. A particular emphasis is placed on the relationship between colonial structures, sustainability, and environmental issues in the Philippines. Special attention is given to the inequality between former colonizers and the colonized, which is further exacerbated by the global climate crisis. By incorporating Metz's paradigm of compassion and Sen and Nussbaum's capabilities approach, this connection is examined in greater detail. The aim is to raise awareness of this issue, drawing from Philippine and European perspectives, and specifically engaging with a theology of creation.

Decolonial theology; climate justice; compassion; capabilities approach; theology of creation

Introductory words[1]

Postcolonialism refers to the persistence of patterns of colonial power and their after-effects on contemporary societies and cultures. This phenomenon is expressed in various aspects of life, including economic and political systems, cultural attitudes, personal relationships, and environmental issues. The dominance of Western economic and political systems, the persistence of racial and ethnic stereotypes, and the disproportionate impact of environmental degradation on marginalized communities are all examples of postcolonialism. Understanding postcolonialism is crucial for addressing ongoing issues of power, inequality, and injustice in our world today.[2]

In the past, European Powers colonized many countries in Africa and Asia. Today we are faced with this history of oppression, which still has an impact on the present. I would like to explore this history as someone who grew up in a European context in the German-Belgian-Dutch border area, where these three countries have owned colonies mainly in Asia, Africa, and the New World, and thus can be considered former colonial powers. My colleague, with whom I prepared the contribution for the conference, was born in the Philippines. After studying in Germany, he now lives and works back in his homeland, which was colonized by Europeans, i.e. more precisely, mainly Spanish conquerors, and can therefore look back on a history of suppression. We are both particularly aware of this past and want to deal with it responsibly, especially by initiating a dialogue about the impact of colonial history on contemporary life. This article aims to disseminate the knowledge acquired from our collaborative efforts and the conference, with a primary focus on examining the interrelationship between colonial structures and sustainability, specifically in the context of the Philippines. To broaden the perspective, I would like to explore what the former colonial powers could learn from the former colonized about sustainability and environmental protection. Additionally, I will investigate the role that religion and spirituality play in this context.

Before I address these questions, I provide an overview of the structure of this paper. This includes a brief outline of the colonial history of the Philippines under the Spanish conquerors, as well as an examination of the impact of these colonial structures on the environment today. Furthermore, I connect this story

---

1 The present article is a collaborative effort, resulting from the joint contributions of Lougigie Pontillo, a theologian specializing in Mission Theology, and myself. It serves as a follow-up to our presentation at the Twin Conference of KU Leuven and Ateneo de Manila University, entitled "De/colonizing Theologies: Glocal Histories, Contemporary Challenges", which took place from March 27th to March 30th, 2023.

2 KERNER, Ina: Postkoloniale Theorien zur Einführung, Hamburg: Junius, 2012, 9; LIEDHOLZ, Yannick: Berührungspunkte von Sozialer Arbeit und Klimawandel. Perspektiven und Handlungsspielräume, Opladen – Berlin – Toronto: Barbara Budrich, 2021, 41–45.

of injustice with the paradigm of compassion to establish references to the capabilities approach according to Nussbaum. Pope Francis' proclamation Laudato si' and further theological implications are also addressed about unjust living conditions and climate justice.

The Philippines and their colonial history with Spain

Spanish missionaries and conquistadores[3] arrived in the Philippines in the early 16th century. Catholic historians as well as non-Catholic scholars agreed that the Spaniards crossed the seas primarily to Christianize the colonized pagan lands. In addition, there was another interest, as Pedro Gagelonia puts it: "Economic prosperity and political greatness were their secondary goals."[4] They had a strong desire to enter the lucrative oriental trade, particularly that of spices, which was a Portuguese monopoly in the early sixteenth century. They also wanted a geographical base to establish trade and missionary contacts with China and Japan.

To overcome the obstacle of a widely dispersed population in the archipelago, the Spaniards tried to gather the natives in towns and villages to be able to instruct them without enormous difficulty. The people were gathered in different villages of a certain size to make baptismal teaching and baptism easier. This strategy was called *Reduction*. The so-called *visita capilla*, i. e. visiting chapels, was built in the small villages and was visited regularly by missionaries to teach the rural population and celebrate mass.[5]

The encomienda system[6] initially served as an instrument of Spanish colonial policy in Latin America to set and thus systematize government taxes. Conversion to the Christian faith was carried out in this way. The predominantly secular encomenderos were obliged to grant the natives military protection, suppress revolts and carry out public works. "They should collect a certain

3 Conquistadores is a term used to refer to soldiers and explorers of the Spanish and the Portuguese Empire in a general sense. During the Age of Discovery, conquistadores sailed beyond Europe to North and South America, Oceania, Africa and Asia to conquer new territories and open trade routes.

4 GAGELONIA, Pedro: The Filipino Historian. Controversial Issues in Philippine History, Manila: Feuci, 1970, 49–50.

5 MÜLLER, Hilja: Philippinen. Ein Länderporträt (Schriftenreihe 10507), Bonn: Bundeszentrale für Politische Bildung, 2020, 56–58.

6 The encomienda system was a type of wage system used to compensate Spanish conquerors and soldiers who had served in the conquest. It was first used during the Roman period in Spain and then after the Christian reconquest of the Muslim lands. On an even larger scale, this wage system was used during the colonization of America and the Philippines.

amount of taxes from the residents in kind or gold and require certain labor services."[7] They also had the task of briefly instructing the basics of the faith, preparing them for baptism, and building chapels. The missionaries found out, however, that the encomenderos had done little of those spiritual tasks and had been suppressing them through forced labor.

The aftermath of colonial structures: environmental and economic devastation

In dealing with the historicity of climate change, there is a challenge to go back in time to when European nations colonized much of the world, extracting natural resources, forcing millions into slavery, and setting up the plantation system. Before this time, the indigenous peoples of the Philippines lived in a fundamental balance with the environment, using it to obtain food while protecting it. Their alimentary system was independent and interwoven with language, traditional knowledge, and cultural heritage. Moreover, it was the result of well-thought-out management of their land and efficient use of resources without harming the environment. After all, only as much was taken as was needed, so that resources could be renewed.[8]

Colonization largely suppressed this way of dealing with the environment sustainably. When people are conscious of the history of colonialism, they can trace the link between empire-building and exploitation of the land and the subjugation of the native people. Created by practices born of a colonial mindset to create wealth, climate change has become one of our most pressing threats today. There is a need to explore these quite complex legacies and relationships between colonialism and climate change.[9]

People in the countries of the Global South suffer the most from this. Again and again, natural disasters destroy their livelihoods. Moreover, it is mainly people in developing countries who lose their lives due to natural disasters. The World Risk Report, a specialized report on global disaster risks, sees a high risk

---

7 SCHREUERS, Peter: Caraga Antigua 1521–1910: The Hispanization and Christianization of Agusan, Surigao and East Davao, Cebu City: San Carlos Publications, 1989, 89–90.

8 ROUÉ, Marie / NAKASHIMA, Douglas: Co-production between Indigenous Knowledge and Science. Introducing a Decolonized Approach, in: ROUÉ, Marie / NAKASHIMA, Douglas / KRUPNIK, Igor (Hg.): Resilience Through Knowledge Co-Production. Indigenous Knowledge, Science, and Global Environmental Change, Cambridge: Cambridge University Press, 2022, 4–6.

9 ROUÉ / NAKASHIMA 2022 [note 8], 4–6.

of catastrophes, especially in Asia and America. According to the report, the danger is particularly high for the Philippines, India, and Indonesia.[10]

In the Philippine context, environmental crisis includes pollution, illegal mining and logging, deforestation, threats to environmental activists, dynamite fishing, landslides, coastal erosion, biodiversity loss, extinction, global warming, and climate change. In this context, it is worth mentioning that the archipelago is projected to be one of the most vulnerable countries to the impacts of climate change. In 2021, the Philippines ranked as the fourth most affected country by weather-related events.[11] Relevant data shows that destructive land use increased significantly in the eighteenth century when Spanish colonialism enhanced its extraction of the archipelago's resources for the early modern global market.[12] Over the course of the 20th century, the forest cover of the Philippines was depleted from 70 percent down to 20 percent.[13] Due to industrial waste and automobiles, the capital city of Manila suffers from air pollution, affecting 98% of the population. According to the Metro Manila Development Authority (MMDA), the country produces an average of 41 kilotons of garbage daily with almost 10 kilotons per day coming from Metro Manila alone.[14] Climate change in the Philippines is having serious impacts such as increased frequency and severity of natural disasters, sea level rise, extreme rainfall, resource shortages, and environmental degradation.[15] All of these crises have greatly affected the Philippines' agriculture, water, infrastructure, human health, and coastal ecosystems and they are projected to continue causing devastating damage to the economy and society of the Philippines.[16] Furthermore, the archipelago is situated along the Pacific Ocean's typhoon belt, leaving the country vulnerable to an average of 20 typhoons every year.

Formerly colonized regions of the world like the Philippines experience the ramifications of climate change most jarringly "because of their high

---

10 LOUELLA, Desiderio: Natural disasters, debt crises top risks for Philippines, says the survey, in: https://www.philstar.com/business/2023/01/13/2237166/natural-disasters-debt-cri-ses -top-risks-philippines-says-survey. (accessed 21.09.2023).

11 BOQUEST, Yves: Environmental Challenges in the Philippines in The Philippine Archipelago, Dijon France: Springer 2017, 779–829; MÜLLER, Hilja: Philippinen. Ein Länderporträt (Schriftenreihe 10507), Bonn: Bundeszentrale für Politische Bildung, 2020, 135–139.

12 UITAMO, Elina: Land Use History of the Philippines in Environmental Science and Technology Library vol. 10, Dordrecht: Springer Netherlands, 1996, 141–156.

13 LASCO, Rodel / VISCO, Roberto / PULHIN, Juan: Secondary Forests in the Philippines. Formation and Transformation in the 20th Century in: Journal of Tropical Forest Science (13) 2001, 652–670.

14 "Solid Waste Management in Metro Manila 2018," Metropolitan Manila Development Authority (2018), 2022, https://mmda.gov.ph/images/Home/ Infomercial-2018.pdf. (accessed Sep. 23)

15 Ibid.

16 Ibid.

dependence on natural resources, their geographical and climatic conditions and their limited capacity to effectively adapt to a changing climate."[17] Since low-income countries have a history of colonialism and resource exploitation, their environment lacks the diversity necessary to prevail against natural disasters. A lack of biodiversity reduces the resilience of a specific region, leaving it more susceptible to natural disasters and the effects of climate change. With its history of Spanish colonization, the Philippines is neither environmentally nor economically equipped to overcome the environmental issues it is currently dealing with. This inability to recover exacerbates the problem, creating a cycle of environmental and economic devastation in the country.[18]

Raising awareness of the question of justice

The capabilities approach

Having stated the facts of colonialism and its effects on the environment, we find the capabilities approach to be a fundamental theory of justice that aims to enable every human being to flourish and to live in dignity. To this end, existing capabilities are combined with the conditions that contribute to the individual fulfillment of this goal. According to the philosopher and legal scholar Martha Nussbaum, the capabilities approach aims to answer the question: "What is required for a life that is adequate to human dignity?" Based on Aristotle's virtue theory and the political theories of John Rawls, Martha Nussbaum has been developing her version of the capabilities approach in cooperation with Armatya Sen since 1986.[19] The approach is applied as a basic theory of social justice and is therefore also required to include considerations of postcolonial structures in its reflection. In this sense, capabilities in the meaning of liberties can only be realized if they are paired with the political, social, and/or economic conditions that they need to be experienced and contribute to human life in dignity.[20] Given

---

17 SMITH, Paul: "Climate Change, Weak States and the War on Terrorism in South and Southeast Asia," Contemporary Southeast Asia, 2007, 264–285, https://www.jstor.org/stable/25798831. (accessed Sep. 23)

18 DAS GUPTA, Monica: "Population, Poverty and Climate Change," The World Bank Research Observer, 2014, 83–108, https://www.jstor.org/stable/24582389. (accessed Sep. 23)

19 NUSSBAUM, Martha C.: Creating Capabilities, The Human Development Approach, Cambridge – Massachusetts - London: Harvard University Press, 2011, 17-45. NUSSBAUM, Martha C.: The Capabilities Approach and the History of Philosophy, in: CHIAPPERO-MARTINETTI, Enrica / OSMANI, Siddiqur / QIZILBASH, Mozaffar (Hg.): The Cambridge Handbook of the Capability Approach, Cambridge: Cambridge University Press, 2021, 13–39.

20 FREDIANI, Alexandre Apsan / CLARK, David Alexander / BIGGERI, Mario: Human Development and the Capability Approach: The Role of Empowerment and Participation, in:

these objectives, the capabilities approach can also help achieve the 17 sustainable development goals of UNESCO, especially Goal 13: climate action, but also 10: fewer inequalities.

As already stated, not every human being has the opportunity to develop his or her capabilities, due to given circumstances. This makes it all the more important to address this situation of injustice and inequality to bring about change and improvement. A prerequisite for initiating processes of change is first of all a precise examination of the given situation, i.e. of postcolonial structures of injustice, which, however, should not stop at an overall view, but should also take into account the fate of individuals. Such a personal approach can be achieved by drawing on the paradigm of compassion, which will be briefly introduced in the following.

The paradigm of compassion

The term compassion was primarily coined by the fundamental theologian Johann-Baptist Metz against the background of an empathic monotheism and a speech of God sensitive to suffering. Metz wants to remind us that Jesus' gaze was not on sin but above all on the suffering of people, especially those who were hardly noticed or socially disadvantaged (cf. Lev 19). His reference is based on the Christian perspective, according to which God reveals Himself, especially where there is a letting oneself be touched by the suffering of others and compassion in the sense of empathy for others is actively lived. This also involves the effort to enlighten in educational processes, "committed[...] fellow humanity that does not simply indifferently accept the suffering of whatever kind and for whatever reason."[21] Compassion sends us – according to Metz – "to the front of the political, social and cultural conflicts in the world today."[22] Compassion means striving for equality and a way of communication, which should take place as far as possible at eye level.

FREDIANI, Alexandre Apsan / CLARK, David Alexander / BIGGERI, Mario (Hg.): Human Development and the Capability Approach. The Role of Empowerment and Participation. Concepts, Methods and Application, Cambridge: palgrave macmillan, 2019, 3–6.

21 KULD, Lothar: Art. Compassion (2016), in: Das wissenschaftlich-religionspädagogische Lexikon im Internet, online im Internet: https://www.bibelwissenschaft.de/fileadmin/buh_bibelmodul/media/wirelex/pdf/Compassion_2020-04-29_14_56.pdf, [abgerufen am 27.11.2021, 23.33 Uhr], 2. (accessed Sep. 23)

22 METZ, Johann Baptist: Compassion. Zu einem Weltprogramm des Christentums im Zeitalter des Pluralismus der Religionen und Kulturen, in: DERS. / KULD, Lothar / WEISBROD, Adolf: Compassion. Weltprogramm des Christentums. Soziale Verantwortung lernen, Freiburg – Basel – Wien. Herder, 2000, 13–14.

The link between the capabilities approach and the paradigm of compassion

The connection between the capabilities approach and the paradigm of compassion lies in the awareness that in both concepts, not every human being – due to different economic, social, but also ecological factors – can participate in a life of prosperity. In both concepts, attention is given to those who are suffering or disadvantaged. The special feature of the compassion approach consists in going far beyond purely analytical thinking and also addressing the emotional level of human beings and their spiritual-religious dimension. This is done, for example, against the background of the Christian principle of charity, to encourage people to actively share compassion with others. Here it is noteworthy that compassion also addresses the ratio when in the sense of passion, innovative ideas are stimulated in the interest of changing the present for the better. The capabilities approach of Nussbaum contributes above all to concretizing such reflections and measuring them against real-life conditions, which also include disadvantages caused by postcolonial structures and suffering from unjust living conditions and, in this context, environmental disasters.

Laudato si'

By looking at the significance of decolonial theology and the theme of climate justice, there is a need to take a closer look at the encyclical Laudato si' by Pope Francis: In this statement, the pope also refers explicitly to the connection between structures of injustice and disadvantage to the colonial aftermath. In doing so he establishes an explicit link to the climate crisis: "A true ecological debt exists particularly between the global north and south, connected to commercial imbalances with effects on the environment and the disproportionate use of natural resources by certain countries over long periods."[23] Pope Francis points out that the earth's resources are being plundered because of short-sighted approaches to the economy, commerce, and production. The loss of forests and woodlands entails the loss of species that may constitute extremely important resources in the future, not only for food but also for curing disease and other uses. Different species contain genes that could be key

---

23 Pope Francis: Laudato si', Vatican City: Vatican City Press, 2015, sec. 51.

resources in years ahead for meeting human needs and regulating environmental problems.[24] He argues that "The current global situation engenders a feeling of instability and uncertainty, which in turn becomes a seedbed for collective selfishness. [...] Our concern cannot be limited merely to the threat of extreme weather events, but must also extend to the catastrophic consequences of social unrest. Obsession with a consumerist lifestyle, above all when few people are capable of maintaining it, can only lead to violence and mutual destruction."[25] About structures of injustice and increasing devastation of the environment, Pope Francis establishes a connection to a theology of creation, in particular by recalling the biblical mandate, according to which man is to assume responsibility for the house of life on earth and all his fellow creatures. He argues that "If the simple fact of being human moves people to care for the environment of which they are a part, Christians in their turn realize that their responsibility within creation, and their duty towards nature and the Creator, are an essential part of their faith. It is good for humanity and the world at large when we believers better recognize the ecological commitments which stem from our convictions."[26]

At this point, I will now take a closer look at the mandate to protect creation, which Pope Francis dealt with so decisively in his encyclical.

Theological implications

In Genesis 2:15, it is said, "The Lord God took the man and put him in the Garden of Eden to work it and take care of it." First of all, the aspect of working is dealt with here, which means that Man's dominion over the garden, i.e. over the house of life on earth (Gen 1:26), is connected with responsibility for everything in it and with the fulfillment of concrete tasks. These require commitment, also in the sense of servanthood. Furthermore, the aspect of guarding, protecting, and preserving is mentioned in Gen 1:25, which God has entrusted to human beings about their fellow creatures. The garden or the house of life is to be preserved and protected as well as possible.[27]

In Gen 1:26, God creates Man in His image which is basically to be understood as a functional statement, which assigns Man a representative function of God

---

[24] Ibid., sec. 32; Cichos, Katarzyna et al.: Sustainable Development Goals and the Catholic Church. Catholic Social Teaching and the UN's Agenda 2030, London: Routledge, 2021.

[25] Pope Francis 2015 [note 23], sec. 204.

[26] Pope Francis 2015 [note 23], sec. 64.

[27] Berges, Ulrich / Dohmen, Christoph / Schwienhorst-Schönberger, Ludger (Hg.): Herders Theologischer Kommentar zum Alten Testament. Genesis 1–11, übersetzt und ausgelegt von Georg Fischer, Freiburg im Breisgau: Herder, 2018, 202–203.

on earth and is connected with responsibility for his fellow creatures.[28] In this regard, it should be mentioned that recent theological research is largely in agreement that the image of God is not to be understood as a legitimization of human arbitrariness and ruthlessness, but rather as a key moment for the ethical dimension of dealing with fellow creatures and the earth as a living space.[29] In this sense, the divine imperative of Gen 1:28 can be understood as a call to arrange the earth as a habitat for everybody.[30] God empowers human beings to enter, take possession of, protect and defend the earth for the benefit of all living beings.[31]

The responsibility for fellow human beings and the environment arising from this biblical mandate can, moreover, not only be brought into connection with Laudato si', but also with the paradigm of compassion. Here, again, it is about responsibility in the form of an active engagement for the preservation of creation as well as a special sensitivity to the needs of other living beings. A prerequisite for the development of such a commitment is first of all an awareness of or attention to unjust conditions, but also the will for wanting to change them.

At this point it should be mentioned that the interpretation of the Genesis passages just presented can in no way be understood as a romanticizing logic of preservation: Thus, the biblical mandate to cultivate and work the earth is not about the conservation of primordial states, but about responsible further development against the background of respective temporal contexts. Such an impetus also includes inventiveness in a postmodern understanding, i.e. concretely, for example, scientific expertise to counteract the problem of environmental destruction. The distinct mandate and perspective on the world

---

28 LIENKAMP, Andreas: Herrschaftsauftrag und Nachhaltigkeit. Exemplarische Überlegungen zum Umgang mit der Bibel im Kontext theologischer Ethik, in: HEIMBACH-STEINS, Marianne / STEINS, Georg (Hg.): Bibelhermeneutik und Christliche Sozialethik, Stuttgart: Kohlhammer, 2012, 189–190.

29 REMELE, Kurt: Die Würde des Tieres ist unantastbar. Eine neue christliche Tierethik, Kevelaer: Herder, 2016, 62–63. For a long time, the biblical mandate of dominion was understood as an invitation to utilize and dominate the Earth and its resources. The focus was on human dominance over nature, a perspective that provided a fertile ground not only for the exploitation of nature but also for the establishment of colonial structures. It is only in more recent interpretations that the mandate of dominion has been understood within the context of stewardship and the preservation of creation. Therefore, this perspective should not be taken for granted as having always been present. It is crucial to critically engage with this history of interpretation. DOMSEL, Maike Maria / TANNHOF, Julia: Wie der Hirte vom Schaf lernen kann – Die transformative Kraft der Tiergestützten Pädagogik im religionspädagogischen Setting, in: Theo-Web. 21 (2022) H. 1, 95-114 ; WHITE, Lynn Townsend / BOURG, Dominique: Les Racines historiques de notre crise écologique, Paris : PUF, 2019.

30 LIENKAMP 2018 [note 28], 8.

31 LÖHNING, Karl / ZENGER, Erich: Als Anfang schuf Gott. Biblische Schöpfungstheologien, Düsseldorf: Patmos, 1997, 152–153.

derived from a religious standpoint and belief in God offers a meaningful purpose and interpretation. According to theologian Andreas Benk, the creation narratives depict an ideal state in accordance with God's will, a utopian vision of a perfect world that has yet to be actualized. This vision of a restored world, aligned with God's desires, carries significant implications and serves as a driving force for Christians to actively engage and advocate for justice. Therefore, religion can serve as a powerful motivator in the pursuit of fair and equitable conditions.[32]

In discussing the importance of respecting the knowledge of indigenous peoples, it is essential to recognize the exploitation and fetishization that often accompanies interactions with these communities. Such exploitation often results in the extraction of their resources and the romanticization of their poverty. However, true respect for indigenous knowledge involves reflecting on and adapting it to specific historical and local contexts. This approach is similar to the cautious-critical approach needed when interpreting biblical texts. One cannot simply transfer biblical texts one-to-one to contemporary contexts; they must be considered against the background of their time of origin.

Conclusion and outlook

Decolonization is an engagement that is aimed to end the wheels of oppression and inequity. Colonial enterprise still has a multitude of (negative) impacts on people living today and their natural environments. A sensitive approach to colonial history and its effects on people and the environment can help to draw attention to structures of injustice. This represents a first step towards changing them. Also, in the interests of UNESCO's Global Sustainability Goals – here especially Goal 17: Partnerships to achieve the goals – it is an impetus in building communities that work together and collectively create a more sustainable and equitable future.

In the spectrum of decolonial theology, we face not only theological but also sociopolitical challenges as well. Facing this conundrum, decolonial theology requires the readiness to dialogue with both the formerly colonized and colonizers for a constructive engagement vis-a-vis socio-economic justice. In the sense of the capabilities approach according to Zen and Nussbaum, special attention should be paid to those conditions that either promote or rather restrict individual freedom and well-being. My considerations have shown that postcolonial structures have an effect in this regard that should be counteracted as far as possible. Decolonial theology provides a space of thought, providing an

32 BENK, Andreas: Schöpfung – eine Vision von Gerechtigkeit. Was niemals war, doch möglich ist, Ostfildern: Grünewald, 2016.

opportunity to rethink power relations that have religious, political, economic, and intellectual implications especially in "building their own religious identity, in the political struggle to end the foreign interventions, in search for independence and the epistemic emancipation from colonial thought."[33]

As far as the role of religion in the colonization process is concerned, it was possible to work out that missionary work supported the exploitation of the indigenous population, at least to a large extent. In this way, valuable knowledge was also lost, in the sense that the indigenous population cultivated a very sustainable approach to the environment. Exactly here lies the insightful potential or the possibility to learn from the way indigenous peoples deal with nature and the environment. The main point here is to take only as much as is needed so that nature can recover. In addition, the relationship to the environment and the closeness to nature are deeply connected to the respective culture, so that special closeness to fellow creatures exists, which in turn promotes an attitude of collaboration. The Indigenous Peoples of the Philippines have a unique way of life that is based on sustainable and harmonious relationships with nature. Their traditional ecological knowledge, conservation of biodiversity, sustainable resource management, community-based conservation, and spiritual connection to nature offers valuable insights into sustainable living and environmental protection. By learning from the Indigenous Peoples, we can develop more effective approaches to managing and protecting the environment, as well as promote the longterm sustainability of our planet. It is essential to recognize and respect the Indigenous Peoples' contributions to sustainability and work towards incorporating their knowledge and practices into modern environmental management strategies. In this regard, it should be implicit that this process does not occur without their meaningful involvement; instead, continual dialogic engagement on equal terms is paramount.

Even if this article refers to a theology of creation, it is necessary to broaden the perspective here as well. Thus, reflections on the integrity of creation or a sustainable approach to the environment are always also about the ethical question "How or according to which principles do we want to live (together)?" It is necessary to investigate this question further (theologically) with a view to a sustainable future for people and the environment, and to learn from indigenous peoples in particular.

About the role of religion and/or mission, it must be emphasized that here, too, a sensitive and, above all, critical examination of the (colonial) past is necessary. This contribution highlighted the correlation between missionary works and colonization processes, emphasizing their substantial role in

33 TONELLI, Deborah: Decolonial Theology and Changing the Global Church, [https://berkleycenter.georgetown.edu/responses/decolonial-theology-and-changing-the-global-church]. (accessed Sep. 23)

establishing and consolidating colonial structures. Even if in the meantime a new understanding of mission has developed, which wants to distance itself from any Euro-centeredness and advocates for just structures etc., this burdening past should not be suppressed or forgotten, because only in this way can we learn from it.

In general, it is important to deal with the past in such a way that the effects of colonial structures on the present are recognized in order to be able to counteract them as far as possible. For this to succeed, dialogue between the formerly colonized and the respective colonial masters should be established or cultivated, because only in this way can learning and knowledge processes be set in motion, especially on the part of the representatives of the former colonial masters. The cooperation between my college and me can be understood as an example of this kind of dialogue. Through our intercultural exchange, knowledge has emerged that goes far beyond factual expertise and also touches on the relational and spiritual levels. In the sense of the paradigm of compassion, a reference is created here to the respective fates of the people concerned, to be able to deal more sensitively with their needs and with what particularly concerns and affects them. Certainly, many necessary theoretical implications have been discussed in this article, but it is the personal encounter between my colleague and me that has led to a deeper examination of the legacy of a burdensome colonial past, the effects of which are especially noticeable today, particularly about the topic of climate justice.

This expertise is not only relevant for research and teaching at universities, but also for school-based education. In the field of pedagogy in general and religious education in particular, addressing the effects of colonial structures in the here and now, especially regarding their theological or religious dimensions, is still anything but a matter of course. Thus, it is a desideratum that this changes in the future and that suitable didactic teaching formats can be made available that make people aware of this important and complex topic.

References Cited

BENK, Andreas: Schöpfung – eine Vision von Gerechtigkeit. Was niemals war, doch möglich ist, Ostfildern: Grünewald, 2016.

BERGES, Ulrich / DOHMEN, Christoph / SCHWIENHORST-SCHÖNBERGER, Ludger (Hg.): Herders Theologischer Kommentar zum Alten Testament. Genesis 1–11, übersetzt und ausgelegt von Georg Fischer, Freiburg im Breisgau: Herder, 2018, 202–203.

BOQUEST, Yves: Environmental Challenges in the Philippines in The Philippine Archipelago, Dijon France: Springer, 2017.

CICHOS, Katarzyna, et al.: Sustainable Development Goals and the Catholic Church. Catholic Social Teaching and the UN's Agenda 2030, London: Routledge, 2021.

DAS GUPTA, Monica: "Population, Poverty and Climate Change," The World Bank Research Washington D.C.: Observer, 2014, 83–108, https://www.jstor.org/stable/24582389. (accessed Sep. 23)

DOMSEL, Maike Maria / TANNHOF, Julia: Wie der Hirte vom Schaf lernen kann – Die transformative Kraft der Tiergestützten Pädagogik im religionspädagogischen Setting, in: Theo-Web. 21 (2022) H. 1, 95–114.

FREDIANI, Alexandre Apsan / CLARK, David Alexander / BIGGERI, Mario: Human Development and the Capability Approach. The Role of Empowerment and Participation, in: FREDIANI, Alexandre Apsan / CLARK, David Alexander / BIGGERI, Mario (Hg.): Human Development and the Capability Approach. The Role of Empowerment and Participation. Concepts. Methods and Application, Cambridge: palgrave macmillan, 2019, 3–6.

POPE FRANCIS: Laudato si', Vatican City: Vatican City Press, 2015.

GAGELONIA, Pedro: The Filipino Historian: Controversial Issues in Philippine History, Manila: Feuci, 1970.

LIEDHOLZ, Yannick: Berührungspunkte von Sozialer Arbeit und Klimawandel. Perspektiven und Handlungsspielräume, Opladen – Berlin – Toronto: Barbara Budrich, 2021.

LOUELLA Desiderio: Natural disasters, debt crises top risks for Philippines, says the survey, in: https://www.philstar.com/business/2023/01/13/2237166/natural-disasters-debt-crises-top-risks-philippines-says-survey. (accessed Sep. 23)

KERNER, Ina: Postkoloniale Theorien zur Einführung, Hamburg: Junius, 2012.

KULD, Lothar: Art. Compassion (2016), in: Das wissenschaftlich-religionspädagogische Lexikon im Internet, online im Internet: https://www.bibelwissenschaft.de/fileadmin/buh_bibel-modul/media/wirelex/pdf/Compassion__2020-04-29_14_56.pdf (accessed Sep. 23).

LASCO, Rodel / VISCO, Roberto / PULHIN, Juan: Secondary Forests in the Philippines. Formation and Transformation in the 20th Century in: Journal of Tropical Forest Science (13) 2001, 652-670.

LIENKAMP, Andreas: Herrschaftsauftrag und Nachhaltigkeit. Exemplarische Überlegungen zum Umgang mit der Bibel im Kontext theologischer Ethik, in: HEIMBACH-STEINS, Marianne / STEINS, Georg (Hg.): Bibelhermeneutik und Christliche Sozialethik, Stuttgart: Kohlhammer, 2012, 187–216.

LÖHNING, Karl / ZENGER, Erich: Als Anfang schuf Gott. Biblische Schöpfungstheologien, Düsseldorf: Patmos, 1997.

MÜLLER, Hilja: Philippinen. Ein Länderporträt (Schriftenreihe 10507), Bonn: Bundeszentrale für Politische Bildung, 2020.

METZ, Johann Baptist: Compassion. Zu einem Weltprogramm des Christentums im Zeitalter des Pluralismus der Religionen und Kulturen, in: DERS. / KULD, Lothar / WEISBROD, Adolf: Compassion. Weltprogramm des Christentums. Soziale Verantwortung lernen, Freiburg – Basel – Wien: Herder, 2000, 9–18.

NUSSBAUM, Martha C.: Creating Capabilities, The Human Development Approach, Cambridge – Massachusetts – London: Harvard University Press, 2011.

NUSSBAUM, Martha C.: The Capabilities Approach and the History of Philosophy, in: CHIAPPERO-MARTINETTI, Enrica / OSMANI, Siddiqur / QIZILBASH, Mozaffar (Hg.): The Cambridge Handbook of the Capability Approach. Cambridge. Cambridge University Press, 2021, 13-39.

REMELE, Kurt: Die Würde des Tieres ist unantastbar. Eine neue christliche Tierethik, Kevelaer: Herder, 2016.

ROUÉ, Marie / NAKASHIMA, Douglas: Co-production between Indigenous Knowledge and Science. Introducing a Decolonized Approach, in: ROUÉ, Marie / NAKASHIMA, Douglas / KRUPNIK, Igor (Hg.): Resilience Through Knowledge Co-Production. Indigenous Knowledge, Science, and Global Environmental Change, Cambridge: Cambridge University Press, 2022, 3–23.

SCHREUERS, Peter: Caraga Antigua 1521–1910. The Hispanization and Christianization of Agusan, Surigao and East Davao, Cebu City: San Carlos Publications, 1989.

SMITH, Paul: "Climate Change, Weak States and the War on Terrorism in South and Southeast Asia," Contemporary: Southeast Asia, 2007, 264–285, https://www.jstor.org/stable/25798831. (accessed Sep. 23)

Solid Waste Management in Metro Manila 2018, Metropolitan Manila Development Authority (2018), 2022, https://mmda.gov.ph/images/Home/Infomer-cial-2018.pdf. (accessed Sep. 23)

TONELLI, Deborah: Decolonial Theology and Changing the Global Church, [https://Berkley-center.georgetown.edu/responses/decolonial-theology-and-changing-the-global-church]. (accessed Sep. 23)

UITAMO, Elina: Land Use History of the Philippines in Environmental Science and Technology Library vol. 10, Dordrecht: Springer Netherlands, 1996.

WHITE, Lynn Townsend / BOURG, Dominique: Les Racines historiques de notre crise écologique, Paris: PUF, 2019.

Compassion als empathische Mitleidenschaft – Einige moralpsychologische Perspektiven

Christian Feichtinger

Der Begriff *Compassion* stützt sich zentral auf die allgemeinmenschliche Fähigkeit der Empathie. Jedoch weisen neuere moralpsychologische Diskussionen auf Fallstricke eines allzu optimistischen Zugangs zu Empathie hin. Der Beitrag stellt aktuelle Perspektiven aus der Moralpsychologie zu Grenzen und problematischen Aspekte von Empathie vor. Abschließend werden Leitlinien und Hinweise für das Konzept einer empathischen Mitleidenschaft diskutiert, die auf Defizite von Empathie adäquat reagieren.

Moralpsychologie; Empathie; ethische Bildung; Altruismus

The concept of compassion is centrally based on the general human capacity of empathy. However, recent discussions in moral psychology point to the pitfalls of an overly optimistic approach to empathy. The article presents current perspectives from moral psychology on the limits and problematic aspects of empathy. Finally, guidelines and indications for the concept of empathic compassion are discussed, which adequately respond to deficits of empathy.

moral psychology; empathy; moral education; altruism

Der Begriff *Compassion* stützt sich wesentlich auf die allgemeinmenschliche Fähigkeit der Empathie und deutet diese als *Mitleidenschaft*[1] handlungsorientiert aus. Durch diesen anthropologischen Zugang weist Compassion das Potenzial auf, kulturelle und religiöse Differenzen zu transzendieren. Studien legen zudem einen Konnex von Empathiefähigkeit und positiven Sichtweisen auf Nachhaltigkeit sowie Umwelt- und Klimaschutz nahe.[2] Zugleich weisen neuere moralpsychologische Diskussionen auch auf Fallstricke eines allzu optimistischen Zugangs zu Empathie als moralischer Grundfähigkeit hin. Im folgenden Beitrag sollen daher aktuelle Perspektiven aus der Moralpsychologie zur Bedeutung von Empathie für moralisches Verhalten beschrieben und damit auch Grenzen und

---

1 KULD, Lothar: Sympatheia – Compassion. Ein Projekt und ein Hinweis auf John Henry Newman, in: TZSCHEETZSCH, Werner (Hg.): Zwischen Exodus und Exil. Religionspädagogik in der Pluralität, Ostfildern: Schwabenverlag, 2000, 72.

2 Vgl. PFATTHEICHER, Stefan: SASSENRATH / Claudia / SCHINDLER, Simon: Feelings for the Suffering of Others and the Environment. Compassion Fosters Proenvironmental Tendencies, in: Environment and Behavior 48/7 (2016), 929–945. DOI: 10.1177/0013916515574549; FEINBERG, Matthew / WILLER, Robb: The Moral Roots of Environmental Attitudes, in: Psychological Science 24/1 (2013), 56–62. DOI: 10.1177/0956797612449177.

problematische Aspekte empathiegestützter Konzepte aufgezeigt werden. Abschließend wird diskutiert, ob Empathie und Compassion konzeptuell stärker voneinander getrennt werden sollten.

Empathie und Mitleidenschaft als Themen der Moralpsychologie

Die Moralpsychologie ist eine vergleichsweise junge Wissenschaft, die gegenwärtig von einer Vielzahl unterschiedlicher, bisweilen konkurrierender Schulen und Ansätze geprägt ist. Vor allem in den letzten zwanzig bis dreißig Jahren haben sich der Bereich und die Fragestellungen der Moralpsychologie stark verändert: Bedingt durch den enormen Einfluss des Stufenmodells von Lawrence Kohlberg (1927–1987)[3] war sie bis dahin vor allem mit entwicklungs- und kognitionspsychologischen Fragestellungen befasst und erschien verhältnismäßig homogen. Dieser weitgehende Konsens ist nun aufgebrochen; in den letzten zwei Jahrzehnten wurde Moral auch zu einem Thema etwa der Sozialpsychologie oder der evolutionären Psychologie, wodurch neue Perspektiven und Theorieansätze entstanden.[4] Diese Fragmentierung betrifft zugleich auch die ethische Bildung, die in ihrer Konzeption wesentlich von moralpsychologischen Grundlagen abhängt.[5]

Eine weitere prägende Entwicklung war ein neuer Fokus auf den Einfluss von Emotionen, Affekten und Intuitionen auf moralische Urteilsprozesse. Seit Jonathan Haidts bahnbrechendem Beitrag *The Emotional Dog and its Rational Tail* aus dem Jahr 2001[6] gibt es einen immer breiteren Konsens über die Bedeutung von Emotionen für menschliche Moral.[7] Allerdings ist das kolportierte hohe Aus-

---

3 Vgl. Kohlberg, Lawrence: Die Psychologie der Moralentwicklung, Frankfurt: Suhrkamp, 1996 (= stw 1232).

4 Vgl. Ellemers, Naomi / van der Toorn / Jojanneke / Paunov, Yavor / van Leeuwen, Thed: The Psychology of Morality. A Review and Analysis of Empirical Studies Published from 1940 through 2017, in: Personality and Social Psychology Review 23/4 (2019), 332–366. DOI: 10.1177/1088868318811759.

5 Vgl. Kristjánsson, Kristján: Moral Education Today. Ascendancy and Fragmentation, in: Journal of Moral Education 46/4 (2017), 339–346. DOI: 10.1080/03057240.2017.1370209.

6 Vgl. Haidt, Jonathan: The Emotional Dog and its Rational Tail. A Social Intuitionist Approach to Moral Judgment, in: Psychological Review 108/4 (2001), 814–834.

7 Vgl. Bucher, Anton A.: Mehr Emotionen und Tugenden als kognitive Stufen. Skizze der aktuellen Moralpsychologie, in: Englert, Rudolf / Kohler-Spiegel, Helga / Naurath, Elisabeth / Schröder, Bernd / Schweitzer, Friedrich (Hg.): Ethisches Lernen, Neukirchen-Vluyn: Neukirchener, 2015 (= Jahrbuch der Religionspädagogik 31), 87–97.

maß dieses Einflusses weiterhin Gegenstand von Debatten und wurde von jüngeren Beiträgen auch wieder in Frage gestellt.[8] Vor diesem Hintergrund wird klar, dass die Bedeutung von Empathie oder Mitleidenschaft für Moral und Ethik zunächst von Philosophie und Religion in den Diskurs eingebracht[9] und erst in jüngerer Zeit auch Gegenstand der Moralpsychologie wurde.

Für das Anliegen, Compassion als verbindende Grundlage über Kulturen und Religionen hinweg zu etablieren, sind Erkenntnisse der evolutionären Psychologie von besonderem Interesse. Diese können Aufschluss darüber geben, inwiefern Empathie und Compassion allgemeinmenschliche Fähigkeiten sind, über die gemeinsames Handeln möglich wird. Gerade vor dem Hintergrund von Pluralität und Heterogenität können Verweise auf menschliche Grundfähigkeiten und *human universals* (Donald Brown)[10] gewinnbringend sein. Aus evolutionsbiologischer Sicht ist die Annahme plausibel, dass Menschen als ‚hypersoziale' Lebewesen zentrale Grundfähigkeiten für das Zusammenleben mit anderen entwickelt haben, die neben Kooperation oder Kommunikation eben auch Einfühlungsvermögen und Mitleidenschaft umfassen. Dafür sprechen auch Studien zu Hirnaktivitäten und zum Einfluss von Hormonen wie Oxytocin; darüber hinaus auch Studien mit Kindern, bei denen bereits im ersten Lebensjahr empathisches Verhalten beobachtet werden kann.[11] Kulturvergleichende Studien legen ebenfalls nahe, dass Empathie und Mitgefühl als menschliche Grundfähigkeiten evolutionär grundgelegt sind, wenngleich diese Fähigkeiten dann je nach Kultur und sozialem Kontext unterschiedlich entfaltet und ausgedeutet werden.[12] Als entwickelte menschliche Fähigkeiten haben sie zudem stets eine kognitive Komponente, sind begleitet von einem *Wissen* um sich und andere, worin sie sich von mitfühlendem Trostverhalten bei Tieren zentral unterscheiden.[13]

Der erste Befund fällt somit positiv aus: Einfühlungsvermögen und Mitgefühl sind evolutionär angelegte menschliche Grundfähigkeiten, die kulturelle und soziale Differenzen transzendieren. Auch ihr Konnex zur Moralentwicklung lässt sich gut argumentieren: Die Wahrnehmung von (menschlichem) Leid und

---

8 Vgl. PÖLZLER, Thomas: Moral Judgments and Emotions. A Less Intimate Relationship than Recently Claimed, in: Journal of Theoretical and Philosophical Psychology 35/3 (2015), 177–195. DOI: 10.1037/teo0000022.

9 Beispiele für ein solches Verständnis sind die christliche geprägte Moralphilosophie von Joseph Butler (1692–1752), die politische Theologie von Johann Baptist Metz (1928–2019) oder allgemeiner der Begriff karuna in der buddhistischen Tradition.

10 Vgl. BROWN, Donald: Human Universals, New York: McGraw-Hill, 1991.

11 Vgl. DECETY, Jean: The Neuroevolution of Empathy and Caring for Others. Why It Matters for Morality, in: DECETY, Jean / CHRISTEN, Yves (Hg.): New Frontiers in Social Neuroscience, Cham u. a.: Springer, 2014, 852–870.

12 Vgl. GOETZ, Jennifer L. / KELTNER, Dacher / SIMON-THOMAS, Emiliana: Compassion. An Evolutionary Analysis and Empirical Review, in: Psychological Bulletin 136/3 (2010), 351–374. DOI: 10.1037/a0018807.

13 Vgl. SAPOLSKY, Robert M.: Gewalt und Mitgefühl. Die Biologie des menschlichen Verhaltens, München: Hanser, 2017, 673–676.

die Fähigkeit, darauf fürsorglich zu reagieren, wird häufig als wichtige Basis für Moralentwicklung gesehen.[14] Empathie ist daher nach Irina Spiegel ein wichtiger Bestandteil des menschlichen Urteilsvermögens.[15] Damit verbunden ist freilich auch eine erste Einschränkung, da mit *Wahrnehmung* schon konkrete kulturelle und soziale Ausfaltungen verbunden sind: Schein & Gray weisen darauf hin, dass Verletzung oder Leiden keine objektiven Beobachtungen sind, sondern im Wahrnehmungsprozess konstruiert werden. Menschen verfügen zwar über ein prinzipielles evolutives Sensorium für Leiden und Schadenszufügung und entsprechendes Einfühlungsvermögen; wer oder was aber als leidensfähig gilt und welche Akte als Verletzung eingestuft werden, ist sozial geprägt und daher heterogen.[16] Auch wenn Menschen daher eine prinzipielle Empathiefähigkeit teilen, ist dies keineswegs ein Garant für Konsens in moralischen oder anderen Handlungsfragen: Ob etwa Tiere, Embryonen oder größere Entitäten wie die Natur oder das Klima als leidensfähig betrachtet werden und welche Handlungen als verletzend gelten, ist zwischen unterschiedlichen Menschen und moralischen Systemen umstritten. Dies hat jedoch zugleich großen Einfluss auf empathische Reaktionen und entsprechende Handlungsmotivationen.[17]

Daher: Auch wenn Empathie eine allgemeinmenschliche soziale Fähigkeit ist, folgt daraus nicht automatisch eine präskriptive Implikation mit Blick auf nachhaltige Entwicklung oder Umweltethik. Es ist erst zu begründen, ob und warum empathische Mitleidenschaft als Unterstützung oder sogar Fundament entsprechender Bildungsansätze gelten und entsprechend gefördert werden sollte, oder ob nicht vielmehr andere – beispielsweise strikt vernunftbasierte oder auf andere Emotionen gründende – Zugänge angemessener wären.[18] Spricht man von ‚empathischer Mitleidenschaft' oder Compassion, weist man Affekten eine positive und präskriptive Bedeutung zu. Indem man sich auf diese Fähigkeiten stützt, übernimmt man allerdings auch Schwierigkeiten und mögliche Probleme affektiver Moral in den Ansatz. Es ist daher kritisch zu diskutieren, worin die Stärken, aber auch möglichen Grenzen und Risiken liegen, wenn Empathie und

---

14 Vgl. HAIDT, Jonathan / KESEBIR, Selin: Morality, in: FISKE, Susan / GILBERT, Daniel / LINDZEY, Garner (Hg.): Handbook of Social Psychology, Hoboken: Wiley, [5]2012, 799.

15 Vgl. SPIEGEL, Irina: Empathie- und Compassion-Training, in: NIDA-RÜMELIN, Julian / SPIEGEL, Irina / TIEDEMANN, Markus (Hg.): Handbuch Philosophie und Ethik. Band 1: Didaktik und Methodik, Paderborn: Schöningh, [2]2017, 245.

16 Vgl. SCHEIN, Chelsea / GRAY, Kurt: The Theory of Dyadic Morality. Reinventing Moral Judgment by Redefining Harm, in: Personality and Social Psychology Review 22/1 (2018), 32–70. DOI: 10.1177/1088868317698288, 34–37.

17 Vgl. dazu auch BATSON, C. Daniel: A Scientific Search for Altruism. Do We Care Only About Ourselves?, Oxford: University Press, 2019.

18 Vgl. die Überlegungen in PRINZ, Jesse J.: Is Empathy Necessary for Morality?, in: COPLAN, Amy / GOLDIE, Peter (Hg.): Empathy. Philosophical and Psychological Perspectives, Oxford: University Press, 2011, 211–229; affirmativ hingegen SPIEGEL 2017 [Anm. 15].

Compassion für Bildung nutzbar gemacht werden sollen.[19] In einem Zwischenschritt sollen zunächst mögliche Verhältnisbestimmungen der Begriff ‚Empathie' und ‚Compassion' vorgenommen werden.

Empathie und Compassion – mögliche Verhältnisbestimmungen

Die Begriffe ‚Empathie' und ‚Compassion' (im Sinne von *Mitleidenschaft*) stehen in einem oft diffusen Begriffszusammenhang mit anderen Ausdrücken wie ‚Mitgefühl' oder ‚Mitleid' und werden nicht selten synonym verwendet. Elisabeth Naurath unterscheidet Empathie und Mitgefühl dadurch, dass sie Empathie als Fähigkeit betrachtet, sich in einen anderen hineinzuversetzen, während Mitgefühl auch ein positives Anteilnehmen, ein In-Beziehung-Treten mit dem anderen einschließt. Im Unterschied zu Mitleid wiederum bezieht sich Mitgefühl auf alle Gemütszustände einer anderen Person, schließt also auch etwa Mitfreuen ein.[20] Wichtig ist, dass Naurath mit Mitgefühl keine Verschmelzung meint, sondern Mitgefühl immer um die Identität des anderen weiß: Mitgefühl ist daher kein ‚blindes' Fühlen, keine Gefühlsansteckung, sondern kognitiv von einem Wissen um die Differenz zwischen sich und dem anderen begleitet, die jedoch eine Differenz in Verbundenheit ist.[21] Robert Sapolsky hingegen argumentiert, dass sich Mitgefühl, Mitleid und Empathie trotz unterschiedlicher begrifflicher Akzentuierungen nicht eindeutig voneinander trennen lassen und spricht daher verallgemeinernd von einem ‚empathischen Zustand', der die Begriffe Mitgefühl, Mitleid und Empathie in einer Schwebe hält.[22]

Und Compassion? Grundsätzlich kann der englische Begriff *compassion* einfach mit ‚Mitgefühl' übersetzt werden und ist dann synonym zu verstehen. Wird aber im Deutschen von Compassion gesprochen, wird Mitgefühl noch einmal explizit handlungsorientiert als ‚Mitleidenschaft' verstanden und weist damit eine ethisch-präskriptive Dimension auf. Beim Begriff ‚Mitgefühl' steht zunächst das Wahrnehmen und Ernstnehmen des anderen im Vordergrund, ein In-Beziehung-Treten. Damit ist zwar eine gewisse positive Handlungsdisposition schon

---

19 Vgl. BUSSMANN, Bettina / HAASE, Volker / PÜHRINGER, Angela (2021): Empathie-Förderung im Unterricht, in: https://www.praefaktisch.de/emotionen/empathie-foerderung-im-unterricht/ [abgerufen am 16.02.2023].

20 Vgl. NAURATH, Elisabeth: Mit Gefühl gegen Gewalt. Mitgefühl als Schlüssel ethischer Bildung in der Religionspädagogik, Neukirchen-Vluyn: Neukirchener, [3]2010, XV.

21 Vgl. Ebd., 284–285.

22 Vgl. SAPOLSKY 2017 [Anm. 13], 673–676.

nahegelegt, aber nicht unbedingt klar zum Ausdruck gebracht.[23] Der Begriff Compassion, wie er im Deutschen verwendet wird, macht diese Handlungsposition deutlicher sichtbar: Compassion ist dann Mitgefühl und Anteilnahme in untrennbarer Verbindung mit einer ethisch motivierten Handlungsbereitschaft. Insofern sind also Empathie und Compassion zu unterscheiden: Letzteres ist ein eigener affektiver Zustand, der zudem auch von anderen Emotionen begleitet werden kann, etwa Zorn darüber, wie mit jemandem umgegangen wurde, oder Abscheu gegenüber möglichen Täter*innen. Compassion als Handlungsmotivation wird also nicht allein durch das Mitfühlen mit anderen angeregt, sondern berührt auch weitere moralische Bereiche, wie etwa Gerechtigkeit.[24]

Letztlich stützen sich aber alle qualitativ konnotierten Begriffe – Mitgefühl, Mitleid, Mitleidenschaft – auf die Grundfähigkeit der Empathie.[25] Empathie ist jedoch ein aus normativer Perspektive kein unumstrittener Begriff, da mit dieser Fähigkeit auch Facetten verbunden sind, die aus ethischer Sicht problematisch sind; „if compassion (or sympathy) is to be a *bone fide* emotion, it must involve empathy with some individual sufferers, and it will thus inherit the defects of empathy."[26] Ein Ansatz empathischer Mitleidenschaft muss sich daher mit den Schwächen und Problemen von Empathie auseinandersetzen und auf diese in seiner Konzeption reagieren. Es wäre ein Trugschluss anzunehmen, dass es eine unmittelbare kausale Verknüpfung von Empathie und Mitleidenschaft gibt.

Empathie: ein brüchiges ethisches Fundament?

Im Jahr 2016 publizierte der Psychologe Paul Bloom ein Buch, das denselben Titel trug wie ein Aufsatz, den der Philosoph Jesse Prinz bereits fünf Jahre zuvor geschrieben hatte: *Against Empathy*.[27] In beiden Fällen handelt es sich um leiden-

---

23 Vgl. LENZ, Viktoria: Empathie-Lernen. Moralpsychologische Perspektiven, in: SAUTERMEISTER, Jochen / ZWICK, Elisabeth (Hg.): Religion und Bildung: Antipoden oder Weggefährten? Diskurse aus historischer, systematischer und praktischer Sicht, Paderborn: Schöningh 2019, 349–361, 355; In der Bedeutung des Englischen compassion schwingt diese Handlungsdisposition stärker mit als in der deutschen Entsprechung ‚Mitgefühl': „compassion [...] is characterized by feelings of warmth, concern and care for the other, as well as a strong motivation to improve the other's wellbeing", SINGER, Tania / KLIMECKI, Olga M.: Empathy and compassion, in: Current Biology 24/18 (2014), R875–R878. DOI: 10.1016/j.cub. 2014.06.054, R875.

24 Vgl. GOETZ / KELTNER / SIMON-THOMAS 2010 [Anm. 12], 352–361.

25 Vgl. PERSSON, Ingmar: Morality from Compassion, Oxford: University Press, 2021, 72.

26 Ebd.

27 Vgl. BLOOM, Paul: Against Empathy. The Case for Rational Compassion, New York: Ecco, 2016; PRINZ, Jesse J.: Against Empathy, in: The Southern Journal of Philosophy 49 (2011),

schaftliche Argumente gegen den Versuch, Ethik und Moral auf Empathiefähigkeit zu gründen. Bloom eröffnet sein Werk dabei geradezu mit einem Frontalangriff:

> Empathy is biased, pushing us in the direction of parochialism and racism. It is short-sighted, motivating actions that might make things better in the short term but lead to tragic results in the future. It is innumerate, favoring the one over the many. It can spark violence; our empathy for those close to us is a powerful force for war and atrocity toward others.[28]

Beide Autoren stellen die positive Bedeutung von Empathie für das unmittelbare Zusammenleben sowie die Moralentwicklung bei Kindern nicht in Frage. Sie zeigen jedoch die Grenzen und Fallstricke menschlicher Empathiefähigkeit auf, die sie aus ihrer Sicht ungeeignet für ‚höhere Zwecke' machen. In diesem Abschnitt sollen daher einige dieser Probleme diskutiert werden: Personengebundenheit, *bias* und *empathy gap*, Empathieerschöpfung sowie Kostenvermeidung.

Personengebundenheit

Das Problem der Personengebundenheit von Empathie ist vor allem unter dem Begriff *identified victim effect* bekannt. Damit beschrieben wird das Phänomen, dass es Menschen leicht fällt, Empathie für einzelne, bekannte Individuen zu empfinden. Je größer die Zahl und je abstrakter die Beschreibung der Betroffenen ist, umso weniger Empathie wird ihnen entgegengebracht.[29] Entscheidend für den Effekt ist die Kombination aus beidem, Zahl und Personalisierung: Je kleiner die Zahl der personalisierten Betroffenen ist, umso eher reagieren Menschen empathisch. Dies gilt sogar im Mikrobereich; ein einzelnes, personalisiertes Opfer löst mehr Empathie aus als eine Kleingruppe personalisierter Opfer.[30] Dies hat zur Folge, dass Menschen konkretes personales Leid stärker und bedeutsamer erfahren als das größere Leiden einer größeren Zahl. Katastrophen mit sehr

---

214–233. DOI: 10.1111/j.2041-6962.2011.00069.x. Vergleichbar auch Breithaupt, Fritz: Die dunklen Seiten der Empathie, Frankfurt: Suhrkamp, 2017 (= stw 2196).

28 Bloom 2016 [Anm. 27], 9.

29 Vgl. Kogut, Tehila / Ritov, Ilana: The "Identified Victim" Effect: An Identified Group, or Just a Single Individual?, in: Journal of Behavioral Decision Making 18 (2005), 157–167. DOI: DOI: 10.1002/bdm.492.

30 Vgl. Ebd., 165; ebenso Slovic, Paul / Västfjäll, Daniel: The More Who Die, the Less We Care. Psychic Numbing and Genocide, in: Kaul, Susanne / Kim, David (Hg.): Imagining Human Rights, Berlin/München/Boston: de Gruyter, 2015, 55–68, 61. In einer klassischen Studie hatten Jenni und Loewenstein keinen Personalisierungs-Effekt festgestellt, doch hatten sie ausschließlich mit Gruppen gearbeitet und den Aspekt der geringeren Zahl außer Acht gelassen, vgl. Jenni, Karen E. / Loewenstein, George: Explaining the „Identifiable Victim Effect", in: Journal of Risk and Uncertainty 14 (1997), 235–257. Entscheidend ist also die Kombination aus Personalisierung und Zahl.

hohen (sogenannten ‚statistischen') Opferzahlen sowie komplexe Ereignisse wie Umweltzerstörung haben daher nur geringes empathisches Potenzial:

> As a result, intuition fails us in the face of genocide and other disasters that threaten human lives and the environment on a large scale. We cannot trust it. [...] Left to its own devices, moral intuition will likely favor individual victims and sensational stories that are close to home and easy to imagine.[31]

Ein beliebter ‚Ausweg' aus diesem Problem ist die Konzentration von Darstellungen auf einzelne, ausgewählte Schicksale, dies fördert allerdings Viktimisierung und verschleiert den Blick auf größere Zusammenhänge.

Bias und empathy gap

Verbunden mit dem Problem der Personalisierung sind kognitive Verzerrungen (*bias*) und die Anbindung von Empathie an Ähnlichkeit und Nähe, die zum Phänomen des *empathy gap* führen, des Nicht-Auftretens von empathischen Reaktionen, wo diese eigentlich zu erwarten wären. Evolutionär betrachtet ist die Fähigkeit zu Mitgefühl und Fürsorge zunächst bezogen auf persönliche Nähe und Bindung: Sie wird im Besonderen bei den eigenen Kindern empfunden. Empathie korreliert daher mit Ähnlichkeit und Bindung und kann in der Folge schnell zu Bevorzugung und Ungleichbehandlung führen.[32] Es fällt leicht, gegenüber Kindern oder engen Freund*innen empathisch zu sein, es ist gut möglich bei uns ähnlichen Menschen, schon schwerer bei Fremden und noch schwerer bei Menschen, die sich in ihrem Auftreten und ihren Anschauungen stark von uns unterscheiden. Dies gilt vor allem dann, wenn es sich bei den Betroffenen um eine dezidierte Outgroup handelt.[33] Noch mehr, kann das Leiden anderer sogar negiert oder ins Positive gewendet werden, wenn diese zu einer Bedrohung stilisiert oder dehumanisiert werden.[34] Ebenso können Psychopath*innen ihre Empathiefähigkeit für manipulative Zwecke nutzen: Sie nehmen die Gefühle anderer wahr, an diesen jedoch keinen Anteil.[35]

Hinzu kommt das Problem der räumlichen Nähe: Empathie ist etwas, das vor allem durch unmittelbare Erfahrungen entsteht und mit Nähe korreliert. Es ist jedoch umso schwieriger, Mitleid zu empfinden, je abstrakter und weiter weg

---

31 Slovic / Västfjäll 2015 [Anm. 30], 61.

32 Vgl. Prinz 2011 [Anm. 26], 227–229.

33 Vgl. Decety 2014 [Anm. 11], 141.

34 Vgl. dazu Haslam, Nick: Dehumanization. An Integrative Review, in: Personality and Social Psychology Review 10/3 (2006), 252–264.

35 Vgl. Prinz 2011 [Anm. 27], 221–222.

das Leid ist, worauf etwa Peter Singer in seiner bekannten ‚Teichanalogie' hinweist.[36] Die Fähigkeit des Menschen, Empathie zu empfinden, ist also eingeschränkt.[37] Bindung und Nähe können zudem zu Konflikten im Empathieempfinden führen: Empathie mit Familienmitgliedern oder nahestehenden Personen ist bei Interessenskonflikten stärker als mit fernstehenden oder abstrakten Betroffenen, und zwar auch dann, wenn deren Leiden ‚objektiv' schwerer wiegt. Die partikulare Bevorzugung von Familienmitgliedern und nahen Verwandten gehört daher im interkulturellen Vergleich zu den universellsten moralischen Grundorientierungen.[38]

Empathieerschöpfung

Ein weiterer Faktor, der Empathie zu einer unsicheren Grundlage präskriptiver Ansätze macht, ist Empathieerschöpfung. Empathie kann durch äußere oder innere Belastung negativ beeinflusst werden: Menschen werden weniger empathisch, wenn sie unter Druck oder unter kognitiver Belastung stehen.[39] Empathie kann auch, wenn als zu drückend empfunden, selbst zu dieser Belastung werden: Menschen, die zu stark empathisch reagieren und sich von ihren eigenen Gefühlen nicht distanzieren oder diese kaum kontrollieren können, sind von Überforderung oder, auf lange Sicht, von Burnout bedroht. Dies gilt besonders, wenn sie den Eindruck haben, nicht adäquat auf die Situation reagieren zu können.[40] Der Fokus richtet sich dann nicht mehr auf die Betroffenen, sondern auf sich selbst und die eigenen Gefühle, was altruistische Handlungsoptionen einschränkt oder verunmöglicht.[41] Empathie braucht daher die Fähigkeit zur Distanzierung und Emotionsregulation sowie das Gefühl, entsprechend handeln zu können.

Empathie und Kostenvermeidung

Doch gerade auch Distanzierung und Emotionsregulation machen Empathie zu einem brüchigen ethischen Fundament: Empathie stellt sich im Regelfall spontan und von selbst ein. Ob Empathie intentional herbeigeführt werden kann, ist unsicher, kognitive Anstrengungen dienen eher ihrer Regulierung.[42] Weil Men-

---

36 Vgl. SINGER, Peter: Praktische Ethik, Stuttgart: Reclam, ^{2}1994, 292–293.

37 Vgl. PERSSON 2021 [Anm. 25], 67–68.

38 Vgl. SAPOLSKY 2017 [Anm. 13], 471–481.

39 Vgl. Ebd., 688–691.

40 Vgl. BLOOM 2016 [Anm. 27], 133–146.

41 Vgl. GOETZ / KELTNER / SIMON-THOMAS 2010 [Anm. 12], 368.

42 Vgl. MCAULIFFE, William H. / CARTER, Evan C. / BERHANE, Juliana / SNIHUR, Alexander C. / MCCULLOUGH, Michael E.: Is Empathy the Default Response to Suffering? A Meta-

schen um dieses spontane Sich-Einstellen wissen und auch um die damit verbundenen Handlungsimpulse, tendieren sie dazu, Situationen zu meiden, die ‚unerwünschte' empathische Reaktionen hervorrufen könnten. Empathisch motivierte Handlungen können Zeit, Energie oder finanzielle Aufwendungen fordern – und Menschen sind nicht bereit, diese ohne Weiteres allen zur Verfügung zu stellen.[43] Wer seine Emotionen gut regulieren kann, ist zudem in der Lage, die Stärke seiner empathischen Empfindung mit seinen anderen Interessen in Ausgleich zu bringen: Wer helfen will, lässt seine Emotionen zu, wer unwillig ist, unterdrückt sie oder sucht sie von vornherein zu vermeiden. Wer weiß, dass er in einer Situation nicht selbst helfen muss, kann seiner Empathie leichter freien Lauf lassen, als wenn er selbst helfen und entsprechende Ressourcen bereitstellen muss, dies aber nicht will.[44]

Zu einem breiteren Verständnis von Compassion

Trotz aller aufgezeigter Probleme lehnt auch Bloom Empathie nicht grundsätzlich ab und anerkennt ihre Bedeutung in sozialen Beziehungen – problematisch wird es für ihn, wenn Empathie präskriptiv aufgeladen wird.[45] Vor diesem Hintergrund ist also erst genauer zu begründen, warum sich ethische oder allgemeine Bildungsansätze auf Empathie stützen oder diese fördern sollten. Dies gilt umso mehr, wenn Empathie unkritisch mit anderen Begriffen des moralisch guten Handelns gleichgesetzt wird.[46] Eine starke moralische ‚Aufladung' empathischer Zustände kann zudem einen unerwünschten Nebeneffekt haben: Wenn Empathie selbst als moralisch gilt, kann dies den subjektiven Eindruck erwecken, dass eine entsprechende Empfindung schon eine adäquate moralische ‚Handlung' darstellt, ohne dass weitere Handlungen gesetzt werden müssen.[47] Eine Person kann die moralische Forderung, die eine Situation stellt, schon allein durch das Empfinden von Mitgefühl als erfüllt betrachten und dies auch noch sozial kommunizieren (*virtue signalling*).

Fällt daher mit dem brüchigen Fundament Empathie auch das Konzept von Compassion als empathischer Mitleidenschaft? Lassen sich Compassion und Em-

---

Analytic Evaluation of Perspective Taking's Effect on Empathic Concern, in: Personality and Social Psychology Review 24/2 (2019), 141–162. DOI: 10.1177/1088868319887599.

43 Vgl. Ebd., 157.

44 Vgl. CAMERON, C. Daryl / PAYNE, B. Keith: Escaping Affect. How Motivated Emotion Regulation Creates Insensitivity to Mass Suffering, in: Journal of Personality and Social Psychology 100/1 (2015). DOI: 10.1037/a0021643, 11–12.

45 Vgl. BLOOM 2016 [Anm. 27], 212.

46 Vgl. BUSSMANN / HAASE / PÜHRINGER 2021 [Anm. 19].

47 Vgl. SAPOLSKY 2017 [Anm. 13], 688–691.

pathie stärker voneinander differenzieren? Und kann mit den aufgezeigten Defiziten von Empathie doch konstruktiv gearbeitet werden? Denn wenn Mitgefühl positiv mit Themen wie Nachhaltigkeit, Umwelt- und Klimaschutz korreliert,[48] ist es angebracht, die entsprechenden Potenziale auch nutzbar zu machen.

Am Beginn steht hier sicherlich ein kritisches Bewusstsein um die angesprochenen Probleme, die ein unverzichtbarer Teil der bildungsorientierten Auseinandersetzung mit Empathie sind.[49] Hinzu kommt, dass Menschen unterschiedlich stark empathisch oder überhaupt auf affektive Impulse reagieren. Statistisch lassen sich etwa Unterschiede im Empathieempfinden zwischen den Geschlechtern konstatieren,[50] und bestimmte Menschen sind insgesamt weniger für (moralische) Emotionen aller Art ansprechbar. Sie sind also nicht nur weniger empathisch, sondern reagieren auch weniger auf Lob, Zorn oder Schuld. Im Besonderen trifft dies auf Psychopath*innen zu.[51] Affektiv orientierte Bildungsansätze können also nicht davon ausgehen, dass sie alle Personen gleichermaßen ansprechen, und sie werden manche kaum bis gar nicht ansprechen. Ein ausschließlicher Fokus auf Empathie oder Affekte greift also zu kurz, wie Bickel & Preston auch mit Blick auf Einstellungen zu Umweltschutz aufweisen.[52] Die Bereitschaft zu altruistischem Handeln könnte daher zusätzlich auch als soziale Pflicht oder Leistung für die Gesellschaft begründet werden und müsste nicht allein in Empathie gründen.[53]

Zwar kommt ein Compassion-Ansatz nicht gänzlich ohne diese affektive Dimension aus, doch sollte diese nach Prinz breiter und handlungsorientierter ausgestaltet werden. Empathie zielt stark auf die Identität des/der Betroffenen ab. Demgegenüber könnte das moralische Empfinden stärker auf problematische *Handlungen* ausgerichtet werden: Nicht Einfühlen mit den Betroffenen, sondern Reaktionen auf Handlungen und Situationen könnten dann handlungsmotivierend wirken, unabhängig davon, ob oder wie stark man mit den Betroffenen

---

48 Vgl. PFATTHEICHER / SASSENRATH / SCHINDLER 2016 [Anm. 2].

49 Vgl. SPIEGEL 2017 [Anm. 15], 248–249.

50 Vgl. GREENBERG, David M. / WARRIER, Varun / ALLISON, Carrie / BARON-COHEN, Simon: Testing the Empathizing-Systemizing theory of sex differences and the Extreme Male Brain theory of autism in half a million people, in: Proceedings of the National Academy of Sciences 115/48 (2018), 12152–12157. DOI: 10.1073/pnas.1811032115.

51 Vgl. PRINZ 2011 [Anm. 18], 216–218.

52 Vgl. BICKEL, Logan A. / PRESTON, Stephanie D.: Environmental impassivity. Blunted emotionality undermines concern for the environment, in: Emotion 22/5 (2022). DOI: 10.1037/emo0001072.

53 Der bekannte Ansatz des Compassion-Projekts führt sich begrifflich auf John F. Kennedy (1917–1963) zurück, der diesen Begriff stark gemacht hatte. Hier ist zu anzumerken, dass Kennedy compassion zunächst als patriotische Pflicht verstand und der Ansicht war, das Individuum müsse der Gemeinschaft etwas zurückgeben. Compassion bei Kennedy hatte somit eine klar definierte Gruppen- sowie Pflichtendimension, vgl. KENNEDY, Ted (2013): Remembering JFK's legacy of compassion, in: http://deseret.com/2013/11/22/20530074/remembering-jfk-s-legacy-of-compassion [abgerufen am 16.02.2023].

mitfühlt. Dann könnten auch andere moralische Emotionen wie Zorn, Abscheu oder Empörung wirksam werden und zu Mitleidenschaft führen.[54] Dieselbe Handlungsbereitschaft kann auch durch das vorbildhafte Handeln anderer und dadurch ausgelöster positiver Emotionen wie Bewegtsein, Erhebung oder Bewunderung ausgelöst werden. Compassion wäre damit konzeptuell nicht ausschließlich auf Empathie angewiesen, sondern könnte sich auch auf andere moralisch relevante affektive Zustände beziehen.

Dies würde auch positiv zur Bildung für Nachhaltige Entwicklung beitragen: Feinberg und Willer haben gezeigt, dass eine zu stark an Empathie, Mitgefühl und Fürsorge orientierte Klimaschutz-Metaphorik nicht breitenwirksam ist, sondern vor allem an höher gebildete, urbane Schichten mit sozial-liberalen Einstellungen appelliert, deren Moralverständnis stark durch Mitgefühl und universelle Fürsorge geprägt ist. Auch sie plädieren daher für einen insgesamt breiteren Ansatz, der unterschiedliche Menschen und Moralvorstellungen anspricht.[55]

Trotz dieser Einschränkungen gibt es Anzeichen, dass mitfühlende Haltungen bis zu einem gewissen Grad trainierbar sind.[56] Ein erprobter Ansatz für Compassion-Training sind etwa buddhistisch inspirierte Meditationstechniken, die weniger auf die Entwicklung von Empathie abzielen als auf die Entwicklung einer wohlwollenden Haltung gegenüber anderen:

> The most widely used technique is called 'loving kindness training'. This form of mental practice is carried out in silence and relies on the cultivation of friendliness towards a series of imagined persons. One would usually start the practice by visualizing a person one feels very close to and then gradually extend the feeling of kindness towards others, including strangers and, at a later stage, also people one has difficulties with. Ultimately, this practice aims at cultivating feelings of benevolence towards all human beings.[57]

Techniken dieser Art können Mitgefühl und entsprechende Handlungsdispositionen nicht ‚herstellen', können aber ergänzend herangezogen werden, um den Compassion-Ansatz zu vertiefen und zu stärken, dazu gehören auch Übungen in Selbstempathie.[58]

---

54 Vgl. PRINZ 2011 [Anm. 27], 230. Zum Umgang mit negativen moralischen Emotionen im Unterricht vgl. etwa FEICHTINGER, Christian: Zorn. Ekel. Ethik. Auseinandersetzung mit negativen moralischen Emotionen als Beitrag zur ethischen Bildung, in: ÖRF 26/2 (2018), 91–103. DOI: 10.25364/10.26:2018.2.7 sowie ROMMEL, Herbert: Lernen an „negativer Moral", in: LINDNER, Konstantin / ZIMMERMANN, Mirjam (Hg.): Handbuch ethische Bildung. Religionspädagogische Fokussierungen, Tübingen: Mohr Siebeck 2021 (= UTB 5604), 326–331.

55 Vgl. FEINBERG / WILLER 2013 [Anm. 2].

56 Vgl. KLIMECKI, Olga M. / LEIBERG, Susanne / RICARD, Matthieu: Differential pattern of functional brain plasticity after compassion and empathy training, in: Social Cognitive and Affective Neuroscience 9/6 (2014), 873–879. DOI: 10.1093/scan/nst060.

57 SINGER / KLIMECKI 2014 [Anm. 23], R 876.

58 Vgl. SPIEGEL 2017 [Anm. 15], 247–248.

Ein weiterer Beitrag zur Entwicklung von Compassion, der auf die skizzierten Probleme reagiert, ist das Aufzeigen und Einüben von Handlungsmöglichkeiten. Wie dargestellt, vermeiden Menschen Situationen, auf die sie empathisch reagieren könnten, oder versuchen entsprechende Reaktionen zu regulieren, weil sie nicht handeln wollen oder das Gefühl haben, nicht handeln zu können. Compassion-Ansätze profitieren daher, wenn sie nicht nur Wahrnehmung und Empfindung schulen, sondern diese auch mit konkreten Handlungsoptionen verknüpfen, Lösungsmodelle entwickeln und das Vertrauen in Selbstwirksamkeit stärken.[59]

Im Angesicht der aufgezeigten positiven Perspektiven im Umgang mit den problematischen Seiten von Empathie sind dennoch auch Grenzen des Ansatzes anzuerkennen. Dort, wo Empathie und Mitleidenschaft in ein Konkurrenzverhältnis von nahestehenden Personen im Hier und Jetzt und entfernten, komplexen, zukünftigen Konstellationen treten, werden erstere die Oberhand behalten. Zwar ist es möglich, den empathischen Horizont bis zu einem gewissen Grad auszuweiten, da menschliche Empathiefähigkeit immer auch reflexiv durchdrungen und geprägt werden kann.[60] Dies gilt jedoch nicht uneingeschränkt, und das kurzfristige Schicksal der eigenen Familie oder der eigenen Kinder wird im Regelfall Oberhand über komplexe Themen wie Nachhaltigkeit und Klimawandel haben. Wer sich täglich um das Wohlergehen, vielleicht sogar Überleben seiner Nächsten sorgen muss, dessen Fähigkeit zur Empathie ist davon umfassend beansprucht. Mitleidenschaft ist damit nie nur eine Sache von Individuen, sondern auch von sozialer Sicherheit und Verteilungsgerechtigkeit.

Literatur

Batson, C. Daniel: A Scientific Search for Altruism. Do We Care Only About Ourselves?, Oxford: University Press, 2019.

Bickel, Logan A. / Preston, Stephanie D.: Environmental impassivity. Blunted emotionality undermines concern for the environment, in: Emotion 22/5 (2022). DOI: 10.1037/emo0001072.

Bloom, Paul: Against Empathy. The Case for Rational Compassion, New York: Ecco, 2016.

Brown, Donald: Human Universals, New York: McGraw-Hill, 1991.

Bussmann, Bettina / Haase, Volker / Pühringer, Angela (2021): Empathie-Förderung im Unterricht, in: https://www.praefaktisch.de/emotionen/empathie-foerderung-im-unterricht/ [abgerufen am 16.02.2023].

Bucher, Anton A.: Mehr Emotionen und Tugenden als kognitive Stufen. Skizze der aktuellen Moralpsychologie, in: Englert, Rudolf / Kohler-Spiegel, Helga / Naurath, Elisabeth /

59 Vgl. Goetz, Keltner, Simon-Thomas 2010 [Anm. 12], 360 sowie Spiegel 2017 [Anm. 15], 249–250.

60 Vgl. Decety 2014 [Anm. 11], 134.

SCHRÖDER, Bernd / SCHWEITZER, Friedrich (Hg.): Ethisches Lernen, Neukirchen-Vluyn: Neukirchener, 2015 (= Jahrbuch der Religionspädagogik 31), 87–97.

CAMERON, C. Daryl / PAYNE, B. Keith: Escaping Affect. How Motivated Emotion Regulation Creates Insensitivity to Mass Suffering, in: Journal of Personality and Social Psychology 100/1 (2015), 1–15. DOI: 10.1037/a0021643.

DECETY, Jean: The Neuroevolution of Empathy and Caring for Others. Why It Matters for Morality, in: DECETY, Jean / CHRISTEN, Yves (Hg.): New Frontiers in Social Neuroscience, Cham u. a.: Springer, 2014, 127–151.

ELLEMERS, Naomi / VAN DER TOORN, Jojanneke / PAUNOV, Yavor / VAN LEEUWEN, Thed: The Psychology of Morality. A Review and Analysis of Empirical Studies Published from 1940 through 2017, in: Personality and Social Psychology Review 23/4 (2019), 332–366. DOI: 10.1177/1088868318811759.

FEICHTINGER, Christian: Zorn. Ekel. Ethik. Auseinandersetzung mit negativen moralischen Emotionen als Beitrag zur ethischen Bildung, in: ÖRF 26/2 (2018) 91–103. DOI: 10.25364/10.26:2018.2.7.

FEINBERG, Matthew / WILLER, Robb: The Moral Roots of Environmental Attitudes, in: Psychological Science 24/1 (2013), 56–62. DOI: 10.1177/0956797612449177.

GOETZ, Jennifer L. / KELTNER, Dacher / SIMON-THOMAS, Emiliana: Compassion. An Evolutionary Analysis and Empirical Review, in: Psychological Bulletin 136/3 (2010), 351–374. DOI: 10.1037/a0018807.

GREENBERG, David M. / WARRIER, Varun / ALLISON, Carrie /BARON-COHEN, Simon: Testing the Empathizing-Systemizing theory of sex differences and the Extreme Male Brain theory of autism in half a million people, in: Proceedings of the National Academy of Sciences 115/48 (2018), 12152–12157. DOI: 10.1073/pnas.1811032115.

HAIDT, Jonathan: The Emotional Dog and its Rational Tail. A Social Intuitionist Approach to Moral Judgment, in: Psychological Review 108/4 (2001), 814–834.

HAIDT, Jonathan / KESEBIR, Selin: Morality, in: FISKE, Susan / GILBERT, Daniel / LINDZEY, Garner (Hg.): Handbook of Social Psychology, Hoboken: Wiley, 52012, 797–832.

HASLAM, Nick: Dehumanization. An Integrative Review, in: Personality and Social Psychology Review 10/3 (2006), 252–264.

JENNI, Karen E. / LOEWENSTEIN, George: Explaining the 'Identifiable Victim Effect', in: Journal of Risk and Uncertainty 14 (1997), 235–257.

KENNEDY, Ted (2013): Remembering JFK's legacy of compassion, in: http://deseret.com/2013/11/22/20530074/remembering-jfk-s-legacy-of-compassion [abgerufen am 16.02.2023].

KLIMECKI, Olga M. / LEIBERG, Susanne / RICARD, Matthieu: Differential pattern of functional brain plasticity after compassion and empathy training, in: Social Cognitive and Affective Neuroscience 9/6 (2014), 873–879. DOI: 10.1093/scan/nst060.

KOGUT, Tehila / RITOV, Ilana: The "Identified Victim" Effect: An Identified Group, or Just a Single Individual?, in: Journal of Behavioral Decision Making 18 (2005), 157–167. DOI: 10.1002/bdm.492.

KRISTJÁNSSON, Kristján: Moral Education Today. Ascendancy and Fragmentation, in: Journal of Moral Education 46/4 (2017), 339–346. DOI: 10.1080/03057240.2017.1370209.

KULD, Lothar: Sympatheia – Compassion. Ein Projekt und ein Hinweis auf John Henry Newman, in: TZSCHEETZSCH, Werner (Hg.): Zwischen Exodus und Exil. Religionspädagogik in der Pluralität, Ostfildern: Schwabenverlag, 2000, 71–75.

LENZ, Viktoria: Empathie-Lernen. Moralpsychologische Perspektiven, in: SAUTERMEISTER, Jochen / ZWICK, Elisabeth (Hg.): Religion und Bildung. Antipoden oder Weggefährten? Diskurse aus historischer, systematischer und praktischer Sicht, Paderborn: Schöningh, 2019, 349–361.

McAuliffe, William / Carter, Evan / Berhane, Juliana / Snihur, Alexander / McCullough, Michael: Is Empathy the Default Response to Suffering? A Meta-Analytic Evaluation of Perspective Taking's Effect on Empathic Concern, in: Personality and Social Psychology Review 24/2 (2019), 141–162. DOI: 10.1177/1088868319887599.

Naurath, Elisabeth: Mit Gefühl gegen Gewalt. Mitgefühl als Schlüssel ethischer Bildung in der Religionspädagogik, Neukirchen-Vluyn: Neukirchener, [3]2010.

Persson, Ingmar: Morality from Compassion, Oxford: University Press, 2021.

Pfattheicher, Stefan / Sassenrath, Claudia / Schindler, Simon: Feelings for the Suffering of Others and the Environment. Compassion Fosters Proenvironmental Tendencies, in: Environment and Behavior 48/7 (2016), 929–945. DOI: 10.1177/0013916515574549.

Prinz, Jesse J.: Against Empathy, in: The Southern Journal of Philosophy 49 (2011), 214–233. DOI: 10.1111/j.2041-6962.2011.00069.x.

Prinz, Jesse J.: Is Empathy Necessary for Morality?, in: Coplan, Amy / Goldie, Peter (Hg.): Empathy. Philosophical and Psychological Perspectives, Oxford: University Press, 2011, 211–229.

Pölzler, Thomas: Moral Judgments and Emotions. A Less Intimate Relationship than Recently Claimed, in: Journal of Theoretical and Philosophical Psychology 35/3 (2015), 177–195. DOI: 10.1037/teo0000022.

Rommel, Herbert: Lernen an „negativer Moral“, in: Lindner, Konstantin / Zimmermann, Mirjam (Hg.): Handbuch ethische Bildung. Religionspädagogische Fokussierungen, Tübingen: Mohr Siebeck, 2021 (= UTB 5604), 326–331.

Sapolsky, Robert M.: Gewalt und Mitgefühl. Die Biologie des menschlichen Verhaltens, München: Hanser, 2017.

Schein, Chelsea / Gray, Kurt: The Theory of Dyadic Morality. Reinventing Moral Judgment by Redefining Harm, in: Personality and Social Psychology Review 22/1 (2018), 32–70. DOI: 10.1177/1088868317698288.

Singer, Tania / Klimecki, Olga M.: Empathy and compassion, in: Current Biology 24/18 (2014), R875–R878. DOI: 10.1016/j.cub.2014.06.054.

Slovic, Paul / Västfjäll, Daniel: The More Who Die, the Less We Care. Psychic Numbing and Genocide, in: Kaul, Susanne / Kim, David (Hg.): Imagining Human Rights, Berlin/München/Boston: de Gruyter, 2015, 55–68.

Spiegel, Irina: Empathie- und Compassion-Training, in: Nida-Rümelin, Julian / Spiegel, Irina / Tiedemann, Markus (Hg.): Handbuch Philosophie und Ethik. Band 1: Didaktik und Methodik, Paderborn: Schöningh, [2]2017, 245–251.

Teil II

Ethik der Compassion – Zum Potenzial gesellschaftlich-transformatorischen Handelns

Die Haltung des Mitgefühls gegenüber allen Lebewesen – Die Bewegung des Engagierten Buddhismus

Peter Ramers

In der ersten Hälfte des 20. Jahrhunderts entstand in einigen Ländern Asiens eine neue Bewegung, die inzwischen unter der Bezeichnung *International Network of Engaged Buddhists* aus der Haltung eines unbegrenzten Mitgefühls und in einem bewussten Handeln für das Wohl aller Wesen weltweit Stellung gegen die Missachtung der Menschenrechte und dessen politische und soziale Ursachen bezieht und sich für gerechte Wirtschaftsverhältnisse, den Umweltschutz, die Gesundheitsvorsorge, die Gleichberechtigung der Geschlechter, den Dialog der Religionen und den Frieden in der Welt einsetzt.

Compassion; frühbuddhistische Spiritualität; Bodhisattva-Prinzip; Netzwerk engagierter Buddhisten; Thich Nhat Hanh

In the first half of the 20th century, a new movement arose in some Asian countries, which, under the name of *International Network of Engaged Buddhists*, has since taken a stand against the disregard for human rights and its political and social causes, out of an attitude of unlimited compassion and in a conscious action for the well-being of all beings worldwide, and has campaigned for just economic conditions, environmental protection, health care, gender equality, dialogue between religions and peace in the world.

Compassion; early-Buddhist-spirituality; Bodhisattva-principle; network of engaged Buddhists; Thich Nhat Hanh

Dem Theologen Johann Baptist Metz verdanken wir den Begriff *Compassion* als Schlüsselwort und Grundvokal des Christentums.[1] Da Jesus primär das Leid der Menschen im Blick habe, stehe im Mittelpunkt der Mystik des Christentums, so Metz, eine Mystik der *Mitleidenschaft*, also das Angerührtsein vom Leid *der ande-*

---

1 Metz greift auf den englischen Begriff *compassion* zurück, weil die Wiedergabe dieser Haltung durch das deutsche Wort *Mitleid* viel zu sentimental und unpolitisch ausgedrückt wird. Außerdem ist *Mitleid* eine „problematische Vokabel, wenn damit eine Haltung von Starken gegenüber Schwachen gemeint ist, die in Menschen, die Betreuung brauchen, schlichtweg nur bedauernswerte Kreaturen sieht". Mitleid ist vielmehr „die Haltung engagierter Mitmenschlichkeit, die Leiden, welcher Art und aus welchen Gründen auch immer, nicht einfach indifferent hinnimmt" (KULD, Lothar: Art. Compassion, 1–7, hier 2, in: WiReLex Online. https://www.bibelwissenschaft.de/fileadmin/buh_bibelmodul/media/wirelex/pdf/Compassion_2020-04-29_14_56.pdf (zuletzt aufgerufen am 22.02. 2023).

ren und die Reaktion darauf. Ungeachtet der Tatsache, dass alle großen Religionen der Menschheit um eine Mystik des Leidens konzentriert sind,[2] sieht er gerade in der „Empfindlichkeit für das Leid der anderen"[3] „*die* Mitgift, die das Christentum in die entstehende Weltgemeinschaft einbringen kann",[4] und stellt in diesem Zusammenhang die Frage, wie „sich zwei klassische Formen dieser Leidensmystik zum Umgang mit fremdem Leid" verhalten:

> Zum einen handelt es sich um die Leidensmystik der biblisch-monotheistischen Traditionen, zum anderen um die Leidensmystik in den fernöstlichen, speziell in den buddhistischen Traditionen, die auch in der postmodernen Welt des Westens, in der Welt nach dem proklamierten ‚Tod Gottes' immer mehr Anhänger gewinnt. Die Mystik der Bibel – in monotheistischen Traditionen – ist in ihrem Kern eine politische Mystik, näherhin eine Mystik der politischen, der sozialen Compassion. Ihr kategorischer Imperativ lautet: Aufwachen, die Augen öffnen! Jesus lehrt nicht eine Mystik der geschlossenen Augen, sondern eine Mystik der offenen Augen und damit der unbedingten Wahrnehmungspflicht für fremdes Leid. [...] Aus den Gründungslegenden des Buddhismus wird deutlich, dass auch Buddha in der Begegnung mit fremdem Leid sich wandelt, gewiss. Doch schließlich flieht er in den Königspalast in seinem Inneren, um in der Mystik der geschlossenen Augen die Landschaft zu finden, die immun ist gegen alles Leid. Demgegenüber ist die biblisch-monotheistische Mystik, ist die Mystik Jesu eine ‚schwache' und ‚verletzbare' Mystik. Jesus kann sich über die Landschaft des Leidens nicht erheben, seine Mystik mündet in einen Schrei. Und die Wege der Nachfolge führen in die Compassion.[5]

Wie ist diese undifferenzierte Schwarzweißmalerei zu erklären angesichts der Tatsache, dass *Mitgefühl* für alle Formen des Buddhismus – besonders in den Formen des Mahayana-Buddhismus – ein zentrales spirituell-ethisches Ideal darstellt und „die Buddha-Legende dort erst eigentlich beginnt, wo Metz sie enden lässt: nämlich mit der Erleuchtung, und dass der Buddha", wie Thomas Wagner in seiner Dissertation über *Profile engagierter Mystik* richtig herausstellt,

> nach seiner Erleuchtung aus ‚Mitleid' fünfundvierzig Jahre lang ein Leben in aktiver Weltzuwendung führte? Die vermutlich naheliegendste Antwort lautet, dass Metz einfach einem verbreiteten Klischee folgt, das nur zu gut ins eigene theologische

---

2 Vgl. METZ, Johann Baptist: Compassion – Weltprogramm des Christentums (in Forum 27), in: https://www.schulstiftung-freiburg.de/eip/media/forum/pdf_156.pdf (zuletzt aufgerufen am 22.02.2023).

3 METZ, Johann Baptist: Die Autorität der Leidenden. Compassion – Vorschlag zu einem Weltprogramm des Christentums, in: Süddeutsche Zeitung 24./25./26. Dezember 1997, Nr. 296, 57.

4 KULD, Lothar: Compassion I. Theologie der Compassion. Biblische Grundlagen und theologische Reflexion sozialen Handelns", hier 4, in: https://www.schulstiftung-freiburg.de/eip/media/forum/pdf_182.pdf (zuletzt aufgerufen am 22.02.2023). Lothar Kult begleitet und evaluiert seit vielen Jahren das Compassion-Projekt, das in einigen Schulen seit Jahrzehnten Teil des Curriculums ist. Zu seinen Publikationen zur Thematik siehe auch: https://katholische-theologie.ph-weingarten.de/fileadmin/redaktuere/Subdomains/Katholische_Theologie/Lehrende/Publikationen_Kuld.pdf (zuletzt aufgerufen am 22.02.23).

5 METZ [Anm. 2].

Programm passt: der weltflüchtige Buddhismus auf der einen Seite und das der Welt in Liebe zugewandte Christentum auf der anderen Seite.[6]

Dieses Klischee prägte und prägt auch nach wie vor das Bild, das viele Menschen hier im Westen vom Buddhismus haben, zumal viele Westler zumeist die meditativ-welt-flüchtige Seite dieser Weltreligion interessiert, verbunden mit der Hoffnung, mittels der dort praktizierten Rituale und Versenkungsmethoden den in seiner Unübersichtlichkeit, Wechselhaftigkeit und Eindimensionalität als belastend empfundenen Alltag zu transzendieren und inneren Halt zu finden.

Es ist zwar richtig, dass sich das buddhistische Denken nach wie vor aufs Ganze gesehen relativ selten gesellschaftlichen Fragen und Problemfeldern zuwendet, keine ausgereifte Sozialphilosophie entwickelt[7] und „einen eher naiven Begriff von sozialen Angelegenheiten“[8] hat. So sucht man auch vergeblich in den frühbuddhistischen kanonischen Zeugnissen nach einem Engagement, dem es beispielsweise um die Behebung gesellschaftlicher oder politischer Missstände geht. Der Buddha hatte keine politischen Ambitionen. Ein Aufruf zu einem aktiven Einsatz für die Welt ist der altbuddhistischen Tradition, soweit sie in den kanonischen Texten greifbar ist, fremd.

So gilt es in der traditionellen Sicht beispielsweise des Theravada-Buddhismus Sri Lankas, Myanmars oder auch Thailands bis heute „als ausgemacht, dass der Buddhismus eine eher weltabgewandte Religion darstellt, der es um die Befreiung des Menschen aus der Verstrickung seines Karma geht und die sich wenig um die Veränderung der Lebensbedingungen, um soziale Gerechtigkeit und soziales Engagement kümmert.“[9]

Umso bemerkenswerter ist es, dass in der ersten Hälfte des 20. Jahrhunderts in einigen Ländern Asiens eine neue Bewegung des Denkens entstand, die eine *Relecture* traditioneller Vorstellungen im Hinblick auf gegenwärtige gesellschaftliche Probleme versucht, um auf diese Weise „die buddhistische Spiritualität ihrem Rufe der *Weltentrücktheit* und Bejahung des sozialen Status Quo“[10] zu entreißen, wobei den Lehren eine besondere Bedeutung zukommt, die zur Förderung von Mitleid und Toleranz in Politik und Gesellschaft dienen können.

---

6 WAGNER Thomas: Profile engagierter Mystik. Eine erziehungswissenschaftliche Untersuchung zu politisch-mystischen Identitätskonzepten im interreligiösen Vergleich. Dissertation, Frankfurt a. M.: Johann Wolfgang Goethe-Universität zu Frankfurt a. M., 2005, 135, in: https://publikationen.ub.uni-frankfurt.de/frontdoor/deliver/index/docId/2949/file/WagnerThomas.pdf (zuletzt aufgerufen am 22.02.2023).

7 Vgl. SUNGTAEK, Cho: Selbstlosigkeit. Zu einer buddhistischen Vision von sozialer Gerechtigkeit, in: Polylog. Zeitschrift für interkulturelles Philosophieren 6 (2000), 34–35.

8 Ebd., 30.

9 EVERS, Georg: Land der Mönche. Der Buddhismus Thailands im gesellschaftlichen Wandel, in: Herder Korrespondenz 56.5 (2002), 243.

10 NEUMANN, Mareke: Engagierter Buddhismus. Eine interkulturelle Orientierung, Nordhausen: Bautz, 2005 (Bausteine zur Mensching-Forschung. N.F., Bd. 11), 12.

Neben Erfahrungen von Leid und Schuld im Kontext von Unterdrückung, Ausbeutung und kriegerischer Auseinandersetzungen als Wurzeln dieses sozial und politisch engagierten Buddhismus erfährt die Bewegung zunehmend Anstöße durch den weltweit wachsenden Austausch von Ideen, wobei auch christliche Vorstellungen und Praktiken – nicht zuletzt die durch die Befreiungstheologie gegebenen Impulse – eine große Rolle gespielt haben und spielen.[11] So werden gerade im Rahmen der *Bewegung des Engagierten Buddhismus* inzwischen beachtenswerte politische und soziale Aktivitäten entfaltet. Die im Westen noch immer vertretene Auffassung, solches Engagement vertrage sich nicht mit buddhistischer Spiritualität, gehört deshalb ebenfalls in die Kategorie *orientalistisches Phantasieprodukt.*

Die Vier unbegrenzten Geisteszustände

Im Folgenden sollen Geist und Praxis dieser Bewegung, besonders im Hinblick auf die zentrale Bedeutung der Haltung der *Compassion*, wie sie das Denken und Handeln ihrer Protagonist*innen bestimmt, näher in den Blick genommen werden.[12]

Werfen wir zunächst einen Blick in den Pāli-Kanon, den alten, nach der Überlieferung im 1. Jahrhundert v. Chr. in Ceylon schriftlich fixierten Korpus autoritativer Texte der Überlieferungstradition des Theravāda, einer frühen Schule des Buddhismus, die heute noch in Sri Lanka und Südostasien beheimatet ist.

Für die *Relecture* altbuddhistischer Spiritualität seitens des engagierten Buddhismus sehr bedeutsam ist der alte buddhistische Erlösungsweg, der sog. *Vier unbegrenzten Geisteszustände*, der mit den beiden Polen buddhistischer Spiritualität – einer, auf den ersten Blick *sozialen* (altruistischen) Komponente, die durch

11 Vgl. LUKOSCHEK, Barbara: Ethik der Befreiung. Engagierter Buddhismus und Befreiungstheologie im Dialog, Paderborn u. a.: Ferdinand Schöningh, 2013 (= Beiträge zur Komparativen Theologie, Bd. 16).

12 Nicht behandelt werden wichtige Gestalten wie der XIV. Dalai Lama bsTan-'dzin-rgyamthso (geb. 1935), der japanische Zen-Meister und Philosoph Shin'ichi Hisamatsu (1889–1980) und die F.A.S.-Society (Formless Self, All-humankind, Superhistorical); der indische Politiker und Sozialreformer Bhimrao Ramji Ambedkar (1891–1956); Sangharakshita (1925–2018) (mit bürgerlichem Namen Dennis Lingwood), der Gründer der *Friends of the Western Buddhist Order* (FWBO) und des *Western Buddhist Order* (WBO), und die buddhistische Reformgemeinschaft Soka Gakkai. Zu Shin'ichi Hisamatsu vgl. BRÜCK, Michael von: Die Bewegung „Engagierter Buddhismus", in: RIßE, Günter / SONNEMANS, Heino / THESS, Burkhard (Hg.): Wege der Theologie. An der Schwelle zum dritten Jahrtausend. Festschrift für Hans Waldenfels zur Vollendung des 65. Lebensjahres, Paderborn: Bonifatius, 1996, 662–667. Zu Ambedkar, Sangharakshita und Soka Gakkai vgl. NEUMANN 2005 [Anm. 10], 119–130 und 131–137.

Haltungen wie *Wohlwollen, Mitleid* und *Mitgefühl* charakterisiert werden kann,[13] und einem dieser entgegenstehenden, aber für die Erlösung förderlichen, wenn nicht gar konstitutiven (egozentrischen) Geisteszustand, der im älteren Buddhismus höchste Wertschätzung genießt und sich mit den Quasisynonymen *Gleichmut, Untangiertheit, Indifferenz* beschreiben lässt, konfrontiert.[14]

Bei der spirituellen Übung der „Vier unbegrenzten [Geisteshaltungen]“ (Pali: *appamāṇa, appamaññā*, Sanskrit: *apramāṇa*), auch „brahmische [Geistes-]Zustände“ (*brahmavihāra*)[15] genannt, sendet der Meditierende Gefühle von Wohlwollen (Pali: *mettā*, Sanskrit: *maitrī*), Mitleid / Mitgefühl (*karuṇā*), [Mit-]Freude (*muditā*) und Gleichmut (Pali: *upekkhā*, Sanskrit: *upekṣā*) – als eine Art Fluidum – in alle Himmelsrichtungen über alle Wesen aus.[16]

Ursprüngliches Ziel dieser Übung ist es, die Emotionen systematisch zu kultivieren, schädliche Geisteszustände zu beseitigen und schließlich in den Zustand einer reinen emotionalen Untangiertheit (Gleichmut) einzutreten. Die stereotype Formel, mit der diese Übung an verschiedenen Stellen des Pali-Kanons beschrieben wird, lautet:

> Mit von Wohlwollen, Mitleid / Mitgefühl, Freude und Gleichmut begleitetem Geist / Gemüt (begleiteter Gesinnung / Geisteshaltung) erfüllt / durchdringt er – eine Zeitlang – eine Himmelsrichtung, desgleichen eine zweite, desgleichen eine dritte, desgleichen die vierte; ebenso aufwärts, abwärts, seitwärts: allseits, ganz und gar, die ganze Welt erfüllt er – eine Zeitlang – mit von Wohlwollen begleitetem Geist, weitem, großen, grenzenlosen, von Feindseligkeit und Übelwollen freiem [Geist].[17]

Sucht man nach einem Übersetzungsäquivalent für *Mitgefühl* im Sinne von *Compassion*, bietet sich hier der Begriff *karuṇā* („Mitleid / Mitgefühl“) an. Im Unterschied zur späteren *Relecture* des Textes durch die Protagonist*innen des *Engagierten Buddhismus*, ist jedoch dort, wo in den Texten des Pali-Kanons die *karuṇā*

---

13 Unbestreitbar ist gerade der buddhistischen (Laien)-Ethik eine starke soziale Komponente zu eigen.

14 Auf die bis heute kontrovers geführte Diskussion, welchem dieser beiden Pole altbuddhistischen Heilsstrebens – dem egozentrischen oder dem altruistischen – die Vorrangstellung gebührt, geht ausführlich Mudagamuwe MAITHRIMURTHI in seiner profunden Dissertation ein: Wohlwollen, Mitleid, Freude und Gleichmut. Eine ideengeschichtliche Untersuchung der vier apramāṇas in der buddhistischen Ethik und Spiritualität von den Anfängen bis hin zum frühen Yogācāra, Stuttgart: Franz Steiner, 1999 (= Alt- und Neu-indische Studien, 50), 161–185. MAITHRIMURTHI setzt sich hier u. a. mit der Position Harvey B. ARONSONS (Love and Sympathy in Theravāda-Buddhism, Delhi: Motilal Banarsidass, 1980) auseinander, der versucht, auf der Grundlage der alten kanonischen Schriften, aber auch postkanonischer Werke sowie der Kommentarliteratur nachzuweisen, dass schon dem Theravāda-Buddhismus eine altruistisch-mahāyānistisch orientierte Ethik eigen war.

15 Vgl. NYANATILOKA (Übers.): Visuddhi-Magga oder der Weg zur Reinheit, Konstanz: Christiani, ³1975, 338–371 (Kap. IX: „Die göttlichen Verweilungszustände [*brahma-vihāra*]“).

16 Diese Übung gehört nach Tilmann VETTER (The Ideas and Meditative Practices of Early Buddhism, Leiden u. a.: Brill, 1988, 20) zur ältesten Schicht der urbuddhistischen Lehre.

17 Ich folge der Übersetzung MAITHRIMURTHIS 1999 [Anm. 14], 35.

thematisiert wird, zumeist diese im Kontext der genannten Übung angesiedelte Haltung gemeint, die in erster Linie der spirituellen Läuterung des Meditierenden selbst dient.[18] Er betrachtet auf dieser Stufe alle Lebewesen als der Hilfe bedürftige, leidende, schwache Wesen, um auf diesem Wege ihm eigene emotionale Fehlhaltungen wie Aggressivität, Grausamkeit und Hass zu beseitigen. Zumindest im Kontext der Übung der *Vier unbegrenzten Geisteshaltungen* ist an ein aktives, konkretes Eingreifen zum Zwecke der Beseitigung des Leidens anderer nicht gedacht. Wie das „Wohlwollen" (*mettā*) beschränkt sich auch das „Mitleid / Mitgefühl" (*karuṇā*) hier weitgehend auf den Wunsch, dass die unglücklichen Lebewesen von Leiden befreit werden mögen, was natürlich auch für das praktische Verhalten insofern Konsequenzen hat, als der Meditierende Handlungen, die anderen Schmerz oder Leid zufügen, selbstverständlich unterlässt.

Fragt man nach der inneren Struktur der Übung der *Vier unbegrenzten Geisteshaltungen* und nach dem spirituellen Rang und der Beziehung der einzelnen Glieder zueinander,[19] so scheint es sich hier um die aufsteigende Reihe eines spirituellen Weges zu handeln, der auf den Vorstufen des Wohlwollens, der Freundlichkeit und des Mitleids / Mitgefühls schrittweise von allen egoistisch konnotierten emotionalen Verhaftungen befreit und in der Stufe der „Untangiertheit" (*upekkhā*), also einer – *idealiter* – vollständigen emotionalen Distanziertheit, gipfelt.

Zumindest im Frühbuddhismus geht es im Rahmen der *Vier unbegrenzten Geisteshaltungen* dabei also weniger um Taten oder gar eine Anleitung zu praktischem Handeln[20] als vielmehr „um eine Geisteshaltung, die der Meditierende vor allem kultiviert, um selbst auf dem Weg zur spirituellen Vervollkommnung weiterzukommen."[21] Letztendlich stand damit bei jedem nach Erleuchtung Strebenden primär die eigene (allerdings nicht in einem egoistisch-exklusivistischen

---

18 Daneben findet sich in den frühbuddhistischen Lehrtexten das Mitgefühl als wichtige Motivation für die Predigt der Lehre durch den Buddha und die Erleuchteten in seiner Gefolgschaft. Vgl. dazu ausführlich Bhikkhu Anālayo: Compassion in the *Āgamas* and *Nikāyas*, in: Dharma Drum Journal of Buddhist Studies 16 (2015), 1–31; Schmidt-Leukel, Perry: Compassion im Buddhismus, in: Wege zum Menschen 65.2 (2013), 127–144, bes. 128–131.

19 Zu den verschiedenen Auffassungen der Tradition vgl. Maithrimurthi 1999 [Anm. 14], 146, Anm. 24.

20 Das Leben der Mönche, wie es der Pali-Kanon beschreibt, zeichnet sich durch ihre Abkehr von der Gesellschaft aus. Sie sollen weder gesellschaftliche Pflichten übernehmen noch sich in die weltlichen Angelegenheiten der Laienanhänger*innen involvieren lassen. Nur dort bestehen noch Berührungspunkte, wo Mönche die sie materiell unterstützenden Laienanhänger im Gegenzug belehren und ihnen durch ihren heiligen Wandel als Vorbild dienen. Mudagamuwe Maithrimurthi kann im gesamten Pali-Kanon „keine einzige Stelle finden, wo darüber hinaus den Mönchen noch andere Hilfeleistungen für Laien nahegelegt werden" (Maithrimurthi 1999 [Anm. 14], 164).

21 Maithrimurthi 1999 [Anm. 14], 117. Das legt auch der Vergleich mit anderen soteriologischen Begriffsreihen nahe. Vgl. dazu Ramers, Peter: Buddhistische Übungen zur Erlangung der Indifferenz und das Mitleid mit allen Lebewesen. Ein Beitrag zur Spiritualität und Ethik des frühen Buddhismus, in: Bsteh, Petrus / Proksch, Brigitte (Hg.): Spiritualität

Sinne anderen missgönnte) Befreiung im Mittelpunkt des persönlichen Bemühens, – sei es die Befreiung von der Angst vor Alter, Krankheit und Tod in der gegenwärtigen Existenz[22] oder die endgültige Befreiung (*nirvāṇa*) aus dem leidvollen Kreislauf des Immer-wieder-Geborenwerdens-und-Sterbens (*samsāra*).

Das heißt keineswegs, dass moralisch einwandfreies Verhalten (*sīla*) in der Spiritualität des älteren Buddhismus einfach über Bord geworfen würde, nachdem man die Erleuchtung erlangt hat. Vielmehr bleibt das nun geläuterte sittliche Verhalten ein integraler (wenn auch für die persönliche Befreiung nicht hinreichender) und für den Vollendeten schließlich zur Selbstverständlichkeit gewordener Bestandteil[23] auf dem Stufenweg zur Erlösung.

Es kann also festgehalten werden, dass im Mittelpunkt des spirituellen Strebens der religiösen Virtuosen im älteren Buddhismus eindeutig die Bemühung um die Ausbildung einer gleichmütig-indifferenten inneren Haltung steht, bei der der Geist – wenigstens zeitweise – frei und unberührt von allem Leid und Glück der Lebewesen den Lauf der Welt ganz neutral betrachten und in einem friedvoll-gleichmütigen Zustand völliger Emotionslosigkeit verharren soll, der nicht nur das entscheidende und höchste Element auf dem Weg zur Erlösung bildet, sondern letztendlich das Unterpfand der Erlösung selbst darstellt. Zugleich wird deutlich, dass auch dem frühen Buddhismus altruistische Aspekte nicht abgesprochen werden können, darf doch das Streben des Religiosen nach eigenem Heil keinesfalls zu Lasten anderer erfolgen. Haltungen wie Mitgefühl, Anteilnahme und Fürsorge allen Wesen gegenüber stellen sich jedoch nicht als automatische Frucht der Erlösung ein, sondern verdanken sich nach dem Zeugnis des Pāli-Kanons einer der Goldenen Regel vergleichbaren Überlegung und bilden eine, wenn auch hochgeschätzte, so doch freiwillige *Zugabe*. Mudagamuwe Maithrimurthi spricht in diesem Zusammenhang von einem „passiven Altruismus", wobei letztlich offenbleiben kann, ob dieser „im Rahmen des privaten Heilsstrebens verbleibt oder nicht. Eine gewisse Eigendynamik, die sich

im Gespräch der Religionen I, Wien/Berlin: LIT, 2009 (= Spiritualität im Dialog, Bd. 1), 216–231.

22 In den meisten der Texte, die den Auszug Siddhartha Gautamas aus dem Haus in die Hauslosigkeit behandeln, steht als Motiv für die Weltflucht eindeutig das Problem des *eigenen* Lebens: das persönliche Betroffensein von Alter, Krankheit und Tod, letztlich die Erwartung des Sterbenmüssens und die Angst vor dem Sterben im Mittelpunkt. Nicht von ungefähr nennt der Buddha das in der Befreiungserfahrung erlangte das „Todlose" (Pali: *amata*, Sanskrit: *amṛta*, „das, wo Sterben nicht stattfindet"). Vgl. VETTER, Tilmann: Die Lehre des Buddha. Mittlerer Weg – Achtfacher Pfad – Vier edle Wahrheiten", in: BSTEH, Andreas, (Hg.): Der Buddhismus als Anfrage an christliche Theologie und Philosophie, Mödling: St. Gabriel, 2000 (= Studien zur Religionstheologie, Bd. 5), 59–66.

23 Nach den kanonischen Texten ist es unmöglich für einen Erlösten (Arhat), dass er eine unmoralische Handlung begeht, beispielsweise absichtlich ein Lebewesen schädigt oder gar tötet.

bei Bedarf in spontaner Hilfeleistung äußern kann, dürfte aber schwer abzustreiten und im Mahāyāna zu voller Entfaltung gekommen sein."[24] Jedenfalls kann hier von einem Interessenkonflikt zwischen dem eigenen Heil und dem Heil der anderen Lebewesen, also zwischen *Egoismus* und *Altruismus*, nicht gesprochen werden.[25]

Das Bodhisattva-Prinzip

Vor allem das im Mahāyāna-Buddhismus zur vollen Entfaltung kommende Bodhisattva-Prinzip bietet als wesentlicher hermeneutischer Schlüssel eines engagiert-buddhistischen Denkens und Handelns „mit der Forderung nach Kultivierung einer *mitleidvollen Empathie*"[26] mit allen Lebewesen auch „gute Gründe für ein *aktives Eintreten* für die Menschenrechte bzw. für deren *konkrete Umsetzung*",[27] heilt doch der Bodhisattva sich selbst, indem er andere Wesen heilt.[28]

In einem wichtigen Kompendium der buddhistischen Dogmatik, dem *Śikṣāsamuccaya* des mahāyānistischen Philosophen Śāntideva (7. Jh. n. Chr.), wird das unendliche Mitgefühl eines Bodhisattva mit folgenden Worten beschrieben:

> Ein Bodhisattva nimmt sich vor: Ich nehme die Last alles Leidens auf mich, dazu bin ich entschlossen, und ich will es alles ertragen. Ich kehre nicht um, noch laufe ich davon, ich zittere nicht, schrecke nicht zurück, noch fürchte ich mich, wende mich nicht ab, noch verzweifle ich.
>
> Und warum? Um jeden Preis muss ich die Lasten aller Wesen tragen. Darin folge ich nicht meinen eigenen Neigungen. Ich habe doch das Gelübde getan, alle Wesen

---

24 MAITHRIMURTHI 1999 [Anm. 14], 185.

25 Entsprechend ist auch für den großen Buddhistischen Gelehrten Buddhaghosa (4./5. Jh. n. Chr.), der in seinem Kompendium des *Visuddhimagga* (NYANATILOKA ³1975 [Anm. 15], 358–360 u. ö.) die Praxis der Meditation zur Zeit der voll entwickelten Kommentarliteratur zusammenfasst, das Mitleid „eingebunden in eine komplexere Haltung, die sich als die Verbindung von liebender Zuwendung mit innerem Loslassen, mit Anhaftungslosigkeit, charakterisieren lässt. Das ist nicht Weltflucht, sondern ein Wirken in der Welt, ohne der Welt verhaftet zu sein. Hier begegnen wir dem typisch buddhistischen Verständnis des Mitleids, das eben immer mit der Weisheit innerer Loslösung von Weltverhaftung einhergeht: Es ist Zuwendung ohne Anhaftung" (SCHMIDT-LEUKEL 2013 [Anm. 18], 137). Vgl. dazu auch HOFFMANN, Cosmas: „Selig die Barmherzigen" – Barmherzigkeit und Mitgefühl als spirituelle Grundhaltungen und gemeinsame Herausforderung für Christen und Buddhisten in der Welt von heute, in: Jahrbuch der PTH SVD St. Augustin, St. Ottilien: EOS, 2014, 213–229.

26 Kursivierung durch Autor.

27 USARSKI, Frank u. a.: Menschenrechte in Buddhismus / Hinduismus / Islam / Judentum / Katholizismus / Protestantismus, in: KLÖCKER, Michael / TWORUSCHKA, Udo (Hg.): Ethik der Weltreligionen. Ein Handbuch, Darmstadt: WBG, 2005, 204.

28 Auf die dieser Idee zugrundeliegende sog. *Advaita*-Lehre wird später noch näher eingegangen.

> zu erlösen. Alle Wesen muss ich befreien. Die ganze Welt der Lebewesen muss ich erretten von den Schrecken der Geburt, des Alterns, der Krankheit, des Todes und der Wiedergeburt, von allen Arten von sittlichen Vergehen, allen Leidenszuständen, dem ganzen Kreislauf von Geburt-und-Tod [...] – von all diesen Schrecken muss ich alle Wesen befreien [...].[29]

Das vom Mitgefühl bestimmte aktive Handeln eines Bodhisattva steht auch im Mittelpunkt der *Bodhisattvabhūmi*, des 14. Kapitels der *Yogācārabhūmi*, eines enzyklopädischen Werks, das die Grundlage der *Yogācāra-Vijñānavāda*-Schule des Mahāyāna-Buddhismus legt und traditionell dem Bodhisattva Maitreya und / oder dem buddhistischen Gelehrten Asanga (4./5. Jh. n. Chr.) zugeschrieben wird. Dementsprechend führt das Mitgefühl

> [...] nicht nur zum Wunsch, dass alle Lebewesen zu Heil und Glück finden sollten, sondern auch zum entsprechenden Handeln, zur aktiven Hilfe: Die Unterstützung des *Bodhisattva* besteht darin, dass er den Lebewesen bei allen Unterfangen hilft, bei Reisen auf gefährlichen Wegen, bei allen guten Arbeiten, beim Schützen von Besitz, beim Zusammenbringen auseinandergegangener Leute und (überhaupt) im Leiden. Er pflegt die Kranken, die Blinden leitet er und zeigt ihnen den Weg, Taube informiert er durch die Hand- oder andere Zeichen, Behinderte trägt er auf seinem Kopf und befördert sie mit einem Wagen. Selbst wenn er wegen eigener Knappheit an Mitteln zunächst zögern sollte, ringt sich ein *Bodhisattva* doch rasch dazu durch, Gaben an Bettler zu spenden, selbst wenn er dadurch selbst unter Knappheit leiden muß.[30]

Die Bewegung des *Engagierten Buddhismus* und ihre Progagonist*innen

Buddhadasa Bhikkhu

Einer der wichtigsten Protagonisten der Bewegung des *Engagierten Buddhismus* ist der thailändische Mönch Buddhadasa (1906–1993). In Opposition zum Mainstream des orthodoxen thailändischen Mönchsbuddhismus mit seinem Festhalten an überlieferten monastischen Observanzen, seinem Ritualismus und seiner wenig kreativen Interpretation und Weiterentwicklung der Schriften des Pāli-Kanons versuchte er, zentrale buddhistische Begriffe und Inhalte zu aktualisieren und gründete im Jahre 1932 ein Waldkloster in Chaya (Provinz Surat Thani), das unter dem programmatischen Namen Suan Mokkhabalarama, „Gar-

---

29 Übersetzung in: Conze, Edward (Hg.): Im Zeichen Buddhas. Buddhistische Texte, Frankfurt am Main/Hamburg: Fischer, 1957 (= Fischer-Bücherei 144), 113–114. Vgl. Schmidt-Leukel 2013 [Anm. 18], 138–140.

30 Maithrimurthi 1999 [Anm. 14], 240.

ten der Befreiung", zum Zentrum einer „Erneuerung des thailändischen Buddhismus aus dem Geist der Meditation und der Anwendung buddhistischer Ethik auf die sozialen Probleme Thailands"[31] wurde. Von entscheidender Bedeutung waren für ihn dabei die Ausführungen des Buddha über die Leidhaftigkeit des individuell wie auch gesellschaftlich verfassten Daseins. Neben der meditativen Praxis als unverzichtbare Voraussetzung, das eigene Begehren zu meistern und so einen Geisteszustand innerer Freiheit und tiefen Friedens zu erlangen, ist für ihn jedoch – im Unterschied zur frühbuddhistischen Spiritualität – ebenso entscheidend ein dem Gemeinwohl verpflichtetes moralisches Handeln, um diejenigen Leiden zu mindern – wenn nicht gar zu beseitigen – die Folge gesellschaftlicher, wirtschaftlicher und politischer Missstände sind. Damit gab Buddhadasa einen „starken Impuls für die Entwicklung der sozialen Dimensionen des Buddhismus, die andere Reformer später näher ausführen sollten."[32]

Phra Kruba Srivicha und Prayudh A. Payutto

So wurden Buddhadasas Impulse im Hinblick auf einen sozial engagierten Buddhismus von den sog. „Entwicklungsmönchen" (*development monks*) wie Phra Kruba Srivichai (1878–1938) und Prayudh A. Payutto (geb. 1938) aufgegriffen, die auf der Grundlage einer von ihnen entwickelten neuen Arbeitsethik Arbeit als spirituelle Übung betrachteten und sich in verschiedenen Entwicklungsprojekten, sei es der Verbesserung der ländlichen Infrastruktur, dem Ausbau des Gesundheitswesens und des Erziehungssystems bis hin zum Kampf gegen Alkoholismus und Drogenmissbrauch engagierten.

Phra Pothirak (Santi Asoke Buddhist Reform Movement)

Auch die Anfang der 1970er Jahre ins Leben gerufene „Santi Asoke Bewegung" (*Santi Asoke Buddhist Reform Movement*) betont die soziale Verantwortung des Buddhismus. So kritisiert ihr Gründer, Phra Pothirak (Bodhirakía, geb. 1934), das mangelnde soziale Engagement der thailändischen buddhistischen Mönchsgemeinschaft und konstatiert: „A religious institution should help the society in solving its problems; otherwise, the existence of the religious institution be-

---

[31] Brück 1996 [Anm. 12], 661.

[32] Ebd.

comes meaningless, which has happened to the mainstream Buddhist institutions in Thailand."[33] Vielmehr müsse sich auch die in der „Meditationspraxis erworbene Kraft zu einer moralischen, d.h. vor allem einfachen und selbstlosen Lebensweise [...] sozial verwirklichen".[34]

Sulak Sivaraksa

Die Ideen Buddhadasa Bhikkhus wurden in besonderer Weise von dem weltbekannten Soziologen, Publizisten, sozialen Aktivisten und Träger des Alternativen Nobelpreises (1995), dem thailändischen Laien-Buddhisten Sulak Sivaraksa (geb. 1933), aufgegriffen und umgesetzt.

Für Sulak Sivaraksa steht außer Frage, dass die Lehre des Buddha nicht individualistisch verengt interpretiert werden dürfe, sondern ein stets kritisches Engagement in gesellschaftlichen, wirtschaftlichen und politischen Dingen impliziere.

Entsprechend interpretiert er auch die oben beschriebene spirituelle Übung der *Vier unbegrenzten Geisteshaltungen* sozial und sieht darin die Grundhaltungen, die die zwischenmenschlichen Beziehungen ebenso wie den politisch-ökonomischen Bereich bestimmen müssten, wobei er eine enge Parallele zwischen dem „Wohlwollen" (Pali: *mettā*, Sanskrit: *maitrī*) und dem christlichen Verständnis der Liebe zieht.

Von ebenso zentraler Bedeutung für die Verwirklichung einer gerechten Welt- und Wirtschaftsordnung sind für Sivaraksa außerdem das in allen wichtigen Normenkatalogen des Pali-Kanons genannte Gebot, nicht zu stehlen und die Spiritualität der „Gewaltlosigkeit" (*ahimsā*) und der Bewahrung des Lebens.[35]

---

33 Zitiert nach ESSEN, Juliana M.: Santi Asoke Buddhist Reform Movement. Building Individuals, Community, and (Thai) Society, in: Journal of Buddhist Ethics 11 (2004), 1–20. hier 6.

34 BRÜCK, Michael von / LAI, Whalen: Buddhismus und Christentum. Geschichte, Konfrontation, Dialog, München: Beck, 1997, 404.

35 So heißt es in einem buddhistischen Lehrtext: „Nachdem er die Tötung von Lebewesen aufgegeben hat, enthält er sich [förderhin] der Tötung von Lebewesen. Den Stock niedergelegt, das Schwert niedergelegt, zurückschreckend [vor jeglicher Art von Gewaltanwendung], voll Güte allen Lebewesen gegenüber, enthält er sich – sogar angefangen von Lebewesen wie Wurm und Ameise – der Tötung von Lebewesen" (*Samghabhedavastu*, Gilgit Manuscripts, fol. 508 *verso*). Übersetzung nach RAMERS, Peter: Die „Drei Kapitel über die Sittlichkeit" im Śrāmaṇyaphalasūtra. Die Fassungen des Dīghanikāya und Samghabhedavastu verglichen mit dem Tibetischen und Mongolischen. Einführung, Text, Übersetzung, Kommentar. Dissertation, Bonn: Rheinische Friedrich-Wilhelms-Universität, 1996, 40.

Ahangamage Tudor Ariyaratne (Sarvodaya Shramadana Movement)

Im Jahre 1958 gründete in Sri Lanka der buddhistische Laie und Lehrer Ahangamage Tudor Ariyaratne (geb. 1931) mit der *Sarvodaya Shramadana Bewegung* eine wichtige Gruppierung des *Engagierten Buddhismus*, der es zentral um die Verwirklichung von Mitleid und Mitgefühl (*karuṇā*) auf gesellschaftlicher Ebene und um „Wohlstand / Wohlfahrt für alle" (*sarvodaya*) geht. Auch für Ariyaratne stellen die *Vier unbegrenzten Geisteshaltungen* weniger einen auf den geistlichen Fortschritt des Einzelnen zielenden Übungsweg dar, sondern dienen als Richtschnur für soziales Engagement („compassionate action").[36]

Thich Nhat Hanh

Eine prägende Gestalt des aus der konkreten Meditationserfahrung erwachsenden sozial und politisch engagierten Buddhismus ist neben den bereits genannten Protagonisten vor allem der vietnamesische buddhistische Mönch, Schriftsteller, Lyriker und Zenmeister Thich Nhat Hanh (1926–2022), der den Begriff *Engagierter Buddhismus* prägte[37] und im Jahre 1966 den inzwischen auch in Europa und Amerika verbreiteten „Tiep-Hien-Orden" gründete, eine aus Laien, Mönchen und Nonnen bestehende Gemeinschaft mit dem Ziel, „den Buddhismus zu studieren, zu experimentieren und in intelligenter und wirksamer Weise auf das moderne individuelle wie soziale Leben anzuwenden [...].[38] Dabei räumte Thich Nhat Hanh vor allem dem Dialog mit dem Christentum einen besonderen Stellenwert ein.

Den Ordensnamen, der aus den vietnamesischen Wörtern „tiep" („in Kontakt sein mit") und „hien" („realisieren / verwirklichen") zusammengesetzt ist, hat Thich Nhat Hanh – orientiert an der Mahāyāna-Philosophie des *Avatamsakasūtras*[39] – mit dem englischen Neologismus „Interbeing" wiedergegeben, was im Deutschen etwa mit „Intersein", „Zwischensein" oder auch „Durchdrungensein" wiedergegeben werden kann. Gemeint ist damit die Allverwobenheit sämtlicher Phänomene, das stete Eingebundensein aller Dinge in ein unendlich komplexes Beziehungsgeflecht. Von besonderer Bedeutung sind in diesem Zusammenhang auch philosophische Lehren, die im *Prajñāpāramitāhṛdayasūtra*

---

36 Vgl. ARIYARATNE, Ahangamage T[udor]: Collected Works, Vol. 2, Ratmalana: Sarvodaya Vishva Lekha Publ., ²1999, 49.

37 In seinem Buch: Vietnam. Lotus in a Sea of Fire, New York: Hill and Wang, 1967.

38 THICH, Nhat Hanh, zitiert nach BRÜCK 1996 [Anm. 12], 673.

39 Auszüge in deutscher Übersetzung mit Kommentaren finden sich EBD., 101–198.

(kurz: „Herz-Sūtra")[40] und im zenbuddhistischen Denken eine zentrale Rolle spielen:

- „die Lehre von der Nicht-Dualität, nach der man selbst und jedes andere Wesen nicht-zwei (*advaita*) ist, weshalb Sorge um sich selbst und Fürsorge für andere als zwei Seiten einer Sache erscheinen, und
- die Lehre von der Nicht-Form (*arūpa*), nach der alle Dinge keine Substanz haben, sondern in gegenseitiger Abhängigkeit entstehen und vergehen, weshalb soziale Hierarchien, das Handeln nach dem Modell miteinander rivalisierender Gruppen usw. unrealistisch sind."[41]

Um die Fähigkeit zu solch einer nicht-dualistischen Betrachtungsweise der Wirklichkeit zu kultivieren und sich von den Unfrieden erzeugenden Geisteshaltungen wie Gier und Hass zu befreien, fordert er eine auf dem Weg meditativer Übungen anzustrebende stete Wachheit und Achtsamkeit „in Bezug auf alles, was sich im Körper, in den Gefühlen, im Bewußtsein und in der Welt ereignet"[42] und die Praktizierung eines, die ganze Wirklichkeit umfassenden Mitgefühls.[43] Für Thich Nhat Hanh besteht kein Zweifel daran, dass derjenige, der „wach ist, [...] gar nicht anders [kann], als barmherzig zu handeln, damit das Leiden vermindert wird, das man um sich herum genau wahrnimmt", weshalb der Ausdruck *Engagierter Buddhismus* eigentlich eine Tautologie sei.[44] Wenn er nicht engagiert ist, ist er kein Buddhismus.

*Das internationale Netzwerk engagierter Buddhist*innen*

Angestoßen durch Sulak Sivaraksa, führte eine gemeinsame Initiative von ihm, dem XIV. Dalai Lama, Thich Nhat Hanh und Buddhadasa Bhikkhu zur Gründung des *International Network of Engaged Buddhists* (INEB), weil man der Überzeugung war,

> dass Meditation allein nicht ausreicht, um Leiden zu lindern; man muss auch handeln. [...] Wenn Gesellschaften ungerecht, ausbeuterisch und gewalttätig sind, dann sollte man wie ein *bodhisattva* handeln: bescheiden, ernsthaft, ungebunden, mit Bewusstsein, Kraft, Geduld und Schwur, Dinge zu ändern.[45]

---

40 Deutsche Übersetzung Ebd., 234–241.

41 Brück 1996 [Anm. 12], 672.

42 Ebd., 674.

43 Die Kultivierung der Haltung des Mitgefühls steht auch im Mittelpunkt der sog. 14 Achtsamkeitsübungen des Intersein-Ordens. Siehe dazu Thich, Nhat Hanh: 'Interbeing': Fourteen Guidelines for Engaged Buddhism, Berkeley, CA: Parallax Press, ^{3}1999.

44 Brück 1996 [Anm. 12], 674.

45 Van den Bosch, Lourens P.: Stimmen eines kritischen Buddhismus im modernen Thailand, in: Hutter, Manfred (Hg.): Religionsinterne Kritik und religiöser Pluralismus im gegenwärtigen Südostasien Frankfurt am Main u. a.: Peter Lang, 2008 (= Religionswissenschaft, Bd. 15), 22.

Im Frühjahr des Jahres 1989 fand in einem thailändischen Kloster die Gründungsversammlung statt, an der Mönche, Nonnen und Laien aus elf Ländern teilnahmen.[46]

Über folgende zentrale Prinzipien als hermeneutische Schlüssel eines engagiert-bud-dhisti-schen Denkens und Handelns herrscht unter sämtlichen Vertreter*innen der Bewegung – seien sie wissenschaftlich-publizistisch oder sozial aktiv – Übereinstimmung:[47]

- das Prinzip universeller Verantwortung angesichts jeglichen Leidens auf der Grundlage universellen „Mitleids / Mitgefühls" (*karuṇā*);
- das Prinzip der Wachheit und Achtsamkeit für die persönlichen Denkmuster, Gefühle und Bewusstseinszustände (Gier, Hass, Verblendung usw.), um so immer »selbst«-loser zu werden und den Blick zu schärfen für das, was Not tut, um Leiden zu mindern;
- das Prinzip der Non-Dualität, das die Verbundenheit aller Wesen und Dinge impliziert und ihren konkreten Ausdruck findet in der mahāyānistischen Idee des Bodhisattva, der im Hinblick auf alle Lebewesen die Idee entwickeln soll: „(Dies ist meine) Mutter, (mein) Vater, (mein) Sohn, (meine) Tochter, ja (dies bin) ich selbst. Wie ich selbst von allen Leiden gänzlich frei sein möchte, so möchten alle Wesen [...] frei sein;"[48]
- das Prinzip der Gewaltfreiheit allen politischen und gesellschaftlichen Handelns.

Die Haltung des unbegrenzten Mitgefühls erstreckt sich dabei nicht nur auf andere Menschen, sondern alles Lebendige, was eine stark ökologische Orientierung impliziert.

Die Bewegung des *Engagierten Buddhismus* kann somit gleichsam als weitere Drehung des Rades der Lehre verstanden werden, die eine Aktualisierung der

---

46 Inzwischen gehören zu diesem Netzwerk Einzelpersonen und Vertreter*innen angeschlossener Gemeinschaften aus über 30 Ländern. Dazu zählen beispielsweise auch Organisationen wie die *Buddhist Compassion Relief Tzu Chi Foundation* in Taiwan und der *Zen Peacemaker Order*. Das Netzwerks engagierter Buddhist*innen für den deutschsprachigen Raum wurde bei der 5. Jahreskonferenz des INEB im Februar 1993 in Thailand gegründet wurde. Zur Spiritualität und den Schwerpunkten der Arbeit vgl. www.buddha-netz.org (zuletzt aufgerufen am 28.06.2022). Ein wichtiger Teil des Netzwerkes vor allem für den nordamerikanischen und australischen Bereich ist die im Jahre 1978 durch den amerikanischen Zen-Meister Robert Aitken Roshi (Zen als Lebenspraxis, Kreuzlingen/München: Hugendubel 2003), seine Frau Anne, Nelson Foster und andere gegründete *Buddhist Peace Fellowship* (BPF) mit ihrem, vor allem durch Thich Nhat Hanh inspirierten Engagement in der Friedensarbeit und für den Schutz und die Bewahrung ökologischer Lebensverhältnisse.

47 Zum Folgenden vgl. NEUMANN 2005 [Anm. 10], 42.

48 Aṣṭasāhasrikā Prajñāpāramitā, ed. P.L. Vaidya (Darbhamga 1960) I, 14. Zitiert nach: SCHUMANN, Hans Wolfgang: Mahāyāna-Buddhismus. Die zweite Drehung des Dharma-Rades, München: Diederichs, 1990, 38–39.

Lehren des Buddha in Theorie und Praxis angesichts gegenwärtiger Herausforderungen in einem bewussten Handeln für das Wohl aller Wesen zu praktizieren versucht. Die *Compassion*, die „Empfindlichkeit für das Leid der anderen“, von der Metz spricht, ist also nicht *die* Mitgift, die *allein* das Christentum in die entstehende Weltgemeinschaft einbringen kann.[49]

Literatur

ARIYARATNE, Ahangamage Tudor: Collected Works, Vol. 2, Ratmalana: Sarvodaya Vishva Lekha Publ., ²1999.

BHIKKHU ANĀLAYO: Compassion in the *Āgamas* and *Nikāyas*, in: Dharma Drum Journal of Buddhist Studies 16 (2015), 1–31.

BRODBECK, Karl-Heinz: Erkenntnis und Mitgefühl. Argumente für einen sozial engagierten Buddhismus, in: STOSCH, Klaus von (Hg.): Wirtschaftsethik interreligiös, Paderborn: Ferdinand Schöningh, 2014, 111–128 (Beiträge zur Komparativen Theologie, Bd. 12).

BRÜCK, Michael von: Die Bewegung „Engagierter Buddhismus“, in: RIßE, Günter / SONNEMANS, Heino / THESS, Burkhard (Hg.): Wege der Theologie. An der Schwelle zum dritten Jahrtausend. Festschrift für Hans Waldenfels zur Vollendung des 65. Lebensjahres, Paderborn: Bonifatius, 1996, 662–667.

BRÜCK, Michael von / LAI, Whalen: Buddhismus und Christentum. Geschichte, Konfrontation, Dialog, München: Beck, 1997.

BRÜCK, Michael von: Weisheit der Leere. Sūtra-Texte des indischen Mahāyāna-Buddhismus, Zürich: Benziger, 1989.

CONZE, Edward (Hg.): Im Zeichen Buddhas. Buddhistische Texte, Frankfurt am Main/Hamburg: Fischer, 1957 (= Fischer-Bücherei 144).

EPPSTEINER, Fred (ed.): The Path of Compassion: Writings on Socially Engaged Buddhism in the West, Berkeley: Parallax Press, ²1988.

ESSEN, Juliana M.: Santi Asoke Buddhist Reform Movement. Building Individuals, Community, and (Thai) Society, in: Journal of Buddhist Ethics 11 (2004), 1–20.

EVERS, Georg: Land der Mönche. Der Buddhismus Thailands im gesellschaftlichen Wandel, in: Herder Korrespondenz 56.5 (2002), 242–246.

HAMILTON, Clarence H.: The Idea of Compassion in Mahayana Buddhism, in: Journal of the American Oriental Society 70.3 (1953), 145–151.

HEIKKILÄ-HORN, Marja L.: Two Paths to Revivalism in Thai Buddhism. The Dhammakaya and Santi Asoke Movements, in: Temenos 32 (1996), 93–111.

HOFFMANN, Cosmas: „Selig die Barmherzigen“ – Barmherzigkeit und Mitgefühl als spirituelle Grundhaltungen und gemeinsame Herausforderung für Christen und Buddhisten in der Welt von heute, in: Jahrbuch der PTH SVD St. Augustin, St. Ottilien: EOS, 2014, 213–229.

JENKINS, Stephen Lynn: The Circle of Compassion. An Interpretive Study of Karuna in Indian Buddhist Literature. Dissertation, Cambridge (Massachusetts): Harvard University, 1999, in: https://philpapers.org/rec/JENTCO-9 (zuletzt aufgerufen am 22.02.2023).

KOTLER, Arnold (Hg.): Mitgefühl leben. Engagierter Buddhismus heute, Frankfurt am Main: Fischer, 1999.

[49] Siehe Anmerkung 4 und 5.

KULD, Lothar: Art. Compassion, 1–7, in: Wissenschaftliches Religionspädagogisches Lexikon im Internet. Onine https://www.bibelwissenschaft.de/fileadmin/buh_bibelmodul/media/wirelex/pdf/Compassion__2020-04-29_14_56.pdf (zuletzt aufgerufen am 22.02. 2023).

KULD, Lothar: Compassion I. Theologie der Compassion. Biblische Grundlagen und theologische Reflexion sozialen Handelns", 1–12, in: https://www.schulstiftung-freiburg.de/eip/media/forum/pdf_182.pdf (zuletzt aufgerufen am 22.02.2023).

LUKOSCHEK, Barbara: Ethik der Befreiung. Engagierter Buddhismus und Befreiungstheologie im Dialog, Paderborn u. a.: Ferdinand Schöningh, 2013 (= Beiträge zur Komparativen Theologie, Bd. 16).

MAITHRIMURTHI, Mudagamuwe: Die Meditation des Wohlwollens als Versenkungspraktik, in: www.buddhismuskunde.uni-hamburg.de/pdf/4-publikationen/buddhismus-in-geschichte-und-gegenwart/bd8-k06maithrimurthi.pdf (zuletzt aufgerufen am 22.02.2023).

MAITHRIMURTHI, Mudagamuwe: Wohlwollen, Mitleid, Freude und Gleichmut. Eine ideengeschichtliche Untersuchung der vier apramāṇas in der buddhistischen Ethik und Spiritualität von den Anfängen bis hin zum frühen Yogācāra, Stuttgart: Franz Steiner, 1999 (= Alt- und Neu-indische Studien, 50).

METZ, Johann Baptist / KULD, Lothar / WEISBROD, Adolf (Hg.): Compassion. Weltprogramm des Christentums. Soziale Verantwortung lernen, Freiburg im Breisgau/Basel/Wien: Herder, 2000.

METZ, Johann Baptist: Compassion – Weltprogramm des Christentums (in Forum 27), in: https://www.schulstiftung-freiburg.de/eip/media/forum/pdf_156.pdf (zuletzt aufgerufen am 22.02.2023).

METZ, Johann Baptist: Die Autorität der Leidenden. Compassion – Vorschlag zu einem Weltprogramm des Christentums, in: Süddeutsche Zeitung 24./25./26. Dezember 1997, Nr. 296, 57.

METZ, Johann Baptist: Im Eingedenken fremden Leids. Zu einer Brückenkategorie zwischen Theologie und Ethik, zwischen Religion und Moral, in: KatBl 122.1 (1997), 78–87.

METZ, Johann Baptist: Memoria Passionis. Ein provozierendes Gedächtnis in pluralistischer Gesellschaft, Freiburg im Breisgau/Basel/Wien: Herder, 2017 (= Gesammelte Schriften / Johann Baptist Metz, Bd. 4).

NEUMANN, Mareke: Engagierter Buddhismus. Eine interkulturelle Orientierung, Nordhausen: Bautz, 2005 (Bausteine zur Mensching-Forschung. N.F., Bd. 11).

NYANATILOKA (Übers.): Visuddhi-Magga oder der Weg zur Reinheit, Konstanz: Christiani, [3]1975.

OHASHI, Rysuke: Phänomenologie der Compassion. Pathos des Mitseins mit den Anderen, Freiburg im Breisgau/München: Karl Alber, 2018.

RAMERS Peter: Die „Drei Kapitel über die Sittlichkeit" im Śrāmaṇyaphalasūtra. Die Fassungen des Dīghanikāya und Samghabhedavastu verglichen mit dem Tibetischen und Mongolischen. Einführung, Text, Übersetzung, Kommentar. Dissertation, Bonn: Rheinische Friedrich-Wilhelms-Universität, 1996.

RAMERS, Peter: Buddhismus zwischen klösterlicher Abgeschiedenheit und sozialpolitischem Engagement. Eine Weltreligion angesichts der Herausforderungen der Moderne, in: Religionen unterwegs 26.1 (2020), 4–9.

RAMERS, Peter: Buddhistische Übungen zur Erlangung der Indifferenz und das Mitleid mit allen Lebewesen. Ein Beitrag zur Spiritualität und Ethik des frühen Buddhismus, in: BSTEH, Petrus / PROKSCH, Brigitte (Hg.): Spiritualität im Gespräch der Religionen I, Wien/Berlin: LIT, 2009 (= Spiritualität im Dialog, Bd. 1), 216–231.

RAMERS, Peter: Die Bewegung des »engagierten Buddhismus«. Spiritualität und Praxis, in: BSTEH, Petrus / PROKSCH, Brigitte (Hg.): Spiritualität im Gespräch der Religionen II, Wien/Berlin: LIT, 2010 (= Spiritualität im Dialog, Bd. 2), 238–254.

RAMERS, Peter: Immanente Welten oder soziopolitisches Engagement? Zur politischen Rolle des Buddhismus in Sri Lanka, Myanmar und Thailand, in: Religionen unterwegs 16.3 (2010), 16–22.

SCHMIDT-LEUKEL, Perry: Buddhistische und christliche Ethik, in: https://www.buddhismuskunde.uni-hamburg.de/pdf/4-publikationen/buddhismus-in-geschichte-und-gegenwart/bd7-k04schmidtleukel.pdf (zuletzt aufgerufen am 22.02.2023).

SCHMIDT-LEUKEL, Perry: Compassion im Buddhismus, in: Wege zum Menschen 65.2 (2013), 127–144.

SCHMITHAUSEN, Lambert: Mitleid und Leerheit. Zu Spiritualität und Heilsziel des Mahāyāna, in: BSTEH, Andreas (Hg.): Der Buddhismus als Anfrage an christliche Theologie und Philosophie, Mödling: St. Gabriel, 2000, 437–455.

SCHUMANN, Hans Wolfgang: Mahāyāna-Buddhismus. Die zweite Drehung des Dharma-Rades, München: Diederichs, 1990.

SIVARAKSA, Sulak: Loyalty Demands Dissent. Autobiography of an Engaged Buddhist, Berkeley, CA: Parallax Press, 1998.

SIVARAKSA, Sulak: Seeds of Peace. A Buddhist Vision for Renewing Society, Berkeley, Calif.: Parallax Press, 1992.

SUNGTAEK Cho: Selbstlosigkeit. Zu einer buddhistischen Vision von sozialer Gerechtigkeit, in: Polylog. Zeitschrift für interkulturelles Philosophieren 6 (2000), 30–37.

SWEARER, Donald K.: Drei Vermächtnisse von Buddhadasa Bhikkhu, in: Evangelisches Missionswerk in Deutschland (Hg.): Wege zu einer gerechten Gesellschaft. Beiträge engagierter Buddhisten zu einer internationalen Debatte, Hamburg: EMW, 1996, 134–154 (= Weltmission heute, Nr 23).

THICH, Nhat Hanh: 'Interbeing': Fourteen Guidelines for Engaged Buddhism, Berkeley, CA: Parallax Press, [3]1999.

THICH, Nhat Hanh: Das Wunder der Achtsamkeit. Einführung in die Meditation, Bielefeld: Theseus, 2010

THICH, Nhat Hanh: Interbeing. Commentaries on the Tiep Hien Precepts, Berkeley, CA: Parallax Press, 1987.

THICH, Nhat Hanh: Liebe handelt. Wege zu einem gewaltlosen gesellschaftlichen Wandel, Heidelberg: Kristkeitz, 1997.

THICH, Nhat Hanh: Vietnam. Lotus in a Sea of Fire, New York: Hill and Wang, 1967.

USARSKI, Frank u. a.: Menschenrechte in Buddhismus / Hinduismus / Islam / Judentum / Katholizismus / Protestantismus, in: KLÖCKER, Michael / TWORUSCHKA, Udo (Hg.): Ethik der Weltreligionen. Ein Handbuch, Darmstadt: WBG, 2005, 204–216.

VAN DEN BOSCH, Lourens P.: Stimmen eines kritischen Buddhismus im modernen Thailand, in: HUTTER, Manfred (Hg.): Religionsinterne Kritik und religiöser Pluralismus im gegenwärtigen Südostasien Frankfurt am Main u. a.: Peter Lang, 2008 (= Religionswissenschaft, Bd. 15), 9–35.

VETTER, Tilmann: The Ideas and Meditative Practices of Early Buddhism, Leiden u. a.: Brill, 1988.

VETTER, Tilmann: Die Lehre des Buddha. Mittlerer Weg – Achtfacher Pfad – Vier edle Wahrheiten", in: BSTEH, Andreas (Hg.): Der Buddhismus als Anfrage an christliche Theologie und Philosophie, Mödling: St. Gabriel, 2000 (= Studien zur Religionstheologie, Bd. 5), 59–66.

WAGNER Thomas: Profile engagierter Mystik Eine erziehungswissenschaftliche Untersuchung zu politisch-mystischen Identitätskonzepten im interreligiösen Vergleich. Dissertation, Frankfurt a. M.: Johann Wolfgang Goethe-Universität zu Frankfurt am Main 2005, in: https://publikationen.ub.uni-frankfurt.de/frontdoor/deliver/index/docId/2949/file/WagnerThomas.pdf (zuletzt aufgerufen am 22.02.2023).

ZÖLLNER, Hans-Bernd: Buddhadasa Bhikkhu (1906–1993). Buddhismus im Garten der Befreiung Frankfurt am Main u. a.: Peter Lang, 2006 (Religionswissenschaft, Bd. 12).

Compassion and Moderatism in Contemporary Indonesian Islamic Education

Asfa Widiyanto

In diesem Beitrag werden die Herausforderungen und Strategien der islamischen Bildung im Kontext der heutigen Zeit untersucht, wobei der Schwerpunkt auf den Erfahrungen Indonesiens liegt. Der Beitrag konzentriert sich auf zwei miteinander verknüpfte Fragen. Erstens: Welche Herausforderungen stellt der Radikalismus für die heutige islamische Bildung in Indonesien dar? Zweitens: Welche Strategien müssen entwickelt werden, um religiösen Mäßigung und Mitgefühl in der indonesischen islamischen Bildung zu fördern?

religiöse Mäßigung, Mitgefühl, indonesisch-islamische Bildung, Radikalismus

This paper investigates the challenges and strategies of Islamic education in the context of the contemporary age by exemplifying Indonesia's experiences. This paper focuses on two interrelated concerns. First, which challenges arise with the issue of radicalism in contemporary Indonesian Islamic education? Second, which strategies must be adopted to promote religious moderatism and compassion in Indonesian Islamic education?

religious moderatism, compassion, Indonesian Islamic education, radicalism

Introduction

Islamic education may impact the future of religious moderation and vice versa due to the possibility of a reciprocal process between the two. Islamic Religious Education (IRE) in Indonesia can support religious moderation in the country. For instance, some scholars claimed that IRE in Indonesia significantly impacts the future of religious moderation. Students will typically be radical if, for example, IRE teachers in Indonesia have extremely limited conceptual understandings. The impact of this narrow understanding is that they are the most righteous and pious. Others are not true, so they may be suppressed, and so on.

Islam was given to the earth to bring safety and mercy to everyone. The hadith refers to this: *wama arsalnaka illa rahmatan lil ͨ alamin* (the Prophet Muhammad was not sent except to give mercy to the whole world). The word *ͨalam* in Arabic has a different meaning from the word *kawn*. *Kawn* is the universe, a natural landscape, for example, mountains, rivers, etc. The word *ͨalam* in Arabic may include all biological creatures such as humans, plants, and animals. The term

ʿalam can also have non-biological creatures such as rivers, skies, etc. So, in Arabic, the meaning of each word is different, so in the Qur'an, it is called *ʿalamin*.

Islamic education must be understood broadly and globally, not just in the learning management framework but also in social politics, history, philosophy, and other factors. Educators can create modest learning models that are anticipated to benefit the people and nation, especially humanity, with the help of this vast understanding.

Even in a secular state, religious education is significant. This can be seen, for instance, in the context of Austria, which, despite being a secular state, also recognizes Islamic law. The justification for this can be found in Ernst-Wolfgang Böckenförde's view, a former constitutional judge in Germany. According to him, even a free and secular state could not exist freely; it depended on factors the state could not control.[1]

Laws and state officers alone cannot guarantee the sustainability of a secular state. Morality is still needed by the state. Additionally, it requires religion as the protector of that morality and a crucial tenet of social order. No matter how complicated the regulations are, if no moral, social, or religious principles require us to respect the government, they will not function properly. Religion offers guidelines for family and social interactions. Religion is crucial in this area because the state cannot intervene when people are, for instance, at home, with their families, or elsewhere.

Islamic education in Indonesia is interesting when compared to Israel and Malaysia. Tayeb explained that topics on *nushuz* (disobedience), polygamy, and others are still being taught to junior and senior high school students in Malaysia.[2] These topics are found in classical books of Islamic law but are not appropriate to be disseminated transparently to junior and senior high school students. This is considering that some Islamic teachings that are revealed without comprehending the context, can mislead listeners and lead to incorrect behaviors.

For example, if people do not understand a verse in the proper context, for instance, the verse "kill the non-believers wherever you find them" (al-Baqarah 191): there were students who visited the Borobudur Temple in Central Java, where many non-Muslim tourists were then killed. If this happens, IRE teachers will also be responsible because they cannot understand the Qur'an verse in the proper context. The verse was revealed in the context of warfare, not in a peaceful situation, if one consults the literature regarding the historical context of the revelation of the verse (*asbab al-nuzul*). Teachers of IRE should be aware of this.

1 Böckenförde, Ernst-Wolfgang: Constitutional and political theory. selected writings, Ocford: Oxford University Press, 2017, 5–8.

2 Tayeb, Azmil Mohd: Islamic education in Indonesia and Malaysia. shaping minds, saving souls, Abingdon/New York: Routledge, 2018, 10–14.

Religious education in Indonesia and Israel has been studied by Künkler and Lerner. One of the main findings is that Indonesian religious education is more progressive than Israeli religious education. The main emphasis of religious education in Israel is on preparing future rabbis (Jewish religious leaders). According to this research, they frequently reject differences and disrespect those practicing other religions.[3]

Religious education in Indonesia has the benefit of teaching a deep understanding of religion while also emphasizing respect for others. People typically neglect other religious teachings if they intently seek one particular religious doctrine. It turns out that Indonesia is different from Israel in terms of religious instruction. According to the study, Israel's religious education includes moderate and unmoderated religious instruction.

Künkler and Lerner emphasized that, while religious education in Indonesia does have strengths, there are still shortcomings. The focus on nation-building and multiculturalism, which enables pupils to coexist with other people's religions, is an interesting aspect of Islamic education in Indonesia. Due to its emphasis on helping students understand religion broadly rather than narrowly, religious education in Indonesia can help nurture Islamic religiosity and nationalism simultaneously.[4]

In a smaller context, Salatiga City in Central Java has been named the most tolerant city in Indonesia for 2022. Salatiga is unique because the followers of Islam can coexist with the followers of Christianity. Islamic traditionalism allows the Muslim community in Salatiga to appreciate other cultures and religions, especially Christianity.

Religious Moderatism: Features and Dynamics

In the Western tradition, moderatism has a broad meaning, and there are occasionally paradoxes. Paradoxes are contradictions. As an illustration, the question "Are you moderate?" was posed to an Australian Muslim leader who met an Australian Christian. The Muslim said, "Yes, I am moderate." The Australian Christian continued asking, "Why are you still praying?"[5] In this instance, it seems that different Western societies have different viewpoints on moderation. Some think the term "moderatism" refers to religious perspectives less faithful to ceremonial obligations.

---

3 KÜNKLER, Miriam / LERNER, Hannah: A private matter? Religious education and democracy in Indonesia and Israel, in: *British Journal of Religious Education* 38, no. 3 (2016), 279–307.

4 Ibid., 279–307.

5 Personal conversation with Nadirsyah HOSEN.

Varying perspectives on moderatism and liberalism can also be observed in the context of Indonesia. This can be seen, for example, in the incident of the Muslim community member who asked, "How come I saw Professor 'A' still praying even though he is a liberal?" Due to his progressive and moderate viewpoints, Professor "A" is regarded as a liberal. He frequently employs a contextual approach when reading verses from the Qur'an and hadith. From the viewpoint of this ordinary Muslim, liberal Muslims do not perform prayer because they do not adhere to the stringent teachings of Islam.

Islamic moderatism refers to adherence to Islamic teachings, and understanding them broadly, so that they can appreciate different religious thoughts and cultures. Islamic moderatism (*wasatiyya*) accordingly signifies the middle path. Al-Imam al-Shafi'i (767–820) is known for saying, "Our opinion is correct, but it contains errors, while the opinion of others is wrong, it contains the truth." Al-Shafi'I's statement underlines a kind of moderatism, in the sense of not absolute our thoughts but does not inflame other people's thoughts. The Egyptian Muslim thinker Nasr Hamid Abu Zayd (1943–2010), in his book, *al Imam al-Shafi'i* wa *ta'sis al-aidulujiyya al-wasatiyya*, said that one of the pioneers of Islamic moderatism is al-Imam al-Shafi'i. This legacy was then continued by Yusuf al-Qaradawi (1926–2022) and other thinkers in the 21st century. This is the perspective of the history of ideas.[6]

In teaching the history of Islamic culture in high schools and universities in Indonesia, some educators present historical events chronologically without appreciating the history of ideas. For example, the explanation of the term *al-amr bi al-maruf wa al-nahy ʿan al-munkar* (Commanding Right and Forbidding Wrong) appears differently in each dynasty. During the Abbasid dynasty, for instance, Commanding Rights and Forbidding Wrong manifested as *wilayat al-hisba* (an institution that has the responsibility to oversee the implementation of Islamic law).[7] What is more fundamental than memorizing chronological events, is to enlighten students regarding the most important scientific and cultural contributions from a dynasty. For example, during the Seljuq dynasty, many sects of Islam were very harmonious. At that time, the Sunnites and Shi'ites shared power. This kind of socio-cultural context allows for the emergence of interpretations of the Qur'an among Shiites, who tend to be sympathetic towards Sunnis.

Islamic moderatism can be observed in three domains, namely, theology (*ʿaqida*), ethics (*akhlaq*), and spirituality (*tasawwuf*). In the realm of theology, Islamic theology is the middle ground between atheism and polytheism. Islam and Judaism fall within the category of strict monotheism. Christianity also claims to be a monotheistic religion.

---

6 ZAYD, Abu: al-Imam al-Shafi'i wa ta'sis al-aidulujiyya al-wasatiyya, Kairo: Sina, 1992, 20–21.

7 COOK, Michael: Commanding right and forbidding wrong in Islamic thought. Cambridge: University Press, 2001, 22–25.

Buddhism actually does not recognize the notion of God but only acknowledges the concept of nirvana (emptiness). Hence, in the Indonesian context, Buddhists try to conform to the first principle of Pancasila (which is the basis of the state), which reads 'Belief in One Supreme God.' To respond to the first precept of the Pancasila, they brought up the concept of *Sang Adhi Buddha*, who is considered God. Hindus know many Gods. The pinnacle of divinity in Hinduism is the Tri Murti, which includes three gods: Vishnu, Shiva, and Brahma. Hindu adherents in Bali are also trying to conform to the first precept of Pancasila by bringing up the concept of *Sang Hyang Widhi Wasa* (The One God), which is unknown to Hindus in India.[8]

In the Indonesian context, teaching IRE in public schools (elementary school, junior high school, and senior high school) is more challenging than teaching IRE in Islamic Schools. This is because students in public schools come from various religions, even though the teaching of IRE is specifically for Muslim students. With this plural religious background, Muslim students still associate with students of other religions at school. If IRE teachers in public schools teach Islamic material narrowly without being given an understanding of religious differences, it will cause problems in the school environment specifically, as well as in society in general.

In terms of spirituality (*tasawwuf*), Islamic moderatism seeks to maintain a balance between *khawf* (fear of God) and *raja'* (hope for God's pleasure). From the theological point of view, Islamic moderatism seeks to be in the middle point between determinism (*jabbariyya*) and free will, free act (*qadariyya*). *Jabariyya* emphasized that God arranged everything. This differs from *qadariyya*, which emphasizes that humans have freedom of will and action. The middle way between these two tendencies is taken by the Ash'ariyya and Maturidiyya schools, emphasizing that humans make efforts, but the final results are in the hands of God. So, *tawakkul* (reliance on God) must begin with the endeavor.

For example, somebody who understands fate in a deterministic way, when dealing with the Covid-19 pandemic, will insist that, if they are not destined to be infected by Covid-19, then they will not be infected, even though they do not wear a mask and do not comply with social distancing. Whereas in classical Islamic books, it is stated that God's destiny is unknown until it happens. In that context, educators must understand the text of Islamic law and the higher goals of Islamic law (*maqasid al-shariʿa*). This *maqasid* seeks to see the most profound spirit and highest goal of Islamic law, especially by paying attention to *daruriyyat al-khams* (five basic necessities); namely defending religion, reason, offspring, property, and the soul.[9] Wearing a mask and observing social distancing during

---

8 FRANKE, Edith / PYE, Michael: Religionen nebeneinander: Modelle religiöser Vielfalt in Ost-und Südostasien. Münster: LIT Verlag, 2006, 15–16.

9 AUDA, Jasser: Maqasid al-shariah: an Introductory guide, Herndon: International Institute of Islamic Thought, 2008, 5–8. See also: ASHUR, Ibn Ashur: treatise on maqasid al-shariah, Herndon: International Institute of Islamic Thought, 2006, 2–3.

the Covid-19 pandemic is primarily to protect the soul, which is one of the highest goals of Islamic law.

Understanding the greater purposes of Islamic law is crucial, particularly for Islamic education teachers. There are stories that the companions of the Prophet namely ʿUmar ibn Khattab (584–644) did not punish someone for stealing because he believed that the person was acting out of hunger. In this vein, Umar ibn Khattab understood Islamic law contextually and dynamically rather than textually and strictly as he strived to reflect the true spirit and essence of Islamic law.

Islamic moderation also affects ethics, namely, in the domain of tolerance (*tasamuh*), which is defined as respecting and being open to something different without having to embrace it. It does not need to be believed, but it does need to be recognized. IRE Teachers must educate their students on the importance of tolerance. Other religions are not required to be believed in. However, it is enough to recognize that followers of other religions are also human beings with the same right to co-exist in the world. Mutual consultation (*shura*), which em phasizes the importance of speaking with and listening to many people to find the best ideas and answers, is another facet of Islamic moderation in the domain of ethics.

Different interpretations are implied by the concept of *wasatiyya* (moderatism) in Islamic scholarship tradition. First, it denotes justice. Therefore, a moderate community is also a just community. By maintaining a balanced attitude, our community aims to uphold fairness. This is in contrast to the tendency of certain people to defend whatever is aligned with their beliefs and pre-existing knowledge. This propensity reveals a person's unfairness. Fairness, then, seeks to strike a balance while not defending anyone other than what is true and supported by solid evidence.

Moderatism is particularly crucial in the post-truth era to uphold fairness. People today often confirm the truthfulness of information if it supports their personal opinions or beliefs. Contrarily, information that conflicts with a person's beliefs and preferences will be considered false. Fairness and impartiality are required in this situation so that people can respond to whether the information is truthful without losing their composure. IRE teachers should serve as examples of how to maintain an epistemic balance in responding to the abundance of information on the internet.

Another meaning of *wasatiyya* (moderatism) in classical Islamic scholarship is creating balance (*tawazun*).[10] *Tawazun* seeks to create harmony between words and deeds. Moderation, in this vein, is the antithesis of radicalism and extremism. Another implication of *tawazun* is maintaining consistency (*istiqama*),

10 Kamali, Mohammad Hasin: The middle path of moderation in Islam: The Qur'anic principle of wasatiyyah, Oxford: Oxford University Press, 2015, 6–9.

namely finding a middle ground between being too fast and too slow while emphasizing discipline and persistence in doing something.

Radicalism and its Challenges to Islamic Education

The other end of moderatism or *wasatiyya* is fundamentalism and radicalism. Fundamentalism and radicalism are not only found in Muslim societies but also in other societies. Even the root of the word fundamentalism comes from the Christian tradition in the USA. Around the 17th century, fundamentalism was widely used to refer to militant piety. In this vein, fundamentalism is considered an antithesis to the European Renaissance (which made European society more secularized).[11] In the 20th century, however, we observe an interesting development, namely that fundamentalism was also addressed to Muslims.

After the Renaissance, some Europeans (namely fundamentalist groups) expressed their disapproval of secularization in Europe by stating that European culture must return to the fundamental roots of society, namely, religion. According to fundamentalists, religion must re-enter politics and even into all domains of social life. Fundamentalists argue that religion and state, or in other words, church and state, must come together again. This is a primary characteristic of the Christian fundamentalist movement that emerged in the 17th century.[12] This fundamentalist movement divides the world into two groups that support God and one that is against God. The dichotomy between the 'God Group' and the 'Anti-God Group' can be found in the Christian fundamentalist movement. This movement then seeks to reject secularism, pluralism, and tolerance. The Christian fundamentalist movement in Europe later poses a threat to world peace and freedom of speech.[13]

Since the 20th century, this fundamentalism has also been addressed by Muslims.[14] The Islamic fundamentalism movement here refers to some Islamic groups that seek to deculturate Islamic teachings. So, Islam is considered to have been completed at the time of the Prophet Muhammad and should not be mixed with any culture. Supporters of this movement are adamant that anything in-

11 AMSTRONG, Karen: The battle for God, New York: Alfred A. Knoft, 2000, 55–56.

12 Ibid.

13 JOSEPH, Craig M. / RIDEL, Barnaby: Islamic Schools, assimilation and the concept of Muslim American Character, in: PRATT EWING, Katherine (Hg.): Being and Belonging: Muslims in the United States since 9/11, New York: Russel Sage, 2008.

14 FEALY, Greg: Islamic radicalism in Indonesia. The faltering revival?. Southeast Asian Affairs 2004, no. 1 (2004), 105–111.

consistent with the Prophet Muhammad's traditions must be opposed. Advocates of this movement argue that Islam is a religion and a state, so Islamic laws must be implemented in a state.

For some supporters of the fundamentalist movement in Indonesia, there are only two choices for that state model: an Islamic state (*dar al-Islam*) or an infidel state (*dar al-harb*). This kind of opinion comes from the classical tradition of Islamic political law. This stands in contrast with Muhammadiyah and Nahdlatul Ulama scholars, who try to find a middle ground from the deadlock of the *dar al-harb* versus *dar al-Islam* dichotomy by offering the concept of '*dar al-ʿahd* (state of agreement). The idea of a state of agreement was applied by Muhammadiyah and Nahdlatul Ulama scholars to the Unitary State of the Indonesian Republic (NKRI), which was born in 1945. The consideration is that the NKRI was born from an agreement between various kinds of religious leaders and elements of society that existed at that time and agreed to establish a new state called NKRI. Thus, the NKRI is an agreement, and people may not violate the collective agreement.

According to members of Muhammadiyah and Nahdlatul Ulama, the Indonesian people respect the Republic of Indonesia not because it is an Islamic state but because it is a manifestation of *dar al-ʿahd*. From this point of view, it can be seen that Indonesian clerics have offered new legal reasoning (*ijtihad*) regarding the binary opposition or dichotomy between *dar al-harb* and *dar al-Islam*. This kind of *ijtihad* offers a middle way for harmony between national and religious commitments.

Several ex-terrorists realized that one way to recruit potential terrorists was to ask a brainwashing question: "Which one is better, the Prophet Muhammad or the President Joko Widodo "? (r. 2014-now) This question implies that the two things are not comparable, considering the Prophet was chosen by God, while Joko Widodo was selected by the people.

Some radicals sometimes ask, "Which is better, the Islamic State or the Republic of Indonesia (NKRI)"?[15] This question implies that the two things are not comparable, considering that the NKRI does not need to be opposed to an Islamic state since the NKRI is a manifestation of *dar al-ʿahd* (state of agreement).

Another question that is sometimes raised by radicals is, "Which is better, the Qur'an or Pancasila (Indonesian state ideology)?" Even though this question implies that the two things are not comparable, it is due to the consideration that the Qur'an is God's revelation, while Pancasila is the common agreement of the Indonesian people. When being asked tricky questions like this, some students become confused. In this case, IRE teachers are expected to be able to provide a counter-culture and counter-narrative related to radicalism.

---

15 SURATNO, Suratno: Ideology and identity transformation in the deradicalization of Muslim extremists in Indonesia, in: IJoReSH: 1, no. 2 (2022), 189–214.

When one takes into account history, radicalism first appeared in the 18th century and was more associated with political issues than religious issues. In this context, radicalism refers to a movement that seeks to change the order of society.[16] But in the following century, the word radicalism was drawn into the realm of religion. In the 21st century, radicalism is widely addressed to Muslims, especially after the bombing of the World Trade Center Building in New York on September 11, 2001. In this case, the war on terror commanded by the USA allegedly partially targets Muslim terrorist groups.

Multiculturalism and Nation-Building in Contemporary Indonesian Islamic Education

Islamic education should be able to strengthen multiculturalism and nationhood. In this case, Islamic education is not to be understood in the context of the classical era but in the contemporary era. The modern era necessitates a nation-state's existence, which is a historical imperative. In a nation-state context, one has to respect his / her fellow citizens, regardless of their religious or ethnic background.

Another challenge in the contemporary era is how to ground and contextualize Islamic education. Current Islamic education should appreciate local wisdom, which is in harmony with the spirit of Islamic teachings. This local wisdom does not have to be the same as Islamic teachings, but what is important is that its spirit is in line with Islamic teachings. The substance of Islamic education is not only related to moral conservation but also the development of students' autonomy, discipline, creativity, cognitive flexibility and the like. Islamic education is, accordingly, concerned with both improvement (*tanmiyya*) and empowerment (*tamkin*).

In Islamic scholarship, one may find an explanation that Islamic Education aims to create perfect human beings (*insan kamil*). The concept of *insan kamil* itself is actually borrowed from the tradition of Sufism. This concept is rooted in the adage *takhallaqu bi akhlaqi-llah* (behave according to God's morals). This concept necessitates that students should emulate God's attributes, for example, by listening carefully (*sami'*), behaving wisely (*hakim*), being gentle (*halim*), being compassionate towards people and other creatures (*rahman*), and so on.

Moderate Islamic education should be able to teach students to become integrated personalities. Integrated personality is not to be confused with split

16 BITTNER, Thomas: Radicalism and the organization of radical movements, in: American Sociological Review (1963), 928–940.

personality. In this context, an example of a split personality can be found in someone who prays diligently but steals or hurts people of different beliefs.

Islamic education is mainly about forming character (*ta'dib*) to become an integrated personality that embraces ritual, social, and professional piety. In the digital age, digital piety needs to be added. Digital piety refers to mental balance and thoughts in expressing opinions in the digital space. A ritually pious person is not necessarily digitally pious. For example, some people worship diligently, but on social media they like to insult and hurt other people or provoke their groups to attack other people.

Indonesian Islamic Education and its Role in Nurturing Moderatism and Compassion

Islamic education should try to respond to the locality and modernity. In this vein, Islam is comprehended within the context of Indonesianness and modernity. Thus, it is crucial to recognize Nahdlatul Ulama's and Muhammadiyah's contributions, particularly in balancing Islam, Indonesianness, and modernity.[17] Accordingly, Azra stated that the sustainability of the Unitary State of the Republic of Indonesia (NKRI) and diversity in Indonesia would continue to exist as long as Muhammadiyah and Nahdlatul Ulama are recognized as legitimate organizations that actively uphold their moderate religious tenets. However, Indonesia's future of religious plurality and moderation could likely grow more problematic if the two Islamic civil society organisations fail. [18]

This indicates that, if someone wants to be a moderate and progressive Muslim, he does not have to give up his cultural heritage. Several tribes with distinct cultural histories can be found, for instance, in Indonesia. Radical Muslim organizations frequently believe that having a name other than of Arabic origin is against Islam. This can be observed, among other things, in certain extremist Muslims with Javanese names who say that the Islamic faith and Javanese identity and culture are incompatible. They also changed their names to Arabic names because Javanese names were viewed as less Islamic.

In Southeast Asia, including Indonesia, one may observe religious education which emphasizes diversity and intercultural understanding. Indonesian state

---

17 SULISTIYONO, Susilo / DALIMUNTHE, Reza Pahlevi: Moderate Southeast Asian Islamic education as a parent culture in deradicalization. Urgencies, strategies, and challenges, in: Religions 10, no. 1 (2019), 45–46; See also: WARNK, Holger: Alternative education or teaching radicalism? New literature on Islamic education in Southeast Asia, in: Journal of Current Southeast Asian Affairs 28, no. 4 (2009), 111–132.

18 AZRA, Azyumardi: Indonesia, Islam, and democracy. Dynamics in a global context, Southeast Asia: Equinox Publishing, 2006, 23–24.

Islamic higher education institutions play a significant role in nurturing multiculturalism and religious moderation. In addition, both the Muhammadiyah and Nahdlatul Ulama have universities that work to integrate Islam, democracy, and citizenship.

Suppose this can be implemented in the IRE curriculum. In that case, it is hoped that the output will be that students can accommodate differences and minimize feelings of hatred towards different people. Islamic education should place more emphasis on *hanafiyya samha* (borrowing the term of Nurcholish Majid), namely *hanafiyya* (straight in understanding religion) but also *samha* (broad). The concept of *hanafiyya samha* is the antithesis of a straight but narrow style of religious understanding.[19]

The notion of *hanafiyya samha* can be found in its illustration in the phrase *al-sirat al-mustaqim* (the right path). In Arabic, the word *sirat* refers to a broad and wide road. This is different from the word *sabil* which refers to a narrow path. The concept of *hanafiyya samha* emphasizes the need to have a straight comprehension, yet, try to remain open-minded, understand other people's religions, and respect other people's cultures. IRE in Indonesia is expected to shape individuals with the characteristics of *hanafiyya samha*, who have deep spirituality, but are also wise and tolerant. The educational process with such a goal certainly requires hard work from educators, with the support of parents.

In a broader sense, religious education should work toward making people more human. Keeping in mind that God does not require religion, the revelation of religion was made for the benefit of people. So that all religious teachings are to be understood within the context of advancing human welfare.

Religiosity with the qualities of *hanafiyya samha* serves as an antithesis to egocentric and superficial spirituality. In this sense, superficial religiosity refers to surface-level religious practices; namely, emphasizing the performance of religious rituals *per se*. This form of piety disregards other factors, such as respecting other people and avoiding corruption. The main criteria for those who follow this type of religiosity include assiduous participation in prayer, pilgrimage, and other acts of worship. A person is regarded as pious solely for engaging in such worship. Adherents to this type of religiosity give little attention to whether devotion to worship also has consequences for enhancing the common good.

Islamic religious educators' efforts to reconcile ritual piety with the human common good undoubtedly take time. Islamic religious educators must therefore be committed to balancing these two aspects. The fact that a few people defend superficial and egotistical religious practices and propagate misconceptions like "the important thing is to pray diligently, even though corruption, insulting and hurting other people are also active" is one of the obstacles to the ideal goal of Islamic education.

---

19 Majid, Nurcholish: Islam, kemodernan, dan keindonesiaan, Bandung: Mizan Pustaka, 2008, 45–47.

Multiculturalism and progressivism may serve as the foundation of the Islamic educational curriculum. In the context of Islamic intellectual history, one may observe a tendency towards ambiguity tolerance.[20] This is demonstrated by the numerous ambiguous verses in the Qur'an. These verses encourage tolerance and openness to different points of view.

ʿAli ibn Abi Talib (599–661), a companion of the Prophet, once compared the messages of the Qur'an to diamonds that emanate different colours. Therefore, when reading the Qur'anic verses, one should not assume that the color shown is the truest. However, readers of the Qur'anic verses should be aware that their interpretation only encompasses one aspect of the verse's meanings and must be supplemented by another viewpoint to have a whole comprehension.

The Covid-19 outbreak illustrated how Islamic teachings have been contextualized to reflect the spirit of the times. In this situation, avoiding a stagnant understanding of Islamic beliefs is best. For instance, in early 2020, some Muslim clerics claimed that because only 10,000 persons had been infected with the virus, it could not be classified as a pandemic (*ta'un*). Ultimately, they continued participating in Friday congregational prayers and did not observe social distancing. Here, it is essential to have an understanding of Islam that takes into account not just its literal meaning but also its social and scientific contexts.

The term *ta'un* indicates a possible trend rather than something that needs to be comprehended quantitatively, such as 10,000 or 20,000 people. Science, particularly epidemiology, is used to determine whether or not a disease falls within the category of a pandemic.

In particular, for individuals who do not understand science, the responsibilities of religious leaders should not exceed and interfere with science. This is in line with a verse from the Qur'an "Do not pursue something of which you do not know" (al-Isra' 36). This verse emphasizes that both knowledge and ignorance have their boundaries. Religious leaders and educators should not fall into the trap of thinking they are all-knowing and then try to judge everything according to their limited perspective. Islam should not, in contrast, be opposed to science.

Islamic Religious educators should emphasize the ability to listen to others. This is in line with a verse of the Qur'an "God is all-hearing and all-knowing" (al-Nisa' 148). This passage can be interpreted from an anthropocentric angle namely it teaches Muslims and humans, in general, on the importance of reading and listening and becoming more knowledgeable. This anthropocentric viewpoint is crucial because the Qur'anic verses were revealed for human benefit, not for the benefit of God.

IRE in Indonesia should strongly emphasize the value of a comprehensive understanding of religion since this will foster a tolerance for difference and a

---

20 BAUER, Thomas: Die Kultur der Ambiguität. Eine andere Geschichte des Islams, Berlin: Verlag d. Weltreligionen, 2011, 55–56.

humanistic attitude toward it. In this instance, it is being amiable to other people and animals. On the other hand, a strictly and narrowly defined religion will produce people who may be religious on an individual level but lack regard for other people.

In Islamic history, Abdurrahman ibn Muljam (d. 661) is one of many pious individuals who lacked respect for others. Ibn Muljam was a person who constantly prayed each night and memorized the whole chapters of the Qur'an. Nevertheless, he murdered ʿAli ibn Abi Talib, a companion of the Prophet, simply because he disagreed with 'Ali ibn Abi Talib's viewpoint. Although 'Ali ibn Abi Talib was pious, even he was listed by the Prophet as the ten companions who would enter heaven immediately (*al-ʿashrah al-mubashsharuna bi al-janna*).

IRE pays attention to nurturing both ritual and social piety. This must be emphasized to avoid the emergence of students who are ritualistically religious but deficient in social piety. They are quite obedient, for instance, during worship, but when there is a conflict, they become inspired to use violence against others. The Prophet Muhammad has been portrayed as a good personage throughout Islamic history. He once received insults from a blind beggar of a different religion, but he did not offend him but instead responded with kindness.

Social piety as a form of compassion should be developed within Islamic education institutions. The core of social piety is the notion that each person has a social obligation to their family and community. IRE instructors are supposed to be able to introduce students to those who live in poverty, inspire compassion for them, and, if possible, meet their needs to help them develop this sense of social piety.

Additionally, Islamic education is anticipated to foster empathy among students. One component of compassion is empathy. Teachers of Islamic religious education might arrange for their students to travel to various settings to learn about other people's lifestyles and perspectives. As a result of their increased empathy and understanding, students will be better able to appreciate diversity. Suppose pupils live and interact in a uniform setting. In that case, their sensitivity to different things will not grow effectively, making it impossible for them to acquire the capacity to appreciate and love different individuals.

Islamic religious teachers must emphasize and instill in students that compassion constitutes one of the important virtues of Islam. This can be seen in Islamic teachings, which emphasize compassion (*rahma*) and doing good (*birr, ihsan*) to other creatures. Islamic teachings strongly emphasize the idea that helping others extends beyond one's fellow humans. This is due to the Islamic belief that humans are God's vicegerents and are in charge of maintaining nature. Such accountability is demonstrated through deeds that are beneficial to nature.

One of the Islamic values that IRE teachers often instill in Indonesia is forgiveness (*al-ʿafw*). This forgiveness allows students to hold back their egos by not directly attacking those who hurt them without careful consideration. He will try to open his chest to receive forgiveness if the one who screwed up apologizes. The value of forgiveness is frequently linked in Indonesian culture to other qualities that are emerging there, particularly harmony. This principle highlights the need for community members to control their egos to preserve amicable relationships among community members. Because community members are urged to place a greater emphasis on harmony, it is said that this idea, particularly in Java, can lessen the possibility of social conflict that already exists in society. This idea is consistent with contemporary sociological ideas like social cohesion. Community members who uphold compassion and kindness will foster genuine social cohesion, not merely because they are wary of the law or government officials. It is in this realm that Islamic education is expected to play a role.

References Cited

ABU ZAYD, Nasr Hamid: al-Imam al-Shafi'i wa ta'sis al-aidulujiyya al-wasatiyya (Imam Shafi'i and the Formation of Moderate Ideology), Kairo: Sina, 1992.

ASHUR, Muhammad Al-Tahir Ibn: Ibn Ashur. treatise on maqasid al-shariah, Herndon: International Institute of Islamic Thought, 2006.

AUDA, Jasser: Maqasid al-shariah. an introductory guide, Herndon: International Institute of Islamic Thought, 2008.

AMSTRONG, Karen: The Battle for God, New York: Alfred A. Knoft, 2000.

AZRA, Azyumardi: Indonesia, Islam, and democracy. Dynamics in a global context, Southeast Asia: Equinox Publishing, 2006.

BAUER, Thomas: Die Kultur der Ambiguität. Eine andere Geschichte des Islams (The Culture of Ambiguity: Another History of Islam), Berlin: Verlag d. Weltreligionen, 2011.

BÖCKENFÖRDE, Ernst-Wolfgang: Constitutional and political theory. selected writings, Oxford University Press, 2017.

BITTNER, Egon: Radicalism and the organization of radical movements, in: American Sociological Review (1963), 928–940.

COOK, Michael: Commanding right and forbidding wrong in Islamic thought, Cambridge: University Press, 2001.

FEALY, Greg: Islamic radicalism in Indonesia. the faltering revival?, in: Southeast Asian Affairs 2004, no. 1 (2004), 104–121.

FRANKE, Edith / PYE, Michael: Religionen nebeneinander. Modelle religiöser Vielfalt in Ost- und Südostasien (Religions side by side: models of religious diversity in East and Southeast Asia), Münster: LIT Verlag, 2006.

JOSEPH, Craig M. / RIDEL, Barnaby: Islamic Schools, assimilation and the concept of Muslim American Character, in: PRATT EWING, Katherine (Hg.): Being and Belonging: Muslims in the United States since 9/11, New York: Russel Sage, 2008.

KÜNKLER, Mirjam / LERNER, Hanna: A private matter? Religious education and democracy in Indonesia and Israel, in: British Journal of Religious Education 38, no. 3 (2016), 279–307.

KAMALI, Mohammad Hashim: The middle path of moderation in Islam. The Qur'anic principle of wasatiyyah, Oxford: Oxford University Press, 2015.

MAJID, Nurcholish: Islam, kemodernan, dan keindonesiaan (Islam, modernity and Indonesianness), Mizan: Pustaka, 2008.

SURATNO, Suratno: Ideology and identity transformation in the deradicalization of Muslim extremists in Indonesia, in: IJoReSH 1, no. 2 (2022), 189–214.

SUSILO, Sulistiyono / REZA, Pahlevi Dalimunthe: Moderate southeast Asian Islamic education as a parent culture in deradicalization: Urgencies, strategies, and challenges, in: Religions 10, no. 1 (2019).

TAYEB, Azmil Mohd: Islamic education in Indonesia and Malaysia. Shaping minds, saving souls, Abingdon/New York: Routledge, 2018.

WARNK, Holger: Alternative education or teaching radicalism? New literature on Islamic education in Southeast Asia, in: Journal of Current Southeast Asian Affairs 28, no. 4 (2009), 111–132.

Erzählend Brücken bauen – Zur Bedeutung von Narrativen für Compassion in der interreligiösen Begegnung

Lukas Wiesenhütter

Johann Baptist Metz stellt die Bedeutung von Erzählungen für die Theologie heraus. In besonderer Weise gilt diese für die Praxis der Compassion. Der Beitrag stellt zunächst seine Position dar und fragt dann nach der Rolle von Narrativen im interreligiösen Gespräch. Dafür wird Metz' Ansatz mit Eleonore Stumps Kategorie des franziskanischen Wissens ins Gespräch gebracht. Dies hilft zu beschreiben, warum Erzählungen für eine Komparative Theologie der Compassion unverzichtbar sind: als Vermittlungen interpersonaler Begegnung.

Narrative Theologie; Erzählung; Komparative Theologie; Compassion

Johann Baptist Metz highlights the importance of narratives for theology. This applies in a special way to the practice of compassion. The article first presents his position and then asks about the role of narratives in interreligious conversation. For this, Metz' approach is brought into conversation with Eleonore Stump's category of Franciscan knowledge. This helps to describe why narratives are crucial for comparative theology: as mediations of interpersonal encounters.

Narrative theology; narrative; comparative theology; compassion

Die Tatsache, dass Geschichten in die Mitte des christlichen Glaubens und seiner Vermittlung gehören, verwundert nicht. Zunächst entspricht dies der Praxis Jesu selbst, der seinerseits mit den Erzählungen der Hebräischen Bibel aufwuchs. Wenn Johann Baptist Metz daher auch im Blick auf die von ihm immer wieder eingeforderte Compassion, die engagierte Mit-Leidenschaft mit den Leidenden, auf die Bedeutungen von Erzählungen insistiert, so steht er damit in dieser biblischen Tradition. Auch für einen Text, der nach der systematischen Rolle von Geschichten fragt, ist es angemessen, zu Beginn eine solche in Erinnerung zu rufen:

> Der Gesetzeslehrer wollte sich rechtfertigen und sagte zu Jesus: Und wer ist mein Nächster? Darauf antwortete ihm Jesus: Ein Mann ging von Jerusalem nach Jericho hinab und wurde von Räubern überfallen. Sie plünderten ihn aus und schlugen ihn nieder; dann gingen sie weg und ließen ihn halbtot liegen. Zufällig kam ein Priester denselben Weg herab; er sah ihn und ging vorüber. Ebenso kam auch ein Levit zu der Stelle; er sah ihn und ging vorüber. Ein Samariter aber, der auf der Reise war, kam zu ihm; er sah ihn und hatte Mitleid, ging zu ihm hin, goss Öl und Wein auf seine Wunden und verband sie. Dann hob er ihn auf sein eigenes Reittier, brachte ihn zu einer Herberge und sorgte für ihn. (Lk 10, 29–34)

Die Botschaft einer solchen, über die Jahrhunderte tradierten Geschichte lässt sich kaum in eine nicht-narrative Sprache übersetzen. Was aber leisten derartige Erzählungen, das argumentierend-abstrakter Sprache nicht in gleicher Weise möglich ist? Diese Frage steht im Mittelpunkt des vorliegenden Beitrags. Sie wird dabei auf die auch im biblischen Text greifbare Praxis der Compassion in der interreligiösen Begegnung zugespitzt.[1] In einem ersten Schritt soll dafür knapp rekonstruiert werden, wie Metz die kultur- und religionsübergreifende Relevanz der Compassion profiliert und welche Bedeutung er dabei der Kategorie der Erzählung zuschreibt (I.). Um deren Relevanz konkretisieren und mit einem gegenwärtigen Ansatz vermitteln zu können, wird Metz' Zugang anschließend mit dem Werk der amerikanischen Religionsphilosophin Eleonore Stump ins Gespräch gebracht (II). Von dieser theoretischen Grundierung ausgehend, wird abschließend die Frage reflektiert, welche Bedeutung Erzählungen in der interreligiösen Begegnung zukommt. Dafür wird deren Rolle für das Anliegen Komparativer Theologie fruchtbar gemacht und so die Grundlage für eine mögliche religionsdidaktische Rezeption gelegt (III.).

Compassion und Erzählung bei Johann Baptist Metz

Die von Metz entwickelte Neue Politische Theologie rückt die Kategorie der Erinnerung in den Mittelpunkt und verknüpft sie eng mit denen der Erzählung und Solidarität.[2] Mit seinem Zentralbegriff der *memoria passionis* markiert Metz „jene gefährliche Erinnerung, die unsere Gegenwart bedrängt und in Frage stellt, weil wir uns in ihr an unausgestandene Zukunft erinnern."[3] Gefährlich ist sie, insofern sie zur Praxis der Nachfolge Jesu herausfordert und einen Widerspruch gegen ein unpolitisches Sich-Abfinden mit dem Status Quo markiert. In der Formulierung ist ebenfalls der Verweis auf den eschatologischen Vorbehalt bereits angedeutet, der Metz' gesamtes theologisches Denken durchzieht. Es bleibt einer solchen Theologie daher verwehrt, die Leidenden der Geschichte zu ignorieren, auch dann, wenn sie der Erlösung durch Christus und seiner Auferstehung nachdenkt. Das Leiden bleibt vielmehr protest- und klagewürdig, so dass Metz

---

1 Vgl. die Rezeption der Erzählung bei METZ, Johann Baptist: Memoria passionis. Ein provozierendes Gedächtnis in pluralistischer Gesellschaft. In Zusammenarbeit mit Johann Reikerstorfer, in: DERS.: Gesammelte Schriften, hg. v. Johann Reikerstorfer, Freiburg im Breisgau: Herder, 2017 (= JBMGS 4), 155.

2 Vgl. METZ, Johann Baptist: Glaube in Geschichte und Gesellschaft. Studien zu einer praktischen Fundamentaltheologie, in: DERS.: Gesammelte Schriften, hg. v. Johann Reikerstorfer, Freiburg im Breisgau: Herder, 2016 (= JBMGS 3/1), §11–§13.

3 METZ, Johann Baptist: „Politische Theologie" in der Diskussion (1969), in: DERS.: Gesammelte Schriften, hg. v. Johann Reikerstorfer, Freiburg im Breisgau: Herder, 2016 (= JBMGS 3/2), 46.

in einem eindringlichen Appell formuliert: „Redet von der Osterbotschaft so, dass darin die Karfreitagsschreie Jesu nicht unhörbar geworden sind.“[4] Seine grundsätzliche Kritik gilt der *Verblüffungsfestigkeit*[5], jener theologischen Versuchung, die das Leiden relativierend ins größere Ganze des göttlichen Plans einordnet und so die Solidarität mit den Leidenden verrät – eine Kritik, die *mutatis mutandis* auch noch politischen Utopien gilt, die eine heile Welt der Zukunft unter Inkaufnahme der Schrecken der Vergangenheit versprechen.[6]

Es ist genau „diese gesteigerte Wahrnehmung und Berücksichtigung fremden Leids im eigenen Leben und Handeln“,[7] die Metz als *Compassion* bezeichnet und die sich in narrativer Form in oben zitierter Parabel findet. Diese Mitleidenschaft *ist* die Praxis christlichen Glaubens. Insofern er selbst in biblischer Tradition steht, gilt dies zugleich für den Monotheismus überhaupt, der, ebenso wie das Christentum, in der Gefahr steht, das biblisch inspirierte Erbe der Leidempfindlichkeit zu ignorieren.[8] Die Vehemenz, mit der Metz für sein Programm eintritt, ist sicherlich auch darin begründet, dass er der christlichen Theologiegeschichte eine solche Blindheit attestiert. Besonders drückt sich dies in seinem Hinweis aus, die Frage nach der Dauer des Leids sei zugunsten der Frage nach der Schuld des Menschen zurückgedrängt worden.[9] Demgegenüber ist die Praxis der Compassion von politischer und von universaler Bedeutung. Denn nicht der Minimalkonsens kann Metz zufolge Grundlage und Kriterium eines Weltethos sein, sondern nur die „Autorität der unschuldig und ungerecht Leidenden.“[10] In diesem Sinne entwirft er, mit verschärfter Dringlichkeit vor dem Hintergrund der Globalisierungsfragen im Nachgang der Anschläge vom 11. September 2001, die Vision einer „Ökumene der Compassion unter den Religionen.“[11] Die praktische Solidarität im Wahrnehmen des Leids der Anderen könnte ein Ausgangspunkt sein, der über kulturelle und religiöse Grenzen hinweg Geltung hat, selbst biblisch imprägniert ist und ein Gegenprogramm zur von Papst Franziskus diagnostizierten *Globalisierung der Gleichgültigkeit* bildet.[12] Eine interreligiöse Begegnung in den Spuren der Metzschen Theologie hat also zunächst die leidenden Anderen in den Blick zu nehmen und ihre Gottesrede von da aus zu entwickeln.

---

4 METZ, Johann Baptist: „Sis mihi Deus!“ (2003), in: DERS.: Gesammelte Schriften, hg. v. Johann Reikerstorfer, Freiburg im Breisgau: Herder, 2017 (= JBMGS 8), 196–204, 199.

5 METZ 2017 [Anm.1], 48.

6 Vgl. METZ, Johann Baptist: Unterwegs zu einer nachidealistischen Theologie (1985), in: JBMGS 3/2, 133.

7 METZ 2017 [Anm.1], 106.

8 Vgl. Ebd., 154.

9 Vgl. etwa Ebd.,155; 224–225.

10 METZ, Johann Baptist: „Aufwachen, Augen öffnen, Leid erkennen.“ (2003), in: JBMGS 8, 213.

11 METZ 2017 [Anm.1], 164.

12 PAPST FRANZISKUS: Apostolisches Schreiben Evangelii Gaudium, Vatikan Stadt: Heiliger Stuhl, 54; Vgl. dazu ECKHOLT, Margit: „Compassion“ und „Passion“. Lateinamerikanische Theologie in der Nachfolge Jesu Christi, in: FISCHER, Irmtraud u. a. (Hg.): Mitleid und Mitleiden (= Jahrbuch für biblische Theologie 30), Göttingen: Vandenhoeck & Ruprecht,

Diese Praxis der erinnernden Solidarität ist nun selbst auf die Kategorie der Erzählung verwiesen. Allgemein gilt dies, weil sie die Form ist, in der *gefährliche Erinnerungen* adäquat tradiert werden, so dass Metz ihnen eine „indispensable *Erzählstruktur*"[13] attestiert. Dies konkretisiert er etwa mit dem Verweis auf wichtige literarische Zeugnisse der Gräuel des 20. Jahrhunderts: „Was z. B. bedeutet das literarische Werk von E. Wiesel für das Auschwitz-Gedächtnis, was A. Solschenizyns Literatur für das Gulag-Gedächtnis?"[14] Die Bedeutung von Narrativen gilt aber auch, weil sie dem christlichen Glauben angemessen ist, der wesentlich auf Erzählungen basiert, wie Metz in den Spuren von Harald Weinrich festhält.[15] Er sieht darin zudem einen Charakterzug der Glaubenspraxis Israels bewahrt, der sich nicht in argumentierende Sprache auflösen lässt und der auch für christliches Sprechen über Gott bleibend normativ ist.[16] Obwohl er mitunter schematisch den griechischen „Logos" theologischer Vernunft mit der erzählenden Sprache der Bibel kontrastiert,[17] wird man sein Plädoyer für die bleibende Bedeutung von Erzählungen nicht so verstehen müssen, als werde hier ein Zugang auf Kosten des anderen profiliert. Vielmehr sollen Erzählungen zunächst in ihrer theologischen Dignität wiederentdeckt werden.

Für die Frage nach der interreligiösen Bedeutung von Narrativen ist nun Metz' Überlegung zur Überwindung des Eurozentrismus von besonderem Interesse, die einer Verengung des Theologiebegriffs auf einen bestimmten Typus von Wissenschaftssprache entgegenwirken könnte. Ihnen traut er eine besondere Kommunikationsleistung zu, die zudem der Kirche als *Erinnerungs- und Erzählgemeinschaft* entspricht:

> So wäre es nicht zuletzt Aufgabe der Theologie heute, in der Erzählung eine privilegierte Sprachform im interkulturellen Umgang miteinander zu erkennen und sie quasi als Brückenkategorie zwischen kulturell unterschiedlichen Lebenswelten und Lebensformen zu entwickeln.[18]

Diese Brückenkategorie für das komparativ-interreligiöse Gespräch fruchtbar zu machen, kann schon deshalb sinnvoll sein, weil Metz selbst den Stellenwert der Erzählung im Rekurs auf die jüdische Tradition begründet und dabei neben der

---

2018, 329. die darauf aufmerksam macht, wie sehr das Schreiben vom Motiv der Compassion durchzogen sei.

13 METZ 2016 [Anm.2], 208.

14 METZ 2017 [Anm.1], 218.

15 Vgl. WEINRICH, Harald: Narrative Theologie, in: Concilium 9 (1973), 329–333. Dieser hatte in seinem Plädoyer für „narrative Theologie" etwa herausgestellt, dass zentrale Theologumena nicht ohne Erzählung ausdrückbar seien: „Aber seltsam: auch bei den konsequentesten Entmythologisierern bleibt eine eklatante Ausnahme bestehen, das erzählte Osterereignis: „Er ist auferstanden." (Ebd., 331).

16 Vgl. METZ 2016 [Anm.2], 217.

17 Vgl. die Hinweise zum Geistangebot Israels bei METZ 2017 [Anm.1], 216 sowie 226–227.

18 Ebd., 225.

biblischen Basis vor allem auf die rabbinische Tradition verweist.[19] Zwar ist das Christentum in einer besonderen Weise auf das Judentum bezogen, die nicht einfach generalisiert werden kann, und doch könnte es sich lohnen, diese Lernbewegung auch im Hinblick auf andere Religionen zu erproben. Dass die Kategorie der Erzählung eine Brücke bildet, insofern sie in anderen religiösen Traditionen prominent beheimatet ist, ist das eine. Was aber leistet sie darüber hinaus, das sie zum empathischen Verstehen der Anderen und damit zur Praxis der Compassion unabdingbar macht? Was ist es, das Erzählungen „bei dem produktiven Austausch von unterschiedlichen Kulturwelten kommunikativer als die subjektlose Argumentationssprache der klassischen Metaphysik“[20] sein lässt? Eine erste Antwort liefert Walter Benjamin, auf den Metz explizit rekurriert. Er beschreibt einen Charakterzug des Erzählens, der verdeutlicht, wieso eine das Leiden der Anderen anerkennende Compassion narrativ vermittelt sein kann: „Der Erzähler nimmt, was er erzählt, aus der Erfahrung; aus der eigenen oder berichteten. Und er macht es wiederum zur Erfahrung derer, die seiner Geschichte zuhören.“[21] Mitleidenschaftliche Anteilnahme an der Leidensgeschichte der Anderen könnte demnach ermöglicht werden, indem ihre Geschichten erzählend tradiert werden. Dieser Gedanke soll nun im Blick auf Eleonore Stumps Zugang noch präzisiert werden.

Die Bedeutung von Narrativen bei Eleonore Stump

Eleonore Stump hat in ihrem monumentalen Werk zum Theodizeeproblem ausführlich auf den Unterschied von propositional-argumentierender und narrativer Sprache reflektiert.[22] Ihre Überlegungen können helfen, die bei Metz betonte Bedeutung von Erzählungen vertieft zu begründen. Dabei ist ihre Differenzierung von zwei Erkenntnisweisen besonders fruchtbar. Typologisch unterscheidet Stump *dominikanisches* von *franziskanischem* Wissen, wobei die namensgebenden Heiligen jeweils den entsprechenden Zugang zur Welt verkörpern.

Das *dominikanische Wissen* steht dabei für den analytisch-urteilenden Zugang, wie er besonders in der englischsprachigen Religionsphilosophie der vergangenen Jahrzehnte maßgeblich war, während das *franziskanische Wissen* für

---

19 Vgl. den Verweis von METZ 2016 [Anm.2], 218–219. auf das Werk von Martin Buber. Vgl. auch METZ, Johann Baptist: Welches Christentum hat Zukunft?. Dorothee Sölle und Johann Baptist Metz im Gespräch (1990), in: JBMGS 8, 143.

20 METZ 2017 [Anm.1], 225.

21 Zit. nach METZ 2016 [Anm.2], 218–219.

22 Vgl. STUMP, Eleonore: Wandering in Darkness. Narrative and the Problem of Suffering, Oxford: Clarendon Press, 2010. In der folgenden Darstellung entnehme ich Formulierungen aus meiner Dissertationsschrift: Hiobs Begegnung. Islamische und christliche Perspektiven auf Theodizee und Theodizeesensibilität (bislang unveröffentlicht).

jene durch Erfahrung vermittelten Wissenszugänge steht, die sich nicht auf dominikanisches Wissen reduzieren lassen.[23] Stump verdeutlicht diesen Unterschied anhand der Überlegung, wie jeweils der Umgang mit einem sündigen Menschen aussehen könnte. Der typisch dominikanische Zugang wäre durch eine stringente Argumentation gekennzeichnet: „You engage in acts of type A, but type A acts are morally wrong. The reason type A acts are morally wrong is that they violate moral principles of sort P."[24] Demgegenüber würde der franziskanische Zugang die Bedeutsamkeit eines personalen Gottesverhältnisses betonen, das sich nicht als formalisiertes Argument andemonstrieren ließe:

> For Francis, a person who wants to obey the command implied in the biblical text first has to be rightly related to God. He has to know God and love God and desire to live for God. And, if he is rightly related to God in these ways, then he himself will be on fire [...][25]

Die eingangs in Erinnerung gerufene Erzählung vom barmherzigen Samariter beantwortet die Frage des Schriftgelehrten also nach den Regeln franziskanischen Wissens. Anstatt einer *dominikanischen* Antwort, die Argumente vorträgt, wer der Nächste sei, erfolgt eine Geschichte, die einlädt, sich selbst in ihr wiederzufinden. Erfahrungswissen, das sich nicht dominikanisch fassen lässt, ist etwa auch die Wahrnehmung von Farben. *Wie es ist*, zum ersten Mal im Leben die Farbe Rot zu sehen, lässt sich, so das Fazit des von Stump rezipierten Gedankenexperiments,[26] der fiktiven Person Mary nicht in Form von „knowledge that" durch Bücher vermitteln, sofern sie vorher noch nie eine Farbe wahrgenommen hat.[27]

Eine besondere Kategorie franziskanischen Wissens aber ist die Erfahrung, die wir machen, wenn wir einer anderen Person begegnen. Um das zu illustrieren, verändert Stump das Gedankenexperiment der fiktiven Mary. Wäre sie Zeit

---

23 Ähnlich, aber nicht identisch ist Russels Unterscheidung zwischen knowledge of things und knowledge of aquaintance. Stump selbst diskutiert allerdings, wie sich die von ihr beschriebenen Begriffe inhaltlich absetzen. (vgl. Ebd., 50; 61; 501–502).

24 Ebd., 46.

25 Ebd.

26 Vgl. Ebd., 50. Stump bezieht sich auf JACKSON, Frank: Epiphenomenal Qualia, in: The Philosophical Quarterly 32 (1982), 127–136. Jackson bezeichnet sich darin selbst als „qualia freak" und fasst pointiert ebd., 127 seine Sicht gegen den Physikalismus zusammen: "Tell me everything physical there is to tell about what is going on in a living brain, the kind of states, their functional role, their relation to what goes on at other times and in other brains, and so on and so forth, and be I as clever as can be in fitting it all together, you won't have told me about the hurtfulness of pains, the itchiness of itches, pangs of jealousy, or about the characteristic experience of tasting a lemon, smelling a rose, hearing a loud noise or seeing the sky."

27 Vgl. STUMP 2010 [Anm. 21], 50: „There are certain first-person knowledge states that cannot be adequately acquired or expressed by means of propositional attitudes. That is why, when Mary first knows redness in virtue of perceiving it, it is hard to express what she knows adequately in terms of knowing *that*."

ihres Lebens eingesperrt und hätte Zugang zu sämtlicher wissenschaftlicher Literatur, die ihr darstellte, wie es wäre, Kontakt zu anderen Menschen zu haben, ohne diesen Kontakt in der Einsamkeit ihrer Gefangenschaft tatsächlich aufnehmen zu können, so sei unmittelbar einsichtig, dass ihr bislang Unbekanntes widerführe, wenn sie nach der Zeit ihrer Gefangenschaft zum ersten Mal auf ihre sie liebende Mutter träfe.[28] Was ist das Neue, zuvor nicht Wissbare, dem Mary nun begegnet, wo sie sich doch sämtliche wissenschaftliche Abhandlungen darüber aneignen konnte, was sich im Hirn eines Menschen abspielt, der einen ihn liebenden Menschen trifft? Stump hält die Unterscheidung von Erster- und Dritter-Person-Perspektive an dieser Stelle für nicht hinreichend und grenzt die beschriebene Begegnungserfahrung von beiden Perspektiven ab, um das Spezifikum der Erfahrung auszudrücken:

> But neither first-person nor third-person accounts will be adequate for Mary to describe what is new for her. What is new for her, what she learns, has to do with her personal interaction with another person. What is new for Mary is a second-person experience.[29]

Eine solche *Zweite-Person-Erfahrung*, die wir im Gewahrwerden einer anderen Person machen, ist Stump zufolge also nicht adäquat in propositionale Sprache übersetzbar. Dann drängt sich die Frage auf, ob und wie sie überhaupt an Dritte vermittelbar sein soll, die an der entsprechenden Begegnung nicht beteiligt waren. An dieser Stelle nun werden Narrative bedeutsam. Denn falls Mary beschreiben wollte, wer ihre Mutter für sie ist, und wie ihr dies in der Begegnung deutlich wurde, würde sie von der Interaktion mit ihr *erzählen*. Bis zu einem gewissen Grad würde sie auf diese Weise Dritten einen Zugang zur Zweite-Person-Erfahrung ermöglichen, bei der diese selbst nicht zugegen waren:

> This is generally what we do when we tell a story. A story takes a real or imagined set of second-person experiences of one sort or another and makes it available to a wider audience to share. It does so by making it possible, to one degree or another, for a person to experience some of what she would have experienced if she had been an onlooker in the second-person experience represented in the story.[30]

Die durch eine solche Geschichte vermittelte Zweite-Person-Erfahrung ist freilich nicht mit der gemachten Erfahrung selbst identisch. Schließlich würde, wer eine ausführliche Erzählung von Mary hört, ihrer Mutter deshalb noch nicht persönlich begegnet sein. Und doch könnte eine solche Erzählung dazu beitragen, dass ein lebendiges Bild vom Charakter der Mutter entsteht, das sie als Person erfahrbar werden lässt. Dies ist durchaus anschlussfähig an Momente der

---

28 Vgl. Ebd., 52: „When Mary is first united with her mother, it seems indisputable that Mary will know things she did not know before, even if she knew everything about her mother that could be made available to her in non-narrative propositional form, including her mother's psychological states."

29 Ebd., 53.

30 Ebd., 78.

Alltagserfahrung, in denen wir *Ich habe schon so viel von dir gehört* oder ähnliche Formulierungen verwenden. Stump nennt solche narrativen Vermittlungsversuche einer Begegnungserfahrung „second-person account."[31] Ein solcher ist die begrenzte, jedoch bestmögliche Vermittlung der Begegnungserfahrung an Dritte. So wäre Stump zufolge auch Marys erstes Zusammentreffen mit ihrer Mutter weniger unvorhersehbar gewesen, hätten ihr in der Zeit der Einsamkeit Klassiker der Belletristik zur Verfügung gestanden, die ihr eine Reihe von *second-person accounts* eröffnet hätten.[32]

Die Konsequenzen für die theologische Reflexion sind erheblich. Wo immer es um interpersonale Begegnung geht, spielen *second-person accounts* eine entscheidende Rolle.[33] Dies hilft etwa, die Bedeutung der Parabel aus Lk 10 hervorzuheben. Mindestens ein doppelter *second-person account* ist hier auszumachen. Da der Umgang Jesu mit einer Anfrage an ihn beschrieben wird, ist die Erzählung narrativ vermittelte Antwort auf die Frage: Wer ist Jesus Christus? Wenn Metz von der „Parabel vom ‚Barmherzigen Samariter'" spricht, „mit der sich Jesus in das Gedächtnis der Menschheit hineinerzählt hat",[34] ist dies im Rückgriff auf Stumps Kategorien wörtlich zu nehmen: Die Erzählung lässt einen *second-person account*, eine vermittelte Begegnungserfahrung mit der Person Jesu zu, die in *dieser Weise* franziskanischem, nicht aber dominikanischem Wissen zugänglich ist.[35] In der vom Jesus des Evangeliums vorgetragenen Geschichte finden ebenfalls Begegnungen statt, nämlich die mit dem leidenden Hilfsbedürftigen, den Vorübergehenden und dem helfenden Samariter, so dass den Zuhörenden die geschilderte Situation zur Anfrage und Handelsaufforderung wird. Dies gilt in einem ersten Schritt für den Text, sofern er eine Geschichte erzählt. In Jesu Erzählungen wäre in einem nächsten Schritt zudem die Form dieser Erzählung jeweils eigens zu reflektieren, die mitunter ebenfalls nicht in andere Textgattungen übersetzbar ist.[36]

---

31 Ebd., 77.

32 Vgl. ebd., 79.

33 Vgl. für weitere Analysen KRONAU, Johannes / GRÖSSL, Johannes: Extra narrationem nulla salus. Perspektiven eines narrativitätstheoretischen Ansatzes für die christliche Soteriologie, in: MThZ 73/3 (2022), 230–245; Ebd., 235. weisen sie zu Recht auf die Relevanz der Kategorie der Erzählung für den in Dei Verbum zentralen Gedanken der Selbstoffenbarung hin.

34 METZ 2017 [Anm.1], 155.

35 Auch hier ist wichtig zu betonen, dass dies einen „dominikanischen" Zugang – etwa die Frage nach der logischen Denkbarkeit der hypostatischen Union – keineswegs obsolet macht. Dieser bleibt aber stets rückgebunden an die ihn allererst provozierende Erzählung.

36 Am eindrücklichsten gilt dies für die Gleichnisse. In der Beschreibung bei RICOEUR, Paul: Stellung und Funktion der Metapher in der biblischen Sprache, in: Ders. / JÜNGEL, Eberhard: Metapher. Zur Hermeneutik religiöser Sprache (Sonderheft Evangelische Theologie), München: Kaiser, 1974, 62 schimmern Stumps Kategorien bereits durch: „Das hebrä-

Mutatis mutandis gilt Vergleichbares, wenn wir autobiografische Zeugnisse von Menschen erinnern, die im Krieg leiden oder gelitten haben, und so in Metz' Spuren die memoria passionis lebendig zu halten suchen. Die das Leid des Anderen wahrnehmende und zur Praxis drängende Compassion ist hier als *second-person account* in Szene gesetzt und *deshalb* kommunikativer als andere Vermittlungsformen.

Konsequenzen für die Komparative Theologie und ihre Didaktik

Erzählungen lassen sich als Brücke verstehen, und zwar zwischen der erlebten interpersonalen Begegnung und ihrer Vermittlung an Dritte. Insofern sie dies leisten, können sie angemessene *Brückenkategorie* sein, um über Kultur- und Religionsgrenzen hinweg empathisches Verstehen zu ermöglichen. Dies ist nötig, um sich von der Wahrnehmung fremden Leids berühren und ins Handeln rufen zu lassen, wie es die von Metz eingeforderte Compassion anzielt. „Diese Compassion verlangt vorweg die Bereitschaft zu einem Blickwechsel [...]",[37] hält Metz fest und betont so ebenfalls eine Möglichkeit, die narrativ-franziskanisch gelingen kann. Er verweist etwa auf die Wahrnehmung des Leidens einst verfeindeter Gruppen, um die Praxis der Compassion im Raum der internationalen Friedenspolitik auszumachen.[38] Dabei erhält die Aufforderung zum Erzählen *der* und Hören *auf* die Leidensgeschichten der Anderen eine unmittelbar politische Relevanz, die zugleich immer wieder zur kritischen Frage werden kann, wessen Leidenserzählungen wir nicht wahrnehmen und so nicht zur *gefährlichen Erinnerung* werden lassen.

Bereits diese Anfrage verweist im interreligiösen Kontext auf einen komparativ-theologischen Zugang, der sich müht, die mitunter überraschende oder irritierende Stimme der religiös-Anderen konstitutiv mit einzubeziehen. Zudem lässt sich in der Aufforderung zum grenzüberschreitenden Blickwechsel ein Grundmotiv Komparativer Theologie ausmachen, deren Anliegen es ist, sich

ische *maschal* verbindet direkt die Bedeutung des Spruches und eine entsprechende Disposition in der Sphäre der menschlichen Existenz ohne den Umweg über eine allgemeine ethische Aussage, die das Gleichnis veranschaulichen würde."

37 Metz 2017 [Anm.1], 157.

38 Metz 2017 [Anm.1], 159: „Ich weiß für diese exemplarischen Schritte zum Frieden immer noch keinen anderen Weg als den, den der Israeli Rabin und der Palästinenser Arafat einschlagen wollten, als sie 1993 in Washington erstmals einander die Hand reichten und sich gegenseitig versicherten, dass sie künftig nicht nur auf die eigenen Leiden schauen wollten, auf die Leiden des eigenen Volkes, sondern dass sie bereit seien, auch die Leiden der Anderen, die Leiden der bisherigen Feinde nicht zu vergessen und bei ihrem eigenen politischen Handeln in Betracht zu ziehen."

über Religionsgrenzen hinweg von der Theologie der Anderen bereichern zu lassen. Dies kann gerade auch dort geschehen, wo Differenzen bleiben,[39] so dass keineswegs eine Verklärung anderer Traditionen gefordert ist.[40] Vorausgesetzt ist allerdings ein Mindestmaß an Empathie, mithin jene von Metz eingeforderte Bereitschaft zum Blickwechsel. Dieser drängt, etwas zugespitzt, selbst zu einem komparativ-theologischen Vorgehen und der Bereitschaft zur ständigen Korrekturbedürftigkeit der theologischen Urteile.[41] Vor dem Hintergrund des bisher Gesagten könnte dies bedeuten, sich auf die formativen Geschichten der anderen Tradition einzulassen und so narrative Zeugnisse in ihrer „kommunikativen Würde“[42] ernst zu nehmen: nicht als bloße Illustrationen von Sachverhalten, sondern als *second-person accounts*, der adäquaten Vermittlungsform interpersonaler Begegnung. Auf diese Weise kann etwas von der *memoria passionis* tradiert werden, die Metz einfordert, indem auch die Stimmen der Leidenden der Vergangenheit hörbar gemacht werden. Dies wird, ebenso wie die Praxis Komparativer Theologie selbst,[43] mit Verletzlichkeit einhergehen, zumal so auch eine Konfrontation mit eigenen Schuldgeschichten geschehen kann – wie par excellence am jüdisch-christlichen Gespräch sichtbar wird. Ist ein Blickwechsel allerdings Voraussetzung engagierter Compassion, geht dies notwendig mit einer solchen Vulnerabilität einher. Von Metz' theologischem Grundimpuls her ist offenkundig, dass Erzählung und Praxis nicht zwei separate Größen darstellen, sondern eng verzahnt sind. Auch hier kann die erinnerte Parabel vom barmherzigen Samariter verdeutlichen, was Metz meint, wenn er die Praxis der Nachfolge und die Christologie zusammenrückt.[44] Diese lässt sich so verstehen, dass die Geschichte Jesu in der Geschichte derjenigen Gestalt annehmen soll, die sich auf den Weg der Nachfolge machen – so dass die *Erzählung* des Evangeliums durch sie wahrnehmbare Praxis wird.[45]

---

39 Vgl. Stosch, Klaus von: Komparative Theologie als Wegweiser in der Welt der Religionen (= Beiträge zur Komparativen Theologie 6), Paderborn: Schöningh, 2012, 245–249.

40 Vgl. die Mahnung zu kritischen Fragen im Religionsdialog in Metz 2017 [Anm.1], 165. Einige seiner eigenen Kontrastierungen selbst verlangen freilich nach dem die Komparative Theologie kennzeichnenden mikrologischen Vorgehen, etwa die zwischen der „Mystik der Compassion“ (ebd., 157), die als „Mystik der offenen Augen“ (ebd.) politisch wird, in Abgrenzung zur Mystik der „fernöstlichen Religionen“ (ebd., 157).

41 Vgl. mit Bezug auf Metz Stosch 2012 [Anm. 39], 213–214. Vgl. für die Grundhaltung der Empathie Stosch, Klaus von: Einführung in die Komparative Theologie, Paderborn: Schöningh, 2021, 14–15.

42 Metz 2017 [Anm.1], 225.

43 Vgl. Moyaert, Marianne: In Response to the Religious Other. Ricœur and the Fragility of Interreligious Encounters, London: Lexington Books, 2014, 182.

44 Metz 2017 [Anm.1], 68.

45 Vgl. dazu die Formulierung von Tilley, Terrence: Story Theology (= Theology and life series 12), Wilmington: Del. Glazier, 1985, 176: „To be a disciple of Christ is to be a member of his body, to take the stories of the Christian tradition and adapt or adopt them to be one's own story." Die Relevanz der Erzählung ist hier zunächst strikt an die Praxis gebun-

Damit ist verdeutlicht, dass im Blick auf die Leidensgeschichten der Menschheit und die Praxis der Compassion *second-person accounts* und damit Narrative von zentraler Bedeutung sind. Dies gilt jedoch darüber hinaus überall, wo der komparativ-theologische Zugang zur interpersonalen Dimension von religiöser Praxis und Erfahrung angezielt ist. Eine Reduktion theologischer Relevanz auf eine bestimmte Form propositionaler Sprache verfiele der Gefahr einer Verengung, vor der Metz gewarnt hatte, und würde von vornherein wesentliche Dimensionen religiösen Handels und die ihm zugesprochene Bedeutung nicht in den Blick bekommen. Dies könnte sogar gelten, wenn die Textfixiertheit komparativ-theologischen Arbeitens angemerkt wird. Marianne Moyaert hat etwa zu Recht darauf hingewiesen, dass die Textlastigkeit Komparativer Theologie nicht zu einer Blindheit anderer religiöser Vollzüge gegenüber führen dürfe.[46] Der *ritual turn* erinnert dies: Religion ist eben nicht nur Textstudium, sondern auch rituelles Handeln. Deshalb ist eine Teilnahme am religiös-anderen Ritual, soweit möglich, aus der Sicht Komparativer Theologie sinnvoll, ebenso wie der Hinweis darauf wichtig ist, dass die Privilegierung von Innerlichkeit gegenüber äußeren Praktiken nicht vorschnell universalisiert werden sollte.[47] Häufig lassen sich allerdings auch dann noch Verweise auf die Kategorie der Erzählung ausmachen, wenn dies berücksichtigt wird. Denn es kann konstitutiver Bestandteil des Rituals sein, dass es nicht für alle mitvollziehbar ist, so dass hier eine narrative Form geradezu notwendig ist, um den Vollzug selbst oder die Deutung zu vermitteln, die dem Ritual zugesprochen wird.[48] Ähnlich wie Marys Mutter mir nicht persönlich begegnet ist und ich in der narrativen Vermittlung dennoch einen lebendigen Eindruck von ihr gewinnen könnte, so können Erzählungen Zugang zu religiös-anderen Vollzügen bieten. In diesem Sinne kann die von Navid Kermani referierte Geschichte der Bekehrung des von der Koranrezitation ergriffenen Umar helfen, die wahrnehmbare Schönheit der Rezitation mit ihrer Normativität für die Tradition zu vermitteln.[49] Hinzu kommt, dass auch Liturgien sich häu-

---

den und bedarf keiner vorschnellen Positionierung bezüglich der Frage, ob das menschliche Leben selbst als Erzählung verstehbar sei. Einen Überblick zur Frage bietet THOMÄ, Dieter: Vom Nutzen und Nachteil der Erzählung für das Leben, in: JOISTEN, Karen (Hg.): Narrative Ethik. Das Gute und das Böse erzählen (= Deutsche Zeitschrift für Philosophie Sonderband 17), Berlin: Akademie Verlag, 2007, 75–93.

46 Vgl. MOYAERT, Marianne: Towards a Ritual Turn in Comparative Theology: Opportunities, Challenges, and Problems, in: Harvard Theological Review 111/1 (2018), 1–23.

47 Vgl. Ebd., 9.

48 Vgl. für eine besonders eindrucksvolle Erzählung ästhetischen Erlebens (und damit ihre franziskanisch-narrative Vermittlung an Dritte) die Schilderung ostkirchlicher Liturgie in der Nestorchronik; zit. bei BREMER, Thomas: Kreuz und Kreml. Geschichte der orthodoxen Kirche in Russland, Freiburg im Breisgau: Herder, ²2016, 66.

49 Vgl. KERMANI, Navid: Gott ist schön. Das ästhetische Erleben des Koran, München: Beck, ⁴2011, 34–35.

fig durch narrative Elemente auszeichnen oder gar als gefeierte Erzählung verstehen lassen. So steht etwa im Zentrum der Eucharistiefeier[50] oder des Sederabends[51] explizit die Vergegenwärtigung einer konkreten Erzählung.

In dem Maße, in dem auch der Religionsunterricht Wert auf interpersonales Lernen über konfessionelle Grenzen hinweg legt,[52] ist dies auch didaktisch zu berücksichtigen und der Raum für die Auseinandersetzung mit narrativen Texten der Tradition ebenso zu eröffnen wie der zum eigenen Erzählen. Für die Religionen in der Tradition der Hebräischen Bibel kommt hinzu, dass sie Erzählungen teilen oder, diese fort- und umschreibend, in einen Gesprächsraum eintreten, so dass hier eine komparativ-theologische Auseinandersetzung mit den formativen Texten in besonderer Weise gefordert ist.[53] Der Zusammenhang von Narrativen und Empathie[54] im Unterricht ist ebenso herausgestellt worden wie die dortige Rolle erzählender Texte für die interreligiöse Begegnung.[55] Dabei ist offenkundig, dass sich die Gestalt narrativer Texte erheblich unterscheidet und sie nach Gattungen differenziert bedacht werden müssen. Was sie über die Unterschiede hinweg eint, ist die Möglichkeit zur Vermittlung von Zweite-Person-Erfahrungen. Dies erlaubt es, in einer ersten Annäherung ihren möglichen Wert für die interreligiöse Begegnung in der pädagogischen Praxis zu benennen. Erzählungen aus den Heiligen Schriften und den religiösen Traditionen vermitteln Dritten einen Zugang zur eigenen formativen Geschichte, der nicht nur Sachinformation, sondern Einladung zum Perspektivwechsel ist. Mit Blick auf die abrahamischen Religionen geben sie narrative Antworten auf die Frage, wer der geglaubte Gott ist, indem Gottes Geschichte mit den Menschen erzählt wird. Zweitens sind es, in der Spur von Metz, die Leidensgeschichten, die eine empathische Anteilnahme ermöglichen und so zur Compassion herausfordern. Theologisch gesprochen werden sie zugleich zu einer Anfrage an Gott, dessen ausstehende Gerechtigkeit sich für die Leidenden noch erweisen muss, und die darum die

---

50 Vgl. METZ 2016 [Anm.2], 220 sowie WENZEL, Knut: Narrative Theologie revisited, in: Lebendige Seelsorge 70/6 (2019), 403–404.

51 Vgl. O'DONNELL, Emma: Methodological Considerations on the Role of Experience in Comparative Theology, in: CLOONEY, Francis / STOSCH, Klaus von: How to Do Comparative Theology, New York: Fordham University Press, 2018, 267.

52 Vgl. ROEBBEN, Bert / STOSCH, Klaus von: Religious Education and Comparative Theology. Creating Common Ground for Intercultural Encounters, in: Religions 13/11 (2022). DOI: https://doi.org/10.3390/rel13111014,3: "Religious learning [...] is and should always be an interpersonal thing."

53 Vgl. den Zugang zur Josefsgeschichte bei MAGGIONI, Pietro Lorenzo: Comparative Theology. A Fairy Tale. For an Ethics in Comparison, Rom: Aracne, 2018, 531–549.

54 Vgl. ROMMEL, Herbert: Lernen an „negativer Moral“, in: LINDNER, Konstantin / ZIMMERMANN, Mirjam: Handbuch ethische Bildung, Tübingen: Mohr Siebeck, 2021, 327.

55 Vgl. ZIMMERMANN, Mirjam: Interreligiöses Lernen narrativ. Feste in den Weltreligionen, Göttingen: Vandenhoeck & Ruprecht, 2015, 45–57.

Gläubigen zu einer Praxis drängt, die Gottes Gerechtigkeit als anfanghaft gegenwärtig behauptet.[56] Drittens wirft Gesagtes auch ein Licht auf die Bedeutung fiktiver Texte, moderner Literatur etwa, für die religionsdidaktische Praxis. Bei allen Unterschieden kann auch durch sie franziskanisches Wissen vermittelt werden. Georg Langenhorst benennt dieses Potenzial literarischer Texte unter anderem mit den Begriffen der „Erfahrungserweiterung"[57] und der „Möglichkeitsandeutung"[58], die sich gut mit einem von Metz und Stump inspirierten Zugang zu Narrativen vermitteln ließen.

Metz' Betonung der Brückenkategorie der Erzählung, die den für die Compassion nötigen Blickwechsel ermöglicht, sowie Stumps Unterscheidung von dominikanischem und franziskanischem Wissen liefern zusätzliche Grundlagen, die diese Lehrpraxis theoretisch fundieren können. Denn sie erlauben es, die Bedeutung von Narrativen strikt theologisch rückzubinden. Wenn der Gottesglaube auf ein interpersonales Geschehen abzielt – wie es die Rede vom Bund Gottes mit den Menschen ebenso insinuiert wie die Betonung der Einheit von Gottes- und Nächstenliebe –, dann sind narrative Vermittlungen nicht Illustration von etwas, das sich auch in präzisere Sprache übersetzen ließe, sondern die adäquate Ausdrucksform dieser Beziehung im Modus franziskanischen Wissens. „Und die Menschlichkeit Gottes verlangt wie jede Liebesgeschichte danach, erzählt zu werden [...]."[59]

Es geht im Blick auf diese Hinweise nicht darum, einen Zugang gegen den anderen auszuspielen oder prinzipiell für theologisch überlegen zu erklären, ebenso wenig wie narrative und argumentierende Sprache strikt in Opposition zu denken sind. Auch Metz hatte bereits betont: „Es gibt eine Zeit des Erzählens und eine Zeit des Argumentierens!"[60] Hinzu kommt, dass auch Erzählungen, so wie franziskanisches Wissen überhaupt,[61] selbst ideologieanfällig sein können. Gerade eine Theologie, die den Stellenwert von Narrativen zentral berücksichtigt, kann weiterhin Wert auf einen dominikanisch-argumentativen Zugang legen, nicht als Konkurrenten, sondern als Ergänzung, die auch Erzählungen noch einmal kritisch auf ihre Verlässlichkeit befragt und den hermeneutischen

---

56 Deshalb lässt sich die Reflexion auf Narrative mit tätiger Praxis verzahnen, wie sie im „Compassion-Projekt" angezielt ist. Vgl. dazu KULD, Lothar: Compassion. solidarisch handeln lernen, in: SAUTERMEISTER, Jochen / ZWICK, Elisabeth (Hg.): Religion und Bildung: Antipoden oder Weggefährten? Diskurse aus historischer, systematischer und praktischer Sicht, Paderborn: Schöningh, 2019, 321–335, der in seinem Text bezeichnenderweise auf die Erzählung von Lk 10 eingeht.

57 LANGENHORST, Georg: Literarische Texte im Religionsunterricht. Ein Handbuch für die Praxis, Freiburg im Breisgau: Herder, 2011, 60–61.

58 Ebd., 62–63.

59 JÜNGEL, Eberhard: Gott als Geheimnis der Welt. Zur Begründung der Theologie des Gekreuzigten im Streit zwischen Theismus und Atheismus, Tübingen: Mohr Siebeck, [7]2001, XV.

60 METZ 2016 [Anm.2], 221.

61 Vgl. STUMP 2010 [Anm. 21], 62.

Grundlagen nachdenkt, mit denen sich ihnen genähert wird. Eine Abqualifizierung von Erzählungen ist allerdings kein gangbarer theologischer Weg, sofern die dem Glauben eigene interpersonale Dimension nicht ignoriert werden soll. Für eine Praxis der Compassion, die sich müht, auf die Stimmen der Leidenden zu hören, ist sie unverzichtbar.

Literaturangaben

BREMER, Thomas: Kreuz und Kreml. Geschichte der orthodoxen Kirche in Russland, Freiburg im Breisgau: Herder, [2]2016.

ECKHOLT, Margit: „Compassion" und „Passion". Lateinamerikanische Theologie in der Nachfolge Jesu Christi, in: FISCHER, Irmtraud u. a. (Hg.): Mitleid und Mitleiden (= Jahrbuch für biblische Theologie 30), Göttingen: Vandenhoeck & Ruprecht, 2018, 323–350.

JACKSON, Frank: Epiphenomenal Qualia, in: The Philosophical Quarterly 32 (1982), 127–136.

JÜNGEL, Eberhard: Gott als Geheimnis der Welt. Zur Begründung der Theologie des Gekreuzigten im Streit zwischen Theismus und Atheismus, Tübingen: Mohr Siebeck, [7]2001.

KERMANI, Navid: Gott ist schön. Das ästhetische Erleben des Koran, München: Beck [4]2011.

KULD, Lothar: Compassion. solidarisch handeln lernen, in: SAUTERMEISTER, Jochen / ZWICK, Elisabeth (Hg.): Religion und Bildung. Antipoden oder Weggefährten? Diskurse aus historischer, systematischer und praktischer Sicht, Paderborn: Schöningh, 2019, 321–335.

KRONAU, Johannes / GRÖSSL, Johannes: Extra narrationem nulla salus. Perspektiven eines narrativitätstheoretischen Ansatzes für die christliche Soteriologie, in: MThZ 73/3 (2022), 230–245.

LANGENHORST, Georg: Literarische Texte im Religionsunterricht. Ein Handbuch für die Praxis, Freiburg im Breisgau: Herder 2011.

MAGGIONI, Pietro Lorenzo: Comparative Theology. A Fairy Tale. For an Ethics in Comparison, Rom: Aracne, 2018.

METZ, Johann Baptist: Glaube in Geschichte und Gesellschaft. Studien zu einer praktischen Fundamentaltheologie, in: DERS.: Gesammelte Schriften, hg. v. Johann Reikerstorfer, Freiburg im Breisgau: Herder, 2016 (= JBMGS 3/1).

METZ, Johann Baptist: „Politische Theologie" in der Diskussion (1969), in: DERS.: Gesammelte Schriften, hg. v. Johann Reikerstorfer, Freiburg im Breisgau: Herder, 2016 (= JBMGS 3/2), 27–60.

METZ, Johann Baptist: Unterwegs zu einer nachidealistischen Theologie (1985), in: JBMGS 3/2, 125–142.

METZ, Johann Baptist: Memoria passionis. Ein provozierendes Gedächtnis in pluralistischer Gesellschaft. In Zusammenarbeit mit Johann Reikerstorfer, in: DERS.: Gesammelte Schriften, hg. v. Johann Reikerstorfer, Freiburg im Breisgau: Herder, 2017 (= JBMGS 4).

METZ, Johann Baptist: Welches Christentum hat Zukunft? Dorothee Sölle und Johann Baptist Metz im Gespräch (1990), in: JBMGS 8, 138–160.

METZ, Johann Baptist: „Sis mihi Deus!" (2003), in: DERS.: Gesammelte Schriften, hg. v. Johann Reikerstorfer, Freiburg im Breisgau: Herder, 2017 (= JBMGS 8), 196–204.

METZ, Johann Baptist: „Aufwachen, Augen öffnen, Leid erkennen." (2003), in: JBMGS 8, 210–214.

MOYAERT, Marianne: In Response to the Religious Other. Ricœur and the Fragility of Interreligious Encounters, London: Lexington Books, 2014.

MOYAERT, Marianne: Towards a Ritual Turn in Comparative Theology. Opportunities, Challenges, and Problems, in: Harvard Theological Review 111/1 (2018), 1–23.
O'DONNELL, Emma: Methodological Considerations on the Role of Experience in Comparative Theology, in: CLOONEY, Francis / STOSCH, Klaus von: How to Do Comparative Theology, New York: Fordham University Press, 2018, 259–270.
RICOEUR, Paul: Stellung und Funktion der Metapher in der biblischen Sprache, in: DERS. / JÜNGEL, Eberhard: Metapher. Zur Hermeneutik religiöser Sprache (Sonderheft Evangelische Theologie), München: Kaiser, 1974, 45–70.
ROEBBEN, Bert / STOSCH, Klaus von: Religious Education and Comparative Theology. Creating Common Ground for Intercultural Encounters, in: Religions 13/11 (2022). DOI: https://doi.org/10.3390/rel13111014.
ROMMEL, Herbert: Lernen an „negativer Moral", in: LINDNER, Konstantin / ZIMMERMANN, Mirjam: Handbuch ethische Bildung, Tübingen: Mohr Siebeck, 2021, 326–332.
STOSCH, Klaus von: Komparative Theologie als Wegweiser in der Welt der Religionen (= Beiträge zur Komparativen Theologie 6), Paderborn: Schöningh, 2012.
STOSCH, Klaus von: Einführung in die Komparative Theologie, Paderborn: Schöningh, 2021.
STUMP, Eleonore: Wandering in Darkness. Narrative and the Problem of Suffering, Oxford: Clarendon Press, 2010.
THOMÄ, Dieter: Vom Nutzen und Nachteil der Erzählung für das Leben, in: JOISTEN, Karen (Hg.): Narrative Ethik. Das Gute und das Böse erzählen (= Deutsche Zeitschrift für Philosophie Sonderband 17), Berlin: Akademie Verlag, 2007, 75–93.
TILLEY, Terrence: Story Theology (= Theology and life series 12), Wilmington: Del. Glazier, 1985.
WEINRICH, Harald: Narrative Theologie, in: Concilium 9 (1973), 329–333.
WENZEL, Knut: Narrative Theologie revisited, in: Lebendige Seelsorge 70/6 (2019), 400–406.
ZIMMERMANN, Mirjam: Interreligiöses Lernen narrativ. Feste in den Weltreligionen, Göttingen: Vandenhoeck & Ruprecht, 2015.

Compassion in Pre-Health and Health Professional Education – Inspiration and Sustenance for Action[1]

Kathleen M. Clark & Alexander Rödlach

In diesem Kapitel wird auf der Grundlage des Metz'schen Compassion-Konzepts beschrieben, wie Studierende in der Gesundheitsvorbereitung und in den Gesundheitsberufen angeleitet werden können, Mitgefühl zu kultivieren und eine mitfühlende Antwort auf die Ziele für nachhaltige Entwicklung der Vereinten Nationen zu geben. Die Autor*innen gehen davon aus, dass dies (1) eine Ökologie des Mitgefühls in der Ausbildung, (2) eine Reflexion der Studierenden über Werte, die die berufliche Praxis prägen, (3) eine Mentor*innenschaft zur Verbesserung der Fähigkeiten für gesellschaftliches Engagement, das sich mit den Ursachen von Krankheit und Einschränkungen in der Gesundheitsversorgung befasst, und (4) eine (An-)Teilnahme der Studierenden in das Leben derjenigen, die mit Krankheit kämpfen, erfordert.

Compassion-Learning; Ziele für nachhaltige Entwicklung; gesellschaftliches Engagement; Ökologie des Mitgefühls; integriertes Lernen

This chapter describes, informed by Metz's concept of compassion, how to guide pre-health and health professional students to cultivate compassion and compassionate response to the United Nations' Sustainable Development Goals. The authors posit that this requires (1) ecologies of compassion in educational settings, (2) student reflection on values that inform professional practice, (3) mentorship to hone skills for civic engagement that addresses root causes of ill health and healthcare limitations, and (4) student immersion into the lives of those struggling with illness.

Compassion-Learning; Sustainable Development Goals; Citizen Professional; Ecology of Empathy; Immersive Learning

Introduction[2]

We are faculty at two faith-based universities in the American Midwest that have a strong emphasis on academic programs related to health and healthcare. Clark is Nursing faculty at the Lutheran Augsburg University, teaching graduate students in Nursing Practice and serving as the executive director of the Augsburg

1 The authors are grateful to Dr. Timothy Cook, Professor of Education at Creighton University, who provided thoughtful feedback on a draft of this chapter.

2 As the two authors are in the United States, this chapter uses U.S. American English.

Health Commons, a nurse-led drop-in center that provides basic care for marginalized people in mostly urban settings. Rödlach is a Medical Anthropologist at the Jesuit and Catholic Creighton University, teaching undergraduate courses for students in pre-health professional programs who aspire to a professional career in healthcare. We have collaborated on research exploring the effectiveness of mission, vision, and value statements that motivated us to further study the role of compassion education in pre-health and health professional programs, drawing from Metz's definition of compassion.[3] Metz is a Catholic priest and theologian whose theory of compassion[4] is relevant for compassion education, as it calls for expanding students' awareness of suffering (cognitive component), increasing their sympathetic emotional response to suffering (intentional component), igniting their desire to see the relief of that suffering (intentional component), and developing their readiness to alleviate others' pain (motivational component).[5] The theological framework of Metz's understanding of compassion has been particularly relevant for faith-based universities such as ours that want to "transform society through willing the good of all"[6] by educating "students to be informed citizens, thoughtful stewards, critical thinkers, and responsible leaders."[7] A focus on the United Nations' Sustainable Development Goals[8] (SDGs) is appropriate to guide our reflections on strategies to integrate compassion education into our courses, curricular events, immersive programs, and student-led research to assist aspiring and current healthcare providers to be compassionate professionals.

We first briefly summarize the scholarship on compassion education that informs our approach, followed by a discussion of a compassionate approach to the SDGs. Then we discuss the conceptual framework of the "citizen health professional," arguing that compassionate civic engagement, exemplified through

---

3 Metz, Johann Baptist: In Memory of the Other's Suffering. Theological Reflections on the Future of Faith and Culture. translated by Peter Kenny, in: Pierce, Andrew / Smyth, Geraldyne (Hg.): The Critical Spirit. Theology at the Crossroads of Faith and Culture, Dublin: Columbia Press, 2003, 179–188.

4 Arens, Edmund: Gottespassion und Compassion. Zum Tod von Johann Baptist Metz, 2019, in: Feinschwarz – Theologisches Feuilleton, December 3. https://www.feinschwarz.net/nachruf-j-b-metz/ (last accessed on 24.02.2023).

5 Jazaieri, Hooria: Compassionate Education from Preschool to Graduate School. Bringing a Culture of Compassion into the Classroom, in: Journal of Research in Innovative Teaching and Learning 2018 11(1), 22–66.

6 Creighton University: A Jesuit Education that Leads to a Life Well-Lived. Our Mission, 2022, in: https://www.creighton.edu/arts-sciences/about/about-our-mission (last accessed: 15.11.2022).

7 Augsburg University: The Augsburg Mission, 2010, in: https://www.augsburg.edu/about/mission/ (last accessed on 10.03.2022).

8 United Nations: The Sustainable Development Goals 2015, in: https://www.un.org/millenniumgoals/2015_MDG_Report/pdf/MDG%202015%20rev%20(July%201).pdf (last accessed on 13.12.2022).

the Citizen Nurse, is integral to pre-health and health professional education and foundational to teaching the SDGs. Afterward, we situate our approach within the broader context of compassionate educational institutions. Finally, we discuss some pedagogical tools that we employ to mentor students in developing compassion and a compassionate approach to the SDGs. A concluding section summarizes our thoughts.

Compassion Education

Since the turn of the century, compassion has increasingly been described as a necessary component of education and has more frequently been referenced in educational texts and curricular initiatives,[9] including in pre-health and health professional education. A growing body of scholarship discusses the teaching of compassion in and through informal and formal education, arguing that every level of formal schooling should nurture students' ability to identify with the suffering of others and conceptualizes the association of educators with students as a compassionate relationship.[10] Education scholars point out that young people are already compassionate in many and varied ways before they start schooling.[11] They have developed compassion through a wide range of social processes in other sociocultural units, such as families, religious units, and civic groups, before entering an educational setting.[12]

Nevertheless, formal education is a crucial mechanism for cultivating compassion.[13] Compassion can be taught, learned, and honed through explicit and direct teaching, as well as a wide range of implicit educational processes using a variety of pedagogical practices, such as simulations, role play, and narratives.[14] Narratives, whether in the form of literary works or personal testimonies, are valuable tools for mentoring students to learn from the moral perspectives, characteristics, and actions of others, as well as their mistakes, successes, and

---

9 PETERSON, Andrew: Compassion and Education. Cultivating Compassionate Children, Schools, and Communities, London: Palgrave Macmillan, 2017, 1–12.

10 NUSSBAUM, Martha: Compassion: The Basic Social Emotion, in: Social Philosophy and Policy 1996, 13, 27–58; WHITE, Richard: Compassion in Philosophy and Education, in: GIBBS, Paul (Hg.): The Pedagogy of Compassion at the Heart of Higher Education, Cham: Springer, 2017, 19–32.

11 PETERSON [note 9].

12 ANNAS, Julia: Intelligent Virtue, Oxford: Oxford University Press, 2011; KRISTJANSSON, Kristján: Phronesis as an Ideal in Professional Medical Ethics. Some Preliminary Positionings and Problematics, in: Theoretical Medicine and Bioethics 2015 36(5), 299–320.

13 PETERSON [note 9].

14 NODDINGS, Nel: The Challenge to Care in Schools. An Alternative Approach to Education, 2nd Edition, New York: Teachers College Press, 2005.

limitations.[15] However, while young people may present an empathetic response in a pedagogical exercise, this may lack sincerity. Further, students can perceive compassion as an obligation without the authentic feelings and actions of care for the wellbeing of others, which Cartwright calls "compulsory compassion".[16] To further complicate compassion education, observers warn of the danger of compassion being inappropriately used to refer to any feelings or acts that could be conceived of as good, caring, or kind without critically analyzing what compassion requires us to do.[17]

Compassion education is particularly relevant for the helping professions,[18] for which compassion is an essential professional trait. For instance, compassion is an integral feature of healthcare, a cornerstone of healthcare ethics, and the best indicator of patient satisfaction.[19] Further, compassion is associated with lower burnout rates and improved provider well-being.[20] Educators in health professional programs are increasingly expected to embed aspects of compassion into curricula. For example, as the International Council of Nursing identified compassion as one of its core values,[21] Nursing educators have been exploring strategies to foster compassion in care, often focusing on effective learning for students to encourage compassionate care.[22] The American Association of Colleges of Nursing's accreditation organization lists compassion care as a required concept in curricula for a university to become accredited.[23] Yet studies indicate that patients report that compassion has been missing in their care.[24]

---

15 ZAGZEBSKI, Linda: Moral Exemplars in Theory and Practice, in: Theory and Research in Education 2013 11(2), 193–206.

16 Representations of the Child, Durham: Duke University Press, 2008.

17 PETERSON [note 9].

18 A helping profession is any profession that nurtures the growth of a person, such as medicine, nursing, counseling, social work, education, spiritual direction, and life coaching.

19 SINCLAIR, Shane et al.: What Is the State of Compassion Education? A Systematic Review of Compassion Training in Health Care, in: Academic Medicine 2021 96(7), 1057–1070.

20 PATEL, Sundip et al.: Curricula for Empathy and Compassion Training in Medical Education. A Systematic Review, in: PLoS ONE 2019 14(8): e0221412.

21 INTERNATIONAL COUNCIL OF NURSES: The ICN Code of Ethics for Nurses. Geneva: International Council of Nurses, 2021.

22 YOUNAS, Ahtisham / MADDIGAN, Joy: Proposing a Policy Framework for Nursing Education for Fostering Compassion in Nursing Students. A Critical Review, in: Journal of Advanced Nursing (2018) 75, 1621–1636.

23 AMERICAN ASSOCIATION OF COLLEGES OF NURSING: Compassionate Care Concept Across Multiple Domains, 2014, in: https://www.aacnnursing.org/Essentials/Database/Kit/i/C_Comp_Care_PDF (last accessed on 24.02.2023).

24 AIKEN, Linda et.al.: Nurse Staffing and education and hospital mortality in nine european countries – a retrospective observational study, in: lancet 2014, 383(9931), 1824–1830. BRAY, Lucy / O'BRIAN, Mary / KIRTON, Jennifer / ZUBAIRU, Kate / CHRISTIANSEN, Angela: The Role of Professional Education in Developing Compassionate Practitioners. A Mixed Methods Study Exploring the Perceptions of Health Professionals and Pre-Registration Students, in: Nurse Education Today, 2014, 34(3), 480–486.

Overall, observers conclude that healthcare is experiencing a compassion crisis, an absence of or inconsistency in compassionate patient care.[25]

We have so far used "compassion" without clearly defining the term and distinguishing it from related concepts. Following Aristotle, Thomas Aquinas and Augustine of Hippo defined compassion as co-suffering.[26] Compassion is a cognitive, emotional, and volitional response to the suffering of others, based on a recognition and appreciation of our common humanity that results in an empathetic response, motivating actions in support of sufferers.[27] Defined as such, compassion is different from "sympathy," which refers to caring about other people's suffering, or "empathy," which refers to identifying with the suffering of others. Both sympathy and empathy are constituent elements of compassion but do not include the wish to act. In contrast, compassion not only refers to affectionate aspects but also implies effective aspects, wanting to help another person and improve the social and cultural conditions faced by the suffering person.[28] Metz associates compassion with *memoria passionis, mortis, et resurrectionis Jesu Christi*,[29] which he considers a liberating memory because it aligns Jesus' suffering with the pain of humanity, recognizing the bond between all people, and his suffering and death with his resurrection, relating human suffering with attempts to overcome it. *Memoria*[30] inspires us to empathize and be in solidarity with and take the side of those who suffer and sends us to the front lines of political, social, and cultural conflicts.[31] Compassion for Metz integrates the care for suffering individuals with addressing the root causes of their suffering, supporting their liberation and furthering justice.[32]

This understanding transcends denominational and religious contexts. With national and international organizations, such as the United Nations and the

---

25 Patel et al. 2019 [note 20].

26 Bein, Steve: Compassion and Moral Guidance, Honolulu: University of Hawai'i Press, 2013, 1–49.

27 Peterson [note 9], 1–3.

28 Bosnjakovic, Josip: Compassion. An Expression of Charity in Treatment of Physical and Mental Illness in Individuals and Communities, in: Psychiatria Danubina 2021. 33(4), 902–910.

29 Translation: memory of Christ's passion, death, and resurrection.

30 Translation: memory

31 Metz [mote 3].

32 Habermas, Jürgen: Letter to Johann Baptist Metz on His 90th Birthday. translated by John Downey 2018, in: https://johannbaptistmetz.com/wp-content/uploads/2020/08/Letter-to-Johann-Baptist-Metz-on-his-90th-Birthday.pdf (last accessed on 12.28.2022); Haker, Hille: Compassion as a Global Programme for Christianity, in: Concilium 2001 4, 55–7; Metz, Johann Baptist: Facing the World. A Theological and Biographical Inquiry, in: Theological Studies 2014 75(1), 23–33; Sobrino, Jon: Johann Baptist Metz's Theology and the Theology of Liberation. translated by John Downey, 2018, in: https://johannbaptistmetz.com/wp-content/uploads/2020/ 08/Sobrino-Letter-1.pdf (last accessed on 09.11.2022).

World Health Organization, paying increased attention to compassion in responding to human suffering, Metz's definition of compassion is relevant for programs educating future healthcare providers.[33]

A Compassionate Approach to the Sustainable Development Goals

The United Nations General Assembly (UNGA) adopted the Millennium Development Goals (MDGs) in 2000 to "spare no effort to free our fellow men, women and children from the abject and dehumanizing conditions of extreme poverty" and "to create an environment – at the national and global levels alike – which is conducive to development."[34] While these goals resulted in remarkable gains, improving the well-being and health of millions of people,[35] progress has been uneven and inequalities persist.[36] The UNGA adopted the SDGs in 2015 to succeed the MDGs.[37] They serve as a blueprint for peace and prosperity, putting sustainability at their center and adding an emphasis on climate change.[38]

Yet, the gap between rich and poor continues to grow, and the social conditions that put people at high risk of ill health persist and even worsen.[39] Observers and analysts call for a comprehensive review of these conditions and the health systems responding to their consequences, emphasizing that health systems need to build on global solidarity, which is fundamental to achieving the SDGs.[40] Such calls for solidarity increase the relevance of Metz's understanding of compassion, which implies solidarity to further an equitable distribution of

---

33 World Health Organization: Policy Levers to Enhance Health Workforce Performance for Compassionate and Respectful Care, Geneva: World Health Organization, 2021.

34 United Nations: United Nations: Millennium Declaration, New York: United Nations General Assembly, 2020, in: https://www.ohchr.org/en/instruments-mechanisms/instruments/united-nations-millennium-declaration (last accessed on 14.12.2022).

35 Yong Kim, Jim et al.: Dying for Growth. Global Inequity and the Health of the Poor, in: The International Journal of African Historical Studies 2002, 185–187; United Nations [note 8].

36 Marmot, Michael: The Health Gap – The Challenge of an Unequal World, London: Bloomsbury Publishing, 2015.

37 United Nations [note 8].

38 United Nations Development Programme: New Threats to Human Security in the Anthropocene. Demanding Greater Solidarity, 2022, in: https://hs.hdr.undp.org/pdf/srhs2022.pdf (last accessed on 13.12.2022).

39 Henry, Patrick: Economic Inequality Has Deepened During the Pandemic. That Doesn't Mean It Can't Be Fixed, in: The European Sting - Your Political Newspager 2022, April 7, in: https://europeansting.com/2022/04/07/economic-inequality-has-deepened-during-the-pandemic-that-doesnt-mean-it-cant-be-fixed/ (last accessed on 24.02.2023).

40 United Nations Development Programme [note 46].

resources to promote global well-being and health. Further, a recent report in *The Lancet* named compassion a missing component of the SDGs:

> The experience of a common humanity leads us to compassion and creates a space for trust and care. [...] Compassion is about coming together to alleviate suffering and nurture human flourishing. These two ideas - intentional togetherness and suffering - are at the heart of the SDGs.[41]

This explicitly aligns with Metz's understanding of compassion, which implies a recognition of our shared humanity and a commitment to overcome human suffering and constraints to human flourishing in solidarity. Further, an understanding of common or shared humanity suggests equality among humans, underscoring the importance of engaging with each other as equals, learning about suffering through the eyes of the sufferers, and addressing suffering and its root causes *with* others and not just *for* them. This entails the creation of personal and reciprocal relationships, which go far beyond more formal partnerships.[42] Metz's understanding of compassion critiques top-down and paternalistic approaches to the SDGs, common in international aid and philanthropic capitalism, joining the voices of development and economic scholars and commentators.[43]

As many of the MDGs and SDGs have an explicit or implicit association with health and wellbeing, Clark and Rödlach's courses, curricular events, programs, and research with students familiarize students with the SDGs through the lens of compassion, discuss empathetic responses to ill health related to the SDGs, and identify sustainable ways to work toward justice by addressing root causes of ill health, the so-called social and cultural determinants of health. The following section presents a model of healthcare professionals who, following Metz, provide compassionate care and work toward justice.

The Compassionate Citizen Professional

Metz is explicit that compassion not only aims to alleviate the immediate pain of the sufferer, but also addresses the cultural, political, economic, and other root causes of suffering. Thus, healthcare providers must learn to provide care

41 GRANT, Liz et al.: A Compassion Narrative for the Sustainable Development Goals. Conscious and Connected Action, in: Lancet 2022, 400 (10345), 7–8.

42 ESTEVA, Gustavo / BABONES, Salvatore / BABICICKY, Philipp: The Future of Development. A Radical Manifesto, Bristol: Policy Press, 2013.

43 MOYO, Dambisa: Fifty Years of Economic Folly – And the Stark Choices Ahead, New York: Farrar, Strauss, and Giroux, 2011; DALRYMPLE, Theodore: Aid, Colonialism, and Corruption, 2010, in: https://www.povertycure.org/learn/media/theodore-dalrymple-aid-colonialism-corruption (last accessed on 25.02.2023); SEN, Amartya: Poverty and Famines. An Essay on Entitlement and Deprivation, Oxford: Oxford University Press, 2023.

through action-oriented compassion that recognizes the legacy of historical and current sociocultural conditions that harm those entrusted into their care. Compassion requires healthcare providers to have the knowledge and skills needed to identify and challenge these conditions, particularly unjust social norms and healthcare practices that marginalize individuals, expose them to high risks of ill health, and prevent them from getting the care they need. Clark and her colleagues at Augsburg University developed a concept to describe politically engaged professionals who actively participate in democratic processes that identify root causes of suffering, frame them as unjust and immoral, and inspire collaboration with others to address suffering through the lens of compassion. Familiarizing students with this concept of a compassionate citizen health professional guides them to provide compassionate care and to participate in the creation of cultural, political, economic, and other structures that keep people healthy and enable them to get the care they need if they fall ill. This concept is illustrated through the Citizen Nurse, which has characteristics that can be applied to other professionals in healthcare.

In 2010, Nursing faculty members at Augsburg University worked with community organizers to revise the Nursing curriculum by identifying the skills that Nursing students need to develop to provide effective, culturally respectful, and socially appropriate care. These attempts to reform the curriculum were initiated by faculty who noticed that students nearing graduation often focus on clinical expertise in their chosen field and fulfilling their clinical responsibilities in the work setting only. This narrow clinical gaze reduces students' professional responsibility for the health of those entrusted to their care and ignores their responsibility to work collaboratively with others to solve systemic issues within healthcare systems, the local community, and society. Students also identified this responsibility gap and voiced their frustration with learning about human suffering due to historical, political, and cultural conditions but not getting the skills to change them. Students expressed their concern that political action had not been sufficiently integrated into their professional identity. Such feedback from students underscores the importance of civic skills for future healthcare providers, including Nurses and Nurse Practitioners, and the need to weave civic skills as a learning objective into the Nursing curriculum. This speaks to Metz's understanding of compassion as political action. He stated, "Compassion is not only for our private lives but also for our public, political lives."[44] The suffering of others should lead to civic and political engagement to change disease-generating structures and organizational and social arrangements. Civic engagement of compassionate healthcare providers should be a priority for educational programs. The Nursing curriculum at Augsburg University strives to teach students the skills needed to be effective as Citizen Nurses, which is an example of a compassionate Citizen Healthcare Provider.

---

44 METZ [note 37], 31.

Clark and her colleagues described Citizen Nurses as nurses who "are deeply connected to individuals as co-creators of change through invested public work that is both meaningful and timely. Citizen Nurses realize the importance of de-emphasizing the expert models to form purposeful relationships for the common good and practice from a social justice framework".[45] This concept is at the heart of the community organizing efforts that have been incorporated into the Nursing coursework and mirror many of the values Metz described related to compassion, such as taking action or engaging politically.

In 2022, more than a decade after the curricular changes, the changes to the curriculum were evaluated by interviewing students and alums to understand whether these changes had addressed the concerns raised by faculty, students, and community organizers, and to review strategies adopted to guide students to be Citizen Nurses. All interviewees reported that the concept of the Citizen Nurse has changed their worldview, their understanding of healthcare, and how they approach their professional practice. For example, they reported having a robust understanding of the negative impact of health inequities on people's health and the need to have strong civic skills to improve public health and healthcare systems. They also stated that their sense of professional responsibility expanded beyond a focus on an individual patient to also include the social units and communities of which the patient is a part. They underscored the importance of being responsible *with*, not just *for*, those for whom they care. The transformations students experienced can be illustrated through a quote from one of the interviews:

> My view of being a nurse has changed dramatically since I came to Augsburg. [...] The biases that they teach, [such as] about racism as a public health crisis, and transcultural nursing, just seeing the bigger picture of historical trauma and seeing the world as a whole [...] and bringing you into the community and actually engaging with [...] community members and talking to them and seeing them and learning from them [are meaningful].

Overall, the curricular emphasis on the Citizen Nurse has been effective in enabling students to understand that compassion in Nursing refers not only to clinical care for individual patients, but also implies civic engagement to change, together with the affected communities, the cultural, political, social and other structures that result in negative health outcomes. While not necessarily the initial focus of this curricular change, the emphasis on the compassionate Citizen Nurse and other Citizen Healthcare Providers inspired students to reflect on compassionate health systems and higher education. The latter will be further discussed in the following section.

45 CLARK, Kathleen et al.: The Citizen Nurse: An Educational Innovation for Change, in: Journal of Nursing Education 2017, 54(4), 247–250.

Education's Compassionate Ecology

In today's demand-driven colleges and universities, education is conceptualized primarily as a private good and its character is transactional, with students exchanging tuition payments for credentials that are a means towards procuring salaried employment and a mechanism for social mobility.[46] This starkly contrasts with the ideal that education is a public good, meant to form virtuous leaders for public service and engaged citizens. It is a time for students to reflect, reconsider, and grow as they shift their thinking and develop skills to practice democratic skills in everyday life. Cultivating compassion for those suffering makes much sense when education is considered a public good, yet it creates difficulty when education is commodified as a private good. The model that decision-makers in an institution of higher learning prioritize determines what metrics and processes are used to evaluate curricula, learning outcomes, and performance indicators.[47] For the transactional and demand-driven model, these do not likely pay attention to compassion in an authentic and meaningful manner, while such a focus is probably central in the transformational and civic model. The resulting "compassion gaps"[48] in demand-driven and transactional higher education are often brushed under the carpet by administrators, whose prime objective often is increasing revenue and balancing budgets. In many instances, this objective may clash with the institution's mission statements. Our research on the effectiveness of such statements for doctoral programs in Nursing Practice at three universities in the American Midwest indicates that students quickly recognize an institution's priorities, compare these with the school's mission, vision, and value statements, and identify the statements' disconnect with administrators' priorities, often becoming frustrated and cynical with the mismatch of the values of the institution with what really matters for decision-makers. They recognize that university funds are more likely to go to programs that primarily serve the institution and not to programs that compassionately support communities and help students to develop a compassionate response to human suffering. Students conclude that the university tends to be self-interested and self-serving, does not show leadership in recognizing and responding to suffering, and is unwilling to develop genuine and reciprocal rela-

---

46 FISCHMAN, Wendy / GARDNER Howard: Mission Possible. What Higher Education Is and What It Can Be, in: Trusteeship 2022 30(6), 12–19; MAXWELL, Bruce: Pursuing the Aim of Compassionate Empathy in Higher Education, in: GIBBS, Paul (Hg.): The Pedagogy of Compassion at the Heart of Higher Education, Cham: Springer, 2017, 33–48.

47 BALLATT, John / CAMPLING, Penelope: Intelligent Kindness. Reforming the Culture of Healthcare, London: RCPsych Publications, 2011.

48 WADDINGTON, Kathryn: The Compassion Gap in UK Universities, in: International Practice Development Journal 2016 6(1), 1–9, 2.

tionships and partnerships with the marginalized in its surrounding communities. An institution's "real" priorities represent the context that impinges on academic programs, curricula, individual courses, and curricular programs and events. The latter may include compassion education, but such teaching is challenged and compromised by the "compassion gaps" in the institution. However, our research also suggests that if faculty and staff are role models of compassion, students are likely to develop compassion, despite the institution's compassion gaps. Students who are passionate about the mission and values of the university also recognize when individual faculty and programs are genuinely aligned with the mission and values and are likely to identify with them and their work. With faculty who are good role models of compassion, education for compassion becomes credible and effective even without an institutional "ecology of compassion."[49]

We want to illustrate this through an example. The SDGs call for urgent action to combat climate change and its impacts.[50] The urgency of action is heightened as the world already experiences the effects of climate change, negatively impacting human health and health systems in myriad ways, increasing the severity and frequency of ill health episodes, escalating the burden on health systems and providers, and resulting in human suffering on an immense scale.[51] Students at Creighton University recognized the urgency of action, inspired by what they learned in a wide range of courses offered by various departments, including Rödlach's Global Health course. Students are aware that a compassionate response is needed to adopt a sustainable approach to address climate change and the resulting human suffering. Like other universities in the United States, Creighton University also relies on investments for generating revenue to pay for its operations, provide scholarships to students, and support other areas that require funding. Some of the university's investments are in fossil fuel industry stocks. Such investments support the fossil fuel-burning industries, contribute to climate change, and are in clear contradiction to what students hear and learn in various courses. Students are astutely aware of climate change's association with burning fossil fuels and how it increases human suffering, including by triggering ill health. As students in Rödlach's Global Health course discussed climate change, students referred to the university's complicity in climate change through its investments in fossil fuel industry stocks. They expressed their frustration that the faith-based Catholic institution continues

---

49 FROST, Peter et al.: Emotions in Organizations, London: Sage, 2000; GIBBS, Paul: Higher Education. A Compassion Business or Edifying Experience, in: GIBBS, Paul (Hg.): The Pedagogy of Compassion at the Heart of Higher Education, Cham: Springer, 2017, 8.

50 UNITED NATIONS [note 8].

51 COMMONWEALTH FUND: The Impact of Climate Change on Our Health and Health Systems, 2022, in: https://www.commonwealthfund.org/publications/explainer/2022/may/impact-climate-change-our-health-and-health-systems (last accessed on 23.02. 2023).

investing in stocks accelerating climate change. Instead, they argue, the university should, inspired by Pope Francis's encyclical *Laudato Si' – On Care for our Common Home*[52], as well as the Jesuit's adoption of "caring for our common home" as one of its apostolic preferences,[53] take steps to curb climate change, e.g., through divesting from fossil fuel industry stocks. Such frustrations complicated conversations in the Global Health class about the SDGs, climate change, and compassionate and sustainable responses to create a healthy future for humanity but also led to a recognition of the democratic engagement with the institution to push for change. While the administration and the board of trustees appeared to fail in creating an "ecology of compassion," according to Metz's understanding of compassion, student-driven efforts were highly effective and ultimately pushed the administration to commit, despite its initial reluctance, to phase out all investments in fossil fuels from its endowments within 10 years and to invest instead in sustainable energy.[54] This decision came more than two years after students began pressuring the school leadership. Students pointed out the institution's hypocrisy, failing to translate its mission and values into appropriate action, highlighted ties of some board members to the fossil fuel industry, identified problematic donations to the school from a foundation, a major backer of climate change denial campaigns and rollbacks of fossil fuel regulations, and laid out convincing arguments supporting divestment. Students led a demonstration from the campus church to the university's College of Business, the main recipient of the foundation donations. They named and shamed board members and called for change. They produced a video showing the broad support of students across campus and summarizing the core arguments for divestment.[55] Some participated in a campus panel discussion on climate change and a faculty meeting in the College of Arts and Sciences. One student laid out various arguments for divestment and called for support. The president of the university's Student Union told the attending faculty the following: "You taught us to be critical thinkers that led us to understand the urgency of action and the need to divest. You taught us to be women and men for and with others and divestment is an expression of being for and with others!"[56] The participation of faculty in some of these events, including two Jesuit priests in the department of Biology and the

52 FRANCIS: Laudato Si' – On Care For Our Common Home, Vatican City: Vatican Publishing House, 2015.

53 JESUITS: Universal Apostolic Preferences 2019, in: https://www.jesuits.global/uap/ (last accessed on 01.14.2023).

54 ROEWE, Brian: Creighton University to Divest Fully from Fossil Fuels within 10 Years, in: National Catholic Reporter, January 5, 2021, in: https://www.ncronline.org/earthbeat/justice/creighton-university-divest-fully-fossil-fuels-within-10-years (last accessed on 16.12.2022).

55 MIKEG PRODUCTIONS: Creighton University Fossil Fuel Divestment, October 28, 2019, in: https://www.youtube.com/watch?v=Ktl4M-RSw4s (last accessed on 12.07.2023).

56 "Women and men for and with others" is one of the guiding values of a Jesuit institution of higher learning.

Anthropology programs, highlighted the support of many faculty for this student-driven work but also the disconnect between them and the administration. To conclude, while the administration failed in this instance to support an "ecology of compassion," students succeeded. We want to underscore that this is just a single example, and we don't imply that the university consistently and generally failed to create an ecology of compassion. We selected this example because of its association with the SDGs, illustrating the complexity of teaching compassion and the importance of institutions creating a culture and ecology of compassion. This example also illustrates the importance of faculty as role models of compassion and supporters of students. Teaching compassion is possible and can be effective. The next section discusses selected pedagogical strategies that Clark and Rödlach successfully employed to help students develop a compassionate response to human suffering.

Fostering Compassion in Students

At Augsburg University, Nursing is taught at the undergraduate and graduate levels by focusing on Transcultural Nursing, which integrates Nursing with Medical Anthropology and provides immersion experiences both locally and globally that emphasize holistic health, diverse cultural healing and caregiving traditions, and civic engagement to foster the development of a just and compassionate health system. At Creighton University, the undergraduate program in medical anthropology offers courses that challenge students to think critically about health and healthcare, adopt a holistic approach to health and care, recognize that national health systems influence and are influenced by global health-related realities, and develop foundational dispositions and skills to promote culturally appropriate care, health equity, and a compassionate and merciful health system. We will now discuss three pedagogical approaches that Clark and Rödlach successfully employed, using the lens of compassion in relation to the SDGs.

The first example is Rödlach's Global Health course, the core course in Creighton's undergraduate minor in Global Health Equity, developed by Rödlach. The minor includes courses that describe health-related suffering based on the SDGs and outline healthcare responses to such suffering. However, courses familiarizing students with moral and value frameworks that motivate such responses and frame them in terms of justice are integral to the minor. The minor and the Global Health course encourage a compassionate response to human suffering, inspired by Metz and the anthropologist and physician Paul

Farmer, who calls for mercy and compassion in healthcare and Global Health,[57] and who co-authored a textbook in Global Health that helps students to develop a compassionate response to ill health.[58] This textbook adopts an approach that first familiarizes students with global health issues in light of historical legacies and current sociocultural realities that expose some to higher risk of ill health than is faced by others. This so-called biosocial or biocultural approach focuses students' attention on the broader context of ill health, the SDGs, and determinants of health.[59] Then students interrogate the role of values in Global Health, such as health-for-all,[60] and moral frameworks that motivate practitioners, researchers, policymakers, educators, and others to take up Global Health work, such as utilitarianism, cosmopolitanism, the capabilities approach, human rights approaches, and religious frameworks. Students discuss these in small groups in class, being encouraged to reflect on the values and worldview that inform their relationships with others, their desire or lack of desire to address human suffering caused by ill health, and their actual or intended involvement in alleviating it. As the university is rooted in the Catholic tradition, religious and spiritual frameworks are extensively discussed. Taking significant time to reflect has been invaluable for students' discernment. Reflections in class form the foundation for discussing a specific approach to responding to human suffering: accompaniment. This concept was formulated by Liberation Theology and introduced into Global Health by Paul Farmer and his colleagues.[61] Accompaniment encourages students to engage in relationships of equality with those who suffer ill health caused by disease-generating conditions, learn from those they are in relationships with about their concerns and priorities, and develop strategies with them to address these concerns and priorities. This approach is deeply personal, relational, reciprocal, and long-term. As students' lives are transitional, they cannot easily adopt accompaniment. However, according to the feedback that Rödlach received, students passionate about a compassionate response to addressing human suffering caused by ill health begin framing their professional aspirations in healthcare through accompaniment. They recognize the importance of developing personal and reciprocal relationships to deeply

---

57 Farmer, Paul: We Know How to Confront the Coronavirus Pandemic – Expert Mercy, In: Boston Globe 2020, March 19, in: https://www.bostonglobe.com/2020/03/19/opinion/we-know-how-confront-coronavirus-pandemic-expert-mercy/ (last accessed on 15.01.2023).

58 Farmer, Paul et al.: Reimagining Global Health. An Introduction, Berkeley: University of California Press, 2013.

59 Wiley, Andrea / Allen, John: Medical Anthropology. A Biocultural Approach, Oxford: Oxford University Press, [4]2020.

60 Pandey, Kiran Raj: From Health For All to Universal Health Coverage. Alma Ata is Still Relevant, in: Global Health 2018 14(62).

61 Griffin, Michael / Weiss Block, Jennie: In the Company of the Poor. Conversations between Dr. Paul Farmer and Father Gustavo Gutierrez, Maryknoll: Orbis Books, 2013.

understand ill health, its causes, and how it affects individuals and whole communities. They notice the privileges that buffer them against ill health and the structural realities that expose others to a high risk of falling ill. They acknowledge that they must give up their privileges and make themselves vulnerable to ameliorate suffering effectively. They recognize that values and a moral framework help them to acknowledge their shared humanity with those who suffer, share the pain of suffering with them, motivate them to become involved in soothing their suffering, and become actively involved in caring for them and changing disease-generating conditions. They understand Metz's understanding of compassion and are inspired by Farmer's statement that health systems should strive to be merciful and compassionate.[62]

The second example is immersive programs in Augsburg University's Nursing program, such as local immersive trips to Native American reservations, study abroad programs to Guatemala, Mexico, Namibia, and other countries, and the Augsburg Central Health Commons (ACHC). Eighty percent of students surveyed by Clark[63] said the immersion experiences, such as at the ACHC, had the greatest impact on their learning. In 1992, some Nursing faculty created this health-focused drop-in center in partnership with Central Lutheran Church in downtown Minneapolis. Clark is its current executive director. Most people seeking care at the ACHC are experiencing homelessness or are precariously housed, resulting from the unfortunate consequences of living in an unequal world. The SDGs can frame much of their health, social, and other struggles. They are considered guests at the ACHC, a space where compassionate care is provided, a sense of community and belonging is created, and mutual learning happens for all stakeholders. The guests can meet one-on-one with a Nurse to discuss health-related questions or receive material support from the Nursing faculty, students, and community volunteers. While recognizing the guests' needs, the faculty and students also witness their strengths and resilience in the face of adversity. The hope is that all involved build mutually beneficial relationships with each other, based on the recognition of humanness in each other. As the ACHC is integrated into the Nursing curriculum, it helps with "engaging students in learning moments and allowing them to begin to understand how to decode systems of oppression that contribute to injustices."[64] Faculty, students, volunteers, and guests are together on a journey of health, during which they accompany one another and find ways to engage in joint "action based on solidarity and mutual problem-solving."[65] Students learn during this program that

---

62 FARMER [note 69].

63 CLARK, Kathleen: Evaluating Student Learning: Community-Based Nursing Education as Action to Address Inequities, in: Journal of Nursing Education 2022, 61(9), 525–527.

64 ENESTVEDT, Ruth et al.: Caring in the Margins. A Scholarship of Accompaniment for Advanced Transcultural Nursing Practice, in: Advances in Nursing Science 2018, 41(3), 230.

65 Ibid., 240.

suffering can only be sufficiently understood by paying attention to the voices of those who suffer and can only be appropriately addressed with them as equals with all stakeholders at the decision-making table. Students' immersive learning in this space about care based on the community's expressed needs and acknowledging the systemic social, cultural, political, economic, and other issues that contribute to the marginalization and ill health of these communities helps them to process what they learn in the classroom about the SDGs and develop a compassionate response to human suffering.

A systematic analysis of students' learning outcomes confirmed that students learned during the ACHC experience to reflect on and challenge their personal biases, develop an appreciation of the importance of connecting with others on a human scale, hone their skills to build relationships of equality and respect with the marginalized, and build skills to successfully work toward needed change in our society to prevent human suffering.[66] Students also commented that the ACHC helped them to recognize human suffering, desire to provide care, and become actively involved in addressing the determinants of health. One student stated that the ACHC experience "increased my compassion and gave me skills to be a change-maker for my marginalized neighbors."[67] While the experience at the ACHC and developing a relationship with the guests were important, the example of faculty is also integral to student learning. One student shared, "There's so much depth and weight to seeing that lived out by the professors. Seeing Katie, when I had gone to Augsburg Commons, bring a healthy meal and share part of her meal that she brought for one of the participants because of how much he cared about his health and that she was partnering together with him, there is so much humanity in that action."[68] The value of faculty exemplifying compassionate care for others and in relationship with them is important for student learning. The positive learning experience of students at the ACHC prompted faculty and students to create similar spaces elsewhere: first in the Cedar-Riverside neighborhood in Minneapolis, which is home to the largest population of Somali immigrants in the United States; second in Rochester, a rural area in Minnesota, where many experience poverty; and third in North Minneapolis, the most impoverished area in Minnesota.

The third example is mentoring students to respond compassionately to human suffering through social science research. As the second example indicates, more than knowledge gained in classrooms is required for students to develop a compassionate engagement with the world. Immersive experiences, relationships with those who suffer, and working with them to address their suffering

---

66 CLARK [note 75].

67 Ibid., 527.

68 REICHERT, Theresa: Interview by ESCHENBACHER, Elaine, Oral History Project. Citizen Professionalism, Minneapolis: Augsburg University Archives, 2022, in: https:// archives.augsburg.edu/islandora/object/AUGrepository%3A149677 (last accessed on 02.24.2023), 57.

and its root causes facilitates compassion development. As a medical anthropologist, Rödlach frequently works with students on designing health- and healthcare-related social science research projects. He encourages students to collect qualitative and quantitative data and adopt anthropology's umbrella approach to research, participant-observation, which tends to be at least a few months but often spans several years. This approach encourages researchers to be as much as possible a participant in the lives of those they study but to also have the analytical and critical distance of an observer. During participant-observation, the researchers interact with those they study on a human level, developing deep personal relationships. These are key to a deeper understanding of what is being studied and such an understanding cannot be easily gained otherwise. In other words, researchers need to be willing to go beyond a formal research collaboration or partnership and be open to personal relationships. Long before they start a research project, they are encouraged to get to know a community, join them for family events, visit individual members of the community in their homes, and acknowledge that they can learn from and with them. Most students are intimidated by the prospect of leaving their comfort zone and by the time commitment such an approach requires. However, some are willing to use participant observation, which is then generally transformative for them, their career aspirations, and their engagement with the world. We want to illustrate this through research done by one of the medical anthropology majors at Creighton University. This student asked Rödlach to mentor her in developing and implementing a research project to explore the association between financial literacy and health among low-income single mothers. As a stellar student, she had all the knowledge needed to develop and implement the research project. As an anthropology student, she was committed to being a participant-observer. As a student researcher, she partnered with the university's Financial Hope Collaborative, which offered a financial literacy program for low-income single mothers. She did a series of interviews during the summer, spent time at program events, and interacted with the program participants as much as possible. The project was successful as an academic research project and she presented her findings at several national and regional conferences, receiving two awards for the project. However, Rödlach considers her personal transformation the most important outcome of the project. As she developed relationships with participants in the program, the knowledge she had gained during course work, including the Global Health course, suddenly began to make sense and to shape her personal dispositions and values as well as her approach to healthcare, particularly dentistry. She is now a dentist who practices compassionate care. She does not send patients away who don't have dental insurance or cannot pay for her services; she creates individualized payment plans with them, even accepting non-monetary compensation and the risk of not receiving full payment for her services. In addition to providing compassionate care, she is involved in her county's health system, discussing with others how to keep residents healthy, addressing root causes of ill health, and removing barriers to access to care. She is a compassionate provider and an engaged Citizen Dentist. No single course or research can be credited for such transformations and the development of a compassionate approach to clinical care. Nevertheless, we recognize that her social science research has been an important factor in her transformation.

Conclusions

Our work as educators in pre-health and health professional academic programs includes a significant emphasis on the SDGs, arguing for a compassionate response to human suffering. We guide and mentor students as they develop compassion for their current or future involvement in healthcare as healthcare professionals. Metz's understanding of compassion as liberating *memoria*[69] can easily be adopted by faith-based universities, as its theological foundation is a good fit for them to inform pedagogical strategies to live their mission. Metz motivates us to pay attention to human suffering (*memoria passionis et mortis*[70]), identify with the sufferers by recognizing our shared humanity, be in solidarity with them, and engage in activities with and for them to promote liberation and justice (*memoria resurrectionis*[71]). The three examples in the previous section illustrate our teaching pedagogy. Together, they lay out how we teach compassion in health and healthcare-related courses, programs, and research.

Learning starts with becoming familiar with foundational knowledge about health, illness, and healthcare, identifying health disparities between different demographic, cultural, and other groups, and recognizing the historical, cultural, political, economic, and other root causes of ill health. Such basic knowledge increases students' awareness of human suffering through ill health, which is related to Metz's *memoria passionis et mortis*. This first step is usually the easiest for compassion education. After all, it is just about gaining factual knowledge and identifying connections between sociocultural realities and health.

The next step is to help students go beyond facts and statistics and be moved by the suffering of others that is described by such basic information. Factual knowledge and statistics are often abstract and do not necessarily result in an empathetic response. The latter can more likely be triggered when suffering has a human face. We consider it effective to connect students with individuals and groups through immersive programs and research to create spaces and events

69 Translation: memory.

70 Translation: memory of [Christ's] passion and death.

71 Translation: memory of [Christ's] resurrection.

that allow them to develop personal attachments and relationships with individuals who struggle with their health. This can happen when students regularly spend time at a community center, participate in an immersive study abroad program, or conduct social science research. In such spaces or during such events, suffering gets a human face, mutual learning happens, students begin to understand suffering through the lens of the sufferer, and they can develop an empathetic response to it. Compared to factual learning about suffering, this step is more difficult for students as it requires them to leave their comfort zone, engage with individuals who may have little to nothing in common with them, and temporarily expose themselves to some of the risks others face on a regular and daily basis.

The following step is for students to confront their values and moral frameworks with the suffering of others, which then can trigger a desire to provide care for sufferers, remove what causes their suffering, and promote health equity and healthcare justice, which is aligned with Metz's *memoria resurrectionis*. This step is the most difficult for students but also the most important. It requires them to take a critical look at their privileges and acknowledge that much of their comparably safe and healthy way of life is the result of societal and global injustice and disparities, challenges them to discern what needs to change in their lives and society, and draws them to the margins. We recognize that long and repeated reflections on students' values and moral frameworks in a safe space where they can express their inability to live their values and morals are of utmost importance. Without reflection, a desire to become actively involved in alleviating human suffering is not likely to emerge, and, if it transpires, it is not sustainable and likely to disappear quickly.

The final step is to discern actual areas of engagement and how to be involved. Identifying areas of involvement is relatively easy, as students tend to know which area of human suffering due to ill health they want to be involved in. However, finding an engagement model that facilitates compassionate involvement is more difficult. In our experience, accompaniment is the most promising and effective model of a compassionate response to health-related human suffering. Accompaniment motivates students to join communities, develop long-term and reciprocal relationships of equality with communities and individuals, be on a journey with individuals and communities, and together learn with them about their worries and concerns and how they want them to be addressed. Accompaniment facilitates being a Citizen Healthcare Provider.

We also recognize that some students simply don't care about the suffering of others. They are more concerned with their own personal and professional futures and not interested in or able to empathize with others' pain and struggles, particularly of those who are not part of their social networks or who don't have much in common with them. Further, their moral frameworks and ideological and political worldviews may not be aligned with compassion. Nevertheless, we have planted the seed of compassion that may grow over the years.

References Cited

AMERICAN ASSOCIATION OF COLLEGES OF NURSING: Compassionate Care Concept Across Multiple Domains, 2014, in: https://www.aacnnursing.org/Essentials/Database/Kit/i/C_Comp_Care_PDF (last accessed on 24.02.2023).

AIKEN, Linda et al.: Nurse Staffing and education and hospital mortality in nine european countries – a retrospective observational study, in: lancet 2014, 383(9931), 1824–1830.

ANNAS, Julia: Intelligent Virtue, Oxford: Oxford University Press, 2011.

ARENS, Edmund: Gottespassion und Compassion. Zum Tod von Johann Baptist Metz, 2019, in: Feinschwarz - Theologisches Feuilleton, December 3. https://www.feinschwarz.net/nachruf-j-b-metz/ (last accessed on 24.02.2023).

AUGBUSRG UNIVERSITY: The Augsburg Mission, 2010, in: https://www.augsburg.edu/about/mission/ (last accessed on 10.03.2022).

BALLATT, John / CAMPLING, Penelope: Intelligent Kindness: Reforming the Culture of Healthcare, London: RCPsych Publications, 2011.

BEIN, Steve: Compassion and Moral Guidance, Honolulu: University of Hawai'i Press, 2013, 1–49.

BILLIAS, Nancy: On Becoming a Campus of Compassion, in: GIBBS, Paul (Hg.): The Pedagogy of Compassion at the Heart of Higher Education, Cham: Springer, 2017, 141–154.

BOSNJAKOVIC, Josip: Compassion. An Expression of Charity in Treatment of Physical and Mental Illness in Individuals and Communities, in: Psychiatria Danubina 2021 33(4), 902–910.

BOYTE, Harry: Civic Agency and the Cult of the Expert. A Study for the Kettering Foundation, Dayton: Kettering Foundation, 2009.

BRAY, Lucy / O'BRIAN, Mary / KIRTON, Jennifer / ZUBAIRU, Kate / CHRISTIANSEN, Angela: The Role of Professional Education in Developing Compassionate Practitioners. A Mixed Methods Study Exploring the Perceptions of Health Professionals and Pre-Registration Students, in: Nurse Education Today, 2014, 34(3), 480–486.

CAHILL, Lisa / IRARRAZAVAL, Diego / VILA-CHA, João: Mercy, in: Concilium 2017/4.

CLARK, Kathleen: Evaluating Student Learning. Community-Based Nursing Education as Action to Address Inequities, in: Journal of Nursing Education 2022, 61(9), 525–527.

CLARK, Kathleen et al.: The Citizen Nurse. An Educational Innovation for Change, in: Journal of Nursing Education 2017, 54(4), 247–250.

CARTWRIGHT, Lisa: Moral Spectatorship. Technologies of Voice and Affect in Postwar Representations of the Child, Durham: Duke University Press, 2008.

COMMONWEALTH FUND: The Impact of Climate Change on Our Health and Health Systems, 2022, in: https://www.commonwealthfund.org/publications/explainer/2022/may/im-pact-climate-change-our-health-and-health-systems (last accessed on 23.02.2023).

CREIGHTON UNIVERSITY: A Jesuit Education that Leads to a Life Well-Lived. Our Mission, 2022, in: https://www.creighton.edu/arts-sciences/about/about-our-mission (last accessed on 15.11.2022).

DALRYMPLE, Theodore: Aid, Colonialism, and Corruption, 2010, in: https://www.poverty-cure.org/learn/media/theodore-dalrymple-aid-colonialism-corruption (last accessed on 25.02.2023).

ENESTVEDT, Ruth et al.: Caring in the Margins. A Scholarship of Accompaniment for Advanced Transcultural Nursing Practice, in: Advances in Nursing Science 2018, 41(3), 230–242.

ESTEVA, Gustavo / PRAKASH, Madhu Suri: Grassroots Post-Modernism. Remaking the Soil of Cultures, London: Zed Books, 1998.

ESTEVA, Gustavo / BABONES, Salvatore / BABCICKY, Philipp: The Future of Development. A Radical Manifesto, Bristol: Policy Press, 2013.

FARMER, Paul et al.: Reimagining Global Health. An Introduction, Berkeley: University of California Press, 2013.

FARMER, Paul: We Know How to Confront the Coronavirus Pandemic – Expert Mercy, in: Boston Globe 2020, March 19, in: https://www.bostonglobe.com/2020/03/19/opinion/we-know-how-confront-coronavirus-pandemic-expert-mercy/ (last accessed on 15.01.2023).

FISCHMAN, Wendy / GARDNER Howard: Mission Possible. What Higher Education Is and What It Can Be, in: Trusteeship 2022 30(6), 12–19.

FRANCIS: Laudato Si' – On Care For Our Common Home. Vatican City: Vatican Publishing House, 2015.

FROST, Peter et al.: Emotions in Organizations, London: Sage, 2000.

GIBBS, Paul: Higher Education. A Compassion Business or Edifying Experience, in: GIBBS, Paul (Hg.): The Pedagogy of Compassion at the Heart of Higher Education, Cham: Springer, 2017, 1–18.

GRANT, Liz et al.: A Compassion Narrative for the Sustainable Development Goals. Conscious and Connected Action, in: Lancet 2022, 400 (10345), 7–8.

GRIFFIN, Michael / WEISS BLOCK, Jennie: In the Company of the Poor. Conversations between Dr. Paul Farmer and Father Gustavo Gutierrez, Maryknoll: Orbis Books, 2013.

HABERMAS, Jűrgen: Letter to Johann Baptist Metz on His 90th Birthday. translated by John Downey 2018, in: https://johannbaptistmetz.com/wp-content/uploads/2020/08/Letter-to-Johann-Baptist-Metz-on-his-90th-Birthday.pdf (last accessed on 12.28.2022).

HAKER, Hille: Compassion as a Global Programme for Christianity, in: Concilium 2001 4, 55–7.

HENRY, Patrick: Economic Inequality Has Deepened During the Pandemic. That Doesn't Mean It Can't Be Fixed, in: The European Sting - Your Political Newspager 2022, April 7, in: https://europeansting.com/2022/04/07/economic-inequality-has-deepened-during-the-pandemic-that-doesnt-mean-it-cant-be-fixed/ (last accessed on 24.02.2023).

INTERNATIONAL COUNCIL OF NURSES: The ICN Code of Ethics for Nurses. Geneva: International Council of Nurses, 2021.

JAZAIERI, Hooria: Compassionate Education from Preschool to Graduate School. Bringing a Culture of Compassion into the Classroom, in: Journal of Research in Innovative Teaching and Learning 2018 11(1), 22–66.

JESUITS: Universal Apostolic Preferences 2019, in: https://www.jesuits.global/uap/ (last accessed on 01.14.2023).

KAGAN, Paula / SMITH, Marlaine / CHINN, Peggy: Philosophies and Practices of Emancipatory Nursing. Social Justice as Praxis, Abingdon-on-Thames: Routledge, 2014.

KRISTJANSSON, Kristján: Phronesis as an Ideal in Professional Medical Ethics. Some Preliminary Positionings and Problematics, in: Theoretical Medicine and Bioethics 2015 36 (5): 299–320.

MARMOT, Michael: The Health Gap – The Challenge of an Unequal World, London: Bloomsbury Publishing, 2015.

MAXWELL, Bruce: Pursuing the Aim of Compassionate Empathy in Higher Education, in: GIBBS, Paul (Hg.): The Pedagogy of Compassion at the Heart of Higher Education, Cham: Springer, 2017, 33–48.

METZ, Johann Baptist: In Memory of the Other's Suffering. Theological Reflections on the Future of Faith and Culture, translated by Peter Kenny, in: PIERCE, Andrew / SMYTH, Geraldyne (Hg.): The Critical Spirit. Theology at the Crossroads of Faith and Culture, Dublin: Columbia Press 2003, 179–188.

METZ, Johann Baptist: Facing the World. A Theological and Biographical Inquiry, in: Theological Studies 2014 75 (1), 23–33.

MIKEG PRODUCTIONS: Creighton University Fossil Fuel Divestment, October 28, 2019, in: https://www.youtube.com/watch?v=Ktl4M-RSw4s (last accessed on 12.07.2023).

MOYO, Dambisa: Fifty Years of Economic Folly – And the Stark Choices Ahead, New York: Farrar, Strauss, and Giroux, 2011.

NODDINGS, Nel: The Challenge to Care in Schools. An Alternative Approach to Education, New York: Teachers College Press, ²2005.

NUSSBAUM, Martha: Compassion. The Basic Social Emotion, in: Social Philosophy and Policy 1996, 13, 27–58.

PANDEY, Kiran Raj: From Health For All to Universal Health Coverage. Alma Ata is Still Relevant, in: Global Health 2018 14 (62).

PATEL, Sundip et al.: Curricula for Empathy and Compassion Training in Medical Education. A Systematic Review, in: PLoS ONE 2019 14 (8). e0221412.

PETERSON, Andrew: Compassion and Education. Cultivating Compassionate Children, Schools, and Communities, London: Palgrave Macmillan, 2017, 1–12.

REICHERT, Theresa: Interview by Eschenbacher, Elaine, Oral History Project. Citizen Professionalism, Minneapolis, Augsburg University Archives 2022, in: https://archives.augsburg.edu/islandora/object/AUGrepository%3A149677 (last accessed on 02.24.2023).

ROEWE, Brian: Creighton University to Divest Fully from Fossil Fuels within 10 Years, in: National Catholic Reporter, January 5, 2021, in: https://www.ncronline.org/earthbeat/justice/creighton-university-divest-fully-fossil-fuels-within-10-years (last accessed on 16.12.2022).

SEN, Amartya: Poverty and Famines. An Essay on Entitlement and Deprivation, Oxford: Oxford University Press, 2023.

SINCLAIR, Shane et al.: What Is the State of Compassion Education? A Systematic Review of Compassion Training in Health Care, in: Academic Medicine 2021 96 (7), 1057–1070.

SOBRINO, Jon: Johann Baptist Metz's Theology and the Theology of Liberation. translated by John Downey, 2018, in: https://johannbaptistmetz.com/wp-content/uploads/2020/08/Sobrino-Letter-1.pdf (last accessed on 09.11.2022).

UNITED NATIONS: MILLENNIUM DECLARATION NEW YORK: United Nations General Assembly 2020, in: https://www.ohchr.org/en/instruments-mechanisms/instruments/united-nations-millennium-declaration (last accessed on 14.12.2022).

United Nations: The Millennium Development Goals Report. New York: United Nations General Assembly 2015, in: https://www.un.org/millenniumgoals/2015_MDG_Report/pdf/MDG%202015%20rev%20(July%201).pdf (last accessed on 12.13.2022).

UNITED NATIONS: The Sustainable Development Goals 2015, in: https://www.un.org/millenniumgoals/2015_MDG_Report/pdf/MDG%202015%20rev%20(July%201).pdf (last accessed on 13.12.2022).

UNITED NATIONS DEVELOPMENT PROGRAMME: New Threats to Human Security in the Anthropocene. Demanding Greater Solidarity, 2022, in: https://hs.hdr.undp.org/pdf/srhs2022.pdf (last accessed on 13.12.2022).

WADDINGTON, Kathryn: The Compassion Gap in UK Universities, in: International Practice Development Journal 2016 6 (1): 1–9.

WHITE, Richard: Compassion in Philosophy and Education, in: GIBBS, Paul (Hg.): The Pedagogy of Compassion at the Heart of Higher Education, Cham: Springer, 2017, 19–32.

WILEY, Andrea / ALLEN, John:. Medical Anthropology. A Biocultural Approach, Oxford: Oxford University Press, ⁴2020.

WORLD HEALTH ORGANIZATION: Policy Levers to Enhance Health Workforce Performance for Compassionate and Respectful Care, Geneva: World Health Organization, 2021.

YONG KIM, Jim et al.: Dying for Growth. Global Inequity and the Health of the Poor, in: The International Journal of African Historical Studies 2002, 185–187.

YOUNAS, Ahtisham / MADDIGAN, Joy: Proposing a Policy Framework for Nursing Education for Fostering Compassion in Nursing Students. A Critical Review, in: Journal of Advanced Nursing 2018 75, 1621–1636.

ZAGZEBSKI, Linda: Moral Exemplars in Theory and Practice, in: Theory and Research in Education 2013 11 (2), 193–206.

„Wirst du behindert?!" – Skizzen zu Compassion, Nachhaltigkeit und Inklusion aus der Perspektive der Disability Studies

Janieta Bartz

Mit rund 3 Milliarden stellen Menschen mit Behinderung weltweit betrachtet die größte Minderheit dar und werden als solche auch im Kontext der Nachhaltigkeitsziele der Vereinten Nationen angeführt. Der Beitrag setzt – ausgehend von einem neuen Verständnis von Behinderung – praktisch-theologische Impulse für eine disability-sensible Compassion für eine nachhaltige sowie inklusive Gesellschaft.

Disability Studies; Inklusion; Behinderung; Nachhaltigkeit; Compassion

With about 3 billion people worldwide, persons with disabilities represent the largest global minority group and are also mentioned as such in the context of the United Nations Sustainable Development Goals. Based on a new understanding of disability, this article provides practical-theological insights into disability-sensitive compassion for a sustainable and inclusive society.

Disability Studies; Inclusion; Disability; Sustainability; Compassion

Einleitung

Welche Form von Unterstützung ist im Kontext von Behinderung sinnvoll? Menschen mit sichtbaren Behinderungen, also jenen Einschränkungen, die beispielsweise die Nutzung eines Langstocks, eines Rollstuhls oder eines Hörgerätes erfordern, kennen die Situation, dass sie Hilfe angeboten bekommen, meist oft unabhängig vom eigentlichen Bedarf. Erklärt wird dies mit einem gesellschaftlichen Analphabetismus, der durch den fehlenden Umgang mit Behinderung verursacht wird.[1] Menschen ohne Behinderung reagieren in der Regel mitleidsvoll, wenn sie sichtbare Behinderungen wahrnehmen, und möchten unterstützen. Der vorliegende Beitrag führt in die disability-sensible Hermeneutik des Helfens ein und liefert Impulse für den gleichberechtigten Einsatz für eine nachhaltige Gesellschaft. Ausgangspunkt ist die Darstellung einer neuen Sichtweise auf Be-

---

[1] Vgl. Bösl, Elisbeth: Die Geschichte der Behindertenpolitik in der Bundesrepublik aus Sicht der Disability History, in: APuZ 23 (2010), 6–12.

hinderung, die jahrelange Fremdbestimmung, Unterdrückung und fehlende Unterstützung behinderter Menschen zu überwinden sucht (2) und diese vor dem Hintergrund aktueller gesellschaftlicher Herausforderungen, nachhaltiger Entwicklung und Inklusion reflektiert (3). Hier knüpft das Konzept der disabilitysensiblen Compassion an, welches als hermeneutischer Schlüssel im Umgang mit Behinderung im Kontext von Nachhaltigkeit und Inklusion dient (4) und sich in Impulsen für die Praxis konkretisiert (5).

Neue Modelle von und Sichtweisen auf Behinderung als Ausgangspunkt

Welche drei Begriffe fallen Ihnen ein, wenn Sie an Behinderung denken? Mit dieser Frage werden Teilnehmer*innen meiner hochschulischen Lehrveranstaltungen oder Fortbildungen regelmäßig zum Einstieg in das Thema Behinderung konfrontiert. Die spontanen Assoziationen werden seit 2015 systematisch ausgewertet. Sie zeigen eine vorwiegend defizitorientierte Sichtweise auf Behinderung. Dies konkretisiert sich in Begriffen wie Schicksal, Last, Leid, Einschränkung, Problem und spiegelt aus der unmittelbaren Momentaufnahme auch ein gesellschaftliches Stimmungsbild wider. Die Diskurse in den Veranstaltungen über die geforderte Auswahl von drei Begriffen zeigen: Mit einer Behinderung zu leben scheint aus vorwiegend nichtbehinderter Perspektive etwas zu sein, was den Wunsch nach Veränderung dieses Zustandes, theologisch gesprochen nach Heilung weckt.

Den Disability Studies zufolge, also jenen wissenschaftlichen Diskursen, die von Forscher*innen mit Behinderung über Behinderung geführt werden, ist jedoch nicht die Behinderung einer Person das Problem, sondern die daraus entstehende Benachteiligung.[2] Die Entwicklungen, die diese neue Deutung von Behinderung hervorgebracht haben, werden nachfolgend kurz skizziert.

Vor 1980 dominiert das sog. medizinische Modell von Behinderung, welches auch in der Klassifikation ICD (*International Classification of Diseases*) der Weltgesundheitsorganisation (*WHO*) repräsentiert ist.[3] Einschränkungen körperlicher und / oder psychischer Art werden als individuelles Problem einer Person gedeutet. Diese Einschränkungen werden (medizinisch) diagnostiziert und weitestgehend therapiert; ihre Auswirkungen auf den Alltag sollen von der betroffe-

---

2 Vgl. WALDSCHMIDT, Anne: Disability Studies, in: DEDERICH, Markus / JANTZEN Wolfgang (Hg): Behinderung und Anerkennung, Behinderung, Bildung, Partizipation, Enzyklopädisches Handbuch der Behindertenpädagogik Band 2, Stuttgart: Kohlhammer, 2009, 129–131.

3 Vgl. WELTGESUNDHEITSORGANISATION: Internationale Klassifikation der Krankheiten, Verletzungen und Todesursachen (ICD), Köln u. a. 1979.

nen Person selbst bewältigt werden. Wenn ein Kind mit Behinderung beispielsweise nicht bei der gemeinnützigen Aktion einer Klasse mitwirken kann, weil es einen Rollstuhl nutzt, kann es im Zweifel – aus dieser Sichtweise heraus gedacht – nicht dabei sein, wenn es nicht selbst eine Lösung für das Problem gefunden hat. Solche Denkweisen sind bis in die 1970er Jahre hinein der Regelfall. Behinderung ist demnach ein Defekt, eine Störung, eine Abweichung – etwas Anderes als das, was die Gesellschaft gewohnt ist. Aus der Disability History, welche Exklusions- und Diskriminierungserfahrungen behinderter Menschen untersucht, wissen wir zudem, dass diese defizitäre Sicht auf Behinderung mit der Erwerbsfähigkeit und Produktivität einer Person einhergeht.[4] Somit sind Diskussionen über Behinderung oft medizinisch geprägt und schauen auf den Defekt und fehlenden Nutzen für die Gesellschaft, der daraus entsteht.[5] Dies wird auch in der Definition des Bundesinnenministeriums aus dem Jahr 1958 deutlich:

> Als behindert gilt ein Mensch, der entweder aufgrund angeborener Missbildung bzw. Beschädigung oder durch Verletzung oder Krankheit (…) eine angemessene Tätigkeit nicht ausüben kann. Er ist mehr oder minder leistungsgestört (lebensuntüchtig).[6]

Die Folge eines solchen Verständnisses ist, dass Menschen mit Behinderung als soziales Problem gesehen werden. Sie gelten auch als Belastung der Gesellschaft. Dies bringt eine weitere Folge mit sich: Man möchte aus Sicht der Gesellschaft mit verschiedenen Maßnahmen dem Problem entgegenwirken, dass Menschen mit Behinderung unproduktiv und belastend sein können. Das bedeutet, dass die Menschen, die als abweichend und defizitär klassifiziert werden, an die leistungsbezogenen Erwartungen der Gesellschaft angepasst werden sollen.[7]

Die defizitorientierte Sicht auf Behinderung wird jedoch im Laufe der 1980er Jahre zunehmend in Frage gestellt.[8] Besonders aus gesellschaftswissenschaftlicher Perspektive wird gefragt: Ist die Behinderung einer Person wirklich das einzige Problem? Man ist der Überzeugung, dass produktive und sogenannte normal erwerbstätige Menschen behinderte Menschen ausgrenzen. Behinderte Menschen haben somit gar nicht die Chance Teil der Gesellschaft zu sein, weil sie durch verschiedene Strukturen daran gehindert und benachteiligt werden. Ein weiterer Punkt ist dabei auch, dass Menschen mit Behinderung durch ihre

---

4 Vgl. Bösl 2010 [Anm. 1]; Mattner, Dieter: Behinderte Menschen in der Gesellschaft. Zwischen Ausgrenzung und Integration, Stuttgart: Kohlhammer, 2000, 16–18.

5 Vgl. Fandrey, Walter: Krüppel, Idioten, Irre. Zur Sozialgeschichte behinderter Menschen in Deutschland, Stuttgart: Sildberg, 1990.

6 Bundesministerium des Innern (BMI): Abt. Va1, Schreiben an Abt. Va2, 12. 8. 1958, Bundesarchiv (Barch) B 106 8414.

7 Vgl. Ebd.

8 Vgl. Eberwein, Hans: Verzicht auf Kategoriensysteme in der Integrationspädagogik, in: Friedrich, Albrecht u. a. (Hg.): Perspektiven der Sonderpädagogik, Neuwied/Berlin: Luchterhand, 2000, 95–106, 95; Weltgesundheitsorganisation: International Classification of Functioning, Disability and Health, Genf 2001; Weltgesundheitsorganisation: International Classification of Imparments, Disability and Handicaps, Genf 1978.

Betreuungssituation oft keine eigenen Entscheidungen treffen können und es außerhalb von betreuenden Einrichtungen neue Orte in der Gesellschaft braucht, wo Betreuung und Selbstbestimmung möglich sind.[9]

In dieser Zeit beginnen die sozialwissenschaftlichen Überlegungen, die seit 2001 das soziale Modell von Behinderung geschaffen haben.[10] Das soziale Modell von Behinderung fragt danach, welche Bedingungen der Gesellschaft Menschen mit Behinderung in der Teilhabe einschränken und wie diese korrigiert werden können. Dies wird auch in der Definition von Behinderung in der Klassifikation International Classification of Functioning, Disability and Health 2001 deutlich:

> Behinderung ist gekennzeichnet als das Ergebnis oder die Folge einer komplexen Beziehung zwischen dem Gesundheitsproblem eines Menschen und seinen personenbezogenen Faktoren einerseits und der externen Faktoren, welche die Umstände repräsentieren, unter denen Individuen leben, andererseits.

So manifestiert sich im Zuge verschiedener Entwicklungen ein bedeutsamer Paradigmenwechsel. Es geht nicht mehr nur um die Behinderung einer Person, sondern um die (gesellschaftlichen) Bedingungen, die sich benachteiligend auf das Leben einer behinderten Person auswirken. Sind also die Wege bei der zuvor erwähnten gemeinnützigen Aktion nicht barrierefrei, wird eine Lösung gemeinsam gefunden (neuer Ort, Beseitigung der Barrieren, neue Aktion). In keinem Fall erlebt das Kind eine Aussonderung oder Schuldzuschreibung aufgrund der Behinderung. Die vorhandenen Barrieren sind ein Anliegen der gesamten Klasse.

Das soziale Modell von Behinderung wird im Laufe der 2000er Jahre im Kontext von Kultur und Menschenrechten weiter ausgearbeitet.[11] Hierbei steht die Frage im Vordergrund, ob eine Person behindert ist oder ob sie darüber hinaus auch in ihrer gesellschaftlichen Teilhabe behindert wird.[12] Hintergrund dieser Frage sind verschiedene Konstitutionen und Werte, die die (kulturelle) Teilhabe behinderter Menschen als Menschenrecht identifizieren. Im Sinne des Paradigmenwechsels im Umgang mit Behinderung geht es auch mit Blick auf die UN-Behindertenrechtskonvention (*UN-BRK*) und in den Nachhaltigkeitszielen da-

---

9 Vgl. Mattner 2000 [Anm. 4], 16–18.

10 Vgl. Franke, Alexa: Modelle von Gesundheit und Krankheit, Bern: Hogrefe, 2006; WHO 2001 [Anm. 8].

11 Vgl. Waldschmidt 2009 [Anm. 2], 125–128.

12 Vgl. Bartz, Janieta: Behindern ist heilbar. Dis-/abilitysensible Anmerkungen zu gegenwärtigen Entwicklungen in der katholischen Kirche, In: Beck, Wolfgang / Heyder, Regina / Sattler, Dorothea / Söding, Thomas / Wuckelt, Agnes (Hg.): Aufbruch statt Rückzug. Die römisch-katholische Kirche in der Öffentlichkeit heute, Freiburg/Basel/Wien: Herder, 2022, 179–182.; Theunissen, Georg: Empowerment und Inklusion behinderter Menschen eine Einführung in Heilpädagogik und Soziale Arbeit, Freiburg im Breisgau: Lambertus, ³2013.

rum, Menschen mit Behinderung die Teilhabe an der Gesellschaft in allen Lebensbereichen zu ermöglichen.[13] Es geht also nicht primär um die Beseitigung der Behinderung selbst, sondern um die Beseitigung der aus ihr entstehenden Einschränkungen, die einen Menschen daran hindern, das eigene Leben selbstbestimmt zu gestalten.[14] Für die Konkretisierung einer dis/ability-sensiblen Compassion ist dieses neue Verständnis von Behinderung der Ausgangspunkt im Einsatz für eine nachhaltige Welt. Es geht darum, behindernde (Lebens-)Bedingungen zu identifizieren, die Menschen an der Teilhabe am gesellschaftlichen Leben hindern, und Benachteiligungen zu beseitigen.

Nachhaltigkeit und Behinderung am Beispiel inklusiver Bildung

Selbstbestimmung und Partizipation für Menschen mit Behinderung in allen Lebensbereichen zu gewährleisten, zählt zu den Kernanliegen der UN-Behindertenrechtskonvention aus dem Jahr 2008.[15] Dem voraus gegangen sind zahlreiche Menschenrechtsverletzungen und Diskriminierungen, die Menschen mit Behinderung zum Anlass nahmen, sich zu emanzipieren und für die eigenen Rechte einzusetzen.[16] Die Umsetzung der Forderungen in die Praxis stellt die Vertragsnationen immer noch vor Herausforderungen. Mit Blick auf die Bundesrepublik gibt es nach wie vor noch hohen Handlungsbedarf. So ist es nicht verwunderlich, dass die Nachhaltigkeitsziele (*Sustainable Development Goals*) der Vereinten Nationen im Jahr 2015 auch das Thema Behinderung bewusst fokussieren. Nachfolgend sollen einige Baustellen nachhaltiger Entwicklungen, die eigentlich bis zum Jahr 2030 umgesetzt werden sollen, benannt werden.

Bis 2030 sollen Menschen mit und ohne Behinderung, die von Armut bedroht sind, erfasst und durch ein Sozialsystem abgesichert sein.[17] Darüber hinaus spielen der Zugang zu hochwertiger Bildung[18] sowie chancengerechte und

---

13 Vgl. VEREINTE NATIONEN: Zwischen Deutschland, Liechtenstein, Österreich und der Schweiz abgestimmte Übersetzung „Übereinkommen über die Rechte von Menschen mit Behinderungen", online 2006: https://www.bmas.de/SharedDocs/Downloads/DE/Teilhabe/uebereinkommen-ueber-die-rechte-behinderter-menschen.pdf?__blob=publicationFile& v=2 s.de

14 Vgl. SANDER, Alfred: Behinderungsbegriffe und ihre Integrationsrelevanz, in: Hans EBERWEIN / Sabine KNAUER (Hg.): Integrationspädagogik, Weinheim und Basel: Beltz, 2002, 95–99.

15 Vgl. UN-BRK 2008 [Anm. 13].

16 Vgl. FANDREY 1980 [Anm. 5].

17 Vgl. SDG 1. Indikatoren 1.3 sowie 1.3.1.

18 Vgl. SDG 4. Indikatoren 4.5, 4.a.1

faire Arbeit[19] eine entscheidende Rolle. Letzteres ist vor allem mit Blick auf die Diskussion um die Beschäftigung von Menschen mit Behinderung in Werkstätten für Menschen mit Behinderung entscheidend, die für ihre Erwerbstätigkeit in der Bundesrepublik in der Regel keinen Mindestlohn erhalten.[20] Darüber hinaus ist auch barrierefreies und bezahlbares Wohnen mit Blick auf Behinderung ein nennenswerter Punkt. Städte und Gemeinden stehen bei der Umsetzung dieses Ziels in der Pflicht, Wohnen barrierearm und bezahlbar zu gestalten und Menschen mit Behinderung auch mit Blick auf Mobilität durch gute Verkehrssysteme sinnvoll zu unterstützen.[21] Darüber hinaus fordern die Nachhaltigkeitsziele auch eine angemessene Repräsentation von Menschen mit Behinderung in gesellschaftlich relevanten Funktionen.[22]

Verschiedene Zwischenbilanzen zeigen, dass die Ziele beider Konstitutionen nach wie vor große Baustellen sind, die bisweilen vom Narrativ der Aussichtslosigkeit begleitet werden. An dieser Stelle gehe ich exemplarisch auf die Zugänglichkeit zu hochwertiger Bildung für Menschen mit Behinderung am Beispiel inklusiver Bildung in Deutschland genauer ein.

Die im schulischen Kontext nahezu als inflationär zu bezeichnende Verwendung des Begriffs Inklusion verursacht vermutlich einige Missverständnisse. Denn eine Differenzierung zwischen Inklusion und Integration ist hierbei selten zu beobachten. Dies mag durch die Diskussion zu Integration und Inklusion im englischsprachigen Raum begünstigt sein, da hier die beiden Begriffe synonym zueinander verwendet werden.[23] Im deutschsprachigen Diskurs wird allerdings eine Unterscheidung zwischen dem Integrations- und dem Inklusionskonzept vorgenommen – dies ist für das Verständnis und die Bewertung der Umsetzung von Inklusion an deutschen Schulen hilfreich.

Dem Integrations-Konzept liegt eine Zwei-Gruppen-Theorie zugrunde: Die Exklusion von Mitgliedern einer Minderheiten-Gruppe aus einer Mehrheitsgemeinschaft, die aufgrund ethnischer oder soziokultureller Merkmale, kognitiver Fähigkeiten, gesundheitlicher Voraussetzungen, sexueller Orientierung, Religi-

19 Vgl. DG 8, Indikatoren 8.5.1 und 8.5.2

20 Vgl. KARIM, Sarah: Arbeiten mit Behinderungen. Aushandlungen von Nähe und Distanz am Beispiel einer Werkstatt für behinderte Menschen während der Covid-19-Pandemie, in: Journal für Psychologie, 30. Jg., H. 2 (2022), 90-93. https://doi.org/10.30820/0942-2285-2022-2-90.

21 Vgl. SDG 11, Indikatoren 11.1 sowie z. B. 11.7.1 und 11.7.2

22 Vgl. SDG 16. Indikatoren 16.7.1 und 16.7.2

23 Vgl. GROSCHE, Michael: Was ist Inklusion? Ein Diskussions- und Positionsartikel zur Definition von Inklusion aus Sicht der empirischen Bildungsforschung, in: KUHL, Poldi et al. (Hg.): Inklusion von Schülerinnen und Schülern mit sonderpädagogischem Förderbedarf in Schulleistungserhebungen, Wiesbaden: Springer, 2015.

onszugehörigkeit etc. besteht, soll dadurch überwunden werden, dass die Minderheiten-Gruppe in die Mehrheitsgemeinschaft integriert wird.[24] Dabei werden Möglichkeiten identifiziert, vor allem die für die Minderheiten-Gruppe bestehenden Probleme, auch Barrieren genannt, zu beseitigen. Ein frühes Beispiel für dieses Konzept ist die schulische Integrationsbewegung in den 1990er Jahren, die das Ziel verfolgt hat, Schüler*innen, die vom Unterricht an deutschen Regelschulen ausgeschlossen waren, erfolgreich in das bestehende Regelschulsystem zu integrieren, um diese dort zielgleich zu unterrichten.[25] Alle Lerner*innen sollen also unter identischen Bedingungen gleiche Ziele erreichen, wobei ihre individuellen Voraussetzungen allerdings keine Berücksichtigung finden. Dazu sind neben einer Ausstattung dieser Schüler*innen mit (technischen) Hilfsmitteln in der Regel bauliche und organisatorische Umstrukturierungen notwendig: Schüler*innen mit einer Sehschädigung arbeiten beispielsweise mit Bildschirmlesegeräten, Lupen, Vergrößerungs- und Vorlese-Software und sind auf bestimmte Lichtverhältnisse in Klassenräumen angewiesen.[26]

Die Idee der Inklusion ist demgegenüber dadurch gekennzeichnet, dass Diversität als gesamtgesellschaftliche Normalität anerkannt wird.[27] Die Zwei-Gruppen-Theorie ist damit überwunden: Im Idealzustand einer inklusiven Gesellschaft gibt es keine Minderheiten-Gruppen, da die oben genannten, für diese Gruppen konstitutiven Merkmale ihren stigmatisierenden Charakter verloren haben.[28] Insbesondere über die Ausgestaltung der schulischen Inklusion existieren im deutschsprachigen Raum derzeit allerdings unterschiedliche Auffassungen, es gibt noch kein kohärentes Konzept.[29] Inklusion im schulischen Kontext meint, dass Schüler*innen gemeinsam lernen können, ohne dass sie die Erfahrung von Stigmatisierung, Exklusion und Diskriminierung machen. Dabei geht es auch um Bildungsgerechtigkeit, denn die Idee der Inklusion verfolgt das Ziel, dass jede*r Schüler*in in dem Maße Zugang zu Bildungsprozessen erhält, wie es ihr*ihm nach dem Gleichheitsgrundsatz des Grundgesetzes und der Menschenrechte zusteht.[30] Dies hat zur Folge, dass jede dauerhafte Identifizierung und

---

24 Vgl. BARTZ, Janieta: Jeder bekommt das, was er braucht. Anspruch, Wirklichkeit und Möglichkeiten erfolgreicher Schul- und Unterrichtsentwicklung, in: Lebendige Seelsorge 69 (1) 2018, 53–54.

25 Vgl. Ebd.; WOCKEN, Hans: Das Haus der inklusiven Schule. Baustellen – Baupläne – Bausteine, Hamburg: Feldhaus, 2011.

26 Vgl. BARTZ 2018 [Anm. 24].

27 Vgl. HINZ, Andreas: Von der Zukunft her denken. Inklusive Pädagogik im Diskurs, Bad Heilbrunn: Klinkhardt, 2016.

28 Vgl. Eberwein 2010 [Anm. 8].

29 Vgl. BARTZ, Janieta: Inklusion im Spannungsfeld von Lust und Frust, in: Unterwegs 35 (2) 2017, 16–17. Online: http://www.katecheten-verein.de/de/files/unterwegs/unterwegs.2-17.pdf., 16; REICH, Kerstin: Inklusive Didaktik in der Praxis. Beispiele erfolgreicher Schulen, Weinheim: Beltz, 2017.

30 Vgl. Ebd.

Stigmatisierung von Schülerinnen und Schülern durch Kategorien wie *sonderpädagogischer Förderbedarf, Deutsch als Fremdsprache / Deutsch als Zweitsprache, Migrationshintergrund* oder *sozial schwacher Kontext* zugunsten einer diversitätssensiblen Diagnose und Förderung aller Schülerinnen und Schüler aufgegeben werden muss.[31]

Durch dieses Grundverständnis von Inklusion ergeben sich für die schulische Praxis im Kern folgende Konsequenzen:[32]

1. Jede*r Schüler*in hat Förderbedarf, es gibt keine besonderen Kinder und Jugendliche mit besonderen Bedarfen. Das hat auch zur Konsequenz, dass wir de facto nicht von stigmatisierenden *Inklusionskindern* oder *Inklusionsklassen* sprechen können.
2. Die Grundlage für inklusive Unterrichtsplanung und -durchführung zeichnet sich durch eine diversitätssensible Diagnostik und Förderung aller Schüler*innen aus. Somit ist zieldifferenter Unterricht nicht als Ausnahme, sondern als Regel inklusiven Unterrichts zu betrachten.
3. Die Idee des gemeinschaftlichen Lernens im Klassenzimmer auf der Grundlage von gegenseitiger Anerkennung ist gesellschaftlich betrachtet enorm wichtig.[33] Die Idee der Inklusion verfolgt das Ziel, dass es eines Tages nicht mehr notwendig ist, von Inklusion zu sprechen, da der Umgang mit Heterogenität zur Selbstverständlichkeit geworden ist (vgl. Hinz 2016).

Der hier vorgestellte Inklusionsbegriff bezieht sich auf einen Idealzustand, hinter dem die gesellschaftliche Wirklichkeit definitiv zurückbleibt.[34] Da nun Inklusion in der Schule bildungspolitisch eingefordert wird, ohne dass bereits alle notwendigen strukturellen und materiellen Voraussetzungen bedacht und geschaffen sind, befinden sich viele Lehrkräfte in einem Spagat zwischen Anspruch und Wirklichkeit. Sie haben die Aufgabe, Schüler*innen für Schulabschlüsse zu qualifizieren, ohne auf das Unterrichten in heterogenen Lerngruppen vorbereitet und entsprechend geschult zu sein. Um sich das als notwendig gewertete Wissen nachträglich anzueignen, fehlt im schulischen Alltag die Zeit – zumal oft noch zielgleicher Unterricht erwartet wird und angesichts großer Schüler*innenzahlen als der einzig gangbare Weg erscheint. Die Folge ist, dass inklusive Bildung mit zahlreichen Belastungserfahrungen und Misserfolgen in Verbindung steht.[35]

---

31 Vgl. BARTZ 2018 [Anm. 24].

32 Vgl. Ebd.

33 Vgl. ROEBBEN, Bert: Schulen für das Leben. Eine kleine Didaktik der Hoffnung, Stuttgart: Calwer, 2016.

34 Vgl. Bartz 2018 [Anm. 24]; BARTZ 2017 [Anm. 29].

35 Vgl. BARTZ, Janieta: All inclusive?! Empirical insights into individual experiences of students with disabilities at German universities and implications for inclusive Higher Education, in: Education Sciences 10, 2020.

Diesen Zustand jedoch der Idee der Inklusion selbst anzulasten, wäre ein Trugschluss. Was vielerorts als *Inklusion* umgesetzt wird bzw. mangels adäquater Rahmenbedingungen umgesetzt werden muss, entspricht noch dem alten Integrationskonzept und wird weder den Schüler*innen mit ihrem Bildungsanspruch gerecht, noch den Lehrer*innen mit ihrem Bildungsauftrag.

Eine erfolgreiche Umsetzung der Idee von Inklusion erfordert bestimmte Rahmenbedingungen, die – wie der Band von Kersten Reich (2017) an konkreten Beispielen inklusiver Schulen aller Schulformen in Deutschland zeigt – dazu beitragen, dass Inklusion im schulischen Kontext gelingt. Dazu gehören allen voran kleine Klassen, Teamteaching, ausreichend Zeit zur Unterrichtsplanung, vernetztes Arbeiten mit unterschiedlichen (außer-)schulischen Professionen, neue leistungsbezogene Beurteilungssysteme, partizipative Lernformen, Lebenswelt- und Gesellschaftsbezug und ausreichende materielle Ressourcen. Dies schließt die gezielte Vorbereitung von Lehrer*innen insbesondere auf die neuen Lehr-, Lern- und Beurteilungsformen im Rahmen der Lehrer*innenaus- und Weiterbildung ein.[36]

Abschließend bleibt aus der Perspektive der Disability Studies darauf hinzuweisen, dass es auch eine Frage des Habitus ist, ob die Gesellschaft bereit ist, die Rechte von Menschen mit Behinderung, die ihren Ausdruck in der Behindertenrechtskonvention und Nachhaltigkeitszielen finden, umzusetzen. Die wenigsten Menschen werden für den Umgang mit und die Förderung von Menschen mit Behinderung adäquat vorbereitet, am wenigsten behinderte Menschen selbst oder ihre Angehörigen. Der behindertenpolitische Aktivist Raul Krauthausen formuliert hierzu provozierend: Wer Inklusion will, findet Wege. Wer sie nicht will, findet Ausreden.

Dis/ability-sensible Compassion

Die Kirche, insbesondere die katholische Kirche, hat seit ihrer Gründung das Leitprinzip der Nächstenliebe und Barmherzigkeit, die den sog. Schwachen der Gesellschaft zugutekommen soll. Caritative Maßnahmen sind seit jeher ein fester Bestandteil kirchlichen und auch theologischen Wirkens im Umgang mit Behinderung. Die Geschichte zeigt, dass die Hilfsbedürftigkeit behinderter Menschen bereits in Epochen von Antike, Mittelalter und Neuzeit als Versorgungsfall gelesen wurde.[37] Menschen mit Behinderung konnten und mussten auf die Mild-

---

36 Vgl. ANDERSSOHN, Stefan: Handbuch inklusiver Religionsunterricht. ein didaktisches Konzept. Grundlagen – Theorie – Praxis, Neukirchen-Vluyn: Vandenhoeck & Ruprecht, 2016.

37 Vgl. MATTNER 2000 [Anm. 4], 16–19.

tätigkeit ihrer religiösen Mitmenschen zählen. Was auf den ersten Blick vorteilhaft wirkt, bringt auch Nachteile mit sich: Menschen mit Behinderung werden durch die caritative Ausrichtung zu Hilfe empfangenden Objekten und stehen in Abhängigkeit zu denen, die sie versorgen. Stets besteht die Gefahr, dass das Mitleid als Motor der Caritas ausgeht oder neu entfacht werden muss, um die Versorgung behinderter Menschen zu gewährleisten. Dieses Prinzip besteht zum Teil bis in die gegenwärtige caritative Praxis. Eine Begegnung auf Augenhöhe zwischen Menschen mit und ohne Behinderung ist hierbei deutlich erschwert. Bis heute stellt die Umsetzung von Empowerment und Selbstbestimmung in der caritativen Praxis einen vulnerablen Punkt dar.[38]

Mitleid hat zudem die Folge, dass Menschen mit Behinderung vor allem mit Blick auf ihre Einschränkungen wahrgenommen werden. Sie werden gewollt oder ungewollt auf die Behinderung reduziert – die Sichtweise ist weiter defizitär ausgerichtet und konzentriert sich lediglich auf das Individuum. Orientiert man sich an dem Paradigmenwechsel bei der Sichtweise auf Behinderung, geht es theologisch gesprochen weniger um die Heilung der Person selbst. Vielmehr ist „Behindern ist heilbar" der entscheidende hermeneutische Schlüssel, mit dem benachteiligende Mechanismen und Bedingungen identifiziert und beseitigt werden.[39] Nicht das Behindert-Sein steht im Fokus, sondern das Behindert-Werden. Auch die dis/ability-sensible Bibelhermeneutik kennt diese Orientierung an Bedingungen, die verändert werden sollen. In Mk 10,46–52 erfolgt das heilsame Wirken Jesu beispielsweise nicht nur in der Heilung der Person Bartimäus, sondern auch in der Herstellung einer Annäherung zwischen der Gesellschaft (Volksmenge) und der an ihrem Rand lebenden Person (Bartimäus). Durch Jesu Wirken wird aus der anfangs offensichtlichen Anfeindung eine heilsame Annäherung und Unterstützung, die Bartimäus ermöglicht, den Kontakt zu Jesus herzustellen.[40]

Compassion bietet eine hilfreiche theologische Leitkategorie, die den erweiterten Blick auf Person und Umfeld, also bei der Erkenntnis um Behindert-Sein und Behindert-Werden, wie sie in der Deutung der biblischen Heilungserzählung skizziert wurde, sinnvoll unterstützen kann. Mitleidenschaftlichkeit und Mitleiden nach Metz bezeichnet einen Habitus, der bewusst den Fokus auf eine

---

38 Vgl. THEUNISSEN 2013 [Anm. 12].

39 Vgl. BARTZ 2022 [Anm. 12], 179.

40 Vgl. JESUTHASAN, Janieta: Warum heilt mich dieser Jesus nicht? Die Heilung des blinden Bartimäus und die Erfahrungswelt sehgeschädigter Schülerinnen und Schüler im Religionsunterricht,_http://www.pastoralis.org/IMG/pdf/Fiche_CITP_Rech_12_Jesuthasan.pdf 2013; KAMMEYER, Katharina / JESUTHASAN, Janieta: Behindern ist heilbar. Dis/ability als hermeneutische Leitkategorie im Umgang mit Krankheit und Gesundheit in biblischen Heilungsgeschichten, in: ZIMMERMANN, Mirjam / KLEIN, Constantin / BÜTTNER, Gerhard (Hg.): Kind – Krankheit – Religion. Medizinische, psychologische, theologische und religionspädagogische Perspektiven, Neukirchen-Vluyn: Neukirchner Verlag, 2013, 194–210, 194–197.

gemeinschaftliche Überwindung einer Grenzsituation setzt. Sie beginnt bei der Empathie, die Menschen in Leid- und / oder Grenzsituationen zu Wort kommen lässt. Jesus adressiert Bartimäus in der Heilungserzählung explizit mit Blick auf seine Wünsche: „Was willst du soll ich dir tun?" – dis/ability-sensibel gelesen ermöglicht diese Frage, dass Bartimäus selbst bestimmen kann, ob und wenn ja, welche Form von Hilfe er in Anspruch nehmen möchte. Durch diese Frage nimmt das Gegenüber, also Jesus, das Leid der Person wahr und handelt in angemessener unterstützender Weise. Dieses Handeln kann als Teil disability-sensibler Compassion gedeutet werden, wobei das gesamte Konzept nachfolgend genauer erläutert wird.

Dis/ability-sensible Compassion hat von ihrer Ausrichtung her wichtige Berührungspunkte mit genuin theologischen Themen wie Menschenwürde, Gerechtigkeit und Freiheit.

1. Würde und Ebenbildlichkeit Gottes: Der Mensch ist als Geschöpf und Ebenbild Gottes in seinem So-Sein von Anfang an akzeptiert, geachtet und geliebt.[41] Dis/ability sensible Compassion begegnet Menschen würdevoll und anerkennend, lenkt den Blick bewusst auf die Charismen einer Person und kennt ihre Lebensbedingungen. Eine Fixierung auf Defizite ist obsolet. Der Fokus liegt darauf, vielfältige Fähigkeiten für das Engagement für Nachhaltigkeit zu nutzen. Unterschiede zwischen Menschen als Gottes Geschöpfe werden so normalisiert und nicht problematisiert.
2. Verletzlichkeit und Gerechtigkeit: Das menschliche Dasein auf Erden ist von Verletzlichkeit und Grenzen geprägt.[42] Dis/ability-sensible Compassion weiß um diese Verletzlichkeit und akzeptiert diese. Sie stellt einen kritischen Gegenpol zur allgemein gesellschaftlichen Leistungsorientierung und Selbstoptimierung dar und ist in der Lage, Vulnerabilitäten dann auszuhalten, wenn es erforderlich und sinnvoll ist,[43] ohne wegzuschauen. Das Bewusstsein für die eigene Vulnerabilität hilft, Gerechtigkeit für alle Menschen im Sinne einer nachhaltigen Gesellschaft anzustreben. Compassion meint beispielsweise in diesem Kontext, dass bei expliziter oder impliziter Diskriminierung kein Zuschauereffekt eintritt, sondern die Diskriminierungsmechanismen identifiziert, problematisiert und beseitigt werden.

---

41 Vgl. ROEBBEN, Bert: Religionspädagogik der Hoffnung. Grundlinien religiöser Bildung in der Spätmoderne, Berlin: LIT, 2011.

42 Vgl. BACH, Ulrich: Boden unter den Füßen hat keiner. Plädoyer für eine solidarische Diakonie, Göttingen: Vandenhoeck & Ruprecht, 1980.

43 Vgl. BARTZ, Janieta / JANHSEN, Vera / THÜMMLER, Ramona / KÄPPLER, Christoph: „Philipp verhält sich einfach nur asozial" – Vulnerabilität als hermeneutische Leitkategorie für den Umgang mit Herausforderungen und Dis/ability bei der Planung und Durchführung inklusionsorientierter Lehr-Lern-Prozesse, Erscheint in: SCHRÖTER, Anne et. al. (Hg.): Inklusion in der Lehramtsausbildung: Lerngegenstände, Interaktionen und Prozesse, Münster/New York: Waxmann Verlag GmbH, 2022.

3. Selbstbestimmung, Partizipation sowie Befreiung: Disability-sensible Compassion beinhaltet vor dem Hintergrund von Selbstbestimmung, Partizipation und Freiheit auch eine politisch-theologische Dimension. Dies wird am Beispiel schulischer Inklusion verdeutlicht: Schaut man auf die Nachhaltigkeitsziele der Vereinten Nationen, so ist das zentrale Anliegen die gleichberechtigte Partizipation an einer nachhaltigen Gesellschaft. Gerade im Kontext Bildung ist dies wichtig. Wer ohne Bildung ist, hat selten eine gute Existenzgrundlage für das weitere (Über-)Leben. Dies erinnert an das Anliegen der Befreiungstheologie, als „Stimme der Armen" eine Befreiung der ökonomisch und strukturell Benachteiligten durch die Wiederherstellung sozialer Gerechtigkeit bereits im Diesseits herbeizuführen. Auch für den Glauben an einen gerechten und befreienden Gott ist die Erfahrung entscheidend, dass jede und jeder das bekommt, was er*sie zum Leben braucht (vgl. die Gewährung des Mannas in der Wüste: Num 11 und Ex 16).[44] Im Kontext der Inklusions- und Nachhaltigkeitsdebatte bedeutet dies: Es darf keine Privilegien bei der Verteilung der Bildungsgüter geben, vielmehr hat sich diese nach den individuellen Bedürfnissen der Menschen zu richten. Sie ist in dem Maße gerecht, wie sie diesen Menschen Selbstbestimmung und Partizipation ermöglicht. Für den allgemein gesellschaftlichen Diskurs um Nachhaltigkeit bietet Compassion in diesem Kontext die Chance, Stimmen marginalisierter Gruppen wahrzunehmen und zu verstärken. Bildung, Barrierefreiheit bei Wohnen und Mobilität sind beispielsweise gesamtgesellschaftlich betrachtet als Probleme nicht ausreichend identifiziert.

Impulse für eine neue Hermeneutik des Helfens

Wie konkretisiert sich also die neue Hermeneutik des Helfens? Menschen mit Behinderung möchten die gleiche Behandlung erleben wie alle anderen Menschen auch: Weder Bewunderung noch Benachteiligung sind angebracht, wenn man als nicht betroffene Person miterlebt, wie behinderungsbedingte Probleme bewältigt werden. Vielmehr geht es darum, eine ernst gemeinte persönliche Begegnung als Ausgangspunkt gemeinsamer zu identifizierender Handlungsoptionen zu verstehen. Diese Optionen sind wiederum vielfältig und bilden unterschiedliche Stufen der Unterstützung ab: Die Nachhaltigkeitsziele zeigen, dass es nach wie vor viele Baustellen gibt, die Menschen mit Behinderung an der umfassenden gesellschaftlichen Teilhabe (be-)hindern. Eine Form des Helfens ist, auf diese Baustellen zu achten, diese anzusprechen und / oder die Stimmen der Betroffenen (z. B. auf Social Media) zu verstärken, damit die Baustellen als solche

---

44 Vgl. Bartz 2018 [Anm. 24].

auch gesamtgesellschaftlich identifiziert werden können. Wahrnehmung und Identifikation der Baustellen für behinderte Menschen gründen auf die Bereitschaft, ihnen aktiv zuzuhören, sie verstehen zu wollen und als selbstbestimmt handelnde Menschen ernst zu nehmen. Auf dieser Grundlage ist es auch möglich, sich gemeinsam für ein Anliegen stark zu machen, ohne dass Menschen mit Behinderung bevormundet und / oder fremdbestimmt werden.

Disability-sensible Compassion dient hierbei als theologische Leitkategorie für die Entwicklung einer nachhaltigen Gesellschaft, die die Bedürfnisse und Rechte von Menschen mit Behinderung berücksichtigen will. Ob und welche Unterstützung angemessen ist, stellt die Grundlage eines gemeinsamen Identifikations- und Aushandlungsprozesses dar: Dieser findet auf Augenhöhe statt und berücksichtigt die Selbstbestimmung behinderter Menschen. Compassion, orientiert am Wirken Jesu, beginnt mit Interesse, Aufmerksamkeit und Mitgefühl und konkretisiert sich in Solidarität und Einsatz für die Ziele, die die Lebenssituation von Menschen verbessern. Dabei geht es nicht darum, Unterstützung von Versorgungsfällen zu organisieren, sondern in dem Bewusstsein zu handeln, dass jeder Mensch ein würdevoller Teil einer nachhaltigen Gesellschaft ist und auf seine*ihre Weise wertvoll und gewinnbringend ist.

Literatur

ANDERSSOHN, Stefan: Handbuch inklusiver Religionsunterricht. ein didaktisches Konzept. Grundlagen - Theorie – Praxis, Neukirchen-Vluyn: Vandenhoeck & Ruprecht, 2016.

BACH, Ulrich: Boden unter den Füßen hat keiner. Plädoyer für eine solidarische Diakonie, Göttingen: Vandenhoeck & Ruprecht, 1980.

BARTZ, Janieta: Behindern ist heilbar. Dis-/abilitysensible Anmerkungen zu gegenwärtigen Entwicklungen in der katholischen Kirche, in: BECK, Wolfgang / HEYDER, Regina / SATTLER, Dorothea / SÖDING, Thomas / WUCKELT. Agnes (Hg.): Aufbruch statt Rückzug. Die römisch-katholische Kirche in der Öffentlichkeit heute, Freiburg/Basel/Wien: Herder, 2022, 179–190.

BARTZ, Janieta: All inclusive?! Empirical insights into individual experiences of students with disabilities at German universities and implications for inclusive Higher Education, in: Education Sciences 10, 2020.

BARTZ, Janieta: Jeder bekommt das, was er braucht. Anspruch, Wirklichkeit und Möglichkeiten erfolgreicher Schul- und Unterrichtsentwicklung, in: Lebendige Seelsorge 69 (1) 2018, 53–57.

BARTZ, Janieta: Inklusion im Spannungsfeld von Lust und Frust, in: Unterwegs 35 (2) 2017, 16–17. Online: http://www.katecheten-verein.de/de/files/unterwegs/unterwegs.2-17.pdf.

BARTZ, Janieta / JANHSEN, Vera / THÜMMLER, Ramona / KÄPPLER, Christoph: „Philipp verhält sich einfach nur asozial" – Vulnerabilität als hermeneutische Leitkategorie für den Umgang mit Herausforderungen und Dis/ability bei der Planung und Durchführung inklusionsorientierter Lehr-Lern-Prozesse. Erscheint in: SCHRÖTER, Anne (Hg.): Inklusion in der Lehramtsausbildung: Lerngegenstände, Interaktionen und Prozesse, Münster/New York: Waxmann Verlag, 2022.

BÖSL, Elsbeth: Die Geschichte der Behindertenpolitik in der Bundesrepublik aus Sicht der Disability History, in: APuZ 23 (2010), 6–12.

BUNDESMINISTERIUM DES INNERN (BMI): Abt. Va1, Schreiben an Abt. Va2, 12. 8. 1958, Bundesarchiv (BArch) B 106 8414.

EBERWEIN, Hans: Verzicht auf Kategoriensysteme in der Integrationspädagogik, in: ALBRECHT, Friedrich u. a. (Hg.): Perspektiven der Sonderpädagogik, Neuwied/Berlin: Luchterhand, 2000, 95–106.

FANDREY, Walter: „Krüppel, Idioten, Irre. Zur Sozialgeschichte behinderter Menschen in Deutschland", Stuttgart: Sildberg, 1990.

FRANKE, Alexa: Modelle von Gesundheit und Krankheit, Bern: Hogrefe, 2006.

GABÖSL, Elisabeth / KLEIN, Anne / WALDSCHMIDT, Anne (Hg.): Disability history. Konstruktionen von Behinderung in der Geschichte. Eine Einführung, Bielefeld: transkript, 2010.

GRASSER, Patrick: Inklusion im Religionsunterricht. Vielfalt leben, Göttingen: Vandenhoeck & Ruprecht, 2014.

GROSCHE, Michael: Was ist Inklusion? Ein Diskussions- und Positionsartikel zur Definition von Inklusion aus Sicht der empirischen Bildungsforschung, in: KUHL, Poldi et al. (Hg.): Inklusion von Schülerinnen und Schülern mit sonderpädagogischem Förderbedarf in Schulleistungserhebungen, Wiesbaden: Springer, 2015.

GRÜMME, Bernhard: Bildungsgerechtigkeit. Eine religionspädagogische Herausforderung, Stuttgart: Kohlhammer, 2014.

HINZ, Andreas: Von der Zukunft her denken. Inklusive Pädagogik im Diskurs, Bad Heilbrunn: Klinkhardt, 2016.

JESUTHASAN, Janieta: Warum heilt mich dieser Jesus nicht? Die Heilung des blinden Bartimäus und die Erfahrungswelt sehgeschädigter Schülerinnen und Schüler im Religionsunterricht. http://www.pastoralis.org/IMG/pdf/Fiche_CITP_Rech_12_Jesuthasan.pdf, 2013.

KAMMEYER, Katharina / JESUTHASAN, Janieta: Wie gehen Kinder mit Behinderungen mit Heilungsgeschichten um? Dis/ability als hermeneutische Leitkategorie für Unterrichtsplanung und -analyse am Beispiel der Bartimäus-Geschichte, in: ZIMMERMANN, Mirjam / KLEIN, Constantin / BÜTTNER, Gerhard (Hg.): Kind – Krankheit – Religion. Medizinische, psychologische, theologische und religionspädagogische Perspektiven, Neukirchen-Vluyn: Neukirchner Verlag, 2013, 211–230.

KAMMEYER, Katharina / JESUTHASAN, Janieta: Behindern ist heilbar. Dis/ability als hermeneutische Leitkategorie im Umgang mit Krankheit und Gesundheit in biblischen Heilungsgeschichten, Iin: ZIMMERMANN, Mirjam / KLEIN, Constantin / BÜTTNER, Gerhard (Hg.): Kind – Krankheit – Religion. Medizinische, psychologische, theologische und religionspädagogische Perspektiven, Neukirchen-Vluyn: Neukirchner Verlag, 2013, 194–210.

KARIM, Sarah: Arbeiten mit Behinderungen. Aushandlungen von Nähe und Distanz am Beispiel einer Werkstatt für behinderte Menschen während der Covid-19-Pandemie, in: Journal für Psychologie, 30. Jg., H. 2 (2022), 90-110. https://doi.org/10.30820/0942-2285-2022-2-90.

MATTNER, Dieter: Behinderte Menschen in der Gesellschaft. Zwischen Ausgrenzung und Integration, Stuttgart: Kohlhammer, 2000, 16–74.

REICH, Kerstin: Inklusive Didaktik in der Praxis. Beispiele erfolgreicher Schulen, Weinheim: Beltz, 2017.

ROEBBEN, Bert: Schulen für das Leben. Eine kleine Didaktik der Hoffnung, Stuttgart: Calwer, 2016.

ROEBBEN, Bert: Religionspädagogik der Hoffnung. Grundlinien religiöser Bildung in der Spätmoderne, Berlin: LIT, 2011.

SANDER, Alfred: Behinderungsbegriffe und ihre Integrationsrelevanz, in: EBERWEIN, Hans / KNAUER, Sabine (Hg.): Integrationspädagogik, Weinheim und Basel: Beltz, 2002, 99–108.

THEUNISSEN, Georg: Empowerment und Inklusion behinderter Menschen eine Einführung in Heilpädagogik und Soziale Arbeit, Freiburg im Breisgau: Lambertus, 2013.

VEREINTE NATIONEN: Zwischen Deutschland, Liechtenstein, Österreich und der Schweiz abgestimmte Übersetzung 2006 „Übereinkommen über die Rechte von Menschen mit Behinderungen", online: https://www.bmas.de/SharedDocs/Downloads/DE/Teilhabe/ueber-einkommen-ueber-die-rechte-behinderter-menschen.pdf?__blob=publicationFile&v=2 s.de

WALDSCHMIDT, Anne: Disability Studies, in: DEDERICH, Markus / JANTZEN, Wolfgang (Hg): Behinderung und Anerkennung, Behinderung, Bildung, Partizipation, Enzyklopädisches Handbuch der Behindertenpädagogik Band 2, Stuttgart: Kohlhammer, 2009, 125–133.

WELTGESUNDHEITSORGANISATION: Internationale Klassifikation der Krankheiten, Verletzungen und Todesursachen (ICD), Köln u. a. 1979.

WELTGESUNDHEITSORGANISATION: International Classification of Imparments, Disability and Handicaps, Genf 1980.

WELTGESUNDHEITSORGANISATION: International Classification of Functioning, Disability and Health, Genf 2001.

WOCKEN, Hans: Das Haus der inklusiven Schule. Baustellen – Baupläne – Bausteine, Hamburg: Feldhaus, 2011.

Teil III

Wir sind dran! – Ansätze aus der Schulpraxis zur Vermittlung von Nachhaltigkeitskompetenzen

Den Fähigkeiten gerecht werden – Compassion als Instrument zur Förderung von Klimagerechtigkeit im schulischen Umfeld

Annika Krahn

Die Klimakrise wird die Gesellschaft national sowie international vor die Frage der Klimagerechtigkeit (*climate justice*) stellen. Um eine gesellschaftliche Antwort darauf zu finden, ist die Förderung emotional-sozialer Kompetenzen wichtig. Vor dem Hintergrund des Fähigkeiten-Ansatzes von Martha Nussbaum und mit der Verknüpfung des Compassions-Konzeptes geht dieser Artikel der Frage nach, wie der Religionsunterricht die Wahrnehmung und das Empathievermögen, also die emotional-sozialen Kompetenzen der Schüler*innen fördern kann.

Capabilities-Approach; Fähigkeiten; Compassion; sozial-emotionale Kompetenzen; Unterrichtsmethoden

The climate crisis will confront society nationally and internationally with the question of climate justice. In order to find a social answer to this, the promotion of emotional-social competencies is important. Against the background of Martha Nussbaum's Capabilities Approach and with the linkage of the Compassions Concept, this article explores the question of how religious education can promote perception and empathy, i.e. the emotional-social competencies of pupils.

Capabilities approach; abilities; compassion; social-emotional competencies; teaching methods

„Von der Vision einer solidarischen Gesellschaft, die sich der Klimakrise entgegenstellt und soziale Sicherheit schafft, entfernen wir uns immer weiter",[1] schrieben Luisa Neubauer und Ulrich Schneider in einem Gastbeitrag im Spiegel im Herbst 2022. Und bereits in der ersten Hitzewelle des gleichen Jahres twitterte das deutsche Gesicht der *Fridays-for-Future*-Bewegung: „Wer guten Klimaschutz blockiert, tut das auf dem Rücken der Vulnerabelsten."[2]

Bekanntermaßen ist genau das das Ziel einer Klimagerechtigkeit: Soziale Sicherheit zu schaffen auch für die Vulnerabelsten auf der Welt in der Klimakrise. Denn die klimatischen Veränderungen, die mit dieser einher gehen, u. a. Hochwasser, Überschwemmungen und Hitzewellen, treffen oft Menschen besonders

---

1 NEUBAUER, Luisa / SCHNEIDER, Ulrich: Ökologische Teilhabe. Das Märchen vom unsozialen Klimaschutz, in: https://www.spiegel.de/politik/deutschland/luisa-neubauer-und-ulrich-schneider-das-maerchen-vom-unsozialen-klimaschutz-gastbeitrag-a-cab15eb9-ca7c-494d-9434-6cdf8020610c, zuletzt aufgerufen am 9.5.23.

2 NEUBAUER, Luisa: @Luisamneubauer, Tweet am 19.6.22, 17:38 Uhr.

hart, die sozial benachteiligt sind. Der anthropogene Klimawandel macht somit derzeit eine soziale Schieflage deutlich, die global, aber auch regional deutlich erkennbar ist.

Um eine gewinnbringende religionspädagogische Perspektive auf diese Fragestellung zu eröffnen, wird vor dem Hintergrund des *Capabilities-Approaches* von Martha Nussbaum die Frage beantwortet, wie das theologisch fundierte Konzept des Compassion-Projektes in eine praktisch-religionsdidaktische Überlegung überführt werden kann.

Der *Capabilities-Approach* von Martha Nussbaum

Der *Capabilities-Approach* von Martha Nussbaum ist ein gerechtigkeitstheoretischer Ansatz und stellt die Frage nach einer gelingenden praktischen Lebensführung in den Mittelpunkt der Überlegungen. Seine unverzichtbaren Grundlagen liegen in der aristotelischen Tugendethik.[3] Außerdem rezipiert das von Nussbaum entwickelte Konzept die Vorstellungen des Indischen Ökonom Amartya Sen ein, der Ende der 1970er Jahre mit seinem *Capability-Approach* die individuelle und gesellschaftliche Wohlfahrt unabhängig von der Einkommensgröße berechnet wissen wollte.

Sen setzt voraus, dass die Freiheit eines Menschen als intrinsisches Ziel neben der Abwesenheit von Widerständen (negative Freiheit) ebenfalls bedeutet, nach eigenen Vorstellungen handeln zu können (positive Freiheit). Dabei hat die grundsätzliche (konstitutive) Freiheit Auswirkungen auf die instrumentellen Freiheiten (u. a. politische Freiheit, soziale Chancen), die wiederum die Freiheit im Sinne von Verwirklichungschancen gewährleisten.[4] Die Befähigungen eines Individuums werden also anhand der konkret existenten Freiheiten bemessen.

Im Gegensatz zum von Sen vorgelegten Konzept, hebt Martha Nussbaum mit ihrem *Capabilites-Approach* hervor, dass es die tatsächliche Lebenssituation eines Menschen erlaubt, universell gültige Maßstäbe eines zufrieden geführten Lebens zu formulieren. Dabei will Nussbaum den Ansatz dezidiert nicht als moralische Lehre verstanden wissen:

> The capabilities approach is a political doctrine about basic entitlements, not a comprehensive moral doctrine. It does not even claim to be a complete political doctrine, since it simply specifies some necessary conditions for a decently just society, in the

---

3 NUSSBAUM, Martha C.: The Capabilities Approach and the History of Philosophy, in: CHIAPPERO-MARTINETTI, Enrica / OSMANI, Siddiqur / QIZILBASH, Mozaffar (Hg.): The Cambridge Handbook of the Capability Approach, Cambridge: Cambridge University Press, 2021, 16.

4 Vgl. SEN, Amartya: Commodities and Capabilities, New Delhi: Oxford University Press, 1999, 26–27.

> form of a set of fundamental entitlements of all citizens. Failure to secure these to citizens is a particularly grave violation of basic justice since these entitlements are held to be implicit in the very notions of human dignity and a life that is worthy of human dignity.[5]

Es geht demnach darum, im Rahmen dieses Ansatzes Grundwerte zu beschreiben, die für ein blühendes bzw. gehaltvolles (flourishing)[6] Leben unverzichtbar sind und allen Menschen zustehen. Dabei unterscheidet Nussbaum zwischen den Funktionsweisen (z. B. Sterblichkeit des Menschen) und Verwirklichungschancen oder Befähigungen (z. B. Leben des Menschen) eines Menschen. Nussbaum beschreibt dann zehn grundlegende Fähigkeiten bzw. Befähigungen, „auf deren Ermöglichung Menschen Anspruch haben und die sich als ein Fundament für die Verfolgung und Verwirklichung der verschiedensten Entwürfe eines guten Lebens verstehen lassen".[7] Diese zehn Fähigkeiten erstrecken sich auf folgende Punkte: 1. das Leben, 2. die Gesundheit, 3. Die körperliche Integrität, 4. die Wahrnehmungsfähigkeit, 5. die Gefühlserfahrung, 6. die praktische Vernunft, 7. die Sozialität und die Anerkennung, 8. den Bezug zu anderen Arten von Lebewesen, 9. die spielerische Entfaltung und 10. die Beteiligungsmöglichkeit.[8] Insgesamt können diese Fähigkeiten systematisch zusammengefasst werden, sodass Martha Nussbaum zufolge ein Mensch vollends Anspruch haben sollte auf

- das Erreichen einer durchschnittlich langen Lebensdauer, sodass man weder verfrüht stirbt noch ein derart eingeschränktes Leben lebt, sodass es dem Menschen nicht mehr lebenswert erscheint.
- die Erfüllung aller Voraussetzungen für ein gesundes Leben bzw. der körperlichen Gesundheit und Unversehrtheit. Das bedeutet, dass man in einer gesunden Umgebung ausreichend und ausgewogen ernährt werden kann, eine angemessene Unterkunft besitzt und zudem befähigt ist, sich allerorts frei zu bewegen, vor sexueller und häuslicher Gewalt geschützt ist und frei in Bezug auf Fortpflanzung entscheiden kann.
- die freie Entfaltung der Sinne, der Vorstellungskraft und das Denken. Das inkludiert die Möglichkeit einer hinreichenden Bildung, insbesondere der Lese-, Schreib- und Rechenfähigkeit und das Erleben und Erzeugen religiöser, literarischer, musikalischer oder anders künstlerischer Werke vor dem Hintergrund der politischen und künstlerischen Meinungsfreiheit und der

---

5 NUSSBAUM, Martha: Frontiers of Justice (Tanner lectures on human values 31), Cambridge/MA: Harvard University Press, 2006, 155.

6 Ebd., 182.

7 OTTO, Hans-Uwe / ZIEGLER, Holger: Der Capabilites-Ansatz als neue Orientierung in der Erziehungswissenschaft, in: DIES.: Capabilities – Handlungsbefähigung und Verwirklichungschancen in der Erziehungswissenschaft, Wiesbaden: Verlag für Sozialwissenschaften, ²2010, 11–12.

8 NUSSBAUM, Martha: Frontiers of Justice (Tanner lectures on human values 31), Cambridge/MA: Harvard University Press, 2006, 75.

freien Religionsausübung. Der Mensch sollte befähigt sein, in diesem Zusammenhang angenehme Erfahrungen zu machen und keine unnötigen Schmerzen erleiden zu müssen.
- die Teilhabemöglichkeit, d.h. befähigt zu sein, mit anderen Menschen konstruktiv zu interagieren, sich an diversen Formen des gesellschaftlichen Miteinanders beteiligen zu können. Das bedeutet, dass man über die gesellschaftlichen Grundlagen der Selbstachtung und der Nichtdemütigung verfügt und dazu befähigt ist, anderen Menschen würdevoll und somit nichtdiskriminierend zu begegnen.[9]

Diese vier Ansprüche formulieren demnach eine Grenze unterhalb derer nach Nussbaum ein menschenwürdiges Leben kaum möglich ist. Das oberste gesellschaftliche und politische Ziel sollte es somit sein, diese Grenze für alle Menschen zu überschreiten, sodass der *Capabilities-Approach* mögliche Minimalbedingungen für die soziale Gerechtigkeit einer Gesellschaft formuliert.[10] Um dem Anspruch einer sozialen Gerechtigkeit im Rahmen eines politischen Gesellschaftsvertrages gerecht zu werden, sollten demzufolge die o.g. Minimalbedingungen erfüllt sein – wie hoch das Bruttonationaleinkommen einer Gesellschaft auch sein mag.

> Wenn wir uns die Struktur einer politischen Gesellschaft als das Ergebnis eines Vertrags vorstellen, der in einer Ausgangssituation geschlossen wurde, die in entscheidender Hinsicht fair bzw. ausgeglichen ist, dann kann uns das bei der Bestimmung der Forderungen der Gerechtigkeit helfen. So gelangen wir über ein Verfahren, das auf seiten [sic!] der beteiligten Individuen keinerlei vorgängige Vorteile als gegeben annimmt, zu einer Reihe von Regeln, die die Interessen aller auf angemessene Weise schützen.[11]

Insgesamt wird deutlich, dass sich der Befähigungsansatz nicht nur auf die Frage nach einem individuellen blühenden bzw. gehaltvollen (*flourishing*) Leben erstreckt, sondern auch auf das Leben der Mitmenschen. Somit ist der *Capabilities-Approach* gleichermaßen als soziales Projekt anzusehen.[12] Des Weiteren vertritt Nussbaum die These, dass „eine für partikulare Besonderheiten offene Ethik

---

9 Roder, Sascha: Leben mit einer Neuroprothese. Die Teilhabe von Menschen mit einem Cochlea-Implantat an der Gesellschaft, Wiesbaden: Springer, 2020, 43–44.

10 Vgl. Nussbaum, Martha: Die Grenzen der Gerechtigkeit. Behinderung, Nationalität und Spezieszugehörigkeit, Frankfurt/Main: Suhrkamp, 2014, 137.

11 Ebd., 26.

12 In diesem Sinne ist der Fähigkeiten-Ansatz nicht nur auf die Mitmenschen, sondern im wahrsten Sinne des Wortes auch auf die Mitwelt zu übertragen, für die die Menschen eine kollektive Verantwortung tragen. Vgl. Nussbaum, Martha: Gerechtigkeit für Tiere. Unsere kollektive Verantwortung (Übersetzung von Manfred Weltecke), Darmstadt: WBG, 2023, 356.

nicht ohne Einbeziehen der Gefühle auskommt".[13] Dabei seien ihr zufolge insbesondere zwei Empfindungen zu nennen, die erforderlich sind, um das menschliche Miteinander möglichst blühend bzw. gehaltvoll zu gestalten: Achtung und Mitgefühl. „[I]ndem sie [i.e. Nussbaum] die Tatsache universell geteilter Menschlichkeit ernst nimmt, endet die normative Botschaft dieser beiden moralischen Haltungen nicht an den Grenzen westlicher Industriestaaten, sondern bezieht auch jene ein, die in Unterdrückung, Not und Elend an den Rändern oder jenseits der Welt des Wohlstands leben."[14] In diesem Zusammenhang ist das Nachdenken über eine Hinzunahme des (theologischen) Compassions-Gedankens sachlogisch.

Compassion und die Notwendigkeit des Sehen Könnens, um in Mit-Leidenschaft gezogen zu werden

Der Psychologe Prof. Paul Gilbert – u. a. Begründer der *Compassion focused Therapy* (CFT) und vor seinem Ruhestand Leiter der Mental Health Research-Einheit vom Derbyshire Healthcare NHS Foundation Trust – definiert *Compassion* auf folgende Weise: „[I]n general most researchers see it is as consisting of two basic processes. First is taking an interest in, and having a sensitivity to, distress and suffering, that is turning into it not away from it. Second is a commitment to work out how to alleviate and prevent it. Crucial to compassion is therefore the courage to engage with suffering and risk, along with the wisdom of working out what to do."[15]

Abgesehen vom ca. 15-jährigen Interesse an der Compassion, deren Entwicklungsmöglichkeit und deren (psychologische und soziale) Konsequenzen in der Psychologie wurde das Compassions-Projekt Mitte der 1990er Jahre von den Katholischen Freien Schulen in Deutschland konzipiert, um maßgebliche soziale Haltungen, wie u. a. Solidarität im Rahmen des Sozialen Lernens in den Schulen häufig in Form eines Sozialpraktikums zu fördern. Die Schüler*innen an einer Compassions-Projekt Schule lernen im Rahmen eines nicht nur passiv verstandenen Praktikums die Lebenssituation von u. a. betreuten, gepflegten oder auch ausgegrenzten Menschen kennen und können so einen wichtigen Einblick gewinnen. Insgesamt umfasst das Compassions-Projekt demnach eine sozialpädagogische und eine moralpädagogische Dimension, die im Zusammenspiel das

---

13 PAUER-STUDER, Herlinde: Einleitung, in: NUSSBAUM, Martha (Hg.): Gerechtigkeit oder das Gute Leben. Gender Studies, Frankfurt/Main: Suhrkamp, 92016, 22.

14 Ebd., 23.

15 GILBERT, Paul: The Science of Compassion, in: HAWKINS, Matt / NADEL, Jennifer (Hg.): How Compassion can transform our Politics, Economy, and Society, London/New York: Routledge, 2022, 8.

schulische soziale Lernen profilieren. Lothar Kuld hebt des Weiteren hervor, dass der Theologe Johann Baptist Metz „[u]nabhängig von der Projektentwicklung, aber zeitgleich und in einer merkwürdigen Koinzidenz, [...] *Compassion* das Schlüsselwort des Christentums genannt [hat] und an diesem Begriff die theologische Dimension entfaltet, die das Projekt praktisch macht."[16] Die Empfindsamkeit für das Leid anderer Menschen könne Metz zufolge aus dem Grund als Schlüsselbegriff des Christentums gelten, da die uneingeschränkte Solidarität Jesu den Leidenden und Ausgestoßenen galt.[17] Dabei übersetzt Metz das Wort Compassion mit „Mitleidenschaft" und nimmt ferner an, dass diese Art der Mitleidenschaft für die Weltgemeinschaft nutzbar gemacht werden kann, auch wenn selbstverständlich die anderen zwei abrahamitischen Religionen das Mitleiden, das Erbarmen und die Barmherzigkeit ebenfalls als grundsätzlich für ihre Religion verstehen.[18] Und doch ist die christliche Gottesrede insbesondere in ihrem Kern „leidempfindliche Gottesrede"[19], denn den Leidenden wurde in der Rede und in dem Handeln Jesu Autorität zugesprochen.[20] Compassion bedeutet also für die Nachfolgenden Jesu stets die Augen für ein solches Leiden zu öffnen. Vor dem Hintergrund einer Analysemöglichkeit der Heilung des blinden Bartimäus (Mk 10, 46–52 parr) nennt sich der jesuanische Imperativ demzufolge: Wache auf! Öffne die Augen! „Im Entdecken, im Sehen von Menschen, die im alltäglichen Gesichtskreis unsichtbar bleiben, beginnt die Sichtbarkeit Gottes, öffnet sich seine Spur."[21] Dabei bezog bereits Jesus mögliche „kreatürliche Sehschwierigkeiten" mit ein. „Er kennzeichnet uns als solche, die ‚sehen und doch nicht sehen'. Gibt es womöglich eine elementare Angst vor dem Sehen, vor dem genauen Hinsehen, vor jenem Hinsehen, das uns ins Gesehene unentrinnbar verstrickt und nicht unschuldig passieren lässt?"[22]

---

[16] Kuld, Lothar: Theologie der Compassion. Biblische Grundlagen und theologische Reflexion sozialen Handelns, in: FORUM Schulstiftung. Zeitschrift für die katholischen freien Schulen der Erzdiözese Freiburg (15/2005), S. 3. [Hervorhebung im Original].

[17] Metz, Johann B.: Im Eingedenken fremden Leids. Zu einer Basiskategorie christlicher Gottesrede, in: Metz, Johann B. / Reikerstorfer, Johann / Werbick, Jürgen: Gottesrede (Fundamentaltheologische Studien Bd. 1), Münster: LitVerlag, 1996, 11.

[18] Außerdem lässt sich das auch für die anderen Weltreligionen behaupten. Der Buddhismus beispielsweise gestaltet seine Lehre vor dem Hintergrund einer Analyse des Lebens als Leiden. Vgl. Kuld, Lothar: Art. Compassion (2016), in: WiReLex. https://www.bibelwissenschaft.de/stichwort/100124/, zuletzt aufgerufen am 9.5.23.

[19] Metz, Johann B.: Compassion. Zu einem Weltprogramm des Christentums im Zeitalter des Pluralismus der Religionen und Kulturen, in: Metz, Johann B. / Kuld, Lothar / Weisbrod, Adolf (Hg.): Compassion. Weltprogramm des Christentums. Soziale Verantwortung lernen. Freiburg/Basel/Wien: Herder, 2000, 17.

[20] Metz, Johann B.: Die Autorität der Leidenden. Compassion – Vorschlag zu einem Weltprogramm des Christentums, in: Süddeutsche Zeitung 24./25./26. Dezember 1997 Nr. 296, 57.

[21] Ebd., S. 57.

[22] Metz, Johann B.: Compassion. Zu einem Weltprogramm des Christentums im Zeitalter des Pluralismus der Religionen und Kulturen, in: Metz, Johann B. / Kuld, Lothar / Weisbrod,

Das Konzept der Compassion im Sinne von Metz, das – wie dargestellt – auch interreligiöse Bezugsmöglichkeiten eröffnet, umfasst demnach das metaphorische Sehen, i.e. dem kognitiven und emotionalen Wahrnehmen von gesellschaftlichen Schieflagen bzw. Ausgrenzungssituationen. Ob die Übersetzung von Compassion, die Metz vorstellt, i.e. Mitleidenschaft, wirklich der Bedeutung des Begriffes gerecht wird, kann an dieser Stelle nicht tiefergehend erörtert werden, auch wenn es Anfragen an diese Übersetzung geben sollte und ggf. die Schreibweise Mit-Leidenschaft passender erscheint.[23] Nichtsdestotrotz geht es in dem Konzept der Compassion darum, den Menschen im übertragenen Sinne die Augen zu öffnen und die Frage, die auch im Rahmen dieser kurzen Untersuchung geklärt werden soll, lautet, wie es gelingen kann, den Menschen im Hinblick auf die Frage der Klimagerechtigkeit die Augen zu öffnen bzw. in Mit-Leidenschaft gezogen zu werden.

Zwischenergebnis

Um dieser Frage nachzugehen, ist es sinnvoll eine kurze Zusammenführung der bisherigen Ergebnisse vorzunehmen:

Der Capabilites-Approach von Martha Nussbaum geht der Frage nach, unter welchen Voraussetzungen ein erfüllendes (*flourishing*) Leben gelingen kann. Dafür formuliert Nussbaum zehn Fähigkeiten (*capabilities*), im Rahmen derer sich die Menschen ohne äußerliche und gesellschaftliche Einschränkungen verwirklichen können. Maßgeblich für diesen Ansatz und unabdingbar für die Umsetzung ist die Empfindung des Mitgefühls, die auch das Compassions-Projekt zum Maßstab ihres Handelns macht. Dieses und seine theologische Fundierung durch Johann Baptist Metz fordern dazu auf, Solidarität und Mitmenschlichkeit, u. a. mit gesellschaftlichen Randgruppen zu lernen und zu zeigen. Dabei sind das Sichtbargemachtwerden und das Sehen zwei grundlegende Indikatoren der Compassion.

Adolf (Hg.): Compassion. Weltprogramm des Christentums. Soziale Verantwortung lernen, Freiburg/Basel/Wien: Herder, 2000, 17.

23 In der Stoa galt gerade die Beherrschung der Leidenschaft als Tugend (u. a. Affektkontrolle). Für René Descartes hingegen ist die Leidenschaft zwar eine genuin menschliche Gegebenheit, allerdings sei der Mensch vor dem Hintergrund der Kenntnis der körperlichen Leidenschaft zu ihrer Überwindung verpflichtet, damit beispielsweise emphatisches Verhalten überhaupt möglich sei. Vgl. ALANEN, Lilli: Descartes's Concept of Mind, Cambridge/Ma./London: Harvard University Press, 2003. 178. Vielleicht ist auch die Übersetzung des Wortes *passio* in Bezug auf das Leid und die Leidensgeschichte Jesu hin zu überprüfen, sodass in diesem Zusammenhang die Schreibweise Mit-Leidenschaft vorzuziehen ist.

Praktische Umsetzung in Bezug auf Klimagerechtigkeit

Die Klimakrise hat insbesondere auf Menschen einen negativen Einfluss, die ökonomisch benachteiligt sind, sodass die Frage nach der Klimagerechtigkeit äußerst virulent ist und ihre Relevanz auch in religionspädagogischen Überlegungen haben sollte.[24] Zum Beispiel betrifft die Klimakrise die Verfügbarkeit von sauberem Trinkwasser und Nahrungsmitteln. „The major effect of climate change in terms of global health is the potential increase in water and food insecurity that could impact billions of people."[25] Diesen Menschen wird es nicht mehr möglich sein, ihr Fähigkeiten gemäß des *Cappabilites-Approaches* von Nussbaum zu verwirklichen und somit ein blühendes und erfüllendes (*flourishing*) Leben zu führen. Dieses Verunmöglichen betrifft jedoch nicht nur die genannten Veränderungen in Bezug auf Nahrung und Wasser. Die Grafik der sogenannten Doughnut-Ökonomie zeigt die Auswirkungen der anthropogenen Klimaänderung auf das Leben der Menschen. Außerdem geht sie von planetaren Grenzen aus, die nicht überschritten werden dürfen, wohingegen die sozialen Grenzen nicht unterschritten werden dürfen, sodass alle Menschen innerhalb des Doughnuts leben können (siehe Abb. 1).

Wie die Weltgemeinschaft in dem Anthropozän die schlimmsten Folgen der Klimakrise vermeiden kann, ist eine Frage, die politische, ökonomische und ethische Aspekte inkludiert. Beispielsweise wird ein UBI (*Universal Basic Income*)[26] diskutiert,

> „to give people the right to choose how they live, and rewild the Earth to protect the needs of other species. With carefully designed policies that unleash dynamics that push society towards a new mode of living for a new epoch, we can do what is necessary: to reduce human suffering, enable people to flourish, and not destroy the life-supporting infrastructure of Earth in the process. [...] It will take many initiatives to replace today's unsustainable consumer capitalist mode of living. But if history teaches us anything, it is that we must do something radically different that breaks the productivity rules that have governed all of human history and gives the best chance for people and the rest of life with which we share our home planet all to flourish."[27]

---

24 Vgl. Krahn, Annika: Klimagerechtigkeit und religiöse Bildung, in: Das Wort. Evangelische Beiträge zu Bildung und Unterricht 76 (04/22), 7-10.

25 Maslin, Mark / Lewis, Simon L.: Climate, in: Hawkins, Matt / Nadel, Jennifer (Hg.): How Compassion can Transform our Politics, Economy, and Society, London/New York: Routledge, 2022, 94.

26 Vgl. Ebd., 99.

27 Ebd., 102.

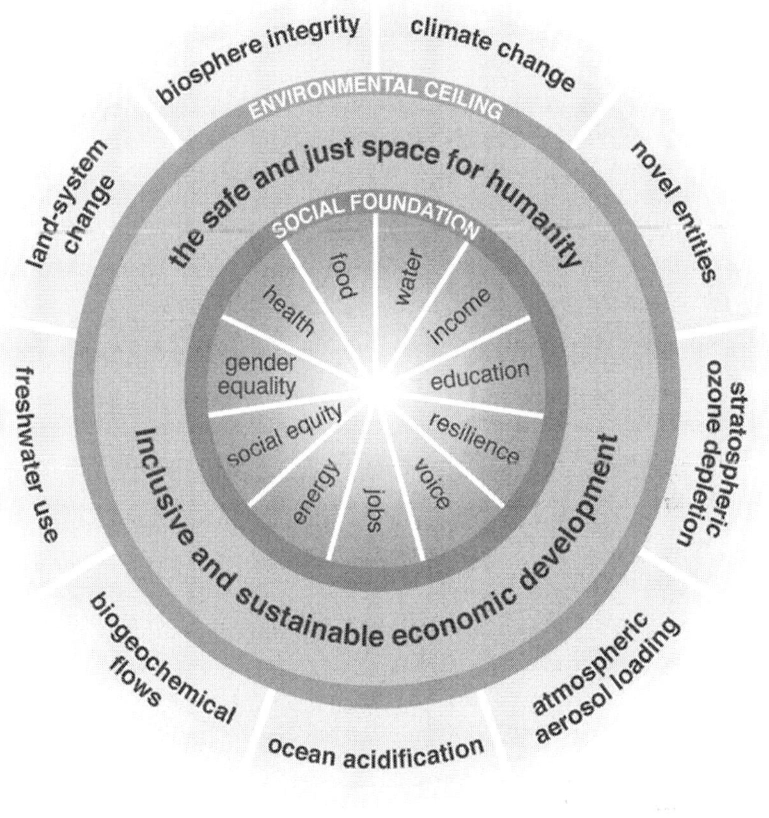

Abb. 1: Adaptation of Raworth's (2017) illustration of doughnut economics and how the physical and social needs of society must be considered together.[28]

Im konkret stattfindenden Religionsunterricht kann nun – abgesehen von einer Diskussion über die Gerechtigkeit eines UBI's im Vergleich mit der Parabel in Mt 20, 1–16 – keine Einführung eines globalen UBI's beschlossen, geschweige denn durchgesetzt werden, sodass zu überlegen ist, wie das Sichtbar-gemacht-werden und das aktive Sehen – also das *in Mit-Leidenschaft Ziehen* – initiiert werden kann. Das metaphorische aktive Sehen konkretisiert sich in diesem Zusammenhang im Religionsunterricht in der Förderung von emotional-sozialen Kompetenzen sowie der Wahrnehmungskompetenz von Kindern und Jugendlichen.

Im Unterricht ist es zuvorderst wichtig, eine Atmosphäre der gegenseitigen Achtung in Bezug auf die Kommunikations- und Beziehungskultur zu schaffen. Insbesondere das Classroom Management ist an dieser Stelle als Basisdimension

28 Ebd., 100.

wirksamen Unterrichts zu nennen.[29] Gerade im Religionsunterricht ist als Anteil des Classroom Managements besonders das ritualisierte Handeln von großer Bedeutung. Grundsätzlich spielen in religiösen Kontexten diverse Rituale (u. a. Gesänge und Gebete) eine große Rolle. Für den Religionsunterricht können auch religiöse Rituale als performatives Handeln im Unterricht etabliert werden, um Orientierung zu bieten und ein Augenöffnen im Sinne der Förderung von emotional-sozialen Kompetenzen zu initiieren. Außerdem ist die Musik ein gewichtiger Faktor, um die Wahrnehmung und das emotionale Hören der Schüler*innen zu fördern.

Von der Theorie zu zwei Beispielen aus der Praxis

Musik

Ein Praxisbeispiel lehnt sich an den Vorschlag von Heike Lindner an, in dem ein Lied zum Unterrichtsgegenstand gemacht wird, in dem der Interpret die Gefühle und Gedanken zum tragischen Unfalltod seines Sohnes verarbeitet und ausgedrückt hat.[30] Zur Förderung der Wahrnehmungskompetenz soll das Lied zunächst assoziativ gehört werden. Dabei sollen die Schüler*innen auf ihre durch das Lied ausgelösten Gefühle und Gedanken achten. Ein weiteres Hören findet dann mit dem Hintergrundwissen statt, über das die Lerngruppe nach dem ersten Hören informiert wurde. Zudem könnten die Schüler*innen beobachten, wie sich das neu erworbene Wissen auf ihre Gedanken und Gefühle auswirkt, also wie die Kenntnisse der Umstände des Liedes beim weiteren Hören möglicherweise verstärkt Mitgefühl auslösen. Über einen Interviewausschnitt wird das Kennenlernen der theoretischen Trauerverarbeitung angeregt. Die Förderung des Empathievermögens werde vor allem durch den im Vordergrund stehenden „autobiographische[n] Kontext einer Vater-Sohn-Beziehung“[31] unterstützt. Der Perspektivwechsel wird vollzogen, indem sich die Schüler*innen in die Gefühls- und Gedankenwelt einer anderen Person versetzen. Konkret schlägt das Umsetzungsbeispiel vor, dass die Schüler*innen in die Rolle des Sohnes schlüpfen, passende Musik auswählen und ein Antwortlied auf den Song des Vaters verfassen. Die Förderung der „Wahrnehmungskompetenz, [des] Empathievermögen[s]

---

29 Vgl. SCHÖNEICH, Sabine: Schwierige Schüler? Wie Lehrer und Schüler besser zusammenarbeiten, Weinheim: Beltz ,2011, 29.

30 Vgl. LINDNER, Heike: Musik für den Religionsunterricht. Praxis- und kompetenzorientierte Entfaltungen, Göttingen: Vandenhoeck & Ruprecht, 2014, 27-29.

31 Ebd., 28.

[und die] Fähigkeit zum Perspektivwechsel“[32] werden als Entwicklungsziele dieser Einheit genannt.

Im weiteren Verlauf der Einheit können nun mit einem ähnlichen Vorgehen musikalischen Beispiele herangeführt werden, die die soziale Schieflage in Bezug auf die Klimakrise deutlich hervorheben, wie beispielsweise „Excuse Me Mr.“ von Ben Harper oder „When You Gonna Learn“ von Jamiroquai. Wichtig sollte es sein, dass die Schüler*innen stets die Möglichkeit haben, mit ihrem eigenen musikalischen Geschmack und mit einer eigens formulierten Antwort zu reagieren. Dabei ist es von Bedeutung, die durch die Musik ausgelösten Gefühle „zu erkennen, zu differenzieren und sie [zu] versprachlichen“,[33] um vor dem Hintergrund der gesteigerten Wahrnehmungskompetenz in Mit-Leidenschaft gezogen zu werden.

Bibliolog

Auch der Bibliolog eignet sich hervorragend, um im Rahmen des Religionsunterrichts die sozial-emotionalen Kompetenzen der Schüler*innen zu fördern. Dieser „bietet einen methodisch strukturierten Weg“, mit den Schüler*innen auf die Art und Weise einen Bibeltext für sich zu entdecken, „das die Bedeutung für das eigene Leben unmittelbar erlebbar wird.“[34] Im Rahmen eines gemeinsam durchgeführten Bibliologs versetzen sich die Teilnehmenden in die Rolle von biblischen Figuren eines bestimmten Erzählabschnittes und beantworten aus ihrer Rolle heraus Fragen, die der Moderierende bzw. die Lehrkraft stellt. Durch das Hineinversetzen in eine Rolle eignet sich diese Methode auch für Schüler*innen, die einer anderen Glaubensrichtung angehören oder nicht religiös sind unter der Voraussetzung, dass eine Beschäftigung mit biblischen Texten akzeptiert wird.

Mit Hilfe des wiederholt stattfindenden Rollenwechsels und des Sich-hinein-Versetzens in die Figuren der biblischen Erzählungen wird insbesondere die Fähigkeit zur Empathie und zum Perspektivenwechsel gefördert. Folglich ist der Bibliolog eine Methode, die im Wesentlichen für den Aufbau von Fertigkeiten im Kompetenzbereich der Fremdwahrnehmung einsetzbar ist. Ein Bezug allerdings

---

32 Ebd., 28.

33 Ebd., 32.

34 Pohl-Patalong, Uta (2016): [Art.] Bibliolog, in: WiReLex Online. http://www.bibelwissenschaft.de/stichwort/100139/ (zuletzt aufgerufen am 12.5.2023). Die Durchführung eines Bibliologs ist in sieben Schritten zu vollziehen und dadurch klar strukturiert (Prolog, Hinführung, Enroling, Echoing, Wiederholung, Deroling, Epilog). Wie genau die einzelnen Schritte durchzuführen sind, ist in der angegebenen Literatur nachzulesen.

zur Selbstwahrnehmung ist stets gegeben, da „die Äußerungen faktisch auch immer Lebenserfahrungen der Teilnehmenden“[35] sind.

Möglichkeiten der Weiterentwicklung bieten sich an, wenn die Lehrkraft gemeinsam mit den Schüler*innen das Verhalten der Figuren in bestimmten Szenen (schriftlich oder mündlich) reflektiert und über die Beweggründe des Handelns und möglichen Handlungsalternativen ins Gespräch kommt. Außerdem ist es ebenso möglich, auf diese Art und Weise mit den Schüler*innen über die sogenannte *Climate Change literature* ins Gespräch zu kommen. Beispielhaft seien an dieser Stelle der Roman von Jessie Greengrass, *The High House* (dt. *Und dann verschwand die Zeit*), *The Line* von Niall Bourke oder *All the Light We cannot See* von Anthony Doerr genannt.

Ergebnis

Mit Hilfe der formulierten Fähigkeiten von Martha Nussbaum ist es möglich, die Komponenten eines erfüllenden (*flourishing*) Lebens zu benennen und gleichzeitig dort einzuschreiten, wo diese Komponenten nicht vollends erfüllt sind. Maßgeblich für die Verwirklichung des Ansatzes von Nussbaum und der Möglichkeit innerhalb des Doughnuts bleiben zu können, ist das Mitgefühl, das den Menschen ermöglicht, im metaphorischen Sinne ihre Augen für das Missverhältnis zu öffnen und demnach in Mit-Leidenschaft gezogen zu werden.

Im Religionsunterricht kann dies insbesondere durch die Förderung von sozial-emotionalen Kompetenzen wie der Wahrnehmungskompetenz oder der Empathie gelingen. Zwei Beispiele aus der Praxis (u. a. die Verwendung von Musik und die Methode des Bibliologs bzw. eines Sich-Hinein-Versetzens) machen deutlich, dass die Fähigkeiten, die für einen Perspektivenwechsel und für das Empathievermögen vonnöten sind, maßgeblich im Religionsunterricht gefördert und unterstützt werden können, sodass die Schüler*innen im Sinne der Metz'schen Compassion in Mit-Leidenschaft gezogen werden und die Relevanz

---

35 Ebd. Abgesehen von diesen Methoden existieren einige evidenzbasierte Förderprogramme zur Förderung bestimmter emotionaler und sozialer Kompetenzen. Eine Möglichkeit ist es, diese im Rahmen des Religionsunterrichts durchzuführen. Eine Möglichkeit ist es, diese ebenfalls im Rahmen des Religionsunterrichts durchzuführen. Eine interessante Weiterentwicklung wäre die Verknüpfung eines solchen Programmes mit religionspädagogischen Inhalten. Als Beispiel wird an dieser Stelle *Lubo aus dem All* genannt. Eine religionspädagogische Perspektive könnte damit erreicht werden, dass ein:e Zeitreisend:e aus der Zeit Jesu als Figur das Programm begleitet. Vgl. HILLENBRAND, Clemens et al.: Lubo aus dem All! – 1. und 2. Klasse: Programm zur Förderung sozial-emotionaler Kompetenzen. Mit zahlreichen Abbildungen und Tabellen, Bildkarten, Postern, einem Spielplan und einer CD-ROM mit Musik, zahlreichen Kopiervorlagen und den Bildergeschichten „Tobi tobt“ und „Sara und Maxi“, München / Basel: Reinhardt, [3]2015.

einer Klimagerechtigkeit verstehen lernen, um diese im Rahmen ihrer Möglichkeiten umzusetzen.

Literatur

ALANEN, Lilli: Descartes's Concept of Mind, Cambridge/Ma./London: Harvard University Press, 2003.

GILBERT, Paul: The Science of Compassion, in: HAWKINS, Matt / NADEL, Jennifer (Hg.): How Compassion can transform our Politics, Economy, and Society, London/New York: Routledge, 2022, 7–38.

HILLENBRAND, Clemens et al.: Lubo aus dem All! – 1. und 2. Klasse: Programm zur Förderung sozial-emotionaler Kompetenzen. Mit zahlreichen Abbildungen und Tabellen, Bildkarten, Postern, einem Spielplan und einer CD-ROM mit Musik, zahlreichen Kopiervorlagen und den Bildergeschichten „Tobi tobt" und „Sara und Maxi", München / Basel: Reinhardt, [3]2015.

KULD, Lothar: Theologie der Compassion. Biblische Grundlagen und theologische Reflexion sozialen Handelns. S. 3. [überarbeitete Version], in: FORUM Schulstiftung. Zeitschrift für die katholischen freien Schulen der Erzdiözese Freiburg (15/2005), 3–12.

KULD, Lothar: Art. Compassion (2016), in: WiReLex. https://www.bibelwissenschaft.de/stichwort/100124/ (zuletzt aufgerufen am 9.5.23).

KRAHN, Annika: Klimagerechtigkeit und religiöse Bildung, in: Das Wort. Evangelische Beiträge zu Bildung und Unterricht 76 (04/22), 7–10.

LINDNER, Heike: Musik für den Religionsunterricht. Praxis- und kompetenzorientierte Entfaltungen, Göttingen: Vandenhoeck & Ruprecht, 2014.

MASLIN, Mark / LEWIS, Simon L.: Climate, in: HAWKINS, Matt / NADEL, Jennifer (Hg.): How Compassion can Transform our Politics, Economy, and Society, London/New York: Routledge, 2022, 91–105.

METZ, Johann B.: Im Eingedenken fremden Leids. Zu einer Basiskategorie christlicher Gottesrede, in: METZ, Johann B. / REIKERSTORFER, Johann / WERBICK, Jürgen: Gottesrede (Fundamentaltheologische Studien Bd. 1), Münster: LitVerlag, 1996, 3–20.

METZ, Johann B.: Compassion. Zu einem Weltprogramm des Christentums im Zeitalter des Pluralismus der Religionen und Kulturen, METZ, Johann B. / KULD, Lothar / WEISBROD, Adolf (Hg.): Compassion. Weltprogramm des Christentums. Soziale Verantwortung lernen. Freiburg / Basel / Wien: Herder, 2000, 9–18.

METZ, Johann B.: Die Autorität der Leidenden. Compassion – Vorschlag zu einem Weltprogramm des Christentums, in: Süddeutsche Zeitung 14./25./26. Dezember 1997 Nr. 296.

NEUBAUER, Luisa / SCHNEIDER, Ulrich: Ökologische Teilhabe. Das Märchen vom unsozialen Klimaschutz, in: https://www.spiegel.de/politik/deutschland/luisa-neubauer-und-ulrich-schneider-das-maerchen-vom-unsozialen-klimaschutz-gastbeitrag-a-cab15eb9-ca7c-494d-9434-6cdf8020610c (zuletzt aufgerufen am 9.5.23).

NUSSBAUM, Martha: Frontiers of Justice (Tanner lectures on human values 31), Cambridge/MA: Harvard University Press, 2006.

NUSSBAUM, Martha: Die Grenzen der Gerechtigkeit. Behinderung, Nationalität und Spezieszugehörigkeit, Frankfurt/Main: Suhrkamp, 2014.

NUSSBAUM, Martha: Gerechtigkeit oder Das Gute Leben. Gender Studies (hrsg. von Herlinde Pauer-Studer), Frankfurt/Main: Suhrkamp, 1998.

NUSSBAUM, Martha C.: The Capabilities Approach and the History of Philosophy, in: CHIAPPERO-MARTINETTI, Enrica / OSMANI, Siddiqur / QIZILBASH, Mozaffar (Hg.): The Cambridge Handbook of the Capability Approach, Cambridge: Cambridge University Press, 2021, 13–39.

NUSSBAUM, Martha: Gerechtigkeit für Tiere. Unsere kollektive Verantwortung (Übersetzung von Manfred Weltecke), Darmstadt: WBG, 2023.

OTTO, Hans-Uwe / ZIEGLER, Holger: Der Capabilites-Ansatz als neue Orientierung in der Erziehungswissenschaft, in: DIES.: Capabilities – Handlungsbefähigung und Verwirklichungschancen in der Erziehungswissenschaft, Wiesbaden: Verlag für Sozialwissenschaften, [2]2010, 9–13.

PAUER-STUDER, Herlinde: Einleitung, in: Martha Nussbaum (Hg.): Gerechtigkeit oder das Gute Leben. Gender Studies, Frankfurt/Main: Suhrkamp, [9]2016, 7–23.

POHL-PATALONG, Uta (2016): Art. Bibliolog, in: WiReLex Online. http://www.bibelwissenschaft.de/stichwort/100139/ (zuletzt aufgerufen am 12.5.2023).

RODER, Sascha: Leben mit einer Neuroprothese. Die Teilhabe von Menschen mit einem Cochlea-Implantat an der Gesellschaft, Wiesbaden: Springer, 2020.

SCHÖNEICH, Sabine: Schwierige Schüler? Wie Lehrer und Schüler besser zusammenarbeiten, Weinheim: Beltz, 2011.

SEN, Amartya: Commodities and Capabilities, New Delhi: Oxford University Press, 1999.

Erzählen will ich von deinem Namen – Zum sinnstiftenden Potenzial des gemeinsamen Erzählens als religionspädagogische Unterrichtsmethode im Kontext einer subjektorientierten konstruktivistischen Didaktik

Maurice Steffens (geb. Andree)

Erzählen ist nicht nur eines der ersten Medien, mit denen Kinder in Verbindung mit der Welt treten, sondern darüber hinaus auch das älteste christliche Tradierungsmedium. Religionsunterricht will in seinem Anspruch eine alternative Weltsicht darbieten. Dieser Beitrag widmet sich der Frage, inwieweit die Kulturtechnik des Erzählens als unterrichtliche Didaktik für dieses Anliegen des Religionsunterrichts und der rBNE fruchtbar gemacht werden kann.

Erzählen; Subjektorientierung; Identitätsbildung; Weltverständnis, rBNE

Storytelling is not only one of the first media through which children make contact with the world, but also the oldest Christian medium of transmission. Religious education aims to offer an alternative view of the world. This article is dedicated to the question of the extent to which the cultural technique of storytelling can be made fruitful for this concern of religious education and rESD as a didactic method of teaching.

narrative; subject orientation; identity formation; understanding of the world, rESD

Relevanz einer Didaktik des Erzählens

„Der gesamte Unterricht ist Kommunikation!“[1] mit diesem Zitat führen Georg Hilger und Hans-Georg Ziebertz in ihre allgemeine Religionsdidaktik in kommunikativer Perspektive ein. So einfach und richtig diese Aussage auf den ersten Blick wirkt, so vielschichtig ist sie gleichzeitig. Gerade der Religionsunterricht nimmt in diesem Kontext eine herausragende Stellung ein, da es zum Proprium

---

[1] Vgl. HILGER, Georg / ZIEBERTZ, Hans-Georg: Religionsdidaktik in kommunikativer Perspektive, in: HILGER, Georg / LEIMGRUBER, Stephan / ZIEBERTZ, Hans-Georg (Hg.): Religionsdidaktik. Ein Leitfaden für Studium, Ausbildung und Beruf, München: [5]2017, 110.

des Religionsunterrichtes gehört, in und durch Kommunikation sich mit dem eigenen Selbst, dem Gegenüber sowie der Welt auseinanderzusetzen.

Das Erzählen gehört hierbei zu einer der Grundlegendsten und ersten Kulturtechniken, die entwickelt wurden und mit denen Kinder und Jugendliche heute in Berührung kommen. Es stellt in der Regel eines der ersten Bildungsmedien dar, durch das sich Kinder in Verbindung mit der Welt setzen. Darüber hinaus ist es jedoch auch das Medium, welches die verschiedenen Kulturen über Jahrhunderte stark prägte und welches als das älteste und wichtigste christliche Tradierungsmedium bezeichnet wird.[2] Das gesamte Schulsystem basiert auf dieser Kulturtechnik, indem es die Bildung derart an epochalen Schlüsselproblemen ausrichtet, dass nach Klafki die Schüler*innen dazu befähigt werden, die zentralen Probleme der Gegenwart und voraussehbaren Zukunft in den Dimensionen der Einsicht, Mitverantwortlichkeit und Bewältigung zu verstehen, diskutieren und argumentativ zu vertreten.[3] Neben überprüfbaren Kompetenzzielen und inhaltlichem Faktenwissen hat es sich gerade der Religionsunterricht zur Aufgabe gemacht, eine alternative Sicht auf die Welt zu bieten. Diese alternative Sicht wird bereits durch die Korrelation der beiden Ausgangspunkte des christlichen Glaubens, der Selbstoffenbarung Gottes in Form der Bibel sowie den konkreten Menschen / Schüler*innen, virulent, da der Wahrheitsgehalt der Religion(en) immer nur in der subjektiven Bedeutungszuschreibung und der lebensvertiefenden Funktion gesehen werden kann und des Ausdrucks bedarf.[4] Diese Subjektorientierung des Religionsunterrichts schließt mithin das Verhältnis von Ich und Welt mit ein, sodass die Aspekte von Natur und Zukunft als gegenwärtige Schlüsselprobleme der jüngeren Generationen die (religiöse) Bildung für nachhaltige Entwicklung (rBNE) nicht nur in den Themen der Gottesebenbildlichkeit oder dem Schöpfungsgedanken zum Gegenstand unterrichtlicher Erzählungen machen, sondern zur Querschnittsaufgabe werden, damit Glaube und Religionsunterricht ihrem Anspruch, hilfreich und sinnstiftend zu sein, gerecht werden können.[5]

Ziel dieses Aufsatzes ist es, die Korrelation aus dem Erzählen als unterrichtliche Didaktik und der Lehrperson als Medium in der Art fruchtbar zu machen, dass sie als religiös Erziehende zu Hilfestellungen in transformativen Prozessen von Kindern und Jugendlichen werden, an deren Ende eine individuelle religiöse Grundhaltung steht, welche sie mit Überzeugung reflexiv vertreten können und

---

[2] Vgl. SEYBOLD, Klaus: Erzählen vom Erzählen. Beobachtungen zu einer biblischen Erzähltheorie, in: Theologische Zeitschrift 61 (2015), 14–16.

[3] Vgl. KLAFKI, Wolfgang: Neue Studien zur Bildungstheorie und Didaktik. Zeitgemäße Allgemeinbildung und kritisch-konstruktive Didaktik, Weinheim: Beltz, [6]2007, 56–57.

[4] Vgl. SCHÜTZE, Stefan: Zum Erzählen biblischer Geschichten, in: Theo-Web. Zeitschrift für Religionspädagogik 14 (2015), 71.

[5] Vgl. BEDERNA, Katrin: Religiöse Bildung für nachhaltige Entwicklung. Ein didaktisches Modell, in: Religionspädagogische Beiträge 44 (2021), 62–63.

so aktiv Gestaltungskompetenzen für die eigene Gegenwart und Zukunft ausgebildet werden.

Erzählungen in unterrichtlichen Kontexten wurden bislang ausführlich im Rahmen verschiedener bibeldidaktischer Theorien untersucht und erläutert. Fraglich bleibt jedoch, ob die Methodik des Erzählens ihren religionspädagogischen Sitz nur im Kontext der Bibeldidaktik finden kann oder vielmehr als durchlaufendes Moment jeglicher religiöser Bildung angesehen werden muss, die gerade in Zeiten gesellschaftlicher Krisen ihre Tragfähigkeit beweist. Wenn das Leitwort „Zur bildenden Kraft des Religionsunterrichts" der Deutschen Bischofskonferenz aus den 1990er Jahren ernstgenommen wird, welches auf ein grundlegendes Verständnis von Religionsunterricht der Würzburger Synode zurück geht, gehört es zu den Kernaufgaben des Religionsunterrichts, die religiös-spirituellen Erzählungen in der Art fruchtbar zu machen, dass sie zum Werkzeug der Verständigung und Identität und somit zu spezifischen Angeboten der Identitätsbildung werden.[6] Dieses Anliegen schließt auch die Ausbildung einer gesellschaftsstiftenden Ethik mit ein, welche die gegenwärtigen Bedarfe achtet. An dieser Stelle wird bereits die zentrale Rolle der Religionslehrkraft als wissender Übersetzer und kritischer Brückenbauer ersichtlich. Erst, wenn Personen durch die Darbietung von Identitäten lernen und gleichsam von der Erzählung und in der Erzählung gelernt wird, kann der Religionsunterricht als subjektiv gewinnbringend, durch das Lernen an Vorbildern und personifizierten Modellen, erlebt werden. Die Gestaltung von Religionsunterricht auf der Grundlage einer subjektorientiert-konstruktivistischen Didaktik entfaltet gerade im Medium des Erzählens das Potenzial intersubjektive Verständigung anzuregen, plurale Einigungsprozesse anzustoßen und den gesellschaftlich-kulturellen Pluralismus mikrokosmisch ins Klassenzimmer wertschätzend hereinzuholen.

Deshalb beschäftigt sich dieser Aufsatz zunächst mit der religionsdidaktisch-kommunikativen Grundlage unterrichtlichen Handelns, bevor der Fokus auf die Technik des Erzählens und das Medium der Lehrkraft gelegt wird. Abschließend werden diese Überlegungen dann auf das gesellschaftliche Schlüsselproblem der Nachhaltigkeit und den Aspekt der rBNE angewandt.

Religionsunterricht in kommunikativer Perspektive

Zweifelsohne bildet das sprachlich-kommunikative Handeln die grundlegendsten Prozesse in unterrichtlichen Kontexten ab. Es wird niemand anzweifeln, dass der Unterricht als Gesamtkonstrukt ein vielschichtiges Handeln darstellt, wel-

---

6 Vgl. DIE DEUTSCHEN BISCHÖFE 56: Die bildende Kraft des Religionsunterrichts. Zur Konfessionalität des katholischen Religionsunterrichts, Bonn: Vandenhoek&Ruprecht [5]2009, 7

ches durch und durch als kommunikatives Handeln auf verbaler und nonverbaler Ebene bezeichnet werden kann. Kommunikative Prozesse können als soziale Dimension verstanden werden, die auf die intersubjektive Verständigung ausgerichtet sind und somit gleichsam subjektorientiert sowie konstruktivistisch zu verstehen sind.[7] Kommunikation und die damit einhergehenden Verständigungshandlungen können nur als Aushandlungsprozess im Spannungsfeld von Verstehen und Verständigung begriffen werden, wodurch als Zweck dieser Handlungen das Subjekt als solches, sowie die dahinterliegende individuelle Repräsentation der Welt zu postulieren sind. Die soziale Dimension der Kommunikation muss mithin nicht nur im genuinen Verständigungshandeln gesehen werden, sondern auch in der Sinn-Stiftung und Sinn-Erhaltung der Selbst-, Fremd- und Weltwahrnehmungen der jeweiligen Individuen.[8]

In Kontexten, in denen die Kommunikation nicht über bekannte Wahrheiten erfolgen kann, sondern aus einem Verstehen und Aushandeln von Wahrnehmungen, Interpretationen, Fraglichkeiten und Unbegreiflichkeiten besteht, kommt den Dimensionen der Verständigung und Subjektorientierung ferner eine herausgehobene Stellung im Kontext der eigenen Ich-Identität und Rollenklarheit zu. Selbstverständlich müssen die dahinterliegenden Kompetenzen in einem kontinuierlichen Prozess durch die verschiedenen Bildungsetappen des Lebens, angefangen in Kindertagesstätten als erste Phase der individuellen Bildungsbiografien, bis hin zum Übergang in das selbstgesteuerte lebenslange Lernen, kontinuierlich weiterentwickelt werden.[9] Dieser Prämisse muss die jeweilige unterrichtlich-didaktische Orientierung Rechnung tragen, die die Fähigkeiten der konkreten Schüler*innen berücksichtigt. Hierbei wird gleichsam partizipative Erziehung im Kontext einer Erziehung zu Freiheit und Mündigkeit vollzogen.[10] Mithin führt unterrichtliche Kommunikation immer zur Ausbildung von Kompetenzen der Perspektivübernahme, die zum Ziel haben, Abstand von der eigenen Perspektive zu gewinnen, um gleichsam die Denkweisen anderer nachvollziehbar erleben zu können. Durch die Abwägung der Ich- und Du-Perspektive hin zu möglichen Formen des „Wir" können sinnstiftende Aspekte aus den verschiedenen Perspektiven entnommen und neu arrangiert werden. Dies birgt in den einhergehenden Aushandlungsprozessen ein gemeinschaftsstiftendes Potenzial, welches aus gemeinsamen Erfahrungen eine neue Normalität und Normativität ableiten lässt, die gleichsam eine Rückendeckung erfährt, da sie durch den erlebten Mikrokosmos getragen wird.[11] Diese Gemeinschaftsdimension speist sich aus Erfahrungen und Erkenntnissen, die mithilfe metakommunikativer Reflexionskompetenzen, gleichsam auch zum Ziel der eigentlichen

---

7 Vgl. HILGER / ZIEBERTZ [Anm. 1], 110–111.
8 Vgl. Ebd., 111–112.
9 Vgl. SCHÜTZE [Anm. 4], 70 sowie 79.
10 Vgl. HILGER / ZIEBERTZ [Anm. 1], 112–113.
11 Vgl. BEDERNA [Anm. 5], 65.

Verständigung werden: Die Erschließung der Lebensbedeutsamkeit in den verschiedenen Kommunikationsebenen, welche zur Ausbildung genuiner Lebens- und Handlungsorientierung und somit zum Identitätsmerkmal führt.[12]

Wenn nun vor diesem Hintergrund der Religionsunterricht mit seinem Anspruch auf Sinnstiftung und Erschließung einer alternativen Weltsicht betrachtet wird, wird virulent, dass durch die fehlenden Wahrheiten und Gewissheiten im Kontext religiöser Kommunikation das Subjekt und seine erwünschte bzw. erhoffte Zukunft zum Ausgangs- und Gipfelpunkt jeglicher unterrichtlicher Kommunikation werden muss. Somit werden kommunikative Handlungen im Religionsunterricht nicht länger zum Instrument oder Medium, sondern zum Ziel und Zweck ihrer selbst, da in der jeweiligen Kommunikation das Subjekt anwesend ist.[13] Bereits die Grundlage religiöser Bildung und somit religiöser Kommunikation ist die göttliche Selbstoffenbarung, in der Offenbarer (Gott) und Geoffenbartes (Inhalt) derart miteinander verwoben sind, dass diese nicht voneinander zu trennen sind. Den Kern religiöser Kommunikation bildet folglich eine dialogische Orientierung, welche durch die Verbindung von Inhalt und Medium die Empfänger*innen (Schüler*innen) dazu auffordert sich zu beiden – Inhalt und Medium – individuell in Beziehung zu setzen. Dies bildet mithin eine genuin konstruktivistische Grundlage des Selbst- und Weltverständnisses ab.[14]

Jürgen Habermas beschrieb Kommunikationsprozesse in drei Dimensionen, welche vor dem Verständnis religiöser Kommunikation noch einmal zusätzlich den Zweck dieser Dimensionen im Verständigungshandeln als Selbstoffenbarung der Personen postuliert. Nach Habermas kann kommunikatives Handeln in einer assetorischen Dimension erfolgen, welche Wahrheiten und Richtigkeiten feststellen will, in einer expressiven Dimension erfolgen, welche Wahrhaftigkeiten im Kontext von Gefühlsäußerungen artikulieren will und in einer normativen Dimension erfolgen, welche Legitimitäten und Begründbarkeiten postuliert.[15] Werden diese Dimensionen nun auf religiöse Kommunikationshandlungen in unterrichtlichen Kontexten bezogen, so wird ersichtlich, dass Wahrheiten, Wahrhaftigkeiten und Legitimitäten sich durch den existenziellen Bezug, der der Religion immanent ist, lediglich in der subjektorientierten–konstuktivistischen Erschließung der Welt und dem damit einhergehenden Verständigungshandeln als lebensweltlichen Erschließung der Bedeutung religiöser Aspekte vollziehen können. Mithin muss kommunikatives Handeln im Religionsunterricht diskursiv konzipiert werden, um zu einer intersubjektiven Verständigung der Lebensbedeutsamkeit des stofflichen Inhalts zu führen, sodass Sinn-Stiftung und Sinn-Erhaltung durch erlebte sowie vollzogene Selbstoffenbarung erfahrbar werden und auf die Zukunft der Subjekte Anwendung finden.

---

12 Vgl. HILGER / ZIEBERTZ [Anm. 1], 113–114.

13 Vgl. Ebd., 111.

14 Vgl. Ebd., 114 sowie 117.

15 Vgl. HILGER / ZIEBERTZ [Anm. 1], 112.

Die Lehrperson als Schlüsselmedium in der unterrichtlichen Erzähltheorie

> „Erzählen will ich von deinem Namen meinen Brüdern, in der Gemeinde will ich dich preisen" (Ps.22,23).

Erzählungen sind eine der ältesten Erziehungsmittel, christliche Tradierungsmedien und Kulturtechniken. Bereits die Bibel zeugt hiervon, da sie als erzählende Literatur eben keine historischen Tatsachen oder Berichte wiedergibt, sondern narrative Wahrnehmungen menschlicher Erfahrungen im Kontext einer conditio humana widerspiegelt. Die erzählende Tradierung religiös-spiritueller Erlebnisse hatte somit schon immer eine transzendierende und gleichzeitig lebensorientierende Funktion, welche durch ihre gesellschaftliche Inszenierung ein mythopoetisches Verständnis ihrer Inhalte im Kontext der ihr eigenen Vieldimensionalität und Ganzheitlichkeit gewährleistet. Religiöse Narrationen stellen demnach keine Wahrheiten dar, sondern schildern individuelle Verstehensansätze für heuristische Wahrheiten und spiegeln mithin die individuellen psychologischen Bilder bezogen auf den Gegenstand der Erzählung bzw. des Erlebnisses wider. Sie stellen Verstehenshilfen für Geschehnisse, die über eine indirekte Erzählebene in der Erzählung vermittelt werden.[16] Religiös Erzählende werden dementsprechend zu wissenden Übersetzer*innen, die eine Vielfalt der Verstehensweisen religiöser Phänomene darstellen und so die Zuhörenden dazu anregen, Urteile und Meinungen selber auszubilden. Von den Erzählenden geht eine hilfreiche und zur Transformation anregende Grundhaltung aus, die ihre Leitideale offen kommuniziert und mit Überzeugung vertritt ohne gleichzeitig bevormundend oder beeinflussend zu sein.[17]

> „Keine sprachlich-textliche Darstellung kann die Realität von Geschehenem komplett wiedergeben. Sie ist nur sehr partiell möglich, konvertiert und umgesetzt ins sprachliche Medium einer Erzählung."[18]

Wenn also das Erzählen selbst als Reflexionsinstrument der Erzählung oder des Erlebnisses fungiert, wird es somit zum Spiegelbild der Erzählung, wodurch die Erzählung selbst zum Thema der Erzählung – Verbindung von Inhalt und Medium - wird. In diesem Spiegelbild eingebettet findet sich eine erzählende – dialogische – Selbstoffenbarung des Erzählers in der Form, dass er durch die Gestaltung der Nacherzählung seine Vorstellung von erzählerischer Objektivierbarkeit und dem was er unter einer guten Erzählung versteht, preisgibt. Hierdurch wird der Erzähler gleichsam zum Zeugen, der Zeugnis von den Tiefenschichten des Geschehens in ihrer Koinzidenz und Konvergenz der Ereigniswahrnehmung

---

16 Vgl. Schütze [Anm. 4], 69–71.
17 Vgl. Schütze [Anm. 4], 78–79.
18 Seybold [Anm. 2], 23.

wiedergibt.[19] Demzufolge ist nicht wichtig, was in der Erzählung auf der inhaltlichen Ebene wiedergegeben wird, sondern wie es wiedergegeben wird. Durch die Art der Inszenierung von Raum, Akteur*innen und Zeit identifiziert sich der Erzählende mit dem Inhalt der Erzählung und intendiert eine spezifische Wirkung auf Hörer*innen und Leser*innen. Auch die Hörenden und Lesenden werden somit in die Erzählung eingebunden und zum Teil der Erzählwelt, sowie die Erzählwelt zum Teil ihrer Wahrnehmung wird.[20]

Finden diese Erzählungen im Klassenraum statt, wird die Lehrkraft somit zum Schlüsselmedium von Unterricht und Erzählung. Diese Rolle als Schlüsselmedium und Realsymbol beinhaltet eine weitreichende Wirkung auf die eigene Identität der Lehrperson, auf die Identität der Schüler*innen sowie auf das Arrangement des Unterrichts.[21] Die Lehrperson muss sich vor dem Hintergrund ihres eigenen Habitus und im Spannungsfeld zwischen Handlungsstrukturen und Handlungsbedingungen zum Unterrichtsgegenstand derart verorten, dass sie es vermag, in der unterrichtlichen Erzählung selbst als Medium sowie mit ihren individuellen Erfahrungen, den Unterrichtsgegenstand betreffend, anwesend zu sein. Sie muss eine Selbstverortung im Sinne einer authentischen Zeugenschaft durchlaufen und so klare Rollenerwartungen an ihr eigenes unterrichtliches Handeln formulieren, ohne dabei ihre Authentizität zu verlieren.[22] Zweifel, Ängste, Ungewissheiten und ähnliches gehören hierbei genauso in die eigene Rollendarstellung und die Verbindung mit dem Unterrichtsgegenstand hinein, wie die sicher geglaubten Wahrheiten und Wahrhaftigkeiten. Gerade die authentische Darstellung der eigenen Person als fragmentarisch Überzeugtem im eigenen Glauben schafft eine Atmosphäre, welche es ermöglicht, den Klassenraum zu einem safe space werden zu lassen, in dem Schüler*innen die Möglichkeit des Identitätslernen gegeben wird. Identitäten werden wesentlich über prozessuale, narrative Strukturen erlernt, wodurch dem unterrichtlichen Erzählprozess, in dem sich das Subjekt des Erzählers selbst zum Gegenstand seiner Wahrnehmung und Reflexion im Medium der Erzählung macht, ein besonderes Potenzial zukommt. Schüler*innen erleben im Medium der Lehrkraft eine Person, die authentisch Zeugenschaft von ihrer Autorentätigkeit hinsichtlich der eigenen (religiösen) Lebensgeschichte gibt und werden gleichsam ermutigt,

---

19 Vgl. SEYBOLD [Anm. 2], 18–20.

20 Vgl. SEYBOLD [Anm. 2], 23–25.

21 Vgl. LEIMGRUBER, Stephan: Woran wird gelernt? Medien im Religionsunterricht, in: HILGER, Georg / ZIEBERTZ, Hans-Georg (Hg.): Religionsdidaktik. Ein Leitfaden für Studium, Ausbildung und Beruf, München:Kösel, [5]2017, 243.

22 Vgl. HEIL, Stefan: Art. Habitus, in: WiReLex Online 2016. http://www.bibelwissenschaft.de/stichwort/100196 (zuletzt aufgerufen am 28.06.2022).

selbst zu Autor*innen ihrer (religiösen) Lebensgeschichten zu werden.[23] In Zeiten hoher pluralistischer Angebote und Unsicherheiten kann diese authentische Zeugenschaft der Lehrkraft schließlich zum Kompass für die Fragen „Wer bin ich?“ „Was ist mir wichtig?“ „Wer will ich sein?“ und „Was soll ich tun?“ werden. Sie füllt mithin eine empowernde Rolle im Sinne eines schulischen Leaderships aus.[24] Hierbei geht es nicht um das Nacheifern oder die Übernahme eines Vorbildes, sondern vielmehr um die Ermutigung und den Ermöglichungsraum, die Signale und Botschaften der Erzählung – in Inhalt und Medium – zu entschlüsseln und so einen eigenen narrativen Umgang mit der erlebten Pluralität auszubilden. Gelingt es der Lehrkraft einen derartigen Ermöglichungsraum im Sinne eines safe spaces im Unterricht zu schaffen, in welchem die Schüler*innen die Erzählung als Erlebnis von Identität begreifen und gleichsam ein kritisches Bewusstsein für die Vielschichtigkeit jeder Erzählung vermittelt bekommen, werden sie dazu angeleitet, sich eigene Urteile hinsichtlich ihrer existenzielle Urfragen im Kontext von Aporien, Kontingenzen und Identitätsdiffusion reflexiv auszubilden.[25]

(Religions-)unterrichtliches Potenzial im Kontext rBNE

Als größte Chance einer derart verstandenen Verbindung aus Erzählmedium (Lehrkraft) und Inhalt der Erzählung (Unterrichtsgegenstand) kann zweifelsohne die religiöse Tiefenorientierung auf Seiten der Lehrkräfte sowie der Schüler*innen gesehen werden.

Wenn die Religionslehrkräfte sich ihrer oben beschriebenen Funktionen als wissende Übersetzer*innen, transparente Spiegel, fragmentarisch Überzeugte und kritische Brückenbauer*innen im Kontext ihres eigenen Professionalitätskonzept und ihres eigenen Rollenverständnisses bewusst werden, so können sie gerade in heutigen krisenhaften Zeiten zu nachhaltigen kultur- und religionsübergreifenden Vermittlern intersubjektiver Verständigungsprozesse werden und so den gesellschaftlich-kulturellen Pluralismus dergestalt mikrokosmisch ins Klassenzimmer holen, dass die Schüler*innen dazu befähigt werden, am Beispiel des Handlungskonzepts der Lehrkraft ihre eigenen reflexiven Handlungskonzepte auszubilden. Voraussetzung hierfür ist das Verständnis des unterrichtlichen Kommunikationsprozesses als doppeldidaktische Selbstoffenbarung. Zum

---

23 Vgl. ZIEBERTZ, Hans-Georg: Wozu religiöses Lernen? Religionsunterricht als Hilfe zur Identitätsbildung, in: HILGER, Georg / ZIEBERTZ, Hans-Georg (Hg.): Religionsdidaktik. Ein Leitfaden für Studium, Ausbildung und Beruf, München: Kösel, ^{5}2017, 148–150.

24 Vgl. ROEBBEN, Bert: Leadership in Times of Rough Coherence. Some Historical and Educational Observations, in: Religious Education 114 (2019), 398–402.

25 Vgl. SCHÜTZE [Anm. 4], 71–72.

einen findet eine Selbstoffenbarung der Lehrkraft durch die Erzählung statt, da sie sich selbst mit ihrer Identität in der Erzählung als anwesend begreifen muss. Zum anderen sind die Schüler*innen dazu aufgefordert, in dialogischen Handlungen in diese Erzählungen einzusteigen und diese weiterzuentwickeln, wodurch sie wiederum eine Selbstoffenbarung ihrer Identität hinsichtlich der Identität und Erzählung der Lehrkraft sowie der Mitschüler*innen vollziehen. In diesen Erzählungen sind wiederum die verschiedenen kritischen und mehrschichtigen Verständnismöglichkeiten eingelagert und müssen durch die jeweils anderen erkannt und interpretiert werden, dass eine indirekte Perspektivübernahme zwangsläufig notwendig wird.

Wird Schüler*innen die reflexive Selbstverortung in dergestalten gelagerten Ermöglichungsräumen (safe space) eröffnet, so führt dies zwangsläufig zu einer positiven Sicht auf Religion. Religiöse Bildung, die in diesem Konzept altersangemessen vermittelt wird, führt dazu, dass heute beliebte kritische Gedanken hinsichtlich Religion, Christentum und Kirche einen positiven Widerhall in den jeweiligen Identitäten finden und zu einer tiefergehenden religiösen Orientierung im Sinne eines religiösen Apriori der Fragilität und Fluidität der eigenen Existenz führen.[26]

Bezogen auf die Lehrkräfte ist bei diesem Konzept wichtig, dass diese den Weg der anatheistischen Auseinandersetzung mit der eigenen Religion bereits beschritten haben. Nur wenn die Lehrkräfte ihren eigenen Glauben in der Art durchdrungen und reflektiert haben, dass dieser zu einer Überwindung übernatürlicher Glaubensvorstellung führt und Gott als immanente Transzendenz der individuellen Wirklichkeitswahrnehmung mit konkreter Lebensbedeutsamkeit wird, können die postulierten Leitideale dazu führen, Schüler*innen für die existenziellen Fragen der anderen zu begeistern und zu gegenseitigen Verstehenshilfen zu werden.[27]

Religionsunterrichtliche Kommunikation wird somit nicht länger zum Medium des Unterrichts, sondern zum Selbstziel, da in den Erzählungen und Kommunikationsmustern sich ereignet, was inhaltlich sowie intersubjektiv geschehen soll. Das Zusammenspiel aus Offenbarer und Geoffenbarten – Inhalt und Medium – wird somit zum unterrichtlichen Ereigniszusammenhang, der als mehrperspektivisch-narrativer Bedeutungszusammenhang verstanden werden muss und folglich eine Verbindung zwischen Wirklichkeit und Möglichkeit der existenziellen Tiefe menschlichen Seins aufspannt.

Diese Subjektorientierung fordert schon deshalb die rBNE und compathisch-theologische Analysen ökologischer Gegenwartsprobleme, da sie die Lebenswelt der Schüler*innen darstellen. Wenn der Religionsunterricht die Zeichen der

---

26 Vgl. SCHÜTZE [Anm. 4], 79.

27 Vgl. Ebd.

Zeit[28] im kommunikativen Handeln ernst nehmen will, muss die vorherrschende ökologische Krise als zentrales und beeinflussendes Problem der jungen Generation zu einer kulturell-ethischen Transformation im compathischen Sinn beitragen. Die von jungen Menschen oft empfundene gesellschaftliche Untätigkeit bei gleichzeitigem Tatendrang, muss demnach als hoffnungsvoller Imperativ verstanden werden, zur gemeinschaftlichen Überwindung der Kluft aus Können und Tun anregt.[29] Nachhaltigkeit wird somit zu einem ethischen Prinzip, welches durch Erzählprozesse ausgehandelt, konkretisiert und derart tradiert wird, dass es zum Identitätsmarker vieler Menschen wird. Dies ist beispielsweise auch am Beispiel der Nachhaltigkeit im Kontext der Ernährung – z. B. Veganismus, Vegetarismus etc. – nachvollziehbar. Das Erzählen als unterrichtliche Dimension einer subjektorientierten-konstruktivistischen Didaktik ist demnach compathisches Lernen, da durch die Subjektverknüpfung von Inhalt und Medium gelernt wird und somit im Sinne einer anamnetisch-antizipativen Dimension das Erzählte gleichsam zum Verheißenen wird.[30] Es beantwortet schließlich im Moment der Erzählung einen Teil der Sinnfrage der Erzählenden und der Hörenden, da andere Sinnsuchbewegungen compathisch erlebt werden und somit zu Motivation, Orientierung und Identität führen.

Literaturverzeichnis:

BERNHARDT, Reinhold: Religiöse Identitätsbildung im religionspluralen Kontext, in: HEIMBACH-STEINS, Marianne / KÖNEMANN, Judith (Hg.): Religiöse Identitäten in einer globalisierten Welt, Münster: Aschendorff Verlag, 2019, 87–94.

BEDERNA, Katrin: Religiöse Bildung für nachhaltige Entwicklung. Ein didaktisches Modell, in: Religionspädagogische Beiträge 44 (2021), 61–71.

BIRKEL, Simone: Warum wir dran sind. Lernen für ein zukunftsfähiges Leben, in: KatBl 3/2019, 177–181.

DAUSNER, Rene: Anatheismus – Richard Kearneys religionsphilosophischer Beitrag zur Gottesfrage heute, in: freinschwarz.net. feinschwarz.net/anatheismus-richard-kearneys-religionsphilosophischer-beitrag-zur-gottesfrage-heute (zuletzt aufgerufen am 28.06.2022)

DIE DEUTSCHEN BISCHÖFE 56: Die bildende Kraft des Religionsunterrichts. Zur Konfessionalität des katholischen Religionsunterrichts, Bonn: Vandehoek&Ruprecht, [5]2009.

HEIL, Stefan: Art. Habitus, in: WiReLex Online, 2016. http://www.bibelwissenschaft.de/stichwort/100196 (zuletzt aufgerufen am 28.06.2022)

---

28 Vgl. PAPST PAUL VI: Gaudium et Spes, 1965, https://www.vatican.va/archive/hist_councils/ii_vatican_council/documents/vat-ii_const_19651207_gaudium-et-spes_ge.html, Kapitel 4.

29 Vgl. BIRKEL, Simone: Warum wir dran sind. Lernen für ein zukunftsfähiges Leben, in: KatBl 3/2019, 178.

30 Vgl. BEDERNA [Anm. 5], 65

HILGER, Georg / ZIEBERTZ, Hans-Georg: Religionsdidaktik in kommunikativer Perspektive, in: HILGER, Georg / LEIMGRUBER, Stephan / ZIEBERTZ, Hans-Georg(Hg.): Religionsdidaktik. Ein Leitfaden für Studium, Ausbildung und Beruf, München: Kösel, [5]2017, 106–120.

KLAFKI, Wolfgang: Neue Studien zur Bildungstheorie und Didaktik. Zeitgemäße Allgemeinbildung und kritisch-konstruktive Didaktik, Weinheim: Beltz, [6]2007.

LEIMGRUBER, Stephan: Woran wird gelernt? Medien im Religionsunterricht, in: HILGER, Georg / ZIEBERTZ, Hans-Georg (Hg.): Religionsdidaktik. Ein Leitfaden für Studium, Ausbildung und Beruf, München: Kösel, [5]2017, 242–253.

PAPST PAUL VI: Gaudium et Spes, 1965, https://www.vatican.va/archive/hist_councils/ ii_vatican_council/documents/vat-ii_const_19651207_gaudium-et-spes ge.html, Kapitel 4.

ROEBBEN, Bert: Leadership in Times of Rough Coherence. Some Historical and Educational Observations, in: Religious Education 114 (2019), 398–402.

SCHÜTZE, Stefan: Zum Erzählen biblischer Geschichten, in: Theo-Web. Zeitschrift für Religionspädagogik 14 (2015), 69–82.

SEYBOLD, Klaus: Erzählen vom Erzählen. Beobachtungen zu einer biblischen Erzähltheorie, in: Theologische Zeitschrift 61 (2015), 14–26.

ZIEBERTZ, Hans-Georg: Wozu religiöses Lernen? Religionsunterricht als Hilfe zur Identitätsbildung, in: HILGER, Georg / ZIEBERTZ, Hans-Georg (Hg.): Religionsdidaktik. Ein Leitfaden für Studium, Ausbildung und Beruf, München: Kösel, [5]2017, 142–154.

Ambiguitätsmanagement als Schlüssel einer (religiösen) Bildung für nachhaltige Entwicklung?

Daniela Zahneisen

Ambiguitätsmanagement stellt eine für den Umgang mit Pluralität notwendige Kompetenz innerhalb religiöser Bildungskontexte dar. Sowohl das Compassion-Projekt als auch der Ansatz (religiöser) Bildung für nachhaltige Entwicklung können diese Kompetenz innerhalb des Religionsunterrichts fördern. Im vorliegenden Beitrag werden diese beiden Ansätze innerhalb des ethischen Lernens verortet, denn das Lernen an ethischen Dilemmata birgt großes Potenzial, einen konstruktiven Umgang mit Mehr- oder Uneindeutigkeit einzuüben.

Ambiguitätsmanagement; Ambiguitätstoleranz; Compassion; (religiöse) Bildung für nachhaltige Entwicklung; ethisches Lernen; Religionsunterricht

Ambiguity management represents a necessary competence for dealing with plurality. Both the Compassion project and the approach of (religious) Education for Sustainable Development can promote this competence. In this paper, these two approaches are located within ethical learning, because learning about ethical dilemmas has great potential for practicing a constructive way of dealing with ambiguity.

Ambiguity management; ambiguity tolerance; compassion; (religious) Education for Sustainable Development; ethical learning; religious education

Hinführung

Klimaschutz und die Frage nach einer nachhaltigen Zukunft auch für kommende Generationen sind Themen, die viele – auch junge Menschen – umtreiben. Klimaaktivist*innen beschmieren Denkmäler, bewerfen berühmte Kunstwerke mit Farbe, kleben sich auf Straßen fest – alles für den Klimaprotest, um auf die Dringlichkeit des Klimaschutzes aufmerksam zu machen und vor dem drohenden Klimanotstand zu warnen.[1] Doch nicht alle für den Klimaschutz engagierten Menschen sind zu zivilem Ungehorsam bzw. zu radikalen Maßnahmen bereit.

---

[1] Vgl. HIRSCH, Christopher / SCHMITT-ROSCHMANN, Verena: „Letzte Generation“. Ein Jahr Kleben fürs Klima, https://www.zdf.de/nachrichten/politik/ein-jahr-letzte-generation-klimakleber-100.html (zuletzt aufgerufen am 14.03.2023).

Fridays for Future initiiert am 3. März 2023 zum fünften Mal den jährlichen Globalen Klimastreik. Weltweit gehen unzählige Menschen auf die Straße, um ein friedliches Zeichen für Klimagerechtigkeit zu setzen.[2]

Die Anfrage, wie radikal Klimaprotest sein darf oder sogar sein muss, um Veränderungen in der Gesellschaft herbeizuführen, Klimaziele zu erreichen und zu einer nachhaltigeren Zukunft beizutragen, soll in diesem Beitrag nicht diskutiert werden. Es soll aber der Frage nachgegangen werden, wie die Dringlichkeit des Klimaschutzes auch im Religionsunterricht wahrgenommen und aufgegriffen werden kann. Hierfür wird eine Möglichkeit vorgestellt, wie der aktuelle Ansatz der (religiösen) Bildung für nachhaltige Entwicklung (rBNE) mit dem des Compassion-Projekts verbunden werden kann. Durch die Verschränkung von BNE- und Compassion-Diskursen kann eine entscheidende Kompetenz, die gerade in Zeiten ökologisch-sozialer Krisen für gesellschaftliche Teilhabe und Mitgestaltung unerlässlich ist, gefördert werden. Hierfür steht das sogenannte Ambiguitätsmanagement, die Fähigkeit, mit Mehrdeutigem, Widersprüchlichem oder Uneindeutigem umgehen zu können. Vor diesem Hintergrund soll im Folgenden dargestellt werden, weshalb die Förderung von Ambiguitätsmanagement von entscheidender Bedeutung ist. Anschließend werden die Konzepte der (religiösen) Bildung für nachhaltige Entwicklung sowie des Compassion-Projekts kurz präsentiert und im Rahmen des ethischen Lernens im Religionsunterricht miteinander verknüpft. Hierdurch soll aufgezeigt werden können, inwiefern der Compassion-Ansatz im Zusammenhang mit der (r)BNE zu einem konstruktiven Umgang mit Ambiguität führen kann.

Ambiguitätsmanagement als gegenwärtige Herausforderung

Umgangsweisen mit Ambiguität

Komplexität nimmt in nahezu allen Lebensbereichen zu. Gegenwärtige gesellschaftliche, religiöse und politische Entwicklungen sind von Pluralisierungsprozessen geprägt, was den Umgang mit Mehr- und Uneindeutigkeiten alternativlos werden lässt. Hier ist die sogenannte Ambiguitätstoleranz, die Kompetenz, mit Mehrdeutigem, Uneindeutigem und / oder Diskrepanzen bzw. Widersprüchen

---

[2] Vgl. KRETSCHMER, Christian: Globaler Klimastreik. Kleben for Future? https://www.tagesschau.de/inland/gesellschaft/fridays-for-future-243.html (zuletzt aufgerufen am 14.03.2023).

umgehen zu können, gefragt.[3] Ambiguitätstoleranz kann als Fähigkeit verstanden werden, „*fluide soziale, ethische wie religiöse Situationen, schwer oder gar nicht lösbare Fragen sowie Vages und Offen-Bleibendes auszuhalten, konstruktiv anzugehen und gegebenenfalls auch als solches stehen zu lassen*“ [Hervorhebung im Original].[4] Ambiguitätstoleranz steht der Vereindeutigung und Vereinfachung von Ambiguität, wenn beispielsweise eine Möglichkeit zur allein gültigen erklärt wird, entgegen.[5] Auch eine indifferente bis gleichgültige Haltung gegenüber Ambiguität spricht gegen eine ambiguitätstolerante Einstellung.[6] Stattdessen geht es darum, mit bleibender Uneindeutigkeit und Komplexität umgehen zu können, ohne diese reduzieren zu wollen: Ambiguität wird akzeptiert und / oder sogar wertgeschätzt.[7]

Von der Ambiguitätstoleranz hin zum Ambiguitätsmanagement

Weshalb im Folgenden von Ambiguitäts*management* statt von Ambiguitäts*toleranz*, der in der Forschungsliteratur geläufigen Formulierung, die Rede sein wird, soll nun im Rahmen einer Begriffsklärung verdeutlicht werden.[8] Der Begriff *Ambiguität* kommt aus dem Lateinischen und findet sich dort, wo es mehr als nur eine mögliche Lesart / Interpretation gibt.[9] Ambiguität kann sich demnach auf Mehr- und Uneindeutiges in unterschiedlichen (Lebens-)Bereichen beziehen.[10] Der *Toleranz*begriff ist ebenfalls lateinischer Herkunft, bedeutet übersetzt *ertragen, erdulden* oder *aushalten* und ist folglich mit einer passivischen Implikation konnotiert. Karlo Meyer plädiert daher dafür, im Zusammenhang mit einem

---

3 Vgl. MEYER, Karlo: Ambiges wird schnell übersehen – ein Plädoyer für einen Lehr-Lern-Ansatz beim „automatischen“ Denken in Stereotypen, in: Zeitschrift für Pädagogik und Theologie 74/2 (2022), 185.

4 Ebd., 189.

5 Vgl. WÖRN, Katharina: Ambiguität. Paul Tillichs Begriff der Zweideutigkeit im Kontext interdisziplinärer Debatten, Tübingen: Mohr Siebeck, 2022 (= Dogmatik in der Moderne 38), 47.

6 Vgl. Ebd.

7 Vgl. MEYER, Karlo: Grundlagen interreligiösen Lernens, Göttingen: Vandenhoeck & Ruprecht, 2019, 277.

8 Einzige Ausnahme bilden direkte oder indirekte Zitate – hier verwende ich die von den jeweiligen Autor*innen präferierte Ausdrucksweise.

9 Vgl. LÖBNER, Sebastian: Semantik. Eine Einführung, Berlin/Boston: De Gruyter, ^{2}2022, 48.

10 Nach Karlo Meyer kann das „Erleben von Uneindeutigkeit [...] auf (mindestens) zwei, sich überschneidenden Gebieten entstehen: Es gibt Dinge, die prinzipiell ungewiss bleiben werden, in diesem Rahmen bezieht sich Ambiguität im allgemeinen, lebensphilosophischen und religiösen Bereich z. B. auf Zufälle und ihre Interpretation, Antworten auf die Frage nach Lebenssinn, aber eventuell auch auf Situationen, in denen Gottes Nähe erfahren wurde usw. Ambiguitätserleben kann sich aber auch spezifisch auf Erfahrungen mit Fremdem und Neuem beziehen, bei denen sich nicht alles, aber doch vieles in einem gewissen Rahmen aufklären lässt.“ MEYER, 2019 [Anm. 7], 270.

fruchtbaren Umgang mit Ambiguität vom klassischen Begriff der Ambiguitäts*toleranz* abzuweichen und stattdessen die aktivische und konstruktive Komponente im Umgang mit Ambiguität zu betonen: Aus Ambiguitäts*toleranz* würde somit Ambiguitäts*management*.[11] Da sowohl der BNE- als auch der Compassion-Diskurs danach fragen, wie mit Ambiguität handlungs- und gestaltungsorientiert umgegangen werden kann, erweist sich diese begriffliche Differenzierung m. E. als besonders zielführend.

Bedeutung von Ambiguitätsmanagement in religiösen Bildungskontexten

Michael Meyer-Blanck konstatiert für den Kontext religiöser Bildung und dessen Reflexion, dass der Begriff der Ambiguitätstoleranz / des Ambiguitäts-managements in der Religionspädagogik lange keine explizite Rolle spielte.[12] Als eine „notwendige Bedingung allen religionspädagogischen Verstehens und Handelns"[13] kommt dem Umgang mit Ambiguität bei der Reflexion theologischer Fragen eine entscheidende Bedeutung zu. Es gibt nur selten klare Antworten auf das, was uns – mit Paul Tillich gesprochen – „unbedingt angeht"[14]: Niemand kann letztgültige und vor allem eindeutige Antworten beispielsweise auf die theologischen Fragen finden, was den Sinn des Lebens ausmacht, was uns nach dem Tod erwarten oder das Reich Gottes bereithalten könnte. Tobias Nicklas betont den Aspekt der Ambiguität biblischer Texte und führt die Deutungsoffenheit bzw. Vielstimmigkeit und Mehrperspektivität biblischer Zeugnisse sowie deren komplexen Entstehungsprozess an.[15] Meyer spricht dagegen vorwiegend von ethischen Dilemmata, dogmatischen Fragestellungen oder dem interreligiösen Lernen, die besonderes Potential für die Förderung von Ambiguitätsmanagement innerhalb religiöser Bildungskontexte bergen.[16]

---

11 Vgl. Ebd., 289.

12 Vgl. Meyer-Blanck, Michael: Ambiguitätstoleranz – eine Dimension religions-pädagogischer Hermeneutik?, in: Zeitschrift für Pädagogik und Theologie 74/2 (2022), 179. Allerdings scheint dieser Befund im Wandel begriffen: Es setzen sich gegenwärtig immer mehr Religionspädagog*innen thematisch mit Ambiguitätstoleranz auseinander, was sich unter anderem darin zeigt, dass 2022 sowohl eine Ausgabe der Zeitschrift für Pädagogik und Theologie als auch eine Theo-Web-Ausgabe zur Thematik erschienen ist.

13 Ebd., 173.

14 Tillich, Paul: Wesen und Wandel des Glaubens, Frankfurt am Main/Berlin: Ullstein, 1961, 9.

15 Vgl. Nicklas, Tobias: Lernen unter Vorzeichen der Ambiguität. Biblische Perspektiven, in: Zeitschrift für Pädagogik und Theologie 74/2 (2022), 125.

16 Vgl. Meyer 2022 [Anm. 3], 189.

Neben diese inhaltsbezogene Begründung für die Förderung von Ambiguitätsmanagement im Religionsunterricht tritt die am Subjekt orientierte. Für Kinder und Jugendliche stellt der Umgang mit Ambiguität „eine der zentralen Herausforderungen im Aufbau des sozialen Ichs dar.“[17] Bernhard Dressler betont zusätzlich das Moment der Positionalität: Bei einer ambiguitätstoleranten Haltung komme es darauf an, „nicht alles für gleich-gültig zu halten, sondern auf eigene Wahrheits- und Geltungsansprüche nicht zu verzichten.“[18] Nur durch die Förderung von Urteilsfähigkeit kann der Religionsunterricht einen Beitrag zur Förderung von Pluralitätsfähigkeit leisten und somit Teilhabe am gesellschaftlichen Leben ermöglichen: Pluralisierung, Individualisierung und Heterogenität, unter anderem bezogen auf Religiosität und deren Ausdrucksformen, „machen die Ambiguitätstoleranz religions-pädagogisch alternativlos.“[19] Die Bereitschaft, sich mit ungewohnten bzw. fremden Positionen auseinanderzusetzen, setzt eine Haltung voraus, die sich nicht von vornherein mit zu vorschnell gefällten und zu eindeutigen Urteilen zufriedengibt. Folglich besteht eine wichtige Aufgabe religiöser Bildungsprozesse darin, durch die Förderung von Ambiguitätsmanagement „für das Ungewohnte sensibel zu machen und zu mehr Akzeptanz dessen zu führen, was einem [und einer] selbst bisher fremd ist.“[20]

(r)BNE und Compassion – Aufgabenfelder innerhalb des ethischen Lernens

„Wir leben in einer dauerhaft verwundeten Welt“[21]

Seit den 1970er-Jahren rücken Themen wie Zukunftsfähigkeit, Gerechtigkeit und Klimawandel mehr und mehr in den öffentlichen Diskurs und fordern dazu heraus, sich zu ihnen zu positionieren und sie zu bearbeiten. Diese Anforderung stellt sich auch in Bildungskontexten, in welchen das Konzept der Bildung für nachhaltige Entwicklung (BNE) zum Tragen kommt. Normativ angelegte BNE-Konzepte und -Theorien verstehen die Klimakrise „als Frage nach den planeta-

---

17 Koerrenz, Ralf / Kumlehn, Martina: Editorial, in: Zeitschrift für Pädagogik und Theologie 74/2 (2022), 119.

18 Dressler, Bernhard: Religionsunterricht. Bildungstheoretische Grundlegungen, Leipzig: Evangelische Verlagsanstalt, 2018, 107.

19 Meyer-Blanck 2022 [Anm. 12], 179.

20 Ebd., 182.

21 Gärtner, Claudia: Klima, Corona und das Christentum. Religiöse Bildung für nachhaltige Entwicklung in einer verwundeten Welt, Bielefeld: transcript, 2020, 7.

ren Grenzen des ökologischen Gleichgewichts verbunden mit einer intergenerativen Perspektive auf soziale und ökonomische Gerechtigkeit."[22] Ausgehend von der Prämisse, dass Gesundheit, Ökologie, Wirtschaft, Soziales und Kultur nicht zielführend unabhängig voneinander in den Blick genommen werden können, fördern BNE-Ansätze ein umfassendes Verständnis von Nachhaltigkeit.[23]

> Bildung für Nachhaltige Entwicklung (BNE) zeigt vor diesem Hintergrund ein großes Potenzial. Sie vereinigt die Berücksichtigung ökologischer, ökonomischer und sozialer Aspekte von notwendigen nachhaltigen Entwicklungsprozessen, bietet interdisziplinäre Zugänge zu Problemlösungsstrategien, unterstützt mit dem Kernelement Partizipation demokratische Vorgehensweisen und nimmt mit der Gleichzeitigkeit lokaler und globaler Bezüge auch den entscheidenden Aspekt der generationalen Gerechtigkeit in den Blick.[24]

Ein Versuch, die BNE-Ansätze theologisch zu durchdringen und auf religiöse Bildungskontexte zu übertragen, liegt in der *religiösen* Bildung für nachhaltige Entwicklung (rBNE) vor.[25] Als „Transformationsbildung in messianischer Perspektive"[26] ist rBNE auf die *„Relativierung eines spezifischen Absolutheitsanspruchs* [gerichtet]: den eines konsumorientierten, raum-, zeit- und zukunftslosen Lebensstils und der ihn stützenden Wirtschaftsweisen [Hervorhebung im Original]."[27]

Ziel und Inhalt von rBNE ist es, den christlichen Glauben als Inspiration, Unterbrechung und Anspruch wahrnehmen zu können, um inmitten von ökologisch-sozialen Krisen an der Transformation der Schöpfung mitzuwirken – hin zu mehr Nachhaltigkeit auf allen gesellschaftlichen Ebenen.[28] Neben ökologischen Fragen können in diesem Kontext, wie bereits angedeutet, auch Themenbereiche wie Demokratie, Frieden und Gerechtigkeit konstruktiv bearbeitet werden. Besonders deutlich wird dies im Grundanliegen von rBNE, das zudem die Möglichkeit der Selbstwirksamkeit und der Handlungsmotivation von Schüler*innen betont: „Religiöse Bildung für nachhaltige Entwicklung will Kinder

---

22 Ebd., 15.

23 Vgl. Ebd.

24 OVERWIEN, Bernd / RODE, Horst: Bildung für nachhaltige Entwicklung. Lebenslanges Lernen, Kompetenz und gesellschaftliche Teilhabe – eine Einleitung, in: DIES. (Hg.): Bildung für nachhaltige Entwicklung. Lebenslanges Lernen, Kompetenz und gesellschaftliche Teilhabe, Opladen/Berlin/Toronto: Barbara Budrich, 2013 (= Schriftenreihe „Ökologie und Erziehungswissenschaft" der Kommission Bildung für eine nachhaltige Entwicklung der Deutschen Gesellschaft für Erziehungswissenschaft (DGfE)), 7.

25 Vgl. BEDERNA, Katrin: Art. Bildung für nachhaltige Entwicklung, in: WiReLex online. https://www.bibelwissenschaft.de/stichwort/200572/ (zuletzt aufgerufen am 10.03. 2023).

26 BEDERNA, Katrin: Every Day for Future. Theologie und religiöse Bildung für nachhaltige Entwicklung, Ostfildern: Grünewald, 2019, 235.

27 Ebd., 237.

28 Vgl. BEDERNA, Katrin: Didaktik religiöser Bildung für nachhaltige Entwicklung, in: KROPAČ, Ulrich / RIEGEL, Ulrich: Handbuch Religionsdidaktik, Stuttgart: Kohlhammer, 2020, 325.

und Jugendliche nicht zu Anwälten für die Schöpfung, die Armen und die Zukunft machen. Sie will, dass sie sich selbst zu Anwälten für die Schöpfung, die Armen und die Zukunft machen."[29] rBNE geht es demnach im Kern um die *Befähigung* der Schüler*innen. Diese sollen gemäß der Gestaltungskompetenz dazu empowert werden, sich für das einsetzen zu können, worauf sie einen Anspruch haben: eine Zukunft für sich, künftige Generationen und die Mitwelt. Die Gestaltungskompetenz kann dann beispielsweise durch Antizipation ihren Ausdruck finden, wenn über mögliche Zukunftsszenarien reflektiert wird, „da Nachhaltigkeit nach zukünftigen Auswirkungen jetzigen Handelns fragt",[30] oder sich im Versuch äußern, sich selbst und andere dazu zu motivieren, Einstellungen und Verhaltensweisen zu überdenken, „da Nachhaltigkeit strukturelle Transformation und Verhaltensänderung vieler verlangt."[31]

Innerhalb von rBNE kann zusätzlich die Wahrnehmungskompetenz der am Lernprozess Beteiligten gefördert werden, die die ethische, politische und religiöse Dimension des Klimaschutzes betont: Die Nachhaltigkeitsdebatte kann dann durch die Wahrnehmung ihrer verschiedenen Dimensionen unter anderem als religiöses Problem verstanden werden und hinsichtlich religiöser Weltdeutung(-en) „auf die krisenhafte Situation und in der Kompetenz zu ethischem und politischem Urteil über Lebensformen und Handlungsoptionen" ausgeweitet werden.[32] Diese letztgenannte Perspektive führt zur Frage, wie rBNE im Rahmen ethischen Lernens im Religionsunterricht verortet werden kann, was im Folgenden mithilfe des Compassion-Ansatzes dargelegt werden soll.

„Empfindlichkeit für das Leid der anderen"[33]

Die Initiatoren des Compassion-Projekts, Adolf Weisbrod, Franz Kuhn und Friedrich Hirsch, verstehen unter dem Begriff *Compassion* „Menschsein für andere".[34] Bewusst wurde die englische Vokabel gewählt und nicht etwa eine der deutschen Übersetzungsmöglichkeiten wie Mitleid. *Mitleid* könnte eine überlegene, diskriminierende Haltung der *Starken* gegenüber *Schwachen* implizieren. Wird Mitleid(-en) allerdings als Haltung engagierter Mitmenschlichkeit verstanden, kann aus menschlichem Mitgefühl soziales Engagement wie selbstverständlich

---

29 Bederna 2019 [Anm. 28], 235.

30 Bederna 2020 [Anm. 30], 326.

31 Ebd.

32 Ebd.

33 Metz, Johann B.: Compassion. Zu einem Weltprogramm des Christentums im Zeitalter der Religionen und Kulturen, in: Ders. / Kuld, Lothar / Weisbrod, Adolf (Hg.): Compassion. Weltprogramm des Christentums. Soziale Verantwortung lernen, Freiburg: Herder, 2000, 11.

34 Kuld, Lothar: Compassion – Raus aus der Ego-Falle, Münsterschwarzach: Vier-Türme-Verlag, 2003 (= Münsterschwarzacher Kleinschriften 138), 24.

erwachsen. Compassion ist in diesem Sinne als „Empfindlichkeit für das Leid der anderen“[35] zu verstehen, was ins Zentrum des Christentums führt.[36]

Im religionspädagogischen Bereich versucht das Handlungsprinzip Compassion, soziales Lernen an Schulen zu fördern und zu verankern: „Ziel des [Compassion-]Projekts ist die Entwicklung sozial verpflichteter Haltungen wie Solidarität, Kooperation und Kommunikation mit Menschen, die [...] auf die Unterstützung und Hilfe Anderer angewiesen sind.“[37] Im Rahmen des Projekts nehmen die Schüler*innen an Praktika in sozialen Einrichtungen teil (z. B. in Altenheimen, Kindergärten, Bahnhofsmissionen, Büros und Unterkünften für Asylsuchende und Geflüchtete oder Behindertenheimen). Lehrkräfte begleiten den Prozess, indem sie im Unterricht auf die Erfahrungen vorbereiten und gemeinsam mit den Schüler*innen reflektieren. Diese Reflexion stellt eine entscheidende Gelingensbedingung des Projekts dar und führt zur Frage, inwieweit Ethik lehrbar ist: „Soziale Haltungen und Hilfsbereitschaft im Bereich des Sozialen beruhen letzten Endes nicht nur auf bloßem Gefühl. [...] Deshalb sind das Gespräch über das Erlebte und die reflektierte Bewertung des Erlebten so wichtig.“[38]

BNE und Compassion im Religionsunterricht

Ethische Dilemmata im Kontext des ethischen Lernens

> Inhalt ethischen Lernens sind die Wertvorstellungen, die persönlich, kirchlich und gesellschaftlich vertreten werden. Ziel ethischen Lernens ist die Fähigkeit, praktische Wertdiskurse zu führen und ein Urteilsvermögen zu entwickeln, das zu verantworteten Entscheidungen befähigt hinsichtlich der Fragen: Was muss ich tun? Was sollen wir tun? Was soll gelten? Was ist wünschbar und haltbar – für mich und für andere.[39]

Ethisches Lernen stülpt keine Wertvorstellungen über, sondern hat die Reflexion von Normen und Werten zum Ziel. Ethisches Lernen verfolgt dementsprechend den Anspruch, eine kritische Urteilsfähigkeit der Schüler*innen zu fördern.[40] Ziebertz’ Ansatz ist stark kognitivistisch angelegt – Bernhard Grümme

---

35 METZ 2000 [Anm. 35], 11.

36 KULD, Lothar: Art. Compassion, in: WiReLex online. https://www.bibelwissenschaft.de/stichwort/100124/ (zuletzt aufgerufen am 10.03.2023).

37 Ebd.

38 KULD 2003 [Anm. 36], 22–23.

39 ZIEBERTZ, Hans-Georg: Ethisches Lernen, in: HILGER, Georg / LEIMGRUBER, Stephan / ZIEBERTZ, Hans-Georg (Hg.): Religionsdidaktik. Ein Leitfaden für Studium, Ausbildung und Beruf, München: Kösel [6]2010, 434.

40 Vgl. z. B. auch Kuld, der hierzu treffend formuliert: „Um zu verstehen, wovon man beim ethischen Lernen spricht, ist zwischen Moral und Ethik zu unterscheiden. Ethik ist die

fragt deshalb an, ob kritische Urteilsbildung nicht zudem auch durch Gefühl / Affektion lehr- und lernbar sei. Demnach besteht für Grümme das Ziel ethischer Bildung nicht nur in der Urteilsbildung, sondern auch in der „Handlungsmotivation im Lichte der Gottesbotschaft […], die dabei auch ihre gesellschaftlichen wie kulturellen Kontexte analysiert und sich kritisch wie produktiv einschaltet in das gesellschaftlich-öffentliche Ringen um ein gutes und gerechtes Leben für alle.“[41] Dieser Ansatz erweist sich m. E. hinsichtlich religionsdidaktischer Überlegungen in Bezug auf (r)BNE und Compassion als sehr anschlussfähig. Denn beiden Ansätzen bzw. Projekten ist es ein Anliegen, Schüler*innen im Sinne des sozialen Lernens dazu zu befähigen, gesellschaftliches Leben selbstwirksam und aktiv zu gestalten – und zwar so, dass ein *gutes und gerechtes Leben für alle* möglich wird. (r)BNE und Compassion sind insofern zusammenzudenken, als sie beide von der Vision geleitet sind, eine gerechte und von Mitgefühl bestimmte nachhaltige Zukunft zu gestalten.

Eine didaktische Methode, die in erster Linie kognitivistisch ausgerichtet ist und im ethischen Lernen verortet wird, in Verbindung mit dem (r)BNE- sowie dem Compassion-Konzept jedoch auch auf das soziale Lernen übertragen werden kann und somit die Ansätze Ziebertz' und Grümmes miteinander vereint, stellt das ethische Dilemma dar.

> Ein Dilemma ist dann gegeben, wenn es in einer konkreten Situation verschiedene Entscheidungs- oder Handlungsmöglichkeiten gibt, die jede für sich genommen Sinn machen, sich aber paarweise gegenseitig ausschließen. […] Das Grundproblem eines Dilemmas besteht somit darin, dass mit jeder Entscheidung für eine Option gleichzeitig ein Verzicht auf eine andere Option gegeben ist. Von einem ethischen Dilemma spricht man, wenn die in der konkreten Situation gegebenen Entscheidungs- oder Handlungsmöglichkeiten Werte oder Normen berühren.[42]

Das Nachdenken über Dilemma-Situationen bzw. -Geschichten kann innerhalb der klassischen Modelle der Werterziehung innerhalb des Modells der Wertentwicklung verortet werden. Die Entwicklung eines eigenständigen, prinzipiengeleiteten ethischen Urteils stellt somit das Ziel der Methode dar.[43] Nach Lothar Kuld bergen Dilemma-Diskussionen als moralische Konflikte das Potenzial, die

---

Reflexion der Moral. Ethisches Lernen führt zum Nachdenken über Moral, es ist reflexiv und insofern bildend.“ KULD, Lothar: Lernen an Dilemmata, in: LINDNER, Konstantin / ZIMMERMANN, Mirjam (Hg.): Handbuch ethische Bildung. Religionspädagogische Fokussierungen, Tübingen: Mohr Siebeck, 2021, 311.

41 GRÜMME, Bernhard: Ethisches Lernen im Kontext des Religionsunterrichts. Ansätze und Herausforderungen, in: SCHRÖDER, Bernd / EMMELMANN, Moritz (Hg.): Religions- und Ethikunterricht zwischen Konkurrenz und Kooperation, Göttingen: Vandenhoeck & Ruprecht, 2018, 112.

42 RIEGEL, Ulrich: Art. Dilemmageschichte, Religionsunterricht, in: WiReLex online. https://www.bibelwissenschaft.de/stichwort/200372/ (zuletzt aufgerufen am 10.03. 2023).

43 Vgl. SAJAK, Clauß P.: Ethisches Lernen, in: DERS. (Hg.): Christliches Handeln in Verantwortung für die Welt, Paderborn: Ferdinand Schöningh, 2015, 286, in Anlehnung an ZIEBERTZ [6]2010 [Anm. 41], 445.

kognitive Seite ethischen Lernens im Religionsunterricht abzubilden, indem unterschiedliche Argumente und Überzeugungen kennengelernt und gegeneinander abgewogen bzw. Wertansprüche miteinander verglichen werden, kurzum: die Urteilskompetenz geschult wird.[44] Darüber hinaus binden Dilemma-Situationen bzw. deren Reflexion „die Diskussion um Moral an die Erfahrungen und den Erfahrungsvorsprung der Kinder und Jugendlichen in ihrer Lebenswelt zurück."[45] Ein Thema, das den Schüler*innen zweifelsohne aus ihrer Lebenswelt bekannt ist, wäre die Diskussion um mehr Nachhaltigkeit und Klimagerechtigkeit. Die schwedische Klimaschutzaktivistin Greta Thunberg und ihr Schulstreik könnten manch eine*n Schüler*in sogar selbst dazu animiert haben, für den Klimaprotest freitags nicht zur Schule zu gehen. Themen wie Nachhaltigkeit und Klimaschutz fordern, sich mit ihnen auf kognitiver wie auch emotionaler Ebene auseinanderzusetzen. Schüler*innen können sich folgende Fragen auch schon unabhängig von unterrichtlichen Settings gestellt haben: Welche Klimaziele müssen erreicht werden, um die Klimakatastrophe zu verhindern? Wie kann ein *gutes und gerechtes Leben für alle* gelingen? Kann ich als Individuum überhaupt etwas tun, um wirkungsvoll zum Klimaschutz beizutragen? In der Spannung „zwischen der ökologischen Belastung des Lebensraumes Erde und der Erfüllung menschlicher Grundbedürfnisse"[46] entsteht ein (ethisches) Dilemma, das es sich im Religionsunterricht zu bearbeiten lohnt. Indem die Schüler*innen die verschiedenen Wertansprüche in einem ersten Schritt ausloten, anschließend miteinander vergleichen bzw. ausdiskutieren und in einem letzten Schritt zu einem begründeten Urteil gelangen, können gemäß dem Modell der Wertentwicklung eigene Einstellungen und Verhaltensweisen reflektiert werden. So finden sich die Schüler*innen letztlich inmitten des (r)BNE- und Compassion-Diskurses wieder, indem sie eigene Antworten auf die Fragen „Was muss ich tun? Was sollen wir tun? Was soll gelten? Was ist wünschbar und haltbar – für mich und für andere?"[47] entwickeln und begründen lernen.

Die Förderung von Ambiguitätsmanagement im Rahmen von (r)BNE und Compassion am Beispiel des ethischen Lernens

Wie bereits dargestellt, fordern Themen wie Klimakrise und Klimaschutz zu Positionierung und ethischer Urteilsbildung heraus. Werden diese Themen innerhalb des ethischen Lernens im Religionsunterricht verhandelt, kann sich daraus die normative Forderung nach mehr Nachhaltigkeit ergeben – sowohl in ökologischer und ökonomischer wie sozialer Hinsicht. An dieser Stelle findet sich ein

---

44 Vgl. KULD 2021 [Anm. 42], 317.

45 Ebd.

46 BEDERNA 2020 [Anm. 30].

47 GRÜMME 2018 [Anm. 43], 111.

entscheidender Berührungspunkt zwischen dem (r)BNE-Ansatz und dem Compassion-Projekt. Denn die Reflexion über die Frage, wie das Ziel einer *guten, gerechten und nachhaltigen Welt für alle* konkret Wirklichkeit werden könnte, kann in einem ethischen Dilemma münden, wenn unterschiedliche und konträre Normen und Werte aufeinandertreffen. Dilemmata sind naturgemäß mehrperspektivisch angelegt, es gibt nicht einfach ein *Richtig* und ein *Falsch*. Kurzum: Dilemmata müssen gedeutet werden, sodass erkennbar wird, was sich konträr und möglicherweise ambig gegenübersteht. Vor diesem Hintergrund verwundert nicht, weshalb Ulrich Riegel ethische Dilemmata bzw. die Diskussion unterschiedlicher ethischer Optionen für besonders geeignet hält, um Perspektivenwechsel und Ambiguitätstoleranz im Religionsunterricht einzuüben.[48] Auch bezogen auf den (r)BNE- wie auch den Compassion-Ansatz würde es zu kurz greifen, gäbe es nur *eine richtige* Haltung, die sich zwangsläufig aus den Diskursen ergeben würde. Wie bereits angedeutet, verstehen sich beide Ansätze als wertentwickelnde. Es kann nicht Ziel religiöser Bildung sein (entsprechend dem Modell der kritisch anzufragenden Wertübertragung), die Vielfalt unterschiedlicher Haltungen und Einstellungen zugunsten des sittlich-moralisch vermeintlich *Richtigen* zu unterbinden.

Ambiguitätsmanagement stellt m. E. dabei nicht nur eine Kompetenz dar, die durch die Thematisierung und Diskussion von Umwelt- und Nachhaltigkeitsfragen im Religionsunterricht gefördert wird, sondern bildet erst die Grundlage dafür, dass die (r)BNE- und Compassion-Ansätze derart Eingang in religiöse Bildungsprozesse finden, dass sie letztlich zu einem Umdenken bzw. Handlungsbereitschaft führen können. In dem Sinne, in dem Ambiguitätstoleranz als „notwendige Bedingung allen religionspädagogischen Verstehens und Handelns“[49] gesehen werden kann, stellt sie nämlich eine entscheidende Voraussetzung dafür dar, die Umweltfrage gemäß Wolfgang Klafki als epochales Schlüsselproblem[50] gegenwarts- und zukunftsorientiert in Kontexte religiöser Bildung einfließen zu lassen und den Blick in ethischer Hinsicht von der Umwelt zur Mitwelt zu weiten[51] – beispielsweise im Rahmen eines sozialen Projekts mit dem Compassion-Konzeptansatz. Emotional aufgeladene Themen wie Umwelt, Klima-

---

48 Vgl. RIEGEL 2018 [Anm. 44]; vgl. auch MEYER 2022 [wie Anm. 3], 189.

49 MEYER-BLANCK 2022 [Anm. 12], 173.

50 Vgl. KLAFKI, Wolfgang: Schlüsselqualifikationen / Allgemeinbildung – Konsequenzen für Schulstrukturen, in: BRAUN, Karl-Heinz / KRÜGER, Heinz-Hermann / OLBERTZ, Jan-Hendrik u. a. (Hg.): Schule mit Zukunft. Bildungspolitische Empfehlungen und Expertisen der Enquete-Kommission des Landtages von Sachsen-Anhalt, Opladen: Leske + Budrich, 1998, 150.

51 Vgl. ADAM, Gottfried: Umwelt, in: LACHMANN, Rainer / GOTTFRIED, Adam / ROTHGANGEL, Martin (Hg.): Ethische Schlüsselprobleme. Lebensweltlich – theologisch – didaktisch, Göttingen: Vandenhoeck & Ruprecht, ²2015 (= Theologie für Lehrerinnen und Lehrer 4), 55–56.

schutz und Nachhaltigkeit sind genuin mit uneindeutigen und widersprüchlichen Einstellungen und Haltungen einer und eines jeden Einzelnen verbunden. Somit ist die Aufgabe religiöser Bildungsprozesse, „die Ambiguität aller Einstellungen vor Augen zu führen und tolerieren zu helfen“,[52] auch bei der unterrichtlichen Behandlung von Umwelt, Klimaschutz und Nachhaltigkeit mitzudenken.

Resümee

Der Klimaprotest hat neben all seinen ernsten und fraglos ernüchternden Facetten auch eine sehr ermutigende: Er zeigt, dass viele – insbesondere junge – Menschen bereit sind, emanzipatorisch und politisch „für die Gestaltung ihrer Zukunft selbst einzutreten.“[53] Im Sinne des Compassion- sowie des BNE-Ansatzes werden diese Menschen selbst aktiv bzw. können beispielsweise durch ethisches Lernen im Religionsunterricht dazu animiert werden, eigene Werte zu entwickeln und zu reflektieren. Aus Reflexion und Urteilsbildung könnte schließlich der Wunsch nach Veränderung und die Handlungsbereitschaft erwachsen, an dieser gewünschten Veränderung selbst mitzuwirken. Dieser Auseinandersetzung liegt *Ambiguitätsmanagement* als Fähigkeit, unlösbare Widersprüche und Ungewissheiten zu akzeptieren, zugrunde, denn es braucht *Ambiguitätsmanagement*, um fremde und gegensätzliche Meinungen akzeptieren und wertschätzen zu können. Insbesondere die Fragen, welche Maßnahmen ergriffen werden müssen und wie man sich zur Klimakrise positioniert, sind vieldiskutierte und sehr unterschiedlich bewertete, ambige gesellschaftliche Schlüsselprobleme der heutigen Zeit.

Deshalb ist abschließend festzuhalten: *Ambiguitätsmanagement* bildet in den Zeiten der Klimakrise und des drohenden Klimanotstands eine unverzichtbare Kompetenz, um im Dialog mit anderen, möglicherweise fremden Perspektiven gemeinsam an einer umfassend nachhaltigen Zukunft arbeiten zu können. So kann das Compassion-Projekt letztlich als Teil des (r)BNE-Ansatzes seinen ganz eigenen Beitrag zum Klimaschutz und dessen bildender Reflexion im Religionsunterricht leisten.

---

52 MEYER-BLANCK 2022 [Anm. 12], 179.
53 GÄRTNER 2020 [Anm. 23], 9.

Literatur

ADAM, Gottfried: Umwelt, in: LACHMANN, Rainer / ADAM, Gottfried / ROTHGANGEL, Martin (Hg.): Ethische Schlüsselprobleme. Lebensweltlich – theologisch – didaktisch, Göttingen: Vandenhoeck & Ruprecht, [2]2015 (= Theologie für Lehrerinnen und Lehrer 4), 49–65.

BEDERNA, Katrin: Art. Bildung für nachhaltige Entwicklung, in: WiReLex online. https://www.bibelwissenschaft.de/stichwort/200572/ (zuletzt aufgerufen am 10.03. 2023).

BEDERNA, Katrin: Didaktik religiöser Bildung für nachhaltige Entwicklung, in: KROPAČ, Ulrich / RIEGEL, Ulrich (Hg.): Handbuch Religionsdidaktik, Stuttgart: Kohlhammer, 2020, 325–331.

BEDERNA, Katrin: Every Day for Future. Theologie und religiöse Bildung für nachhaltige Entwicklung, Ostfildern: Grünewald, 2019.

DRESSLER, Bernhard: Religionsunterricht. Bildungstheoretische Grundlegungen, Leipzig: Evangelische Verlagsanstalt, 2018.

GÄRTNER, Claudia: Klima, Corona und das Christentum. Religiöse Bildung für nachhaltige Entwicklung in einer verwundeten Welt, Bielefeld: transcript, 2020.

GRÜMME, Bernhard: Ethisches Lernen im Kontext des Religionsunterrichts. Ansätze und Herausforderungen, in: SCHRÖDER, Bernd / EMMELMANN, Moritz (Hg.): Religions- und Ethikunterricht zwischen Konkurrenz und Kooperation, Göttingen: Vandenhoeck & Ruprecht, 2018, 111–127.

HIRSCH, Christopher / SCHMITT-ROSCHMANN, Verena: „Letzte Generation“. Ein Jahr Kleben fürs Klima. https://www.zdf.de/nachrichten/politik/ein-jahr-letzte-generation-klimakleber-100.html (zuletzt aufgerufen am 14.03.2023).

KLAFKI, Wolfgang: Schlüsselqualifikationen / Allgemeinbildung – Konsequenzen für Schulstrukturen, in: BRAUN, Karl-Heinz / KRÜGER, Heinz-Hermann / OLBERTZ, Jan-Hendrik u. a. (Hg.): Schule mit Zukunft. Bildungspolitische Empfehlungen und Expertisen der Enquete-Kommission des Landtages von Sachsen-Anhalt, Opladen: Leske + Budrich, 1998, 145–208.

KOERRENZ, Ralf / KUMLEHN, Martina: Editorial, in: Zeitschrift für Pädagogik und Theologie 74/2 (2022), 119–121.

KRETSCHMER, Christian: Globaler Klimastreik. Kleben for Future? https://www.tagesschau.de/inland/gesellschaft/fridays-for-future-243.html (aufgerufen am 14.03.2023).

KULD, Lothar: Lernen an Dilemmata, in: LINDNER, Konstantin / ZIMMERMANN, Mirjam (Hg.): Handbuch ethische Bildung. Religionspädagogische Fokussierungen, Tübingen: Mohr Siebeck, 2021, 311–317.

KULD, Lothar: Art. Compassion, in: WiReLex online. https://www.bibelwissenschaft.de/stichwort/100124/ (zuletzt aufgerufen am 10.03.2023).

KULD, Lothar: Compassion – Raus aus der Ego-Falle, Münsterschwarzach: Vier-Türme-Verlag, 2003 (= Münsterschwarzacher Kleinschriften 138).

LÖBNER, Sebastian: Semantik. Eine Einführung, Berlin / Boston: De Gruyter, [2]2022.

METZ, Johann B.: Compassion. Zu einem Weltprogramm des Christentums im Zeitalter der Religionen und Kulturen, in: DERS. / KULD, Lothar / WEISBROD, Adolf (Hg.): Compassion. Weltprogramm des Christentums. Soziale Verantwortung lernen, Freiburg: Herder, 2000, 9–18.

MEYER, Karlo: Ambiges wird schnell übersehen – ein Plädoyer für einen Lehr-Lern-Ansatz beim „automatischen“ Denken in Stereotypen, in: Zeitschrift für Pädagogik und Theologie 74/2 (2022), 184–197.

MEYER, Karlo: Grundlagen interreligiösen Lernens, Göttingen: Vandenhoeck & Ruprecht, 2019.

MEYER-BLANCK, Michael: Ambiguitätstoleranz – eine Dimension religionspädagogischer Hermeneutik?, in: Zeitschrift für Pädagogik und Theologie 74/2 (2022), 172–183.

NICKLAS, Tobias: Lernen unter Vorzeichen der Ambiguität: Biblische Perspektiven, in: Zeitschrift für Pädagogik und Theologie 74/2 (2022), 122–141.

OVERWIEN, Bernd / RODE, Horst: Bildung für nachhaltige Entwicklung. Lebenslanges Lernen, Kompetenz und gesellschaftliche Teilhabe – eine Einleitung, in: DIES. (Hg.): Bildung für nachhaltige Entwicklung. Lebenslanges Lernen, Kompetenz und gesellschaftliche Teilhabe, Opladen / Berlin / Toronto: Barbara Budrich, 2013 (= Schriftenreihe „Ökologie und Erziehungswissenschaft" der Kommission Bildung für eine nachhaltige Entwicklung der Deutschen Gesellschaft für Erziehungswissenschaft (DGfE)), 7–10.

RIEGEL, Ulrich: Art. Dilemmageschichte, Religionsunterricht, in: WiReLex online. https://www.bibelwissenschaft.de/stichwort/200372/ (zuletzt aufgerufen am 10.03. 2023).

SAJAK, Clauß P.: Ethisches Lernen, in: DERS. (Hg.): Christliches Handeln in Verantwortung für die Welt, Paderborn: Ferdinand Schöningh, 2015, 275–296.

TILLICH, Paul: Wesen und Wandel des Glaubens, Frankfurt am Main/Berlin: Ullstein, 1961.

WÖRN, Katharina: Ambiguität. Paul Tillichs Begriff der Zweideutigkeit im Kontext interdisziplinäre Debatten, Tübingen: Mohr Siebeck, 2022 (= Dogmatik in der Moderne 38).

ZIEBERTZ, Hans-Georg: Ethisches Lernen, in: HILGER, Georg / LEIMGRUBER, Stephan / ZIEBERTZ, Hans-Georg (Hg.): Religionsdidaktik. Ein Leitfaden für Studium, Ausbildung und Beruf, München: Kösel, [6]2010, 434–452.

Schöpfung im Umbruch und Schöpfungsvisionen – Ein Werkstattbericht über die Fortbildungsarbeit zur religiösen Bildung für nachhaltige Entwicklung der Schulabteilung im Erzbistum Köln

Nina Frenzel

Das Thema ‚Schöpfung' ist seit jeher ein dem Religionsunterricht genuines Thema und wird theologisch, anthropologisch und ethisch betrachtet. Seit der Einführung der Rahmenvorgabe für Verbraucherbildung für die Lehrpläne aller Fächer in Nordrhein-Westfalen gilt es, die schöpfungstheologische Perspektive in eine besondere Verbindung mit dem schulischen Auftrag zu einer BNE zu setzen. Wie der Religionsunterricht konkret einen Beitrag zur Schul- und Unterrichtsentwicklung leisten kann, ist auch in der Aus- und Fortbildung bedeutsam. Der Werkstattbericht gibt einen Einblick in die Veranstaltungen der Schulabteilung im Erzbistum Köln zum Thema rBNE.

Verbraucherbildung; Schöpfungsverantwortung; Gerechtigkeit; Haltung; Pädagogische Woche

The topic of 'creation' has always been a genuine subject of religious education and is considered theologically, anthropologically and ethically. Since the introduction of the framework for consumer education for the curricula of all subjects in North Rhine-Westphalia, it is important to put the theological perspective on creation in a special connection with the school's mandate for an ESD. How religious education can concretely contribute to the development of schools and lessons is also significant in education and training. The workshop report gives an insight into the events of the school department in the Archdiocese of Cologne on the topic of rESD.

Consumer education; responsibility for creation; justice; attitude; pedagogical Week

Religiöse Bildung für nachhaltige Entwicklung – Die Perspektive des Glaubens ins Spiel bringen

„Lernen. Handeln. Gemeinsam Zukunft gestalten." So lautet die neue Kampagne des Bundesministeriums für Bildung und Forschung (BMBF), die im Januar 2023 startete, um Bildung für nachhaltige Entwicklung (BNE) und ihre Akteur*innen noch sichtbarer zu machen. Schon lange ist BNE kein Trend und keine Bewegung alternativer Gruppen mehr, sondern integraler Bestandteil in schulischen Bildungskontexten. Mit der Einführung der Rahmenvorgabe für Verbraucherbildung für die neuen Lehrpläne aller Fächer ist sie ein Auftrag für den Lern- und Lebensraum Schule geworden. Im Geographieunterricht setzt man sich mit den Folgen des medialen Konsums und der Ausbeutung von Menschen in Lateinamerika auseinander; in Biologie und Chemie lässt sich die Verschmutzung der Weltmeere ergründen; in Politik und Sozialwissenschaft diskutieren Schüler*innen über die Zusammenhänge und Folgen einer verstrickten globalen Marktwirtschaft. Auch über den Unterricht hinaus spielt BNE in der Schulgemeinschaft eine Rolle. Viele Schulmensen bieten auf Wunsch der Schüler*innen mindestens einen so genannten Veggie-Day an, in Schulgärten stehen selbstgebaute Bienenhotels und ein Teil des Schulstroms speist sich aus Solaranlagen auf der Sporthalle. Kinder und Jugendliche lernen auf unzählige Weise regionale und globale Zusammenhänge zu reflektieren, das eigene Handeln zu überdenken und werden angeleitet, aktiv zu werden für die Zukunft, in der sie selbst handelnde Subjekte für eine Welt von morgen sein werden. Mehr und mehr wird Bildung für nachhaltige Entwicklung so zu einer Vermittlung eines bedachten Umgangs mit den Ressourcen dieser Erde. Geht es um die Entwicklung und Förderung einer grundlegenden Lebenseinstellung, so liegt gerade darin die Chance für den Religionsunterricht, den Compassion-Gedanken wirksam werden zu lassen. Vor dem Hintergrund der christlichen Antwortkontexte wie der christlichen Liebesethik können junge Menschen sensibilisiert werden für eine empathische und compathische Haltung zur Welt. Diese empathische Mitleidenschaft kann junge Menschen verbinden mit Blick auf ihre gemeinsame Zukunft auf dieser Erde.

Für den Religionsunterricht wie auch für die Fort- und Weiterbildung von Religionslehrer*innen stellen sich daher grundlegende Fragen: Wie kann vermieden werden, dass der Religionsunterricht nicht nur auf den Zug einer schulischen Verbraucherbildung aufspringt, sondern weiterhin seinem genuin religiösen Auftrag gerecht wird? Wie dieser Auftrag *innerhalb* der BNE wahrgenommen und in religiösen Lehr- und Lernprozessen zu einer spezifisch *religiösen* BNE werden? Wie ist die Rede von einer Verantwortung des Menschen angesichts einer generationenübergreifenden Aufgabe so ins Wort zu bringen, dass sie nicht trivialisiert? Inwiefern kann die hoffnungsvolle Dimension des Glaubens, die Rede von der Welt als Schöpfung Gottes und dem Menschen als Geschöpf gerade heute noch thematisiert werden? Was kann Schüler*innen Orientierung und Hoffnung geben, eine Haltung zu den großen, drängenden Fragen einzunehmen und daraus Perspektiven für die Zukunft zu entwickeln?

Sicherlich hat die Theologie als Bezugswissenschaft des Religionsunterrichts nicht die Expertise, um die naturwissenschaftlichen wie auch wirtschaftlich-politischen Fragen und Herausforderungen dieser Klimakrise zu lösen. Dies sei den jeweiligen Expert*innen vorbehalten. Doch sind die großen Fragen längst inmitten der Gesellschaft und in vielfältigen Lebensbereichen angekommen. Zu unausweichlich sind die Konsequenzen für eine global gedachte Gerechtigkeit, eine soziale Gesellschaft und einen langfristigen Frieden mit Blick auf gleichberechtigte Lebenschancen und Lebensqualität in allen Ländern dieser Erde. Spätestens seit der Enzyklika *Laudato Si'* von Papst Franziskus hat sich die Kirche die Themen Nachhaltigkeit und Schöpfungsbewahrung auf die Fahnen geschrieben. Seitdem sind unzählige Dokumente entstanden wie die Arbeitshilfe der DBK *Schöpfungsverantwortung als kirchlicher Auftrag* oder auch das Visionspapier *Schöpfungsverantwortung im Erzbistum Köln 2030.* In seiner Enzyklika bringt es Papst Franziskus sehr eindrücklich auf den Punkt, weshalb wir als Kirche unsere Stimme im Diskurs um die Klimakrise erheben müssen: „[....] unsere Schwester, Mutter Erde, [....] schreit auf wegen des Schadens, den wir aufgrund des unverantwortlichen Gebrauchs und des Missbrauchs der Güter zufügen, die Gott in sie hineingelegt hat."[1] Der Papst verwendet Beziehungsbegriffe, die unser Innerstes anrühren, ist der Aufschrei doch unüberhörbar und zunehmend auch für Menschen hierzulande an der eigenen Haut spürbar. Zu dieser Welt, dieser Erde und dem, was auf ihr geschieht, steht der Mensch nicht beziehungslos da. Die biblischen Erzählungen vom Verhältnis des Menschen zu seinem Lebensraum zeugen davon; der biblische Begriff ‚Schöpfung' ist selbst Beziehung zwischen Gott, dem Schöpfer, Geschöpf und Schöpfung. Und doch befindet sich diese Schöpfung in einem Wandel, einem Umbruch, konkret gesagt in einer Krise, die viele Fragen aufwirft.

Der Religionsunterricht war von jeher ein Ort, an dem die großen Fragen des Lebens auf den Tisch kommen. Seit jeher hat auch das Thema ‚Schöpfung' seinen genuinen Ort im Religionsunterricht und wird in vielfältiger Weise biblisch, theologisch, anthropologisch wie auch mit Blick auf je aktuelle gesellschaftspolitisch relevante Diskurse und Anknüpfungspunkte ethisch betrachtet. Spiralcurricular schlägt sich die schöpfungstheologische Perspektive als zentraler Sinnkontext schon immer in einer Vielzahl von Themen des Religionsunterrichts nieder und zieht sich wie einer roter Faden durch die christlichen Antwortkontexte auf die existentiellen Fragen, die im Religionsunterricht verhandelt werden. Das betrifft sowohl die Sorgen wie auch Hoffnungen, die die jungen Menschen von heute bewegen. Es gibt wahrlich vieles, was Kinder und Jugendliche in diesen Zeiten ganz anders bewegt. Katastrophen und Krisen hat es schon viele auf dieser Welt gegeben. Aber vermutlich führt keine andere als die des Klimas vor Augen, wie endlich und fragil diese Welt, wie vulnerabel der Mensch tatsächlich ist. Daher gilt es heute, junge Menschen zu stärken, mit dem Gefühl der Ohnmacht und Hilflosigkeit umzugehen und ihnen Orientierung und Hoffnung zu geben, Perspektiven zu entwickeln. Wie kein anderes Fach vermag es der Religi-

---

[1] Papst Franziskus: Enzyklika Laudato Si'. Über die Sorge für das gemeinsame Haus, Bonn, 2015 (= Verlautbarungen des Apostolischen Stuhls 202), 7.

onsunterricht, Räume zu eröffnen, eine eigene Haltung zu den großen, drängenden Fragen einzunehmen, die motiviert, die Zukunft selbst ein Stück weit in die Hand zu nehmen und Verantwortung zu übernehmen. Diese tragfähige Perspektive des christlichen Glaubens bringen Religionslehrer*innen vor Ort im Religionsunterricht ins Spiel. Es ist die hoffnungsvolle Dimension unseres Glaubens, die junge Menschen als handelnde Subjekte stärken kann. So will rBNE „Kinder und Jugendliche nicht zu Anwälten für die Schöpfung, die Armen und die Zukunft machen. Sie will, dass sie sich selbst zu Anwälten für die Schöpfung, die Armen und die Zukunft machen. Sie versucht, Möglichkeiten dazu zu eröffnen."[2] Eine zentrale Voraussetzung dafür ist eine emphatische Mitleidenschaft mit anderen, so wie es Johann Baptist Metz im Begriff der ‚Compassion' grundgelegt hat. Als Haltung erkennt die Compassion die Autorität der Leidenden an, öffnet die Wahrnehmung auf den Anderen und sein Leid hin – wie Jesus Christus es uns zum Vorbild getan hat. Nicht nur lässt eine compathische Haltung Gott im und durch den Anderen entdecken, sondern fordert in der Konsequenz zu einem gerechten und solidarischen Handeln auf. Wird der Compassion-Gedanke in religiösen Lernprozessen vermittelt und eingeübt, so kann er jungen Menschen konkrete Visionen von einer besseren Welt eröffnen. Dabei ist es die Zielsetzung der rBNE, dass es um ein zukunftsträchtiges Sprechen, Denken und Handeln geht. Es gilt, junge Menschen nicht im Potentialis zukunftsfähig zu machen, sondern vielmehr in der Erwartung einer Realisierung dieser neu gedachten Zukunft im Realis stark zu machen. So spricht Bederna davon, dass erst zukunftsträchtiges Verhalten die neue Zukunft in sich trage und neues Leben eröffne.[3] Der spezifisch religiöse Beitrag des Religionsunterrichts innerhalb der BNE liegt daher darin, dass rBNE eine Transformationsbildung ist, die fragt „nach dem *Sinn-Grund* nicht nur des eigenen Lebens, sondern dem des Lebens der Anderen, der Zukünftigen und der Mitwelt. Sie fragt nach einer guten Ordnung, die ist und doch noch kommen muss. (...) Sie fragt also nach einem Sinn-Grund, auf den zu warten und der zu erflehen ist. Insofern hast sie eine messianische den Fluss der Normalität unterbrechende Perspektive."[4]

In vielen Veranstaltungen der Schulabteilung im Bereich rBNE wurden daher in den vergangenen zwei Jahren die Fragen nach einem nachhaltigen und zukunftsorientierten Leben in den Vordergrund gerückt. Mit Blick auf den christlichen Schöpfungsauftrag eröffnen sich theologische Anschlussfragen nach Visionen von einer besseren, gerechten, weil nachhaltigen Zukunft sowie

---

2 Bederna, Katrin: Every Day For Future. Theologie und religiöse Bildung für nachhaltige Entwicklung, Ostfildern: Matthias-Grünewald, ²2020, 235.

3 Vgl. Ebd., 239 und weiter: „In dieser Intention verhilft der Religionsunterricht zu transformationsrelevantem Wissen, fördert den Erwerb transformationsrelevanter Kompetenzen und erprobt eine bestimmte, demütige, parteiische und zukunftsoffene Weltsicht sowie das aus dieser entspringende gemeinsame verändernde Handeln."

4 Ebd., 237.

eine theologische Reflexion im Hinblick auf ihre Bedeutung für Transformationsprozesse im Denken und Handeln des Menschen in der globalen Welt. Vor diesem Hintergrund ist das religiöse Lernen daraufhin auszurichten, dass es die spezifisch christliche Perspektive auf Heil und Erlösung, Hoffnung und Zukunft ins Spiel bringt. Das gilt für den Religionsunterricht in den Zielperspektiven wie für die vielschichtigen Projekte der Schulpastoral und für die curriculare Eigenprägung aller Fächer an den Katholischen Schulen und folgerichtig auch für die die Fort- und Weiterbildung von Religionslehrer*innen. Exemplarisch werden folgend einige Veranstaltungen der Schulabteilung vorgestellt.

Fortbildungsarbeit im Zeichen der *religiösen* Bildung für nachhaltige Entwicklung

Die Pädagogische Woche 2021: Was uns in Atem hält – Schöpfung im Umbruch

Unter dem Titel *Was uns in Atem hält – Schöpfung im Umbruch* wurden in den Veranstaltungen der Pädagogischen Woche 2021 auf vielfältige Weise Fragen nach einem nachhaltigen und zukunftsorientierten Leben in den Blick genommen. Die Pädagogische Woche ist eine der größten regelmäßigen Fortbildungsveranstaltungen für Religionslehrer*innen in NRW. Jedes Jahr wird sie von der Hauptabteilung Schule / Hochschule des Erzbistums Köln in Kooperation mit dem bischöflichen Institut für Lehrerfortbildung (IfL) organisiert. Seit nunmehr über vierzig Jahren widmet sich die Fortbildungswoche Themen aus Theologie und Gesellschaft sowie ihrer Relevanz für die schulische Bildung. So bietet die Woche für jede Schulform einen eigenen Fortbildungstag. Eröffnet wird diese Fortbildungswoche montags mit einem Gottesdienst und einem Festakt.

Das Thema 2022 fiel in ein Jahr, in dem es für so einige Folgen aus der Klimakrise eines langen Atems bedurfte. Mit Blick auf den Zustand dieser Erde trat deutlich zu Tage, dass wir in einer krisen- und umbruchhaften Zeit leben. Prägend waren Bilder vom verseuchten Marmarameer und von Waldbränden, die wie ein Strohfeuer kaum zu bändigen waren; es gab Bilder von Menschen auf der Flucht und nicht zuletzt von der verheerenden Flutkatastrophe an der Ahr. Letzteres geschah nicht weit weg in fremden Ländern, sondern direkt vor der Haustür. Betroffen waren Familien und Freunde, Kolleg*innen der eigenen Schule sowie die ihnen dort anvertrauten Kinder und Jugendlichen. Im Sommer dann hat der aktuelle Bericht des Weltklimarats IPCC anhand von physikalischen Befunden nur das bestätigt, was längst klar war: Der Klimawandel hält unseren Lebensraum ‚Erde' und die Zukunft der kommenden Generationen in Atem. Die

Coronapandemie und die Flutkatastrophe verschärfen den Blick darauf wie ein Brennglas. Mit dem Titel *Was uns in Atem hält – Schöpfung im Umbruch* schien das Thema von geradezu erschreckender Aktualität zu sein und den Nerv der Zeit getroffen zu haben. Inmitten des Diskurses von ethischen, gesellschaftspolitischen wie ökonomischen Fragen setzte das Thema einen religiös-theologischen Akzent. In den Veranstaltungen wurden die Fragen nach einem nachhaltigen und zukunftsorientierten Leben in den Vordergrund gerückt. Mit Blick auf den christlichen Schöpfungsauftrag eröffneten sich theologische Anschlussfragen nach Visionen von einer besseren und gerechten, weil nachhaltigen Zukunft sowie eine theologische Reflexion im Hinblick auf ihre Bedeutung für Transformationsprozesse im Denken und Handeln des Menschen in der globalen Welt. Stets zu bedenken war dabei die Prämisse, dass der Religionsunterricht einen eigenen, religiösen Beitrag für eine BNE zu leisten hat.

Wichtige Impulse kamen im Festvortrag von Prof. Dr. Armin Grunwald, unter anderem Leiter des Instituts für Technikfolgenabschätzung und Systemanalyse (ITAS) in Karlsruhe sowie Leiter des Büros für Technikfolgenabschätzung beim Deutschen Bundestag (TAB) und Mitglied im Deutschen Ethikrat. Mit seinen vielfältigen Einblicken in ethisch-philosophische und gesellschaftspolitische Diskurse sprach er zum Thema *Anthropozän – das ‚Zeitalter des Menschen'. Von Krisen und Umbrüchen, Hybris und Verantwortung.* In seinem Vortrag erläuterte er, Technikfolgen seien nicht einfach Folgen der Technik, sondern Folgen des Umgangs damit. Demzufolge ermutigte er dazu, durch bewusstes Handeln Verantwortung für eine nachhaltige Entwicklung zu übernehmen. Gleich ob Wissenschaftler*innen oder Christ*innen wüssten wir, dass wir nicht alles tun können, aber etwas könne jeder und jede von uns tun. Dies beginne damit, zu reflektieren wie intensiv man Ressourcen und Techniken nutze, die für die Umwelt und die Folgen für die Klimakrise problematisch sein könnten. Auf diese Weise forderte er dazu auf, eine nachhaltige Zukunft aktiv zu gestalten.

Der schulische Auftrag, Kinder und Jugendliche angesichts der komplexen Herausforderungen des 21. Jahrhunderts zu zukunftsfähigem Denken und Handeln zu befähigen, ist ein Auftrag, dem sich katholische Schulen mit Blick auf die christliche Überzeugung einer Schöpfungsverantwortung besonders verpflichtet wissen. Mit Blick auf das religiöse Schulprofil ist eine rBNE für den gesamten Lern- und Lebensort Schule prägend zu machen. Daher trug der Tag für Katholischen Schulen in freier Trägerschaft den Titel: *Schöpfungsverantwortung als Bildungsauftrag der Erzbischöflichen Schulen.* In Fortbildungsangeboten wurde dem nachgegangen, wie Lehrer*innen junge Menschen an ihren Schulen in Unterricht, in schulischen Projekten und im Schulalltag bei dem Erwerb der dafür notwendigen Kenntnisse und Kompetenzen unterstützen können, handelnde Subjekte zu werden. Im Zentrum stand die Auseinandersetzung mit der Schöpfungsverantwortung und deren Konkretisierung in der schulischen Wirklichkeit. Das Hauptreferat wurde von Dr. Christian Weingarten, Leiter der Abteilung Schöpfungsverantwortung im Erzbistum Köln, mit seinem Vortrag *Schöpfungsverantwortung konkret* gehalten. Er gab Einblick in die vielfältigen nachhaltigen Projekte, Aktionen und Unterstützungsangebote, die es im Erzbistum Köln gibt. Über die Pädagogische Woche hinaus besteht ein fachlicher Kontakt zur Abteilung Schöpfungsverantwortung in Bezug auf die Konkretisierung und Einbindung von Projekten zur rBNE. Im Anschluss an den Vortrag bestand die Möglichkeit, die Thematik in Seminaren für den Schulalltag zu übersetzen. Einige Seminare beschäftigten sich mit der Frage, wie Schöpfungsverantwortung in der Schule institutionalisiert werden kann, um aus einem Trend ein konkretes Konzept zur Schöpfungsbewahrung werden zu lassen (*Vom Trend zum Konzept: Nachhaltigkeit als gelebte Schöpfungsverantwortung in der Schule).* Dazu zählten auch schulpastorale Seminare mit Ideen und Anregungen für die gesamte Schulgemeinschaft. Überdies wurde im Workshop *Zukunft erschließen mit Szenarien – kollaboratives Selberdenken* eine Methode vorgestellt, die die herkömmliche Umweltpädagogik verwendet und Zukünfte entwickelt, die sich radikal voneinander unterscheiden.

Mit Blick auf den konkreten Religionsunterricht gab Dr. Guido Hunze in seinen Vorträgen gewinnbringende Hinweise zu den *Theologischen Herausforderungen und schöpfungsdidaktischen Stolpersteinen.* Immer weniger Kinder und Jugendliche können heute noch etwas mit religiösen Vorstellungen und Glaubensüberzeugungen anfangen. Sie nehmen andere Perspektiven auf Welt und Mensch ein. Daher warnte Dr. Guido Hunze einerseits davor, Nachhaltigkeit beliebig im Religionsunterricht zu thematisieren, gleichzeitig mahnte er an, diese nicht mit Schöpfungsverantwortung gleichzusetzen. Schließlich könne man schon lange nicht mehr selbstverständlich auf ein Verständnis treffen, dass der christliche Glaube von einem Schöpfergott spreche. Didaktisch-methodisch analysierte er gängige Darstellungen des Schöpfungsglaubens und Nachhaltigkeitsgedankens in Unterrichtsmaterialien und Lehrwerken für den Religionsunterricht. Dabei ging es ihm darum, den Blick dafür zu schärfen und zu sensibilisieren, welchen spezifischen Beitrag der Religionsunterricht zu einer BNE leistet und wie die vor dem Hintergrund einer heterogenen, oft nicht mehr kirchlich und religiös sozialisierten Schüler*innenschaft zeitgemäß gelingen kann. Da es im Zuge der Vorbereitung der Pädagogischen Woche stets ein Referent*innengespräch mit dem Hauptreferent*innen und den für die Arbeitskreise gewonnenen Referentinnen und Referenten gibt, waren die Leitungen der Arbeitskreise bereits für die Planung ihrer unterrichtspraktischen Hinweise und Ausarbeitungen sensibilisiert für die genuin religiöse Dimension einer Auseinandersetzung mit Nachhaltigkeit im Religionsunterricht. Im Religionsunterricht gehe es darum, so führte Hunze aus, zu motivieren und anzustoßen, eine eigene Haltung einzunehmen, die das eigene Handeln anstoße und vor dem Hintergrund einer Annahme eines Schöpfergottes verändere. Einen weiteren fachwissenschaftlichen Impuls setzte Frau Prof. Dr. Gärtner mit ihren Ausführungen zu *Klima, Corona und das Christentum.*

Religiöse Bildung für nachhaltige Entwicklung in einer verwundeten Welt. Vor dem Hintergrund der Sustainable Development Goals der UN (Agenda 2030) forderte sie dazu auf, vorliegende BNE-Konzepte kritisch weiterzudenken. BNE sei eine bedeutsame Chance in Bezug auf den Einsatz für eine nachhaltige Zukunft, sei es doch ein global weitverbreitetes und einflussreiches Modell mit unhintergehbaren Zielsetzungen. Eine religiöse Dimension in BNE-Konzepten werfe jedoch die Frage auf, ob es Religion und Christentum für Nachhaltigkeit bedürfe. Christliche Überzeugungen und Traditionen in BNE bewegten sich stets zwischen Normativität und Pluralität, weshalb darauf zu achten sei, inwiefern diese legitim oder doch überwältigend in BNE seien. Hier sei eine kritische Selbstreflexion notwendig. Die Leistung bestehe darin, sie so übersetzen, dass dadurch nichtreligiöse Diskurse unterbrochen und gleichzeitig eine Überwältigung vermieden werde. Doch könne Religion in diesem Kontext als Quelle für Resilienz und Widerstand und zum Dienst am Menschen und an der Welt wahrgenommen werden. Die größte Herausforderung sei, dass Schüler*innen verstrickt seien in nicht-nachhaltigen wie auch nicht-religiösen Systemen und sich doch von einer tiefen Hoffnung auf Veränderung getragen fühlten.

Die Themen der angebotenen Arbeitskreise waren vielfältig. Für die Primarstufe und die Förderschulen gab es u. a. Workshops, die sich mit dramapädagogischen Elementen beschäftigten und auf diese Weise zu einer kreativen und bewegungsorientierten Auseinandersetzung anregten: Unter dem Titel *Gott gab uns Atem. Dramapädagogische Elemente im Religionsunterricht - Erzählen, Spielen und Darstellen: Ideen für eine inklusive Theaterarbeit* lud der Workshop zu einem Perspektivwechsel ein, um den alltäglichen Unterricht aufzubrechen. Indem Grundschulkindern in einem geschützten Rahmen Spielanlässe geboten werden, könne den heterogenen Perspektiven einer Welterschließung ermöglicht werden, dass sie neue Rollen ausprobieren und die eigene Rolle finden. Innerhalb des komplexen Themas *Schöpfungsglauben* könne den Kindern eine Möglichkeit gegeben werden, im Sinne einer rBNE handlungsorientiert verschiedene Lösungsmöglichkeiten zu erforschen. Auch die Enzyklika *Laudato Si'* wurde für die Grundschule aufbereitet. Der Workshop *Laudato Si' – Ein Brief an die Menschenkinder, die Welt zu FAIRändern* nahm sich der Tatsache an, dass der Glaube an die Welt als Geschenk Gottes und der Appell zur Schöpfungsbewahrung nicht voraussetzungslos sei. Damit Kinder das Grundanliegen der Enzyklika *Laudato Si'* elementar verstehen lernten, wurde angeregt, über eine erfahrungsorientierte Auseinandersetzung mit dem Symbol Haus eine Verständnisgrundlage zu schaffen und Impulse für ein verändertes Handeln im Kontext Schule zu geben. Schulpastorale Arbeitskreise wie *Schöpfungspsalmen- ist spirituelle und ökologische Nachhaltigkeit möglich?* nahmen die Lehrkräfte in den Blick und gingen der Frage nach, welche Bedeutung das Stehen in der Psalmentradition für das persönliche wie berufliche Handeln hat. Konkrete Praxisbeispiele wie die sogenannten Müllsheriffs oder die 15-Minuten-Pausenaktion boten Anregungen und Ideen für die eigene Schule.

Für die Sekundarstufe I und II wurde u. a. der Workshop *Durch die Brille der Schöpfung schauen – zwischen Wissen und Partizipation* angeboten, in dem Unterrichtsmodule vorgestellt und diskutiert wurden, die das Thema *Schöpfung* sprachsensibel behandeln, ohne *Schöpfung* dabei auf Naturschutz zu reduzieren. Die Module erörterten die Frage, was Gott für seine gesamte Schöpfung wünsche. Dabei wurde auch zu einer Auseinandersetzung mit Utopien und Zukunftsszenarien sowie der Umgang mit Chaos, Angst, Hoffnung und Verantwortung im Religionsunterricht angeregt, damit Schüler*innen echte Selbstwirksamkeitserfahrungen machen können. Wie ihnen der theologische Wert des Begriffs Schöpfung auch heute noch nahegebracht werden kann, wurde im Workshop *„Ich bin Leben, das leben will, inmitten von Leben, das leben will." – Impulse der Ethik Albert Schweitzers zur Gestaltung von Welt und Gesellschaft im Zeichen des Umbruchs* anhand ausgewählter ethischer Impulse aus dem Werk Albert Schweitzers erarbeitet. In diesem Kontext setzten sich die Teilnehmenden damit auseinander, dass zunehmend und inzwischen fast inflationär der Begriff Schöpfung in unterschiedlichen Komposita verwendet werde. Der wachsenden Bedeutung in diversen theologischen Tagungen und Publikationen stünden bisweilen eine zumindest fragende Haltung aus weiten Teilen der Gesellschaft entgegen, welchen Mehrwert Theologinnen und Theolog*innen in ihrem Sprechen von Schöpfung in die Debatten um die Herausforderungen unserer Zeit eigentlich einbringen könnten und ob die großen Krisen mit den Mitteln der Ökologie, der Ökonomie, der Soziologie etc. nicht hinreichend zu lösen seien. Den Leitungen des Workshops ,*Buen Vivir. Vom Recht auf ein gutes Leben. Schöpfungsbewahrung durch Suffizienz und nicht durch Effizienz* war es ein Anliegen, nach dem Buch von Alberto Acosta den weiten Weg von der traditionellen (kirchlichen) Entwicklungshilfe in einen echten Perspektivwechsel zu gehen. Durch ein Lernen auf unserer Seite des Globus könne das Wissen der Anderen für eine Welt jenseits des Wachstums genutzt werden. Konkrete Projekte an Schulen können so einen Beitrag in der Postkolonialismusdebatte leisten. Auch dem Compassion-Gedanken gingen einige Workshops nach: Zugrunde gelegt wurde die Überlegung, dass es in einer Zeit, in der ein Gemeinschaftssinn dem Individualismus weiche, alternativer sozialer Erfahrungsräume bedürfe. So könne ein Religionsunterricht, der über einen Theologie- und Weltanschauungsunterricht hinausgehe, vor dem Hintergrund des performativen Religionsunterrichts Angebote schaffen. Sozialprojekte eröffnen soziale Erfahrungsräume. So wurden im Arbeitskreis eine Auswahl an digitalen und analogen Compassion-Projektideen vorgestellt und gemeinsam weitere Ideen entwickelt.

Von ‚Schöpfungsvisionen' in der religionspädagogischen Zeitschrift Impulse

Ausgehend von der Pädagogischen Woche widmet sich ein Heft der religionspädagogischen Zeitschrift *Impulse* dem Thema *Schöpfungsvisionen.* Als Titelbild wurde das Bild gewählt, das am 24. Dezember 1968 um die Welt ging. Es zeigt die Erde als Kugel, so wie es Apollo 8 bei der Umkreisung des Mondes erblickte. Per live-Übertragung ging es um die Welt und macht noch heute eindrücklich deutlich, was der Ausspruch „Es ist eine Frage der Perspektive." bedeutet: Wenn wir aus christlicher Perspektive auf diese Erde, die wir Schöpfung nennen, schauen, dann ruft uns unser Glaube aus Ehrfurcht und Bewunderung zur Verantwortung für die Schöpfung auf. Die Hoffnung auf Umwandlung und Erlösung lässt Visionen von einer Schöpfung von morgen entstehen – so die Grundintention des Heftes. In seinem das Heft eröffnenden fachwissenschaftlichen Basisartikel plädiert Dr. Guido Hunze für ein Lernen mit Blick auf eine Haltungsveränderung. In diesem Zusammenhang regt er zu einer Umsetzung von Nachhaltigkeit für die Schule als ganze Institution an, wodurch sich für Schüler*innen Erfahrungen von Selbstwirksamkeit und positiv-emotionaler Bestärkung eröffnen.

Im Anschluss dazu lädt die Geistliche Hinführung *Soli deo gloria. Eine Frage der Perspektive* die Religionslehrer*innen ein, sich selbst damit auseinanderzusetzen, wie es um den eigenen Glauben in Bezug auf die Rede von einem Schöpfergott und dem Menschen als Geschöpf bestellt ist; was Motivation gibt, trotz der eigenen Hilflosigkeit und Ohnmacht aktiv und handelnd zu bleiben und den eigenen Schöpfungsvisionen nachzugehen. Die darauffolgenden unterrichtspraktischen Impulse bieten eine Vielzahl an Materialien und Impulsen u. a. zur Enzyklika *Laudato Si'*, zu den Nachhaltigkeitszielen der UN-Mitgliedstaaten wie auch den biblischen Schöpfungsvisionen als nachhaltige und resilienzfördernde Kraftquellen. Vor diesem Hintergrund regen die Arbeitsaufträge die Schüler*innen an, perspektivisch Visionen für ihr persönliches wie auch gesellschaftliches Leben zu skizzieren. Ein weiterer Beitrag entfaltet die Idee, Tugenden, die das Leben fördern wollen und den Lebensstil von Menschen mit einer Grundhaltung positiv prägen, als einen ethischen Maßstab für das eigene wie das gesellschaftliche Handeln bei den Herausforderungen der Klimakrise anzulegen. Dabei werden sowohl die vier Kardinaltugenden als auch die drei göttlichen Tugenden einbezogen. Überdies geben weitere Unterrichtsbausteine Ideen, wie der Sonntag als Ruhe- und Beziehungstag für die ganze Schöpfung reflektiert werden oder Verantwortung für die Zukunft als theologisch-ethische Kategorie thematisiert werden kann. Zuletzt setzt sich ein Material mit der christlichen Symbolik des Pelikans als Beispiel für das Opfer und die Hingabe Christi auseinander. Reflektiert wird die Schau Gottes in allen Geschöpfen und die Umwandlung der Schöpfung in Jesus Christus bis hin zur Frage, was für die Schüler*innen persönlich in ihrem Leben auf die Anwesenheit eines liebenden Schöpfers verweist und was an der Schöpfung für sie wie ein Sakrament die Existenz der Liebe Gottes greifbar macht. Über die unterrichtspraktischen Ideen hinaus stellt die Schulpastoral das schulpastorale Bildungsangebot ‚Werde WELTfairÄnderer!' für weiterführende Schulen unter dem Motto 2021 *Das Wenige, das du tun kannst, ist viel!* (Albert Schweitzer) vor. Mit vielfältigen Projekten und Aktionen können junge Menschen zu Fairness, Nachhaltigkeit und soziale Gerechtigkeit sensibilisiert und ermutigt werden. Einen praxisbezogenen Erfahrungsbericht, wie eine Schule den Bildungsauftrag der Schöpfungsbewahrung in die Lernkultur konkret integriert, liefert die Erzbischöfliche Liebfrauenschule Köln. Dabei geht das Engagement über konkrete ökologische Umsetzungen wie Bienenstöcke im eigenen Schulgarten hinaus. Das regelmäßig stattfindende Abendformat *LFS im Diskurs* stand bereits mehrfach im Zeichen der BNE. Eingeladen waren Expert*innen aus dem Bereich Ökologie, Ökonomie und Gesellschaft, um zu aktuellen Fragen rund um die Klimakrise zu diskutieren. Außerdem gab es eine Zero-Waste-Week, in dem eine ganze Schulwoche sowohl im Unterricht, in den Gottesdiensten wie auch in außerunterrichtlichen Aktionen ganz im Zeichen der rBNE stand. Jede schulische Aktion wirke in den Unterricht und in das schulische Leben und das Agieren der jungen Menschen hinein – schließlich brauche es im Krisenmodus wache Menschen, die bereits seien, sich reflektiert und vernünftig zu engagieren.

Weitere Fortbildungen im Bereich der religiösen BNE – vom ‚Klimawandel und Gerechtigkeit' und ‚Verbraucherbildung im Religionsunterricht'

Auch die Jahrestagung 2021 der Schulabteilung für katholische Religionslehrkräfte der Sekundarstufe II im Kloster Steinfeld hat sich in Kooperation mit dem IFL dieser Thematik unter dem Titel *Klimawandel und Gerechtigkeit* angenommen. Aufgrund der coronabedingten Einschränkungen wurde sie als online-Tagung durchgeführt. Im Sinne einer theologischen Grundlegung und Vertiefung machte Prof. Dr. Michael Reder von der Hochschule für Philosophie in München den Aufschlag und hielt einen Vortrag über *Klimawandel und Gerechtigkeit: Eine ethische Landkarte der Debatte.* Anhand spezifischer Aspekte erläuterte er zunächst die Herausforderungen des Klimawandels, um dann den ethischen Aspekt der Gerechtigkeit näher in den Blick zu nehmen. Klimaschutz und Armutsbekämpfung müssten wirksam, effizient und gerecht miteinander verbunden werden können, indem u. a. gerechte Institutionen aufgebaut werden. Davon ausgehend skizzierte er den Zusammenhang vom Klimawandel und Menschenrechten mit der Konsequenz zu einer ethisch begründeten Klimapolitik. Im Anschluss referierte Dr. Sebastian Kistler, Mitarbeiter am BMBF-Projekt *Bioökonomie als gesellschaftlicher Wandel* (LMU München und Universität Passau) zum

Thema *Unsere Schöpfungsverantwortung nachhaltig gestalten: Gerechtigkeit in den Enzykliken von Papst Franziskus*. Dabei kam er zu dem Schluss, dass die Enzyklika *Laudato Si'* in der Tradition bisheriger Sozialenzykliken stehe und das Gerechtigkeitsmotiv, einer Option für die Armen, zentral sei. Diese Option gelte nicht nur gegenüber der geschundenen Natur, sondern auch den Einzelnen, sowie zwischen den Ländern. In der Praxis seien internationale Organisationen zu stärken.

Auch im Kontext der Steinfeld-Tagung gab es einen Workshop von Dr. Guido Hunze, der mit Blick auf die Lehrmaterialien der Sekundarstufe II Darstellungsweisen und thematische Verknüpfungen zwischen dem christlichen Schöpfungsglauben und dem heutigen Ruf nach einem nachhaltigen Leben unter die Lupe nahm (*Nachhaltiges Leben - Im Namen Gottes*). Der Proteste und Aktionen von jungen Menschen nahm sich in besonderer Weise der Workshop *Everyday for Future - positive Visionen wecken, eigene Zukünfte denken, um selbstverantwortlich unsere Zukunft zu gestalten* an. In den Impulsen für den Unterricht wurde gewürdigt und ernstgenommen, dass Kinder und Jugendliche bei den Folgen des Klimawandels ihre eigene Zukunft wie auch die der folgenden Generationen gefährdet und bedroht wissen und sich daher auf vielfältige Weise für einen Wandel im Denken und Handeln aller Bereiche des Lebens und der Gesellschaft einsetzen. Der Workshop *Globale Gerechtigkeit und Entwicklungszusammenarbeit - Thema im RU der Sek II* durch Mitarbeiter*innen von Misereor eröffneten den Teilnehmenden die Möglichkeit, sich mit den Intentionen und Hintergründen der entstandenen Unterrichtsbausteine auseinanderzusetzen und neue Impulse einbringen. An einem Nachmittag stand eine Lehr-Lerneinheit mit dem Wuppertal-Institut für Klima, Umwelt und Energie an. Mit dem Titel V*om Spielen zum Handeln - Serious Gaming als Lehrmethode im Kontext von Nachhaltigkeit* wurde der Ansatz spielerischen Lernens im Nachhaltigkeitskontext diskutieren und Erfahrungen mit bestehenden Materialien und Produkten ausgetauscht. Diese sollen Schüler*innen ermöglichen, sich spielerisch Wissen über Ressourcenendlichkeit, Güterproduktion und die ökologischen und sozialen Auswirkungen ihres eigenen Konsums anzueignen, zu reflektieren und anzuwenden.

Am Ende der online-Tagung waren sich alle Beteiligten einig und ermutigt, dass der Religionsunterricht einen tatsächlich eigenen und noch dazu äußerst wertvollen Beitrag innerhalb der BNE leisten kann. Ein Teilnehmender hat es sehr treffend ausgedrückt: Damit der Religionsunterricht einen religiösen Beitrag zur BNE leiste, müssten nur die dem Religionsunterricht eigentümlichen Strickmuster gefunden werden. Dann bietet sich die Chance, junge Menschen stark zu machen, eine Haltung einzunehmen, damit sie in ihrem Alltag Verantwortung für die Zukunft übernehmen in der Hoffnung, dass diese Welt durch einen nachhaltigen Umgang mit Welt und Mensch gerechter werde.

Ebenso online fand Ende 2021 eine implementationsaffine Fortbildung zur *Verbraucherbildung* statt. Diese ist gedacht zur Unterstützung der fachlichen Unterrichtsentwicklung im Nachgang zur Implementation des seit Beginn des

Schuljahres 2019/2020 geltenden neuen Lehrplans für den Katholischen Religionsunterricht. Mit dem Titel *Verantwortung – Gottes Schöpfung in Menschenhand Verbraucherbildung im Religionsunterricht Shirts für 2,50 € vs. Demos für Nachhaltigkeit?* gab es weiterführende und vertiefende Erschließungen zu den Zielen und Anforderungen des kompetenzorientierten Lehrplans, didaktische Impulse sowie konkrete Anregungen für die Unterrichtsgestaltung. Vor dem Hintergrund der 2017 eingeführten Rahmenvorgabe *Verbraucherbildung in Schule* war die Veranstaltung vor allem durch die Frage geleitet, wie der Religionsunterricht als Ort des religiösen Lernens einen eigenen spezifischen Beitrag zur *Verbraucher*innenbildung* leisten könne, ohne den moralisch-ethischen Zeigefinger zu erheben.

Schlussfolgerungen: Von der Erfahrung zur Haltung, von der Haltung zur Handlung

Der Religionsunterricht wie auch Projekte der Schulpastoral haben das Potenzial, Kinder und Jugendliche anzuleiten, selbst handelnde Subjekte einer Welt von morgen zu werden. Existenzielle Fragen nach Gerechtigkeit, Chancengleichheit, Heil und Erlösung, Wert und Würde des Menschen und seiner Arbeit werden mit christlichen Antwortkontexten in Verbindung gebracht. Dazu zählen religiöse und spirituelle Deutungsmuster wie die christliche Liebesethik, der Glaube an einen lebensbejahenden Gott, aber auch Reflexionen über ein gelungenes Menschsein und die Hoffnung auf eine gute und gerechte, weil nachhaltige Zukunft. Schule ist ein Lern- und Lebensort, an dem Denken, Fühlen und Handeln, Erleben und Erfahren Hand in Hand gehen. Das macht Schule zu einem zentralen Ort für und in der Gesellschaft. Ist Schule ein Spiegelbild der Gesellschaft – auch an Heterogenität von gläubigen, nicht-gläubigen, spirituell aufgeschlossenen und nichtreligiösen jungen Menschen – so ist sie ein Mikrokosmos von Gesellschaft vor Ort, an dem Gesellschaft gelebt, ausprobiert, ausgehandelt und erfahrbar wird. Dabei haben Lehrer*innen eine besondere Vorbildfunktion insbesondere, wenn die religiöse Dimension ins Spiel gebracht werden soll. So hat schon Papst Paul VI. in seinem Schreiben *Evangelii nuntiandi* 1975 festgestellt, dass der heutige Mensch lieber auf Zeugen als auf Gelehrte höre, und wenn er auf Gelehrte höre, dann deshalb, weil sie Zeug*innen seien.[5] Es bedarf Religionslehrer*innen, die auskunfts- und sprachfähig ihre Haltung und ihre Perspektive

---

5 Vgl. PAPST PAUL VI.: Apostolisches Schreiben ‚Evangelii nuntiandi'. Seiner Heiligkeit Papst Pauls VI. an den Episkopat, den Klerus und alle Gläubigen der Katholischen Kirche über die Evangelisierung in der Welt von heute, Bonn, 1975 (= Verlautbarungen des Apostolischen Stuhls 2), 29.

auf Mensch und Welt verwurzelt im christlichen Gottes- und Menschenbild leben und erfahrbar machen. Zielperspektive der Fortbildungsarbeit der Schulabteilung ist es daher, Religionslehrer*innen nicht nur in ihrem pädagogischen und theologischen Handwerk, sondern gleichermaßen auch in ihrer – religiösen, ethischen und geistlichen – Haltung zu unterstützen, ihnen Räume und Angebote zu eröffnen, um sich immer neu zu vergewissern und weiterzuentwickeln. Dies umfasst in besonderer Weise auch die Fort- und Weiterbildungsangebote im Bereich der rBNE. In diesem Kontext sei auf zwei schöpfungsthematische Arbeitshilfen hinzuweisen, die mit Blick auf einen heterogenitätssensiblen Religionsunterricht aus dem Projekt ZuRuF der Abteilung Schulische Religionspädagogik entstanden sind: Die Arbeitshilfe für die Grundschule nimmt sich dem ‚Wunder Welt – Gottes Schöpfung?!' an und ist getragen von der Idee, dass der biblischen Rede von der Schöpfung ein befreiender Charakter inne liege, der zum Staunen, Loben, Danken und schließlich zur Verantwortung herausfordere. Die zweite Arbeitshilfe mit dem Titel ‚Fasten für die Schöpfung' bildet die Grundlage eines Arbeitskreises in der o.g. Pädagogischen Woche. In den Materialien wird das breite Spektrum der Begriffe ‚Schöpfung' und ‚Schöpfungsverantwortung' dargestellt und das spezifisch Transzendente bzw. Religiöse herausgearbeitet. Am Fasten kann Schöpfungsverantwortung als christliche Performance charakterisiert werden, als modus vivendi des Geschöpfs, das seine Beziehung zu Gott, seinem Schöpfer, und Mitgeschöpfen bejahend performt.

Was und wie in Schule gelernt, gelebt und kommuniziert wird, kann richtungsweisend für die Zukunft der Kinder und Jugendlichen sein, die die Gesellschaft von morgen sind. Schule ist ein Ort, an dem Haltungen und Einstellungen wie die einer rBNE vermittelt und grundgelegt werden. Dazu zählt in besonderem Maße auch der Compassion-Gedanke. Compassion für die Anliegen der Menschen, dieser Erde, der Schöpfung Gottes ist nicht etwas, was man lernt wie mathematische Formeln oder den Grundwortschatz einer anderen Sprache, um das Gelernte dann punktuell anwenden zu können. Compassion muss tiefgreifend eingeübt und in Begegnung und Beziehung erfahrbar gemacht werden, damit es den Menschen in Gänze ergreift und berührt. Nur so wird Compassion zu einer Haltung, zu einer Lebenseinstellung, die das eigene Handeln prägt und über sich hinaus prägend sein kann. Das gilt auch für den Bereich der rBNE. Erfahrungen und Einüben von Haltungen führen zu einer eigenen Haltung, die es ermöglicht zu handeln, zu verändern und Schöpfungsvisionen zu entwickeln. „Bildung für Nachhaltige Entwicklung ist eine Querschnittsherausforderung mit transformatorischem Anspruch. Jede Anstrengung in diese Richtung ist lohnenswert – der Religionsunterricht bliebe aber weit unter seinen Möglichkeiten, wenn er das Potenzial seines ureigenen Beitrags unterschätzt: er kann – mitten im Chaos –

Schöpfungsvisionen anbieten, die Hoffnung und Mut machen und die Menschen herauslocken, sich in kleinen Schritten einer großen Herausforderung zu stellen.“[6]

Literatur

BEDERNA, Katrin: Every Day For Future. Theologie und religiöse Bildung für nachhaltige Entwicklung, Ostfildern: Matthias-Grünewald, ²2020.

HUNZE, Guido: Schöpfungsvisionen – mitten im Chaos. Herausforderungen für eine religiöse Bildung für Nachhaltige Entwicklung (rBNE), in: impulse 129 (3/2021), 4–7.

PAPST FRANZISKUS: Enzyklika Laudato Si'. Über die Sorge für das gemeinsame Haus, Bonn, 2015 (= Verlautbarungen des Apostolischen Stuhls 202).

PAPST PAUL VI.: Apostolisches Schreiben ‚Evangelii nuntiandi'. Seiner Heiligkeit Papst Pauls VI. an den Episkopat, den Klerus und alle Gläubigen der Katholischen Kirche über die Evangelisierung in der Welt von heute, Bonn, 1975 (= Verlautbarungen des Apostolischen Stuhls 2).

6 HUNZE, GUIDO: Schöpfungsvisionen – mitten im Chaos. Herausforderungen für eine religiöse Bildung für Nachhaltige Entwicklung (rBNE), in: impulse 129 (3/2021), 7.

Lernen in der Natur – Der Schulgarten als Lehrstück der Montessori-Pädagogik zur alltagsintegrierten Vermittlung von compathischen Werten und Nachhaltigkeitshandeln

Christina Steffens

Die aktuelle Jugendgeneration stellt die Themen Umweltschutz und Nachhaltigkeit in den Fokus ihrer Bemühungen, wobei sie gleichsam eine Form des Umsetzungs-Pessimismus verspüren. Ziel des Beitrags ist es aufzuzeigen, wie die intrinsische Motivation der Schüler*innen, welche in der Nachhaltigkeitsbewegung ihren Ausdruck findet, mithilfe von Ansätzen der Montessoripädagogik zur Ausbildung einer gesellschaftsfähigen compathisch-ethischen Wertegrundlage führen kann. Hierbei kommt dem Schulgarten als praktische Lernebene eine Schlüsselrolle zu, in der sich die Ansätze des montessorianischen Erdkinderplans mit dem Aspekt der Schöpfungsverantwortung in Einklang bringen lassen und mithin zu einer nachhaltigen Entwicklung zu selbstständigen und freien Persönlichkeiten beitragen kann. Das EarthKinds-Class-Konzept versteht sich vor diesem Hintergrund als offenes Lernangebot, welches die Bedingungen für die persönliche sowie gesellschaftlich-soziale Entwicklung von Kindern und Jugendlichen nachhaltig fördern möchte.

Montessoripädagogik; Schulgarten; Compassion; Schöpfungsverantwortung; EarthKids-Class

The current generation of young people is focusing their efforts on the topics of environmental protection and sustainability, while at the same time feeling a form of implementation pessimism. The aim of this article is to show how the intrinsic motivation of the students, which is expressed in the sustainability movement, can lead to the formation of a socially acceptable compathic-ethical value basis with the help of Montessori educational approaches. In this context, the school garden plays a key role as a practical learning level in which the approaches of the Montessorian EarthKinds plan can be harmonised with the aspect of responsibility for creation and thus contribute to a sustainable development towards independent and free personalities. Against this background, the EarthKinds-Class concept sees itself as an open learning offer that aims to promote the conditions for the personal as well as socio-social development of children and young people in a sustainable way.

Montessori education; school garden; compassion; responsibility for creation; EarthKids-Class

Thematische Herleitung

> Das ganze bewusste Streben des Kindes geht dahin, sich durch die Loslösung vom Erwachsenen und durch die Selbstständigkeit zur freien Persönlichkeit zu entwickeln. Unsere Erziehung trägt diesem Streben Rechnung: und unser Bemühen ist es, dem Kind zu helfen, selbstständig zu werden. – Maria Montessori

Dieser Grundgedanke der Pädagogin Maria Montessori (1870–1952) ist heute noch genauso aktuell wie damals. Kinder und Jugendliche sollen sich in einer reflektierten Auseinandersetzung mit sich selbst und der Umwelt zu Persönlichkeiten entwickeln, die die Werte einer Gesellschaft verstehen, angemessen hinterfragen und immer wieder neu denken. Es geht darum, sich (selbst-)ständig weiterzuentwickeln und dabei sich selbst aber auch die Gesellschaft, das direkte und auch weite Umfeld in den Blick zu nehmen. Bestehende Regeln und Grenzen aufzubrechen, um Neues zu schaffen und bestehende gute Werte und Ideen zu festigen.

Das Bundesministerium für Umwelt, Naturschutz und nukleare Sicherheit (BMU) veröffentlichte 2018 eine Studie, in der Jugendliche im Alter zwischen 14 und 22 Jahren befragt wurden, ob und inwiefern sie sich für Themen wie Umwelt, Naturschutz und nukleare Sicherheit interessieren. Dabei fiel auf, dass sich diese Altersgruppe für die eben genannten Themenbereiche aus einer intrinsischen Motivation heraus stark interessiert, häufig jedoch in Verbindung mit einer Form von Pessimismus. Das Bewusstsein, dass die Gesellschaft achtsamer mit der Umwelt umgehen muss, ist vorhanden. Gleichzeitig wird jedoch auch bemängelt, dass trotz dieses Bewusstseins keine Veränderung im Handeln zu spüren ist. Eine Schülerin äußerte sich beispielsweise wie folgt:

> ‚Ich glaube, der Zustand [der Umwelt] wird sich weiter verschlechtern. Wir Menschen achten viel zu wenig auf unsere Umwelt und das wird uns schaden. Ohne die Natur haben wir keine Ressourcen oder Artenvielfalt. Pflanzen oder Tiere wird es immer weniger geben, da sie vielleicht auch für Experimente verwendet werden und das Meer wird durch Chemikalien, die ins Wasser kommen, immer mehr verschmutzt.' Lava, weiblich, 18 Jahre[1]

Die sogenannte Nachhaltigkeitsbewegung wurde besonders im Jahr 2018 durch *Fridays for Future* geprägt und sorgte für große mediale Aufmerksamkeit. Schüler*innen schwänzten den Unterricht, um auf die Straße zu gehen und für eine nachhaltige Welt und einen Klimawandel zu protestieren, der jetzt einsetzen muss, um für nachfolgende Generationen eine lebenswerte Welt zu hinterlassen. Diese Haltung kann als gelebte Mitleidenschaft für die Schöpfung verstanden

---

1 Vgl. Bundesministerium für Umwelt, Naturschutz und nukleare Sicherheit (BMU): Zukunft? Jugend fragen! Nachhaltigkeit, Politik, Engagement – eine Studie zu Einstellungen und Alltag junger Menschen, Berlin, ^{2}2018.

werden, die in konkrete Handlungen und reflektierte Wertekonzepte überführt werden sollte.

Diese Diskrepanz zwischen dem Drängen nach Veränderung und dem Pessimismus der Umsetzbarkeit seitens der Jugendlichen muss demnach überwunden werden. Die Lernenden brauchen Handlungsbeispiele und Handlungsmöglichkeiten, um entsprechend der Forderungen aktiv werden zu können. Denn durch die Wissenschaft wurde mehrfach bestätigt, dass die Klimaziele unbedingt erreicht werden müssen. Die Schwierigkeit hierbei stellt sich vor allem vor dem Hintergrund der aktuell hohen Diversität an Weltanschauungen und Wertekontexten, welche dazu führen, dass die (Aus-)Wahl der entsprechenden Handlungsmöglichkeiten überfordernd wird.[2] Die richtige Auswahl der angebotenen Möglichkeiten zu treffen und diese in ein konsistentes Bild bezogen auf die individuell als wichtig deklarierten Ziele und Werte zu überführen stellt hierbei eine annähernd krisenhafte Herausforderung dar, da diese Wahl die Wahrnehmung der eigenen Identität maßgeblich beeinflusst. Hierbei bietet die Montessori-Pädagogik eine (kritische) Brückenbauerfunktion im Sinne eines Leaderships, welche als Unterstützungsangebot an die Schüler*innen zur Ausbildung einer individuellen compathisch-empathischen Wertegrundlage fungiert, die darüber hinaus auch noch gesellschaftlich-konsensfähig ist. Das folgende Handlungskonzept soll ein Beispiel sein, wie im Rahmen des Schulunterrichts die angesprochenen Aspekte verknüpft werden können. Zum einen geht es um die Beachtung der Entwicklungsstufen von Heranwachsenden im sozialen und intellektuellen Kontext nach Maria Montessori, um möglichst sinnstiftende Lernarrangements zu schaffen, die dem Sein der Kinder entspricht. Denn die Schule bietet die Möglichkeit, durch den Schulgarten einen Ansatz für ein nachhaltiges Leben selbst zu erleben, um dann wiederum außerhalb der Schule Anwendung zu finden. Zum anderen geht es um die Entwicklung der Schüler*innen im Sinne des Compassion-Gedankens. Denn die Arbeit im Garten verlangt ein Miteinander als Gruppe als auch ein Mitwirken an vorangestellten gesellschaftlichen und naturbedingten Problematiken. Durch die erlebte Maßnahme in Verbindung mit gelernten Inhalten und einer entsprechenden Reflektion bietet die Arbeit im Garten die Möglichkeit, eine längerfristige Verhaltensänderung zu implementieren. Diese Handlungsfelder sollen zusammengeführt werden, sodass der Garten einer Schule zu einem (Er-) Lebensraum wird, der viele verschiedene Lern- und Arbeitsmöglichkeiten (an-) bietet.

Für ein Verständnis dieses Praxisbeispiels werden zunächst die wichtigen Grundlagen erörtert. So gibt es zunächst einen Einblick in die Theorie des Erdkinderplans nach Maria Montessori sowie einen kurzen Überblick über das

---

[2] Vgl. ANDREE, Maurice / DOMSEL, Maike Maria: Die Paradigmen der Compassion und Freiheit als Bindeglieder zwischen Theologie und Ethik? Möglichkeiten spirituell-reflexiver Praxis im schulischen Kontext, in: ÖRF 30 (2022) 1, 113-115. DOI: 10.25364/10.30:2022.1.7

Schöpfungsverständnis von Heranwachsenden im Alter von etwa 12 bis 16 Jahren (etwa das Alter von Lernenden in der Sekundarstufe I). Fortlaufend wird Bezug genommen auf die Sustainable Development Goals (SDGs), welche für genau dieses Projekt relevant sind. Schlussendlich münden die theoretischen Grundlagen in einem konkreten Praxisbeispiel, welches in einem Schulgarten einer Montessori-Schule mit integrierten Freiarbeitsstunden im Land Nordrhein-Westfalen aktuell erprobt wird.[3] Ebenso ist es aber möglich, dieses Beispiel an anderen Regelschulsystemen in angepasster Form anzuwenden.

Die Montessori-Pädagogik

Der Erdkinderplan für Jugendliche im Alter von 12 – 18 Jahren

Die Montessori-Pädagogik umfasst eine Vielzahl an Themen und Bereichen, die sich mit den intellektuellen und sozialen Entwicklungsbedürfnissen von jungen Heranwachsenden beschäftigen. In diesem Kapitel geht es vor allem um den sogenannten Erdkinderplan, der sich in diesem Fall auf die Jugendlichen im Alter von 12 – 16 Jahren bezieht. Es geht hierbei darum, die „körperlichen, psychisch-geistigen und sozialen Bedürfnisse"[4] zu fördern. Ebenso liegt ein Schwerpunkt darauf, die stetige Suche nach dem Selbstausdruck und dem Streben nach Unabhängigkeit Rechnung zu tragen. In einem weiteren Schritt bezieht sich der Erdkinderplan dann auf ältere Heranwachsende, die nach „gesellschaftlichem Engagement, Partizipation und Anerkennung"[5] streben. Schlussendlich gilt es, die Adoleszenten in ihrer Persönlichkeitsentwicklung zu unterstützen, um unter anderem eine Berufsvorbereitung zu gewährleisten, bei der eine starre Wissensvermittlung jedoch sekundär ist. Das bedeutet also, den Erdkinderplan nicht als eine Art Erziehungsmodell zu sehen, sondern vielmehr als Kompetenzrahmen, in welchem sich die Heranwachsenden entfalten können. Eine wichtige Voraussetzung ist, die Arbeit mit den Jugendlichen immer wieder zu hinterfragen und neue Ansätze auszuprobieren, die zu der jeweiligen Lerngruppe passen.[6]

Der Erdkinderplan möchte aber noch viel mehr als das. Es geht ebenso darum, die

---

3 Das Praxisbeispiel befindet sich aktuell in der Erprobungsphase der Bischöflichen Maria-Montessori-Gesamtschule und stellt das Ergebnis anderthalbjähriger didaktischer Forschungsarbeit und kollegialer Beratung dar.

4 ECKERT, Ela: Erdkinderplan. Maria Montessoris Erziehungs- und Bildungskonzept für Jugendliche, Freiburg im Breisgau: Herder, 2020, 7.

5 ECKERT 2020 [Anm. 3], 7.

6 Vgl. Ebd., 8.

> [...] Kinder so zu erziehen, dass sie den in ihnen angelegten Lebensgesetzen folgen und dadurch zu ausgeglichenen, friedliebenden Erwachsenen heranwachsen können, die in Empathie miteinander und in Solidarität mit anderen Menschen über die Grenzen von Nationen und Ethnien hinaus [...] leben können.[7]

Maria Montessori war davon überzeugt, dass die Heranwachsenden mit sich im Reinen sein müssen, um in einer Welt voller Gewalt und Krieg bestehen zu können. Dies geht nicht, wenn sie von Erwachsenen durch autoritäre Erziehungsstile herangezogen werden, sondern nur dann, wenn sie in einer Umgebung aufwachsen, die durch Kooperation geprägt ist und in der Konflikte friedlich gelöst werden, in der Kritik geäußert werden darf und das nicht nur insofern, dass Erwachsene Kinder kritisieren, sondern dass auch Heranwachsende Handlungsmuster und Entscheidungen von Erwachsenen auf eine respektvolle Art und Weise kritisch hinterfragen dürfen.[8]

Im Folgenden wird auf die Hintergründe des Erdkinderplans für Jugendliche im Altern von 12 bis 18 Jahren genauer Bezug genommen. Um die Heranwachsenden ihrer Entwicklung entsprechend fördern zu können, ist es unerlässlich sich ihres Entwicklungsstandes bewusst zu sein. Sicherlich entwickelt sich jedes Kind individuell und hat eigene spezielle Bedürfnisse. Nichtsdestotrotz gibt es Stadien, die die Kinder in etwa der genannten Zeitspanne erleben und durchleben. Die Pubertät spielt in vielerlei Hinsicht eine entscheidende Rolle, denn die Hormonumstellung und die erhöhte physische Belastung, wie beispielsweise durch das Wachstum, sind die Adoleszenten vermehrt krank und fokussieren sich stärker auf eben diese Entwicklung. Damit einhergehend sind die Jugendlichen häufig psychisch labiler. Aufgrund dieser Entwicklung ist es unerlässlich, die Kinder mit dem nötigen Respekt zu behandeln und sie zu unterstützen sowie ihr Selbstvertrauen zu stärken.[9] In dieser Altersspanne sind Jugendliche durchaus in der Lage auch neue Dinge zu lernen und Wissen aufzunehmen, steht dies jedoch nicht an erster Stelle, sondern eben die individuellen Bedürfnisse.[10] Die Persönlichkeitsentwicklung ist nun ein entscheidendes Element für die Vorbereitung auf die zukünftige Gesellschaft, da diese die individuellen Bedürfnisse, im Kontext des zu entwickelnden gesellschaftlich-konsensfähigen Wertekanons, prägt. Die zu schaffenden Lernarrangements sollen Möglichkeiten bieten, sich selbst kennenzulernen, Dinge auszuprobieren und auch einzuüben. Der Blick geht immer mehr auf die Gesellschaft und auf die mögliche eigene Stellung in

---

7 Ebd., 91.

8 Vgl. Ebd., 92–93.

9 Vgl. Ebd., 41–43.

10 Mit Bedürfnissen sind grundlegend die Bedürfnisse von Jugendlichen nach Brazelton & Greenspaan 2002 (materielle Bedürfnisse, Akzeptanz in der Peergroup, Abnabelung von Erziehungspersonen und Bedürfnis der eigenen Grenzerfahrungen) gemeint. Vgl. BRAZELTON, Berry / GREENSPAN, Stanley: Die sieben Grundbedürfnisse von Kindern. Was jedes Kind braucht, um gesund aufzuwachsen, gut zu lernen und glücklich zu sein, Weinheim/München: Beltz, 2008.

dieser, auch in beruflicher Hinsicht. Daher ist im Erdkinderplan die *Arbeit auf dem Land* ein entscheidender Faktor. Denn hier können sich „praktische Erfahrungen und theoretische Sequenzen einander kontinuierlich ablösen und die Möglichkeiten zu Wahlfreiheit entstehen."[11] Durch eine produktive Arbeit, treffen die Lernenden auf sogenannte *echte Probleme* und können auch *echte Lösungen* finden, denn ein rein akademisches Lernen ist in dieser Lebensphase nicht nachhaltig. Zudem sei anzumerken, dass Heranwachsende in dieser Altersgruppe ein großes Interesse daran haben, auch schwierigere oder komplexere Aufgaben zu lösen, wenn sie den Eindruck haben es erstens im Rahmen ihrer Peergroup bearbeiten zu können und zweitens einen Ansatz haben, wie eine spätere Lösung aussehen könnte, die Aufgabe also demnach zu bewältigen scheint.[12] Die hohe Motivation der Lernenden kann jetzt genutzt werden, um Fähigkeiten und Fertigkeiten einzuüben, die später in einer komplexen Gesellschaft gebraucht werden können. Durch das eigenverantwortliche Handeln übernehmen sie schrittweise eine *echte* Verantwortung und erfahren, wie es ist, für eine (kleine Form der) Gesellschaft aktiv zu werden und etwas zu bewegen. Durch diese Art des Lernens werden drei wichtige Aspekte der Entwicklung von Jugendlichen verknüpft. Zum einen lernen die Adoleszenten in ihren jeweiligen Peergroups, also außerhalb der eigenen (Kern-)Familie. Zu anderen werden Arbeitsprozesse erfahrbar gemacht, welche auch in der Berufswelt zu finden sind. Zu guter Letzt nehmen sie am sozialen Leben und dessen Weiterentwicklung teil.[13] Montessoris Idee ging ursprünglich sogar so weit, die Jugendlichen ab einem Alter von etwa zwölf Jahren der Ursprungsfamilie zu entziehen und gemeinsam mit gleichaltrigen (Altersspanne von etwa 12 – 18 Jahren) auf dem Land zu unterrichten, begleitet durch Erwachsene, die sich ihnen annehmen sollten. Sie war der Überzeugung, dass das das beste Lernsetting wäre, um die Jugendlichen zu fördern. Dieses Konzept wurde jedoch aufgrund der großen Ablehnung seitens der Eltern nicht hinreichend in der Praxis erprobt.[14] Sodann müssen Überlegungen angestrebt werden, inwiefern diese Kompetenzen dennoch gelehrt und gelernt werden können. In den Kinderhäusern und auch in der Grundschule werden kindliche Persönlichkeiten entwickelt und beispielsweise die Pflege und das Sauberhalten des Arbeitsplatzes und der Lernumgebung gelehrt, da diese ebenso wie die Ästhetik notwendig zum nachhaltigen Lernen nach Maria Montessori sind. Es geht also um Handlungen, die für ein gutes Miteinander relevant sind. Diese gelernten Kompetenzen sollen dann in den folgenden Jahren manifestiert und weiterentwickelt werden – auf einem entsprechend höheren Niveau. Im Fokus steht also *die Arbeit*, die mit einer Ernsthaftigkeit, Genauigkeit und in einem individuellen Tempo getan werden soll.

---

11 Vgl. ECKERT 2020 [Anm. 3], 44.
12 Vgl. Ebd., 45.
13 Vgl. Ebd., 46.
14 Vgl. Ebd., 46–47.

> Die gesamte Zivilisation basiere auf der Arbeit von Menschen und der Arbeitsteilung unter ihnen; dabei baue jede Generation auf den Arbeitsleistungen einzelner Individuen wie der kollektiven Arbeit der Menschheit insgesamt auf. Insofern vereine Arbeit die Menschheit über Generationen und Entwicklungen menschlicher Zivilisationen hinweg. Der Jugendliche, der zu arbeiten beginne, trete ein in die Welt der Erwachsenen *seiner* Gesellschaft und *seiner* Epoche; er werde aber zugleich auf neue Weise Teil der Evolution menschlicher Zivilisation insgesamt, der Arbeitsprozesse, die sie prägen – und bewusst verantwortlicher und kreativer Mitgeschalter zukünftiger Entwicklungen.[15]

Die Rolle der Lehrperson nach Maria Montessori im Rahmen des Erdkinderplans

„Die Vorbereitung der Umgebung und die Vorbereitung des Lehrers sind das praktische Fundament unserer Erziehung."[16] Montessori meint hiermit konkret, dass die vorbereitete Lernumgebung[17] der eine wichtige Bestandteil eines gelingenden Lernens ist und andererseits die Lehrkraft selbst konkret weiß, welche Rolle ihr zukommt. Präziser ausgedrückt ist die Lehrkraft im Lernprozess passiv. Passivität sei aber nicht mit Nichtstun misszuverstehen, sondern es geht vielmehr darum, als Lernbegleiter*in zu fungieren, die in erster Linie vorbereitet und im Tun beobachtet. Als wichtige Grundvoraussetzung und Profil der Erzieher*innenrolle sieht Montessori eine angemessene Allgemeinbildung, fachliche Qualifikation und eine pädagogische Grundausbildung. Darüber hinaus spricht sie von einer *inneren Einkehr*, die das pädagogische Selbstverständnis, die Grundhaltung und die persönlichen Eigenschaften in den Blick nimmt. [18] Die genauen Funktionen werden im Folgenden ausführlich erläutert.

Um die Rolle der lehrenden Person zu beschreiben, nutzt Montessori zwei Bilder. Zum einen wird die Lehrperson als Bildhauer*in dargestellt, was nach ihrem Ansatz die schlechte Wahl wäre. Denn die Bildhauerin oder der Bildhauer formt und prägt das Kind nach dem eigenen Ermessen und den eigenen ange-

---

15 Eckert 2020 [Anm. 3], 48; Sowie vertiefend: Montessori, Maria: Die „Erdkinder". Ein Plan für eine Reform der Sekundarerziehung, in: Ludwig, Harald / Klein-Landeck, Michael (Hg.): Von der Kindheit zur Jugend. Grundschule – Sekundarschule – Universität, Freiburg im Breisgau: Herder, [2]2018 (Bd. 14, 98–118).

16 Montessori, Maria: Grundlagen meiner Pädagogik, Heidelberg/Wiesbaden: Quelle & Meyer, 1988, 21.

17 Auf die vorbereitete Lernumgebung wird in Bezug auf das konkrete Beispiel des Schulgartens explizierter eingegangen. An dieser Stelle sei der Hinweis gegeben, dass es darum geht, die Lernlandschaft so zu gestalten, dass sich die Lernenden frei und ohne (große) Einwirkung der Lehrenden mit der Arbeit beginnen kann. Sie soll ansprechend und animierend wirken. (Vgl. Klein-Landeck, Michael / Pütz, Tanja: Montessori-Pädagogik. Einführung in Theorie und Praxis, Freiburg im Breisgau: Herder, [3]2013, 56–62.)

18 Vgl. Ebd., 44–45.

setzten Maßstäben, ohne das Kind als Individuum zu betrachten. Die Kinder werden nach einem festgeschriebenen Plan geschult, belehrt und korrigiert. Arbeitet die Lehrperson hingegen als Gärtner*in, so sorgt diese für gute Bedingungen, um dem Kind eine möglichst gute Grundlage zu bieten, sich selbst zu entwickeln und dabei das Wesen, die Bedürfnisse und den je eigenen Entwicklungsstand zu berücksichtigen. Methodische und didaktische Entscheidungen werden dann nach dem Kind ausgerichtet und nicht nach einem starren Lehrplan. So gibt es durchaus einen Lehrplan, der zur Orientierung dient, welcher aber immer noch Raum für Entscheidungen bietet, die der Situation angemessen sind. Um dieser Rolle wirklich gerecht zu werden, bedarf es unbedingt regelmäßiger Supervisionen oder auch Lerncoachings, wie sie gegenwärtig immer häufiger im pädagogischen Kontext auftreten.[19]

Konkret bedeutet dies, dass sich die Lehrperson über sich selbst und die eigene Rolle im Klaren sein muss. Ziel ist es, den Lernenden eine gute Orientierung zu bieten und eine hilfreiche Stütze zu sein, wenn sie es benötigen. Um dies zu erreichen, sollen Lehrende vor allem die Stärken und das Können der Heranwachsenden in den Fokus nehmen. Hierfür nutzt Montessori einige Schlagwörter, die im Alltag als Erinnerung dienen können, wenn sie denn zuvor verstanden wurden. Die wichtigsten dieser Ansätze sind die Folgenden.

Die Lehrperson sollte dem Kind grundsätzlich zugewandt sein und das Gute im Kind sehen. Im Vordergrund stehen die Wertschätzung und eine realistische Beobachtung. Das Lernen soll so gestaltet werden, dass die Heranwachsenden selbstständig in einer vorbereiteten Umgebung aktiv werden können und die Lehrperson eine Begleitung im Lernen darstellt, die durch das Kind eingefordert werden kann. Die Lehrperson greift erst dann ein, wenn das Kind dauerhaft über einen längeren Zeitpunkt beobachtet, dass das Kind weit unter seinen Möglichkeiten lernt. Entwickelt es sich gut und eigenständig, wird es sich melden, wenn es einer Hilfestellung bedarf. Die Lehrperson muss sich also in Selbstbeherrschung und Zurückhaltung üben und die Lernenden nicht zu etwas drängen, wozu sie intrinsisch motiviert, noch nicht bereit sind. Ein weiterer unumgänglicher Aspekt ist der, dass sich die Lehrperson immer wieder selbst reflektieren muss. Sie kann ein selbstständiges und an Regeln orientiertes Lernen nur einfordern, wenn sie sich selbst regelmäßig reflektiert und Überlegungen anstrebt, ob sie sich denn selbst auch an die geltenden Regeln hält. Erwartet sie von ihren Schüler*innen Pünktlichkeit, so darf sie beispielsweise selbst nicht zu spät kommen. Sollen die Lernenden ihre Materialien immer dabeihaben, sollte auch sie diese immer bereit haben und zu Beginn des Unterrichts vorliegen haben. Die Kinder sollen das Gefühl bekommen, dass die Erwachsenen ihnen auf Augenhöhe begegnen, ohne dabei die natürliche Autorität fallen zu lassen. Das Kind

---

19 Vgl. Ebd., 45–46.

soll „Vertrauen in die Kompetenzen, Erfahrungen und Verantwortung der Erwachsenen [haben].“[20] Die Lehrperson gibt stets eine Orientierung und hilfreiche Stütze durch ihr Dasein.

Neben der eigenen inneren Haltung der Lehrperson ist es ebenso unumgänglich, alle nötigen Materialien zu kennen und genau zu wissen, was zu tun ist. Ein Material muss detailliert ausprobiert und nicht nur theoretisch erarbeitet worden sein. Denn erst im Ausprobieren erkennt man die volle Entfaltung dieser Materialien. Wo sind Fehler verborgen? Wo könnten Schüler*innen Hilfe benötigen? Kann ich vorher schon Hilfestellungen vorbereiten, um mich zurückzunehmen? Welche weiteren Chancen und Möglichkeiten bietet das Material? Es geht beim Lehren und Unterrichten nicht darum, dem Kind vorgefertigte Muster zu erklären und Fachbegriffe auswendig zu lernen. Vielmehr geht es darum, „selbstständig Erfahrungen zu machen, Erkenntnisse zu gewinnen, seine Welt zu entdecken und zu erobern.“[21] Nun gilt es genau zu beobachten und zu erkennen, wann die Lehrperson eingreifen sollte und wann sie Tätigkeiten gewähren lassen kann und auch muss. Dies Bedürfen viel Zeit und Übung und muss immer wieder reflektiert und trainiert werden. Hinzu kommt, dass jedes Kind anders ist und sich unterschiedliche Verhaltensmuster bei Kindern zeigen werden. In kurzen Stichworten zusammengefasst, beinhalten die Kernaufgaben:

- „Kinder beobachten [...]
- Verhaltensweisen interpretieren [...]
- Die [Frei-]Arbeit vor- und nachbereiten [...]
- Den Raum gestalten, ordnen und pflegen [...]
- Freiheit gewähren und Unabhängigkeit ermöglichen [...]
- Die Kinder anregen und anleiten [...]
- Halt geben und lenken [...]“[22]

Und schlussendlich geht es auch darum, sich selbst angemessen zu kleiden, um auch optisch in die Lernlandschaft zu passen. Am konkreten Beispiel des Gartens, um dies an dieser Stelle vorzugreifen, beutet es also, dass die Lehrperson beispielsweise festes Schuhwerk trägt und passende Gartenhandschuhe besitzt, um möglichst effektiv arbeiten zu können. Kinder müssen sehen, dass auch die Lehrenden ihre Rolle ernst nehmen und sich der Sache annehmen. Denn Lehrende sind die Vorbilder der Kinder und orientieren sich an ihnen.

---

20 Klein-Landeck / Pütz 2013 [Anm. 16], 47.

21 Ebd., 49.

22 Ebd., 51–55.

Theologische Grundlagen: Schöpfungstheologie

Die religiöse Erziehung nach Maria Montessori

Maria Montessori betrachtet die Werteerziehung als ein Bindeglied, welches sich an einem religiös-christlichen Wertekanon orientiert. Bindeglied meint in diesem Fall, dass eine religiöse, soziale und *kosmische* Erziehung stattfinden muss, welche den Kindern eine Orientierung gibt. Mit kosmischer Erziehung nach Maria Montessori wird im Allgemeinen die ganzheitliche Perspektive der Verbundenheit des Kindes mit sich selbst und der Welt im Sinne einer Verantwortung für den Kosmos sowie die Verantwortungsübernahme für einen gelingenden Frieden bezeichnet. In jeder Handlung wird somit das Beziehungsdreieck aus Gott, Mensch und Natur sowie die damit einhergehenden Pflichten gegenüber sich selbst, der Familie, Gesellschaft, Umwelt und Gott mitgedacht. Diese Orientierung bietet Erziehung und Bildung im Kontext des eigenen Daseins, denn das Kind, so Montessori, ist auf natürliche Weise moralisch urteilsfähig und muss dies nicht von Grund auf lernen. Das Streben des Kindes beinhaltet vielmehr ein handlungsorientiertes Konkretisieren des moralischen Wertekanons, welches aus den großen Fragen des Lebens erwächst, ein aufeinander-Zugehen im Sinne eines Lernens von- und miteinander erfordert und schließlich im sozialen Geschehen der Liebe seine gesellschaftliche Wurzel und Ausdifferenzierung findet.[23]

Entwicklungspsychologie in der Religionspädagogik

Im konkreten Anliegen geht es um das Verständnis und die Entwicklung von Kindern im Sinne des Schöpfungsverständnisses. So wie die Heranwachsenden unterschiedlich in Bezug auf die soziale und geografische Situation aufwachsen und entsprechend unterschiedliche Erfahrungen hinsichtlich der Natur erlebt und erfahren haben, sind die Kinder auch uneinheitlich in Bezug auf den Schöp-

23 Vgl. Klein-Landeck / Pütz 2013 [Anm. 16], 95–96, 100. Weitere Informationen siehe auch: Schaub, Horst: Kosmische Erziehung in der Montessori-Pädagogik. Die Entstehung des Konzepts der Kosmischen Erziehung – Die Geschichte des Universums und unserer Erde, Freiburg im Breisgau: Herder, 2013.

fungsgedanken aufgewachsen. Ein Schöpfungsverständnis kann nur dann angemessen geschult werden, wenn Naturerfahrungen gemacht werden und im Staunen und Nachempfinden Erfahrungen erlebt werden.[24]

Dabei ist das Thema *Schöpfung* für Kinder in vielerlei Hinsicht relevant und zumeist auch interessant. Wenn auch die Kinder sich nicht immer mit dem konkreten oder bewussten Gedanken der Schöpfung und des Wirkens durch Gott beschäftigen, so befinden sie sich direkt in der Auseinandersetzung mit sich selbst. Zur Erschließung des Ganzen der Welt bedarf es der Fragen nach dem Woher, Wohin und Wozu, welche in dem Thema Schöpfung ihre Konkretisierung und ihren Ursprung finden (können).[25] Ziel der Erziehung ist es, die religiöse Dimension der Wirklichkeit im Spannungsfeld zwischen gesellschaftlicher und individuell-anthropologischer Dimension zu erschließen. Kinder sollen ihre eigene (christliche) Kultur kennenlernen, verstehen und sie in ihrem Alltag leben lernen.[26] Ein Aspekt dessen ist der, dass Kinder darauf vertrauen, dass Gott (oder jemand) die Welt erschaffen hat und dadurch eine Sicherheit vermittelt wird, dass somit auch jemand auf die Schöpfung schaut und sie bewacht. Somit kann durchaus mithilfe der Schöpfung ein erster Zugang zu einer Gottesvorstellung geschaffen werden, um einen konkreten Gedanken herzustellen. In Zeiten der immer stärker werdenden Bedrohungen durch (Umwelt-)Katastrophen hilft der Schöpfungsglaube, das Vertrauen und die Hoffnung nicht zu verlieren. Der Mensch wäre durchaus in der Lage, die Welt zu bewahren, wenn er sich an dem Glauben der christlichen Kirche orientiere. Denn „wer die Welt als Schöpfung und Geschenk Gottes und sich selbst als Teil dieser Schöpfung versteht, wird sich ihr gegenüber umsichtig verhalten."[27] Weiter kann gedacht werden, dass sich exemplarisch an der Schöpfungserzählung zeigen lässt, wie sich die Beziehung zwischen Gott und den Menschen durchzieht. Es wird ein Bild des sich kümmernden und sich sorgenden Gottes vermittelt.[28] Bei den jeweiligen Gedanken geht es nicht darum, den Heranwachsenden den Schöpfungsgedanken aufzudrängen, sondern vielmehr darum, mithilfe der religiösen Dimension der Wirklichkeit, einen Blick auf die Gesellschaft zu forcieren, der den Anspruch hat, die Schüler*innen zu verantwortungsvollen und entscheidungsfähigen Bürger*innen zu machen, die durch ihre Erfahrungen (im Glauben), die Schöpfung

---

24 Vgl. EGGER, Moni: Schöpfung – Biblische und religionspädagogische Aspekte, in: Reli.ch https://www.reli.ch/schoepfung-biblische-und-religionspaedagogische-aspekte/ [abgerufen am 08.04.2023].

25 Vgl. BOSCHKI, Reinhold: Einführung in die Religionspädagogik (Einführung Theologie), Darmstadt: WBG, ^{3}2017, 61–62.

26 Vgl. ZIEBERTZ, Hans-Georg: Warum die religiöse Dimension der Wirklichkeit erschließen?, in: HILGER, Georg u. a. (Hg.): Religionsdidaktik. Ein Leitfaden für Studium, Ausbildung und Beruf, München: Kösel, ^{5}2017, 137–139.

27 EGGER [Anm. 23].

28 Vgl. Ebd.

neu denken und so bewahren können.[29] Einhergehend mit dem Gedanken der Schöpfungsbewahrung stellen sich Schüler*innen häufig die Frage nach der Endlichkeit und sind somit konfrontiert mit der Frage nach dem Sinn des Lebens. Auch Montessori denkt diese Frage in ihrer Pädagogik mit und betrachtet diese als essenziell.[30]

Schöpfungsverantwortung

Dass etwas passieren muss, der Klimawandel immer weiter voranschreitet, Generationen nach Veränderung rufen und drängen, ist keine Neuigkeit, die hier genannt wird. Auch im Rahmen der christlichen Kirchen wird das Thema aufgerufen und bearbeitet. Nun stellt sich jedoch die Frage, welche Ansätze bereits verfolgt werden, auf die Lehrende und Lernende zurückgreifen können und an welchen Stellen Schulen weiterdenken und mit den Heranwachsenden aktiv werden können.

Fakt ist, dass die Menschen lebenswichtige Ressourcen aufbrauchen, Lebensräume und damit Lebewesen ausrotten und nachfolgende Generationen mit den Schäden der Natur zurechtkommen müssen. Globale Systeme funktionieren nicht mehr so, wie sie sollten, weil das Gleichgewicht der einzelnen Komponenten durcheinandergebracht wird. Die Erde wird beispielsweise immer wärmer, was zu einer globalen Erwärmung, und dies wiederum zu einer Lebensraumveränderung führt und so weiter. Die Welt befindet sich in einer Art *ökologischen Krise*, welche nun eine zeitgemäße Theologie verlangt, die das Schöpfungsverständnis neu denkt und die Erfahrungen der Menschen einbezieht. Das Evangelium muss angesichts der Entwicklungen ausgelegt und neu gedacht werden und das nicht willkürlich, sondern mit einem klaren gemeinsamen Ziel.[31]

Wenn von *Schöpfung* gesprochen wird, ist es unumgänglich, über Gen 1 nachzudenken. Hier wird die Schöpfungserzählung dargestellt und für den Menschen anschaulich. Immer wieder stolpert man dann über den Ausdruck *sich die Erde untertan machen*. Was aber nicht meint, die Erde und damit die Schöpfung auszunutzen, ganz im Gegenteil. Es geht darum, diese zu bewahren und zu beschützen.[32] Die Schöpfungserzählungen behandeln demnach nicht Tatsachenberichte oder Mythen, sondern sollen verstanden werden als eine Erklärung, warum die Welt so ist, wie sie ist und wie sie in einem ausgeglichenen Verhältnis

---

29 Vgl. ZIBERTZ 2017 [Anm. 26], 137–139.

30 Vgl. KLEIN-LANDECK / PÜTZ 2013 [Anm. 16], 95.

31 Vgl. SCHAACK, Thomas: Schöpfungszeit. Schöpfung Praktisch, Hannover: UTB, 2004, 4.

32 Vgl. KALLOCH, Christina: „Gott hat die Welt erschaffen – aber eigentlich ist sie so entstanden". Biblische Schöpfungsgeschichten und naturwissenschaftliche Erklärungsmodelle – Ein Dilemma für Grundschulkinder?, in: KALLOCH, Christina / SCHREIBER, Martin (Hg.): Gott hat das in Auftrag gegeben. Mit Kindern über Schöpfung und Weltentstehung nachdenken, Stuttgart: Calver, 55–57.

funktionieren kann. Das Bild des Vaters oder der Mutter, die Verantwortung übernehmen und auf ihr Heim und ihre Familie Acht geben, wird gerne genommen, um die Bedeutung der Menschen für die Schöpfung darzustellen.[33] Lernende sollen animiert werden, Mythos und Logis unterscheiden zu lernen, um dann wiederum Ideen für ein praktisches Handeln entwickeln zu können.[34] Die Lebenswirklichkeit der Schüler*innen spielt hier eine entscheidende Rolle. Je nachdem wie die Adoleszenten aufgewachsen sind, bringen sie andere Grundvoraussetzungen mit. Kinder, die vorwiegend in der Stadt aufgewachsen sind und wenig Berührungspunkte mit der Natur im Sinne von Landwirtschaft haben, bringen einen anderen Wissensstand mit als Kinder, die auf dem Land aufgewachsen sind und (eher) wissen, wo beispielsweise saisonale oder auch tierische Lebensmittel herkommen.[35]

„Aus christlicher Sicht ist Klimaschutz eine Bewährungsprobe für praktizierte Schöpfungsverantwortung." (LS 114) und so wurde im Jahr 2015 die Enzyklika *Laudato si'* veröffentlicht und beschäftigt sich unter anderem mit dem Grundgedanken, dass der ökologische Gedanke und das soziale Miteinander neu gedacht werden müssen. Papst Franziskus äußerte sich wie folgt: „Wenn jemand die Erdenbewohner von außen beobachten würde, würde er sich über ein solches Verhalten wundern, das bisweilen selbstmörderisch erscheint." (LS 55) Diese Äußerung deckt sich mit den Forderungen der kommenden Generation, denn auch diese weiß, dass sich das Verhalten der Gesellschaft ändern muss. Es reicht nicht darüber zu sprechen, nur wenn die Gesellschaft tatsächlich die Schwierigkeiten der Klimakrise aufdeckt, was unter anderem durch Politik und Wissenschaft getan und besprochen wird, und Handlungsmuster entwickelt, die dem aktuellen Handeln entgegenwirkt, hat eben diese Gesellschaft eine reelle Chance, die Schöpfung zu (be-)schützen.

Aufgrund der Forderungen und der zugehörigen Äußerungen der christlichen Kirchen kann es unumgänglich sein, religionspädagogisch anzuschließen und das religiöse Lernen in der Schule weiterzudenken und ökologisch zu arbeiten.[36] Der Schulgarten ist eines von vielen Beispielen, wie der Gedanke des Schöpfungsbewahrens aktiv gelebt werden kann, Sinneseindrücke zu schaffen und reflektiert über verschiedenste Sachverhalte, auch fächerübergreifend, nachzudenken. Im Zuge des *ästhetischen Lernens*[37] wird in der ästhetischen Wahr-

---

[33] Vgl. Scoralick, Ruth: Biblische Schöpfungstheologie in Gen 1-9, in: Münk, Hans J. (Hg.): Schöpfung, Theologie und Wissenschaft. Theologische Berichte XXIX, Freiburg im Breisgau, 2006, 65–67.

[34] Vgl. Ebd.

[35] Vgl. Naurath, Elisabeth: Mehr als Öko-Idylle: Religionsunterricht auf dem Bauernhof, in: KATBL 144 (3/2019) 193.

[36] Vgl. Ebd., 167.

[37] Vgl. Hilger, Georg: Ästhetisches Lernen, in: Hilger, Georg u. a. (Hg.): Religionsdidaktik. Ein Leitfaden für Studium, Ausbildung und Beruf, München: Kösel, [6]2017, 334–343.

nehmungsdimension (aisthesis) die Gartenarbeit mit allen Sinnen wahrgenommen, in der ästhetischen Ausdrucks- und Gestaltungsfähigkeit (poiesis) geht es um die gestalterische Tätigkeit, wie beispielsweise das Anlegen von Blumenbeeten und schlussendlich in der ästhetischen Urteilsfähigkeit (katharsis) und das kritische Urteilen und Reflektieren über die Handlungen und den Fortschritt im Garten. Über die Handlungen im Garten selbst können auch viele Projekte zum Thema angestoßen werden, wie beispielsweise die Diskussion über sogenanntes „krummes Gemüse", die Vermarktung von fair gehandelten Produkten oder aber auch den Anspruch der Konsumenten schön verpackte Lebensmittel zu konsumieren. Wenn Kinder echte Erfahrungen machen, diese ausprobieren und hinterfragen, gegebenenfalls optimieren, fällt es ihnen viel leichter, diese auch in Alltagshandlungen zu übernehmen. Mit diesem Ansatz stehen wir an dieser Stelle wieder im Rückbezug auf die Ansätze des Lernens nach Maria Montessori.

Vortheologische Dimension des Konzepts der Bildung für nachhaltige Entwicklung (SDGs)

Im Lehren und Lernen soll darauf geachtet werden, die Schüler*innen zu Menschen heranzubilden, die in reflektierter Auseinandersetzung mit christlichen Glaubensinhalten und Werten die Schöpfung bewahren und nachhaltig das Leben auf der Erde positiv beeinflussen. Eine kritische Auseinandersetzung, die kreative Lösungsansätze erlaubt, verantwortlich zu handeln und einen eigenen Standpunkt zu vertreten, sollen hier stets im Zentrum stehen. Um dieses Ziel zu erreichen, orientiert sich das Konzept an den SDGs, welche als konkrete Handlungsziele christlicher Nächstenliebe verstanden werden und somit die soziale Umsetzung einer vorspirituellen und vorreligiösen Dimension einer christlichen Liebesethik darstellen.[38]

> […] [Sie] skizzieren eine neue und ehrgeizige weltweite Agenda, um Armut und Hunger zu reduzieren, Gesundheit zu verbessern, Gleichberechtigung zu ermöglichen, den Planeten zu schützen und vieles mehr. Echte Fortschritte werden schwer möglich sein, wenn nicht alle Kinder und Jugendlichen weltweit eine hochwertige Bildung erhalten. Daher spielt Bildung in den SDGs eine zentrale Rolle. Daten, insbesondere des UNESCO-Weltbildungsberichts, zeigen eindeutig, dass Bildung essentiell ist für den Erfolg aller 17 nachhaltigen Entwicklungsziele.[39]

38 Vgl. Deutsche UNESCO-Kommission e.V. et.al.: Unpacking SDG 4. Fragen und Antworten zur Bildungsagenda 2030. Bonn, 2017.

39 Deutsche UNESCO-Kommission: Agenda Bildung 2023. Bildung und die Sustainable Development Goals, in: https://www.unesco.de/bildung/agenda-bildung-2030/bildung-und-die-sdgs [abgerufen am 05.04.2023].

Natürlich kann im Rahmen der *EarthKids-Class*[40] nicht auf alle 17 Ziele eingegangen werden, weswegen verteilt über vier Schuljahre (Klasse 5–8) der Schwerpunkt auf den Zielen 2 (kein Hunger), 4 (Chancengleichheit und hochwertige Bildung), 11 (nachhaltige Städte und Gemeinden), 12 (nachhaltiger Konsum und Produktion), 13 (Klimaschutz und Anpassung) und 15 (Leben an Land) liegt. Diese Schwerpunktsetzung ist im Sinne von Querschnittsaufgaben zu verstehen, welche sich durch die *EarthKids-Class*-Aufgaben der vier Jahre ziehen. In der praktischen Anwendung bedeutet dies, dass die jeweiligen Klassen in einem Schuljahr aktiv auf dem Acker praktische Erfahrungen sammeln und in den weiteren drei Schuljahren diese projektorientiert ausdifferenzieren. Selbstverständlich kann nicht der Anspruch bestehen, jegliches Handeln der Schüler*innen auf die Erreichung der ausgewählten SDGs hin auszurichten. Vielmehr sollen die den SDGs zugrundeliegenden Werte in den eigenen empathisch-compathischen Wertekanon nachhaltig übernommen werden und somit ihren Beitrag zum sozialen Lernen und dessen vortheologischen Dimensionen leisten.

Der Unterricht im Rahmen der EarthKids-Class

Der Anspruch des Konzeptes ist es, möglichst vielen Schüler*innen die Möglichkeit zu geben, in ihrer Schullaufbahn an der *EarthKids-Class* teilzunehmen. Die Schwierigkeit besteht vor allem darin, den Stundenplan, die Ansprüche der einzelnen Lehrkräfte, die Anzahl der Schüler*innen und das Platz- bzw. Lernangebot des Schulgartens in Einklang zu bringen. Die hier gezeigte Projektumsetzung stellt die Idealbedingungen für ein Gelingen in dem oben beschriebenen pädagogischen Anspruch dar.

In diesem Kapitel wird sich vor allem auf die Bedingungen der Praxisschule bezogen und davon ausgehend versucht, möglichst allgemeingültige Hinweise zu geben. Darüber hinaus bietet *Ela Eckert* in ihren Erklärungen zum Erdkinderplan ebenfalls Erfolgsfaktoren für eine gelingende Umsetzung.[41] Wenn das Handlungsbeispiel an einem anderen Lernort ausprobiert wird, müssen die jeweiligen Voraussetzungen und Bedingungen selbstverständlich hinreichend geprüft werden.

---

40 Der Begriff *EarthKids-Class* stellt als Symbolbegriff das pädagogische Nachhaltigkeitskonzept der Autorin sowie die zugrundeliegende Didaktik dar. Dieser Begriff soll hierbei die Verbindung von konkreten Handlungsmöglichkeiten in schulischen Kontexten mit dem Anspruch einer Orientierungsfunktion in pluralistischen Wertevorstellungen darstellen. Das Konzept vertritt hierbei den Anspruch eines compathisch-zukunftsfähigen schulischen Leaderships.

41 Vgl. ECKERT 2020 [Anm. 3], 202–217.

Die Umsetzung des Erdkinderplans lässt sich an einer bestehenden Montessori-Schule mit einer Sekundarstufe I ermöglichen, da diese über das Fach *Freiarbeit*[42] verfügt. In dieser Zeit können sich die Schüler*innen intensiv mit Themen verschiedenster Lerninhalte beschäftigen. Weiterhin ist eine Voraussetzung, dass es einen Schulgarten (entweder auf dem Schulgelände oder in unmittelbarer Nähe) gibt, in welchem die Schüler*innen arbeiten dürfen. Da Schulen über mehrere hundert Lernende verfügen, ist es selbstverständlich, dass nicht alle gleichzeitig im Garten lernen und arbeiten können. Daher wird mittels einer möglichst gerechten Aufteilung ermöglicht, dass alle Interessierten wenigstens ein Schuljahr lang Teil der *EarthKids-Class* sein können. Die folgende Grafik veranschaulicht die Aufteilung in einer möglichen Planung:

Schuljahr	Klasse 6							
	6 A		6 B		6 C		6 D	
SJ 1	Mo	Kind 01–08			Mo	Kind 01–08		
	Di	Kind 09–16			Di	Kind 09–16		
	Mi	Kind 17–24			Mi	Kind 17–24		
	Do	Kind 25–32			Do	Kind 25–32		
SJ 2			Mo	Kind 01–08			Mo	Kind 01–08
			Di	Kind 09–16			Di	Kind 09–16
			Mi	Kind 17–24			Mi	Kind 17–24
			Do	Kind 25–32			Do	Kind 25–32
SJ 3	Mo	Kind 01–08			Mo	Kind 01–08		
	Di	Kind 09–16			Di	Kind 09–16		
	Mi	Kind 17–24			Mi	Kind 17–24		
	Do	Kind 25–32			Do	Kind 25–32		

Schuljahr	Klasse 7							
	7 A		7 B		7 C		7 D	
SJ 1	Mo	Kind 01–08			Mo	Kind 01–08		
	Di	Kind 09–16			Di	Kind 09–16		
	Mi	Kind 17–24			Mi	Kind 17–24		
	Do	Kind 25–32			Do	Kind 25–32		
SJ 2			Mo	Kind 01–08			Mo	Kind 01–08
			Di	Kind 09–16			Di	Kind 09–16
			Mi	Kind 17–24			Mi	Kind 17–24
			Do	Kind 25–32			Do	Kind 25–32
SJ 3	Mo	Kind 01–08			Mo	Kind 01–08		
	Di	Kind 09–16			Di	Kind 09–16		
	Mi	Kind 17–24			Mi	Kind 17–24		
	Do	Kind 25–32			Do	Kind 25–32		

42 Nach Harald Ludwig (Professor für Montessori-Pädagogik): Freiarbeit im Sinne Maria Montessoris ist eine Unterrichtsform, „in welcher der Schüler aus einem differenzierten Lernangebot den Gegenstand seiner Tätigkeit, die Ziele, die Sozialform sowie die Zeit, die er auf den gewählten Aufgabenbereich verwenden will, im Rahmen allgemeiner Vorstrukturierungen selbst bestimmen kann. Für den Ablauf der selbst gewählten Arbeit gilt, dass der Schüler sich frei im Raum bewegen und auch Kontakte mit Mitschülern, aufnehmen darf, etwa um ihnen zu helfen oder sich helfen zu lassen, sofern und soweit die Arbeit mit anderen Schülern, dadurch nicht gestört wird. Mit der Wahl der Arbeit ist die Verpflichtung verbunden, sie möglichst auch zu Ende zu führen." (LUDWIG, Harald: Erziehen mit Maria Montessori. Ein reformpädagogisches Konzept in der Praxis, Freiburg im Breisgau: Herder, [5]2003, 27.)

Geht man davon aus, dass im Jahrgang 6 die Freiarbeit mit 8 Unterrichtsstunden zu jeweils 45 Minuten stattfindet und im Jahrgang 7 mit jeweils 6 Unterrichtsstunden, werden zwei dieser Stunden für ein Schuljahr für die Lernzeit im Schulgarten genutzt. So wird an dieser Stelle vorausgesetzt, dass alle Freiarbeitsstunden in den betroffenen Jahrgängen (siehe Tabelle 1) parallel liegen. Aus diesem Grund werden die jeweiligen Klassen in vier Untergruppen eingeteilt, welche auf die Tage verteilt in den Schulgarten gehen und jeweils ähnliche Tätigkeiten durchführen. Beispielsweise wird an je einem Tag in der Woche in unterschiedlichen Bereichen des Gartens gepflanzt, Unkraut gejätet oder Geräte repariert und gereinigt. Dies bedarf einer langfristigen und detaillierten Planung seitens der betreuenden Lehrkräfte.

Eine maßgebliche Schwierigkeit besteht darin, dass alle Lehrenden das Konzept mittragen müssen. Denn es wird in einem Schuljahr für acht Monate (März – Oktober) so sein, dass nie alle Kinder gleichzeitig die Freiarbeit besuchen werden und andere in der Freiarbeit angelegten Konzepte für diesen Zeitraum individuell verändert werden müssen (z. B. Klassenrat, Klassenleitungsstunden etc.). Dem entgegenzusetzen ist jedoch, dass aufgrund von Krankheit oder weiteren Aktionen innerhalb der Schule ohnehin selten wirklich alle Kinder in der Klasse sind und es meist eine Anzahl von fünf bis acht Schüler*innen betrifft, die nicht anwesend sein wird. Des Weiteren kann beispielsweise für Abstimmungen in Einzelfällen die Absprache getroffen werden, dass die betroffenen Lernenden etwas später in den Schulgarten gehen. Auch ist ein Lösungsansatz, dass innerhalb der Klassengemeinschaft geübt werden kann, eben diese Kinder sachlich über Vorfälle zu informieren, sodass keine Wissenslücken entstehen. Weitere Lösungsansätze sind möglich, werden an dieser Stelle aber nicht weiter erörtert. Die Beispiele sollen an dieser Stelle Anregungen bieten, wie mit etwaigen Schwierigkeiten umgegangen werden kann.

Wie bereits erwähnt, dauert die Zeit der *EarthKids-Class* im Garten von März bis Oktober an und orientiert sich am phänologischen Kalender.[43] Für die Organisation bedeutet es, dass die ersten beiden Klassen nach den Sommerferien mit der voraussichtlichen Ernte beginnen und dann den Ackertätigkeiten bis in den Spätherbst nachgehen. In den folgenden Monaten bis hin in den Frühling gibt es im Garten nur sehr wenige Aufgaben, die nach Absprache getätigt werden. Ab März arbeitet die *EarthKids-Class* wieder aktiv und regelmäßig im Garten bis zu den Sommerferien. Nach den Sommerferien beginnt dann das zweite Jahr und andere Klassen sind mit der Arbeit im Schulgarten an der Reihe. In den Monaten,

---

43 Das phänologische Jahr unterteilt sich nicht nur in die klassischen vier Jahreszeiten, sondern in zehn biologische begründete Zeitfenster, die sich an dem tatsächlichen Pflanzenwachstum orientieren. Dies führt dazu, dass sich diese Jahreszeiten nicht auf den Tag genau festlegen lassen. (vgl. NABU: Der Phänologische Kalender. Die Jahreszeiteneinteilung nach den Erscheinungen in der Pflanzenwelt, in: https://www.nabu.de/tiere-und-pflanzen/pflanzen/pflanzenwissen/jahreszeiten.html [abgerufen am 05.04.2023].)

in denen nicht aktiv im Garten gearbeitet wird, haben die Klassen eine Freiarbeitsstunde in der Woche gemeinsamen Theorie-Unterricht mit einzelnen Experimenten und kleineren Projekten im Klassenraum, um die Thematik des Schulgartens, verbunden mit den eigelagerten vortheologischen Dimensionen des compathisch-empathischen Lernens, weiterhin als einen Schwerpunkt zu fokussieren. Welche Themen wann zu behandeln sind, sind dem entsprechenden Lehrplan des Konzeptes zu entnehmen.[44] Wie die Ferien gestaltet werden, müssen die jeweiligen Schulen beispielsweise mittels eines Gieß- und Ernteplans organisieren oder durch die beteiligten Klassen im Sinne einer Übergabe organisieren lassen.

Bewusst wird die Arbeit im Schulgarten in die Jahrgangsstufen 6 und 7 gelegt, da dies den Entwicklungsstufen nach Montessori (siehe Kapitel 1.1) entspricht. Streng genommen beschreibt Montessori in ihrem pädagogischen Ansatz des Erdkinderplans, dass die Arbeit etwa mit zwölf bis fünfzehn Jahren (Klasse 7 – 9) im Garten stattfinden soll. Jedoch zeigen aktuelle Entwicklungen, dass die Pubertät bei den Schüler*innen immer früher einsetzt[45] und dementsprechend die Arbeit im Schulgarten auch ein Jahr früher angesetzt werden kann. Dem kann entgegengesetzt werden, dass ab Klasse 7 fokussierter auf die jeweiligen Schulabschlüsse hingearbeitet wird, wodurch die Lernenden die ohnehin geringere Anzahl an Freiarbeitsstunden für die Bewältigung der Aufgaben benötigt. Folgt man jedoch dem Ansatz Montessoris, ist es im Jahrgang 7 genau die Zeitspanne, in der die kosmische Erziehung und somit der Erdkinderplan genutzt werden können, um den Bedürfnissen der Heranwachsenden gerecht zu werden. Eltern und auch Lehrende müssen darauf vertrauen, dass die Kinder innerhalb der zweiten Entwicklungsstufe (etwa Klasse 1 – 6) kognitiv deklaratives Wissen besser aufnehmen und verarbeiten können als in der dritten Entwicklungsstufe und das Wissen bezogen auf die oben genannten Softskills in dieser Phase prägender sind und für die Weiterentwicklung hinsichtlich einer gesellschaftlichen Stabilität ebenso wichtig sind (z. B. Ausgeglichenheit, Empathiefähigkeit, Solidarität, Friedfertigkeit). So würde wenigstens im Jahrgang 7 den Heranwachsenden ein Freiraum im Lernen gewährt, welcher den Grundlagen des Erdkinderplans entspricht. „In der Zeit im Kinderhaus und in der Grundstufe werden die Konzepte Montessoris als wohltuend bereichernd und fördernd für die Kinder erlebt. Eltern fällt es in diesen Altersgruppen leicht, die Anforderungen und den ‚Ernst des Lebens' im späteren Alter auszublenden."[46] Ab der Sekundarstufe rücken die Prüfungen und das curriculare Wissen meist in den Fokus

---

44 Eine ausführliche Version des Lehrplans für den Schulgarten kann über den Verlag bei der Autorin angefragt werden.

45 Vgl. Brix, Nils et.al.: Timing in puberty in boys and girls. A population-based study, in: Pediatric and Perinatal Epidemiology 33/1 (2019), 70–7. DOI: https://doi.org/10.1111/ppe.12507.

46 Eckert 2020 [Anm. 3], 207.

und die Sorge, dass etwas zu wenig oder gar nicht gelernt wird, steigt. Aus diesem Grund ist eine Art Mischform in diesem Konzept gewählt worden. Im sechsten Jahrgang haben die Kinder noch mehr Zeit, um Dinge zu lernen und im Jahrgang sieben ist der Druck bezüglich der Abschlüsse noch etwas geringer als in höheren Jahrgängen und dennoch benötigen die Heranwachsenden die Möglichkeit, sich außerhalb starrer Unterrichtsformen zu entwickeln und für ihre Altersstufe angemessen zu lernen. Sollten Lernende höhere Jahrgangsstufen (8 – 10) Lust und Kapazitäten haben, in der Freiarbeit im Schulgarten mitzuwirken, kann beispielsweise nach Absprache mit den Lehrenden eine Art Patenschaft entstehen, sodass ältere Schüler*innen, die bereits im Garten gelernt haben, die jüngeren Schüler*innen unterstützen können. Hilfreich ist das besonders bei Arbeiten, die mehr Kraft oder Körpergröße bedürfen.

> Die tatsächliche Organisation der Sekundarstufe in Deutschland, Vorgaben durch fachbezogene Rahmenpläne, Prüfungsordnungen und Abschlussbedingungen bieten auf den ersten Blick kaum Ansatzpunkte, ein Konzept einer radikalen Entschulung der Sekundarstufe umzusetzen. Insbesondere, wenn auch Schulabschlüsse vergeben werden, die einen Übertritt in die gymnasiale Oberstufe oder in die Berufsbildung ermöglichen, sind die Hürden unüberwindbar.[47]

Betrachtet man die aktuellen Lehrpläne der Schulen jedoch genauer, wird man feststellen, dass die Hürden doch nicht so unüberwindbar sind, wie sie auf den ersten Blick scheinen. Die Bildungsziele der Schulen orientieren sich immer mehr an einer Kompetenzentwicklung und weniger an starren Lerninhalten. Beispiele sollen an dieser Stelle genannt und mit obigen Inhalten in Verbindung gebracht werden:
Bildungs- und Erziehungsauftrag der Schule (§2 SGV NRW)

> „(4) Die Schule vermittelt die zur Erfüllung ihres Bildungs- und Erziehungsauftrags erforderlichen Kenntnisse, Fähigkeiten, Fertigkeiten und Werthaltungen und berücksichtigt dabei die individuellen Voraussetzungen der Schülerinnen und Schüler. Sie fördert die Entfaltung der Person, die Selbstständigkeit ihrer Entscheidungen und Handlungen und das Verantwortungsbewusstsein für das Gemeinwohl, die Natur und die Umwelt. Schülerinnen und Schüler werden befähigt, verantwortlich am sozialen, gesellschaftlichen, wirtschaftlichen, beruflichen, kulturellen und politischen Leben teilzunehmen und ihr eigenes Leben zu gestalten. Sie erwerben Kompetenzen, um zukünftige Anforderungen und Chancen in einer digitalisierten Welt bewältigen und ergreifen zu können. Schülerinnen und Schüler werden in der Regel gemeinsam unterrichtet und erzogen (Koedukation)." (§ 2 Abs. 4 SGV NRW)
> (6) Die Schülerinnen und Schüler sollen insbesondere lernen
> 1. selbstständig und eigenverantwortlich zu handeln,
> 2. für sich und gemeinsam mit anderen zu lernen und Leistungen zu erbringen,
> 3. die eigene Meinung zu vertreten und die Meinung anderer zu achten,
> 4. in religiösen und weltanschaulichen Fragen persönliche Entscheidungen zu treffen und Verständnis und Toleranz gegenüber den Entscheidungen anderer zu entwickeln,

---

47 Ebd., 208.

[...]
7. die eigene Wahrnehmungs-, Empfindungs- und Ausdrucksfähigkeit [...] zu entfalten,
[...] (§ 2 Abs. 6 SGV NRW)
(9) Der Unterricht soll die Lernfreude der Schülerinnen und Schüler erhalten und weiter fördern. Er soll die Schülerinnen und Schüler anregen und befähigen, Strategien und Methoden für ein lebenslanges nachhaltiges Lernen zu entwickeln. [...] (§ 2 Abs. 9 SGV NRW)

Kirchliche Richtlinien zu Bildungsstandards für den katholischen Religionsunterricht in den Jahrgangsstufen 5–10/Sekundarstufe I

Der katholische Religionsunterricht weckt und reflektiert die Frage nach Gott, nach der Deutung der Welt, nach dem Sinn und Wert des Lebens und nach den Normen für das Handeln des Menschen und ermöglicht eine Antwort aus dem Glauben der Kirche, befähigt zu persönlicher Entscheidung in Auseinandersetzung mit Konfessionen und Religionen, mit Weltanschauungen und Ideologien und fördert Verständnis und Toleranz gegenüber der Entscheidung anderer, motiviert zu religiösem Leben und zu verantwortlichem Handeln in Kirche und Gesellschaft und befähigt zur Kommunikation und solidarischen Partizipation über den eigenen Kulturkreis hinaus.[48]
Neben den Haltungen und Einstellungen, die alle Unterrichtsfächer fördern wollen wie z. B. Verantwortungsbereitschaft, Freiheitsliebe, Respekt vor anderen Menschen, Gerechtigkeit und Solidarität, will der Religionsunterricht vor allem folgende christliche Haltungen fördern: [...], Lebensfreude, Dankbarkeit für das eigene Leben und die ganze Schöpfung, Sensibilität für das Leiden anderer, [...]. Einstellungen und Haltungen sind nur begrenzt lehrbar. Oft ist es kaum möglich zu entscheiden, welchen Anteil der Religionsunterricht oder gar eine bestimmte Unterrichtsreihe an der Herausbildung einzelner Haltungen und Einstellungen hat. Sie werden auch nicht ausschließlich im Unterricht erworben, sondern auch in der Familie und in der Freizeit. Einen wesentlichen Beitrag zum Erwerb von Haltungen und Einstellungen leistet die Schulkultur, zu der an manchen Orten auch Angebote der Schulpastoral gehören.[49]

Kernlehrplan für die Gesamtschule in Nordrhein-Westfalen, Katholische Religionslehre

Handlungskompetenz erwächst aus Sach-, Methoden- und Urteilskompetenz. Sie wird im Unterricht angebahnt, weist jedoch über den schulischen Kontext hinaus. Sie zeigt sich einerseits in der Entdeckung und Gestaltung der eigenen Religiosität und des gelebten Glaubens. Andererseits äußert sie sich in der Teilnahme am religiösen und interreligiösen Dialog, in der Mitgestaltung religiöser, kirchlicher und gesellschaftlicher Prozesse sowie im Handeln auf der Basis der eigenen religiösen und moralischen Einsicht. Handlungskompetenz zeigt sich in der Fähigkeit, Einsichten und Erkenntnisse projekt-, produkt- und handlungsorientiert umzusetzen. Zur

---

48 Die deutschen Bischöfe 78 (Hg.): Kirchliche Richtlinien zu Bildungsstandards für den katholischen Religionsunterricht in den Jahrgangsstufen 5–10 / Sekundarstufe I (mittlerer Schulabschluss), Bonn: Sekretariat der deutschen Bischofskonferenz, 2004, 9–10.

49 Ebd., 11–12.

Handlungskompetenz gehört auch, Sprach- und Ausdrucksformen des Glaubens zu erproben, zu gestalten und ihren Gebrauch zu reflektieren.[50]

Festzustellen ist also, dass die benannten Ziele in den Kapiteln 1 und 2 eine große Relevanz in den Lehrplänen und Vorgaben des Landes Nordrhein-Westfalens in Bezug auf die schulische Bildung der Schüler*innen haben. Sowohl die zu erwerbenden Kompetenzen nach Montessori als auch die Inhalte der Kernlehrpläne des christlichen Kontextes widersprechen sich nicht mit dem gedachten Konzept des Erdkinderplans.

Fazit

Neben den bislang genannten Kompetenzen, die sich vor allem auf Fachwissen und Nachhaltigkeit – auch in Bezug auf das Christsein – beziehen, soll die *EarthKids-Class* dazu beitragen, auch die persönliche und soziale Entwicklung zu fördern. Die Klasse muss immer wieder gemeinsam Aufgaben bewältigen, die Schüler*innen sollen sich gegenseitig unterstützen und zusammen an einem großen (Schul-)Projekt arbeiten. Die sogenannten Softskills spielen in dieser Unterrichtsphase eine besondere Rolle, da es sich um ein offenes Lernangebot handelt, in welchem sich die Lernenden frei entfalten können und sich ausprobieren sollen. Dabei wird darauf geachtet, dass nicht für alle Probleme Lösungen durch die Lehrkräfte bereitgestellt werden, sondern die Schüler*innen darin bestärkt werden, als Team mit kreativen Denkansätzen und einer hohen Selbstständigkeit arbeiten sollen. Gleichzeitig wird die Kritik- und Konfliktfähigkeit geschult, da sich viele Personen einigen müssen, um das gemeinsame Ziel zu erreichen.

Durch mögliche Unterrichtsgänge erleben die Schüler*innen weitere Lernräume und interagieren mit Expert*innen. Das erworbene Wissen kann dann im schuleigenen Garten angewandt und vertieft werden.[51]

Bedingt durch das Schulsystem handelt es sich bei den Schüler*innen um weitgehend heterogene Lerngruppen bezogen auf ihr Leistungsvermögen. Das hier dargestellte Konzept arbeitet nach den Prinzipien der Montessori-Pädago-

---

50 Ministerium für Schule und Weiterbildung des Landes Nordrhein-Westfalen: Kernlehrplan für die Gesamtschule in Nordrhein-Westfalen. Katholische Religionslehre, Düsseldorf 2013, 15.

51 Das *EarthKids-Class*-Konzept, welches über die Ausführungen in diesem Beitrag hinausgeht, sieht darüber hinaus noch Möglichkeiten des Austauschs mit anderen Schulen, möglicherweise auch in anderen Ländern und somit in einer fächerübergreifenden Zusammenarbeit mit den Fremdsprachen, vor. Auch werden Wettbewerbe zwischen den Klassen / Schulen, Fortbildungen für Betreuer*innen und Lehrkräfte, die nachhaltige Verarbeitung der erzeugten Lebensmittel in den Schulküchen sowie *EarthKids-Conferences* zum gemeinsamen Austausch mitgedacht.

gik, die der Eigentätigkeit der Kinder einen hohen Stellenwert einräumt. Infolgedessen sind die Schüler*innen besonders ansprechbar für Formen des selbstgesteuerten und kreativen Lernens. Diesen Rahmenbedingungen wird bei der Unterrichtsgestaltung Rechnung getragen. Kreative Elemente und Phasen des eigenverantwortlichen und kooperativen Lernens bieten darüber hinaus gute Möglichkeiten zur Leistungsdifferenzierung. Das gemeinsame Lernen von Schüler*innen mit und ohne Behinderung bildet einen weiteren Pfeiler des pädagogischen Grundkonzepts. Infolgedessen verfügen die Schüler*innen über vielfältige Erfahrungen im Umgang mit eigener und fremder Behinderung und über eine hohe soziale Sensibilität. Hier ergeben sich gerade in der *EarthKids-Class* vielfältige Anknüpfungspunkte und Möglichkeiten, die zuvor bereits angesprochen wurden.

Literatur

Andree, Maurice / Domsel, Maike Maria: Die Paradigmen der Compassion und Freiheit als Bindeglieder zwischen Theologie und Ethik? Möglichkeiten spirituell-reflexiver Praxis im schulischen Kontext, in: ÖRF 30 (2022) 1, 110-127. DOI: 10.25364/10.30:2022.1.7

Boschki, Reinhold: Einführung in die Religionspädagogik (Einführung Theologie), Darmstadt: WBG, [3]2017.

Brazelton, Berry / Greenspan, Stanley: Die sieben Grundbedürfnisse von Kindern. Was jedes Kind braucht, um gesund aufzuwachsen, gut zu lernen und glücklich zu sein, Weinheim/München: Beltz, 2008.

Brix, Nils et.al.: Timing in puberty in boys and girls. A population-based study, in: Pediatric and Perinatal Epidemiology 33/1 (2019), 70–71. DOI: https://doi.org/10.1111/ppe.12507.

Bundesministerium für Umwelt, Naturschutz und nukleare Sicherheit (BMU): Zukunft? Jugend fragen! Nachhaltigkeit, Politik, Engagement – eine Studie zu Einstellungen und Alltag junger Menschen, Berlin, [2]2018.

Deutsche UNESCO-Kommission: Agenda Bildung 2023. Bildung und die Sustainable Development Goals, in: https://www.unesco.de/bildung/agenda-bildung-2030/bildung-und-die-sdgs [abgerufen am 05.04.2023].

Deutsche UNESCO-Kommission e. V. et. al.: Unpacking SDG 4. Fragen und Antworten zur Bildungsagenda 2030, Bonn, 2017.

Die deutschen Bischöfe 78 (Hg.): Kirchliche Richtlinien zu Bildungsstandards für den katholischen Religionsunterricht in den Jahrgangsstufen 5–10 / Sekundarstufe I (mittlerer Schulabschluss), Bonn: Sekretariat der deutschen Bischofskonferenz, 2004, 9–10.

Eckert, Ela: Erdkinderplan. Maria Montessoris Erziehungs- und Bildungskonzept für Jugendliche, Freiburg im Breisgau: Herder, 2020.

Egger, Moni: Schöpfung – Biblische und religionspädagogische Aspekte, in: Reli.ch https://www.reli.ch/schoepfung-biblische-und-religionspaedagogische-aspekte/ [abgerufen am 08.04.2023].

Franziskus: Enzyklika Laudato si'. Über die Sorge für das gemeinsame Haus, Verlautbarungen des Apostolischen Stuhls, 2015, Nr. 202.

Hilger, Georg: Ästhetisches Lernen, in: Hilger, Georg u. a.: Religionsdidaktik. Ein Leitfaden für Studium, Ausbildung und Beruf, München: Kösel, [6]2017, 334–343.

KALLOCH, Christina: „Gott hat die Welt erschaffen – aber eigentlich ist sie so entstanden". Biblische Schöpfungsgeschichten und naturwissenschaftliche Erklärungsmodelle – Ein Dilemma für Grundschulkinder?, in: KALLOCH, Christina / SCHREIBER, Martin (Hg.): Gott hat das in Auftrag gegeben. Mit Kindern über Schöpfung und Weltentstehung nachdenken, Stuttgart: Cavler, 55–57.

KLEIN-LANDECK, Michael / PÜTZ, Tanja: Montessori-Pädagogik. Einführung in Theorie und Praxis, Freiburg im Breisgau: Herder, ^{3}2013.

LUDWIG, Harald: Erziehen mit Maria Montessori. Ein reformpädagogisches Konzept in der Praxis, Freiburg im Breisgau: Herder, ^{5}2003.

MINISTERIUM FÜR SCHULE UND WEITERBILDUNG DES LANDES NORDRHEIN-WESTFALEN: Kernlehrplan für die Gesamtschule in Nordrhein-Westfalen. Katholische Religionslehre, Düsseldorf, 2013, 15.

MONTESSORI, Maria: Grundlagen meiner Pädagogik, Heidelberg / Wiesbaden: Quelle & Meyer, 1988.

MONTESSORI, Maria: Die „Erdkinder". Ein Plan für eine Reform der Sekundarerziehung, in: LUDWIG, Harald / KLEIN-LANDECK, Michael (Hg.): Von der Kindheit zur Jugend. Grundschule – Sekundarschule – Universität, Freiburg im Breisgau: Herder, ^{2}2018 (Bd. 14, 98–118).

NABU: Der Phänologische Kalender. Die Jahreszeiteneinteilung nach den Erscheinungen in der Pflanzenwelt, in: https://www.nabu.de/tiere-und-pflanzen/pflanzen/pflanzenwissen/jahreszeiten.html [abgerufen am 05.04.2023].

NAURATH, Elisabeth: Mehr als Öko-Idylle: Religionsunterricht auf dem Bauernhof, in: KATBL 144 (3/2019) 192–195.

SCHAACK, Thomas: Schöpfungszeit. Schöpfung Praktisch, Hannover: UTB, 2004.

SCHAUB, Horst: Kosmische Erziehung in der Montessori-Pädagogik. Die Entstehung des Konzepts der Kosmischen Erziehung – Die Geschichte des Universums und unserer Erde, Freiburg im Breisgau: Herder, 2013.

SCORALICK, Ruth: Biblische Schöpfungstheologie in Gen 1–9, in: MÜNK, Hans J. (Hg.): Schöpfung, Theologie und Wissenschaft. Theologische Berichte XXIX, Freiburg im Breisgau, 2006, 58–93.

ZIEBERTZ, Hans-Georg: Warum die religiöse Dimension der Wirklichkeit erschließen?, in: HILGER, Georg u. a. (Hg.): Religionsdidaktik. Ein Leitfaden für Studium, Ausbildung und Beruf, München: Kösel, ^{6}2017, 123–141.

Bildung für nachhaltige Entwicklung – Ergebnisse aus einer Befragung von Religionslehrer*innen und Perspektiven für das Compassion-Projekt

Jennifer Jakob & Martin Rothgangel

Compassion und Bildung für nachhaltige Entwicklung (BNE) besitzen unterschiedliche Entstehungskontexte. Gleichwohl können sie als zwei Ansätze verstanden werden, die sich vortrefflich ergänzen. Der vorliegende Artikel basiert auf insgesamt 16 Interviews mit Religionslehrer*innen aus dem Pflichtschulbereich in Österreich, die zu den Themen Nachhaltigkeit und Bildung für nachhaltige Entwicklung befragt wurden. Die Auswertung mit der Qualitativen Inhaltsanalyse führt zu dem Befund, dass aus der Sicht der Religionslehrer*innen BNE Aufgabe bzw. Teil des Religionsunterrichts ist, wobei bestimmte Punkte wie Verantwortung, Vorbildfunktion sowie der im Religionsunterricht spürbare Beziehungsaspekt des Schöpfungsbegriffes hervortreten. Näher betrachtet zeigen diese Punkte wiederum Affinitäten zu und Potenziale für Compassion als religionspädagogischer Schlüsselkategorie auf.

*Compassion; BNE; Religionslehrer*innen; Verantwortung; Vorbildwirkung; Beziehung*

Compassion and Education for Sustainable Development (ESD) have different contexts of origin. Nevertheless, they can be understood as two approaches that complement each other perfectly. This article is based on a total of 16 interviews with religion teachers from compulsory schools in Austria who were asked about the topics of sustainability and education for sustainable development. The evaluation with the Qualitative Content Analysis leads to the finding that, from the perspective of the religion teachers, ESD is a task or part of religious education, whereby certain points such as responsibility, role model function and the relationship aspect of the concept of creation, which is noticeable in religious education, stand out. These points, in turn, show affinities with and potential for compassion as a key religious education category.

Compassion; ESD; religion teachers; responsibility; role models; relationship

Hinführende Überlegungen

Compassion und Bildung für nachhaltige Entwicklung

Im vorliegenden Band wird Compassion als Schlüssel einer Bildung für nachhaltige Bildung (BNE) bedacht. Bekanntlich ist Compassion ein Ansatz, der in theologischer Hinsicht auf Johann Baptist Metz zurückgeht und in religionspädagogischer Hinsicht insbesondere von Lothar Kuld reflektiert wurde.[1] Letztgenannter begleitete wiederum wissenschaftlich ein Projekt, das von den Deutschen Bischofskonferenz in Auftrag gegeben und von Adolf Weisbrod entwickelt wurde.[2]

Systematisch-theologisch ist Compassion motiviert durch eine „leidempfindliche" bzw. „eine für fremdes Leid empfindliche Gottesrede".[3] Darüber hinaus macht Metz auf den biblischen Horizont einer „universellen Verantwortung"[4] aufmerksam, wobei diese weniger „am Universalismus der Sünde, sondern am Universalismus des Leidens in der Welt"[5] orientiert ist. Im schulischen Kontext besteht die Idee des Compassion-Projekts u. a. darin, dass die Schüler*innen nicht einfach nur für eine „globalisierte Wettbewerbsgesellschaft"[6] qualifiziert, sondern auch für ihre „soziale Kehrseite"[7] sensibilisiert werden sol-

---

1 Vgl. Metz, Johann Baptist / Kuld, Lothar / Weisbrod, Adolf (Hg.): Compassion. Weltprogramm des Christentums. Soziale Verantwortung lernen, Freiburg im Breisgau: Herder, 2000.

2 Vgl. Weisbrod, Adolf: Ein Pilotprojket. Genese, Besonderheiten, Ziele, in: Metz, Johann Baptist / Kuld, Lothar / Weisbrod, Adolf (Hg.): Compassion. Weltprogramm des Christentums. Soziale Verantwortung lernen, Freiburg im Breisgau: Herder, 2000, 97–100.

3 Metz, Johann Baptist: Compassion. Zu einem Weltprogramm des Christentums im Zeitalter des Pluralismus der Religionen und Kulturen, in: Metz, Johann Baptist / Kuld, Lothar / Weisbrod, Adolf (Hg.): Compassion. Weltprogramm des Christentums. Soziale Verantwortung lernen, Freiburg im Breisgau: Herder, 2000, 9–18, hier: 11.

4 Ebd., 11.

5 Ebd., 11.

6 Rekus, Jürgen: Compassion – ein erlebnisbezogenes Bildungskonzept, in: Metz, Johann Baptist: Compassion. Zu einem Weltprogramm des Christentums im Zeitalter des Pluralismus der Religionen und Kulturen, in: Metz, Johann Baptist / Kuld, Lothar / Weisbrod, Adolf (Hg.): Compassion. Weltprogramm des Christentums. Soziale Verantwortung lernen, Freiburg im Breisgau: Herder, 2000, 75–88, hier: 75.

7 Ebd., 75.

len. Dementsprechend setzt sich Compassion mit der „Wahrnehmung eines sozialmoralischen Defizits“[8] sowie einer zunehmenden „Entsolidarisierung der Gesellschaft“[9] auseinander und kommen in den Projekten u. a. Menschen mit Beeinträchtigungen, kranke und alte Personen sowie Asylsuchende und Obdachlose in den Blick.[10] Unschwer wird an diesen Ausführungen zu Compassion deutlich, dass dieses im Kontext des sozialen Lernens verortet wird – so führt die Monographie „Compassion. Weltprogramm des Christentums“ den Untertitel „Soziale Verantwortung lernen“.[11] Zusammengefasst liegen demnach die Ursprünge von Compassion im Kontext von Kirche und Theologie und können im Kontext sozialen Lernens verortet werden.

Zugespitzt und pointiert kann demgegenüber festgestellt werden, dass die Ursprünge von BNE im Kontext von UNESCO und Umweltbildung liegen, wobei es auch Affinitäten zum teilweise konkurrierenden Konzept des globalen Lernens gibt. So ist die maßgeblich von der UNESCO geprägte Weltdekade Bildung für nachhaltige Entwicklung (2005–2014) dafür verantwortlich, dass BNE als Leitbild in sämtlichen Ebenen von Bildungssystemen und Bildungsbereichen verankert werden sollten.[12] Dabei ist Bildung für nachhaltige Entwicklung kein neues Schulfach oder nur bestimmten Schulfächern zuzuschreiben. Für das Konzept sind der ganzheitliche und transformative Aspekt bestimmend.[13] Lernende sollen Gestaltungskompetenz erwerben, um aktiv und gestaltend an einer nachhaltigen Entwicklung mitarbeiten zu können.[14] Dabei sollen sie unter anderem sich selbst in Veränderungsprozesse einbringen, Zusammenhänge verstehen, Werte und Normen kritisch reflektieren und selbstständige Entscheidungen treffen können. Demnach sind alle Bereiche von Bildung angesprochen und damit auch der Religionsunterricht. Bislang ist jedoch empirisch nicht geklärt, ob und wie BNE einen Bestandteil in der Praxis des Religionsunterrichts bildet. Die nachstehend dargelegte empirische Studie geht dieser Frage anhand einer Befragung von Religionslehrer*innen nach.

---

8 Kuld, Lothar: Dimensionen der Compassion-Initiative, in: Metz, Johann Baptist: Compassion. Zu einem Weltprogramm des Christentums im Zeitalter des Pluralismus der Religionen und Kulturen, in: Metz, Johann Baptist / Kuld, Lothar / Weisbrod, Adolf (Hg.): Compassion. Weltprogramm des Christentums. Soziale Verantwortung lernen, Freiburg im Breisgau: Herder, 2000, 89–94, hier: 89.

9 Ebd., 89.

10 Vgl. Ebd. 92.

11 Vgl. Metz / Kuld / Weisbrod 2000 [Anm. 1].

12 Vgl. UNESCO: Education for sustainable development goals: Learning objectives, in: https://unesdoc.unesco.org/ark:/48223/pf0000247444 [abgerufen am 17.03.2023], 7.

13 Vgl. Ebd., 7.

14 Vgl. De Haan, Gerhard: Gestaltungskompetenz als Kompetenzkonzept der Bildung für nachhaltige Entwicklung, in: Bormann, Inka / De Haan, Gerhard (Hg.): Kompetenzen der Bildung für nachhaltige Entwicklung. Operationalisierung, Messung, Rahmenbedingungen, Befunde, Wiesbaden: VS Verlag für Sozialwissenschaften, 2008, 23–44.

Design der empirischen Studie

Grundlage dieser empirischen Studie sind Interviews mit 16 evangelischen Religionslehrer*innen aus Österreich, die hauptsächlich im Pflichtschulbereich unterrichten. Dazu wurde ein Interviewleitfaden erstellt, der im Wesentlichen drei große Teilbereiche enthält: Nachhaltigkeit im Privatleben, im Schulalltag und im Religionsunterricht. Erkenntnisleitend waren dabei die Einstellungen der Religionslehrer*innen zu Nachhaltigkeit sowie ihre Rolle in Bezug auf Bildung für nachhaltige Entwicklung (BNE).

Von den 16 befragten Religionslehrer*innen sind vier männlich und 12 weiblich. Zum Befragungszeitpunkt (September – Dezember 2021) waren sie zwischen 24 und 57 Jahre alt und im zweiten bis 24. Dienstjahr. Sie arbeiten in verschiedenen Bundesländern Österreichs, sowohl im städtischen als auch im ländlichen Bereich.

Ausgewertet wurden die Interviews mit der Qualitativen Inhaltsanalyse nach Mayring. Bei der induktiven Kategorienbildungen wurden subjektive Einstellungen, Vorstellungen und Meinungen der Religionslehrer*innen zu Nachhaltigkeit im Privatleben, Schulalltag und Religionsunterricht herausgefiltert.

Im folgenden Teil wird beschrieben, wie die befragten Religionslehrer*innen Bildung für nachhaltige Entwicklung als Teil bzw. Aufgabe des Religionsunterrichts verstehen. Dabei stehen die Schlüsselbegriffe Beziehung, Verantwortung und Vorbildwirkung im Zentrum. Die Reflexion dieser Ergebnisse im Hinblick auf Compassion erfolgt im abschließenden Teil.

Bildung für nachhaltige Entwicklung und die Rolle des Religionsunterrichts

Die Ergebnisse der Befragung lassen darauf schließen, dass Bildung für nachhaltige Entwicklung für die befragten Religionslehrer*innen als Teil und Aufgabe des Religionsunterrichts verstanden wird. Das manifestiert sich nicht nur in thematischen Überschneidungen von BNE und Religionsunterricht, d.h. dass sich Nachhaltigkeitsthemen im Religionsunterricht finden (wie z. B. Gerechtigkeit, Natur- und Umweltschutz), sondern auch im Verständnis von BNE und Religionsunterricht. Manche Religionslehrer*innen legen zum Beispiel den Fokus auf die Ganzheitlichkeit, auf die es im Religionsunterricht ankommt. Diese ist aber auch in der Bildung für nachhaltige Entwicklung zentral, wenn es um das Verstehen von Zusammenhängen und Interdisziplinarität geht. Auf drei wesentliche Aspekte, die von den befragten Religionslehrer*innen benannt werden, soll im Folgenden näher eingegangen werden: der Beziehungsaspekt, das Thema Verantwortung sowie die Vorbildfunktion.

Beziehung

Die Beziehungsthematik kommt auf zweierlei Arten zum Ausdruck: zum einen, wenn die befragten Religionslehrer*innen beim Thema Schöpfung über die Beziehung zwischen Gott und Mensch sowie Mensch und Mitwelt ansprechen, und zum anderen, wenn sie die Beziehungsebene im Religionsunterricht reflektieren.

In der erstgenannten Dimension, der Beziehung zwischen Gott und Mensch sowie Mensch und Mitwelt, geht es vor allem um die in den Schöpfungserzählungen thematisierte Verantwortung. Darauf wird später noch näher eingegangen, so dass hier die Beziehungsebene im Religionsunterricht im Fokus steht. Gerade im evangelischen Religionsunterricht in Österreich finden sich aufgrund der Minderheiten-Situation in der Regel kleine Gruppen zusammen. Religionslehrerin H beschreibt, dass es in den kleinen Gruppen möglich ist, dass „wirklich jedes Kind ausführlich zu Wort kommt und ausführlich seine eigenen Erfahrungen und Einstellungen mitteilen kann." Das bedeutet auch, dass die Schüler*innen nicht nur mit ihren Fragen und persönlichen Anliegen in den Religionsunterricht kommen können, sondern auch kritischen Bemerkungen ausreichend Raum zur Bearbeitung gegeben werden kann. Darin unterscheidet sich laut Religionslehrerin H der Religionsunterricht deutlich vom literarischen Unterricht, weil genügend Zeit und Platz dafür ist, auf jedes einzelne Kind mit seinen Fragen und Meinungen einzugehen. Religionslehrerin M spricht in diesem Zusammenhang von einer „Wohlfühl-Atmosphäre", die den Religionsunterricht einzigartig macht und die Beziehungsebene zwischen Schüler*innen und Lehrperson fördert. Dadurch ist es möglich, dass Religionslehrer*innen „da viel genauer eingehen [...] auf jedes einzelne Kind" (Religionslehrerin C).

Wenn die Schüler*innen merken, dass die Religionslehrer*innen wirklich Interesse an ihnen haben und auf sie eingehen, dann fassen sie Vertrauen und bringen ihre Themen vor. Beispielsweise darf jedes Kind in den Erzählrunden zum Stundenbeginn mitteilen, wie es ihr oder ihm gerade geht. Hier können dann unter anderem Fragen auftauchen, die im Zusammenhang mit dem aktuellen Weltgeschehen stehen oder die das Themenfeld Nachhaltigkeit berühren. Demnach besteht die Chance im Religionsunterricht darin, empathisch auf das einzugehen, was die Schüler*innen gerade bewegt und interessiert, woraus zugleich ein Anknüpfungspunkt zur Lebenswelt der Schüler*innen resultiert.

Verantwortung

Aus den Schöpfungserzählungen leiten die befragten Religionslehrer*innen eine Verantwortung bzw. einen Auftrag ab. Exemplarisch dafür steht der folgende Beleg: „Wir haben ja einen klaren Auftrag bekommen von Gott, dass wir auf die Erde schauen“ (Religionslehrer E). Die Verantwortung für die Erde ergibt sich demnach aus den biblischen Schöpfungserzählung – aber auch ein Gemeinschaftsgefühl, weil alle gemeinsam verantwortlich sind, wie Religionslehrerin H argumentiert.

Dementsprechend wird die Aufgabe des Religionsunterrichts darin gesehen, „wirklich ganz bewusst die Verantwortung des Menschen zu thematisieren“ (Religionslehrerin J). Die Schüler*innen sollen im Religionsunterricht diese Verantwortung reflektieren. Im Religionsunterricht hören sie bewusst von dieser Verantwortung im Zusammenhang mit der Schöpfungserzählung.

Insofern hat der Religionsunterricht die Aufgabe, das große Themenfeld Nachhaltigkeit zu thematisieren und auf die multiplen Krisen einzugehen, die damit im Zusammenhang stehen:

> Religionsunterricht hat für mich da einen Auftrag. Und wenn das meine Kollegen zu wenig machen in ihren anderen Fächern, ich mein, da denk ich mir, das kann nicht sein als Mensch, das kann man nicht aufschieben. Und das haben für mich diese Jugendlichen da nicht zum Narren halten diesbezüglich. Ich find das geht nicht anders. Man kann dem nicht ausweichen, ganz einfach (Religionslehrerin M).

Dass man sich dieser Verantwortung nicht entziehen kann, begründet Religionslehrerin F, folgendermaßen: „Weils mich auch betrifft. Weils auch meine Verantwortung ist. Und wenn wir jetzt ganz am Anfang in der Bibel nachlesen, ich glaub 1. Mose 2,15 steht der Auftrag für die Menschen, dass sie sich um die Welt kümmern sollen, um die Erde kümmern sollen und bebauen und bewahren sollen. Da zähl ich ja auch dazu.“

Gleichfalls möchten die befragten Religionslehrer*innen bei ihren Schüler*innen Kompetenzen fördern, die ihnen dabei helfen sollen, an einer nachhaltigen Entwicklung mitzuarbeiten. Zwei Kompetenzen stechen dabei besonders hervor: einerseits die Vermittlung eines sorgsamen sowie respektvollen Umgangs und andererseits die Vermittlung einer kritischen Haltung sowie Förderung von Kommunikations-Kompetenzen. Beides überschneidet sich mit dem bereits genannten Beziehungsaspekt. In der Vermittlung eines sorgsamen und respektvollen Umgangs geht es nämlich um den Umgang mit Mitmenschen, aber auch den Umgang mit der Umwelt bzw. Mitwelt. Auch das kann besonders gut in den Kleingruppen im Religionsunterricht gefördert werden, weil hier das Miteinander und aufeinander Achten im Fokus stehen. Religionslehrerin I argumentiert, dass das wohl auch andere Lehrer*innen machen würden, aber „ich glaub, wir machens intensiver und anders.“ Zwar werden kommunikative Kompetenzen und eine kritische Haltung von Schüler*innen sicherlich auch in anderen

Fächern gefördert. Die für den evangelischen Religionsunterricht in Österreich typischen Kleingruppen eignen sich jedoch vorzüglich dafür, jede*n zu Wort kommen zu lassen und genauer nachzufragen. In der vertrauten Atmosphäre von Kleingruppen ist es wahrscheinlicher als in einer größeren Gruppe, dass sensible bzw. kritische Punkte angesprochen werden. Somit kann der Religionsunterricht hier auch als ein vertrauensvoller Ort, als ein „safe space" gesehen werden.

Die genannten Kompetenzen finden sich auch in Kompetenzmodellen, die in der BNE diskutiert werden.[15] Zwar können ebenfalls andere Fächer diese Kompetenzen stärken, das Spezifikum des Religionsunterrichts ist jedoch der Bezug zum Schöpfungsglauben und die Einbeziehung dieser Dimension.

Religionslehrer*innen nehmen schließlich auch insofern ihre Verantwortung wahr, als sie selbst als Vorbilder fungieren und den Schüler*innen einen nachhaltigen Lebensstil vorleben. Dieses leitet über zum folgenden Punkt.

Vorbildfunktion

Für die befragten Religionslehrer*innen ist deutlich, dass sie als Vorbilder wirken können. Dies bezieht sich nicht nur auf ihre Schüler*innen, sondern auch auf die Kolleg*innen und auf die Eltern der Schüler*innen. In den Interviews spricht Religionslehrer G sogar davon, dass die Schule als Ganzes eine Vorbildwirkung in der Gesellschaft hat.

Im Religionsunterricht direkt bzw. im Schulalltag geht es für die befragten Religionslehrer*innen um ihr eigenes Tun, um die kleinen Schritte, die sie selbst setzen. Es ist ihnen bewusst, dass ihr Handeln beobachtet wird und es auf die Kleinigkeiten ankommt, wie Religionslehrer B beschreibt:

> Ob ich eine Vorbildfunktion hab? Ja, sicher, weil wenn ich das jetzt in Bezug auf Nachhaltigkeit positiv vermittle, kann ich da natürlich eine Vorbildfunktion haben. Ja. Das sind so Kleinigkeiten, ob ich jetzt eine Trinkflasche hab oder ob ich aus der Plastikflasche trinke. Auch als Lehrer, ja. Oder, wie meine Jause verpackt ist. Ob ich Äpfel esse zur Jause oder ob ich, was weiß ich, eine Leberkäs-Semmel iss. Hab ich sicher auch eine Vorbildfunktion.

Mit der Vorbildfunktion hängt die Authentizität der Lehrperson zusammen. Die befragten Religionslehrer*innen argumentieren, dass sie in ihrem Tun glaubwürdig sein wollen. Das setzt Authentizität voraus – Handeln und Reden sollen im Einklang stehen. Die Schüler*innen würden merken, wenn dies nicht passt. Das geht über den Schulalltag sowie den Religionsunterricht hinaus und betrifft auch das Privatleben der Religionslehrer*innen. Religionslehrerin I erzählt, dass

---

15 Vgl. WIEK, Arnim / WITHYCOMBE, Lauren / REDMAN, Charles L.: Key competencies in sustainability. a reference framework for academic program development, in: Sustainability Science 6/2 (2011), 203–218. DOI: https://doi.org/10.1007/s11625-011-0132-6.

ihr die Stimmigkeit ihres Verhaltens bedeutsam ist. Sie würde sich nicht wohlfühlen, wenn sie sich in der Schule vorbildhaft verhält und es im Privatleben gar nicht umsetzt.

In diesem Zusammenhang wird deutlich, dass die befragten Religionslehrer*innen gut reflektiert mit dem Thema umgehen. Sie erwähnen, dass es ihnen auch wichtig ist, sich einzugestehen, wenn mal etwas nicht so gut gelingt oder sie dabei scheitern, einen nachhaltigen Lebensstil zu etablieren. Das vermitteln sie auch den Schüler*innen, weil sie es wichtig finden, dazu zu stehen und zu sagen, dass nicht immer alles gelingen kann. Auch das gehört zu der Vorbildwirkung von Religionslehrer*innen. Sie vermitteln den Schüler*innen, dass auch sie z. B. Fehler im Blick auf Nachhaltigkeit begehen und man diese zugeben kann. Dies ändert nichts daran, dass man im eigenen Leben kleine Schritte im Blick auf Nachhaltigkeit setzt, wo immer es möglich ist.

BNE und Compassion: Wechselseitige Potenziale

Die vorliegende Befragung von Religionslehrer*innen gibt Hinweise darauf, dass es sich bei BNE und Compassion um zwei affine Konzepte handelt, die sich gegenseitig befruchten können. Es ist bemerkenswert, dass die Religionslehrer*innen beim Thema BNE den Beziehungsaspekt so stark in den Vordergrund rücken. So kann nach ihrer Wahrnehmung im Religionsunterricht erlebt werden, wie gutes Miteinander und wertschätzender Umgang gelingen können. Die Religionslehrer*innen wollen zudem Vorbilder hinsichtlich eines nachhaltigen Handelns sein und Schüler*innen zeigen, wie sie respektvoll miteinander umgehen. Dazu gehört auch, dass die Religionslehrer*innen nicht versuchen, ein perfektes Bild von sich zu zeigen, sondern offen auch gegenüber den Schüler*innen eingestehen, wenn es z. B. nicht gelingt, einen nachhaltigen Lebensstil zu verfolgen. Auf diese Weise wird soziales Lernen im Religionsunterricht erlebbar. Dieses soziale Lernen kann durch die Berücksichtigung von Compassion eine spezifische Tiefenschärfe erhalten, indem die Augen nicht vor dem Leid von Mitschüler*innen, Familie, Freund*innen oder eben von kranken, alten, armen oder beeinträchtigten Menschen verschlossen werden. Darüber hinaus argumentieren befragte Religionslehrer*innen, dass Schüler*innen vor allem oder gerade im Religionsunterricht erfahren, dass sie eine Verantwortung tragen, an einer guten Zukunft für alle mitzuarbeiten. Dies wird nicht selten mit Bezugnahme auf die Schöpfungserzählungen begründet. Jedoch könnte an dieser Stelle gleichfalls weiterführend mit Compassion argumentiert werden: Die universelle Verantwortung für eine gute Zukunft wird in der Compassion-Perspektive mit der Universalität des Leidens begründet.

Genau an diesem Punkt kommen jedoch auch Potenziale in den Blick, welche BNE für das Compassion-Projekt bereithält. Der Fokus und die Stärke von Compassion liegen auf der mitmenschlichen Ebene. Diese steht von frühen religionspädagogischen Publikationen[16] bis hin zu jüngeren[17] im Vordergrund. Demgegenüber kann durch BNE auch für die Dimension von Mensch und Mitwelt sensibilisiert werden, d.h. für das Leid von Tieren sowie durch die von Umweltzerstörung verursachten Leiden. Somit können BNE und Compassion als zwei Konzepte verstanden werden, die sich ungeachtet ihrer verschiedenen Ursprünge wechselseitig hinsichtlich einer lebenswerten Zukunft sowie einer entsprechenden Bildung ergänzen und bestärken.

Literatur

De Haan, Gerhard: Gestaltungskompetenz als Kompetenzkonzept der Bildung für nachhaltige Entwicklung, in: Bormann, Inka / De Haan, Gerhard (Hg.): Kompetenzen der Bildung für nachhaltige Entwicklung. Operationalisierung, Messung, Rahmenbedingungen, Befunde, Wiesbaden: VS Verlag für Sozialwissenschaften, 2008, 23–44.

Kuld, Lothar: Dimensionen der Compassion-Initiative, in: Metz, Johann Baptist / Kuld, Lothar / Weisbrod, Adolf (Hg.): Compassion. Weltprogramm des Christentums. Soziale Verantwortung lernen, Freiburg im Breisgau: Herder, 2000, 89–94.

Kuld, Lothar: Art. Compassion, in: WiReLex Online. https://www.bibelwissenschaft.de/stichwort/100124/ (zuletzt aufgerufen am 16.03.2023)

Metz, Johann Baptist: Compassion. Zu einem Weltprogramm des Christentums im Zeitalter des Pluralismus der Religionen und Kulturen, in: Metz, Johann Baptist / Kuld, Lothar / Weisbrod, Adolf (Hg.): Compassion. Weltprogramm des Christentums. Soziale Verantwortung lernen, Freiburg im Breisgau: Herder, 2000, 9–18.

Metz, Johann Baptist / Kuld, Lothar / Weisbrod, Adolf (Hg.): Compassion. Weltprogramm des Christentums. Soziale Verantwortung lernen, Freiburg im Breisgau: Herder, 2000.

Rekus, Jürgen: Compassion – ein erlebnisbezogenes Bildungskonzept, in: Metz, Johann Baptist / Kuld, Lothar / Weisbrod, Adolf (Hg.): Compassion. Weltprogramm des Christentums. Soziale Verantwortung lernen, Freiburg im Breisgau: Herder, 2000, 75–88.

UNESCO: Education for sustainable development goals: Learning objectives, in: https://unesdoc.unesco.org/ark:/48223/pf0000247444 [abgerufen am 17.03.2023].

Weisbrod, Adolf: Ein Pilotprojket. Genese, Besonderheiten, Ziele, in: Metz, Johann Baptist / Kuld, Lothar / Weisbrod, Adolf (Hg.): Compassion. Weltprogramm des Christentums. Soziale Verantwortung lernen, Freiburg im Breisgau: Herder, 2000, 97–100.

Wiek, Arnim / Withycombe, Lauren / Redman, Charles L.: Key competencies in sustainability. a reference framework for academic program development, in: Sustainability Science 6/2 (2011) 203–218. DOI: https://doi.org/10.1007/s11625-011-0132-6.

16 Vgl. Metz / Kuld / Weisbrod (2000) [Anm. 1].

17 Vgl. Kuld, Lothar: Art. Compassion, in: WiReLex Online. https://www.bibelwissenschaft.de/stichwort/100124/ (zuletzt aufgerufen am 16.03.2023)

Frühstück im Dunkeln – Nachhaltige Gestaltung der Zukunft durch compathische Vermittlung im islamischen Religionsunterricht

Mevlida Mešanović

Der Islam lehrt Muslim*innen, Werte wie Liebe, Frieden und Barmherzigkeit zu verkörpern. Barmherzigkeit umfasst die gesamte Schöpfung und nimmt als Thema im islamischen Religionsunterricht einen wichtigen Platz ein. Unterrichtsprojekte können die Entwicklung von Barmherzigkeit bei den Lernenden beeinflussen und präformieren. In einem Salzburger Gymnasium wurde im Rahmen des islamischen Religionsunterrichts das Projekt *Frühstück im Dunkeln* durchgeführt. Um seine nachhaltige Wirkung zu ermitteln, fand nach einigen Jahren ein Gespräch mit den Lernenden statt, um zu erfahren, ob und was dieses Projekt bei ihnen bewirkt hat.

Islamischer Religionsunterricht; Compassion; Barmherzigkeit; Mitgefühl; Mitleid; Nachhaltigkeit

Islam teaches Muslims to embody values such as love, peace, and mercy. Mercy encompasses all of creation and occupies an important place as a theme in Islamic religious education. Teaching projects can influence and shape the development of mercy in learners. In a Salzburg grammar school, the project Breakfast in the Dark was carried out as part of Islamic religious education. To determine its lasting effect, a discussion was held with the learners after a few years to find out whether and what effect this project had on them.

Islamic religious education; compassion; mercy; sustainability

Einleitung

Gegenwärtig steht die Menschheit vor vielen Herausforderungen wie Krisen, Kriege, Migration und sozialer Distanzierung. Tagtäglich begegnen uns mannigfache Bilder in den Medien, die das Leid der Menschen bezeugen. Um damit umzugehen, muss der Mensch bestimmte Haltungen entwickeln, um seinem Gegenüber barmherzig, mit Mitleid und Mitgefühl zu begegnen und ihm zu helfen. Viele Menschen sehnen sich nach Mitgefühl, aber nicht jeder handelt mitfühlend oder barmherzig, und wenn, dann beschränkt er sich oft auf ihm nahestehende Personen. Einer / Einem völlig Fremden Mitleid oder Mitgefühl entgegenzubringen, erscheint vielen als unmöglich, wenn nicht gar absurd. Mit der Erkenntnis, dass die Gesellschaft, mit der sich jeder Mensch identifiziert, versagt hat und nicht dem Ideal und Vorstellungen einer solidarischen Gesellschaft entspricht, vermeiden viele Menschen „gezielt den Blick auf die Leidenden bzw. den von Schmerz gekennzeichneten, der an den Rand gedrängt ist, weil sie ihre eigene Beschämung vermeiden wollen."[1]

Paul Gilbert und Choden untersuchten das Mitgefühl[2] gestützt auf die Bindungstheorie von John Bowlby, dessen Forschungen feststellten, dass die liebevolle Zuwendung der Mutter sich auf die Entwicklung des Mitgefühls des Säuglings auswirkt und auch noch im späteren Leben des Erwachsenen fortwirkt.[3] Carolyn Zahn-Waxler von der University of Wisconsin wollte herausfinden, ab welchem Alter – und wie – Kleinkinder auf eine*n Familienangehörigen reagieren, der „Aua!" ruft oder vorgibt zu weinen. Sie kam zum Ergebnis, dass bereits Einjährige versuchen, Trost zu spenden, bzw. dass sich bei ihnen Mitgefühl entfaltet.[4] Auf die Entwicklung des Mitgefühls wirkt sich vor allem die Umgebung aus, in welcher Kinder aufwachsen, bzw. das Verhalten der Eltern und Erziehungsberechtigten.[5]

Beim Mitgefühl handelt es sich nicht, wie der deutsche Begriff nahelegt, um ein temporäres oder gar flüchtiges und nur von äußeren Umständen ausgelöstes Gefühl, sondern vielmehr um eine stabile psychische Kompetenz, die dauerhaft gebildet und zu einer Seinsweise des Individuums werden kann.[6] Mitgefühl ist für unser Überleben unverzichtbar. Jeder Mensch ist in der Lage es zu bilden, denn es zählt zu den zentralen Dimensionen der menschlichen Entwicklung.[7]

Beunruhigend sind jedoch Statistiken der OECD[8] in einer Studie von 2015. Dieser zufolge waren 11% aller jungen Menschen zwischen 11 und 15 Jahren im

---

1 Mierzwa, Roland: Compassion – Zwischen Mit-Leid, Mitgefühl und Barmherzigkeit, Hamburg: Verlag Dr. Kovač, 2014, 363.

2 Gilbert, Paul / Choden: Achtsames Mitgefühl. Ein kraftvoller Weg, das Leben zu verwandeln, Freiburg in Breisgau: Arbor Verlag, 2014.

3 Bowlby, John: Über das Wesen der Mutter-Kind-Bindung, in: Psyche 13 (1958), 415–456.

4 Vgl. Maayan, Davidov / Zahn-Waxler, Carolyn / Roth-Hanania, Ronit / Knafo, Ariel: Concern for Others in the First Year of Life. Theory, Evidence, and Avenues for Research, in: The Society for Research in Child Development 7 (2), 2013, 126–131.

5 Ulrich, Dieter / Kienbaum, Jutta / Volland, Cordelia: Empathie mit anderen entwickeln. Wie entwickelt sich Mitgefühl, in: von Salisch, Maria (Hg.): Emotionale Kompetenz entwickeln. Grundlagen in Kindheit und Jugend, Stuttgart: Kohlhammer, 2002, 113.

6 Vgl. Singer, Tania / Bolz, Matthias (Hg.): Mitgefühl. In Alltag und Forschung, München: Max-Planck-Gesellschaft, 2013, Online unter: www.compassion-training.org/?lang=de (abgerufen am 07.03.2023).

7 Vgl. Schloßberger, Matthias: Das Mitgefühl als Gefühl, in: Bermes, Christian / Henckmann, Wofhart / Leonardy, Heinz (Hg.): Vernunft und Gefühl. Schelers Phänomenologie des emotionalen Lebens, Würzburg: Königshausen & Neumann. 2003, 41.

8 Vgl. Organisation für wirtschaftliche Zusammenarbeit und Entwicklung (OECD): Skills for Social Progress. The Power of Social and Emotional Skills, Paris, 2015. Veröffentlicht in der OECD I Library. Abrufbar unter: http://dx.doi.org/10.1787/9789264226159-en (abgerufen am 07.03.2023).

Untersuchungsjahr 2010 Opfer von Mobbing.[9] Österreich war laut diesem Bericht mit einem Wert von 21% negativer Spitzenreiter. Nach einem WHO-Bericht zur Gesundheit junger Menschen in Europa[10] haben 10 bis 20% der Heranwachsenden mentale Probleme, knapp 8% der untersuchten 12- bis 17-Jährigen leiden unter Verhaltensstörungen, 4% unter Depressionen und bei 4,4% wurde eine Aufmerksamkeitsstörung (ADHS) diagnostiziert. Menschen mit diesen Schwächen sind auch im Bildungssystem präsent, ihre Beeinträchtigungen werden nicht selten zum Grund von Mobbing und wirken sich negativ auf den Lehrberuf aus, manchmal mit fatalen Folgen beim Lehrpersonal.[11] Da diese Berichte nicht gerade erfreulich sind, stellt sich die Frage: Wie sieht es mit der Compassion und deren Entwicklung im Bildungsbereich aus? Wie können junge Menschen bei sich Compassion entwickeln und dadurch zu einem besseren Miteinander in der Schule und zugleich in der Gesellschaft beitragen?

Dem schottischen Pädagogen David McMurtry zufolge müssen Lehrende und Lernende dringend die Fähigkeit entwickeln, achtsam und mitfühlend mit sich selbst und anderen umzugehen. Compassion kann bei Schüler*innen durch das Curriculum im Rahmen der sozialen, religiösen und moralischen Bildung gefördert werden. Positive Vorbilder, ein ganzheitlicher Schulansatz und die Wertschätzung für Achtsamkeit sind wichtige Treiber.[12]

Compassion aus islamischer Perspektive

Die Botschaft Gottes an die Muslim*innen und zugleich die primäre Quelle des Islam – der Qur'an[13] – enthält viel mehr als Gebote und Verbote. Wer bereit ist, unter die Oberfläche zu blicken, sich in den Qur'anischen Text zu vertiefen und genauer hinzusehen, wird feststellen, dass der Qur'an über universelle Werte wie Liebe, Mitgefühl, Frieden und Wohlwollen lehrt und eine Fülle von Stellen

---

9 Gemeint sind sowohl Mobbing als auch Bullying – Mobbing in der Schule unter Gleichaltrigen.

10 Vgl. World Health Organization: A Snapshot of the Health of Young People in Europe. Brussels 2009. A report prepared for the European Commission Conference on Youth Health, Brussels, Belgium 9–10 July 2009.

11 Wie die Tageszeitung The Independent berichtet, liegt die Selbstmordrate unter britischen Grundschullehrer*innen um 42% höher als beim Durchschnitt der Bevölkerung.

12 Vgl. McMurtry, David: Compassion in Education, in: Pädagogik der Achtsamkeit. Abrufbar unter: https://bit.ly/3ZHb3jW (abgerufen am 07.03.2023).

13 Für diese Arbeit wurde die Übersetzung von Bubenheim & Elyas herangezogen. Im weiteren Text sind an manchen Stellen nur die Suren- und Verszahlen angeführt, z. B. 49:13.

mit dem Begriff Barmherzigkeit enthält. Der Qur'anische Text weist immer wieder auf die schwächeren Teile der Gesellschaft hin, zu denen er unter anderem Waisen, Witwen, Arme und Ausgebeutete, Sklav*innen und andere politisch, sozial und wirtschaftlich unterdrückte Gruppen zählt. Der Qur'an betont verschiedene Möglichkeiten, den betroffenen Gruppen zu helfen, in erster Linie durch die Barmherzigkeit.

Im Qur'an wird Gottes Barmherzigkeit sehr deutlich betont. In Vers 12 aus Sure 6 verpflichtet Gott sich sogar selbst zu dieser Eigenschaft. Versucht man, den englischen Begriff Compassion[14] zu übersetzen, kann das mit den Worten „mitfühlendes Mitleid und Anteilnahme an den Leiden oder dem Unglück anderer"[15] erfolgen. Aus der islamischen Perspektive betrachtet, kann die Compassion zu den Kernpunkten des Islam gezählt und als Rahma definiert werden; ein Begriff, für den verschiedene Synonyme parallel bestehen, wie Barmherzigkeit / Mitgefühl / Mitleid.[16]

Mit Rahma wird eine Art von Sanftmut und Zärtlichkeit bezeichnet, die in einem den Drang weckt, anderen gegenüber Güte zu zeigen – zu ihnen barmherzig zu sein. Eine der Suren[17] im Qur'an heißt ar-Rahman – *der Barmherzige*. Dieser Begriff ist bezeichnenderweise ein Attribut Gottes und weist darauf hin, dass Gottes Barmherzigkeit und Mitgefühl alle Aspekte Seiner Schöpfung umfassen.[18] Die Muslim*innen werden dazu ermutigt, Basmala (*Mit Namen Gottes, des Allerbarmers, des Barmherzigen)* zu rezitieren, bevor sie eine Handlung beginnen. Dies soll sie daran erinnern, die göttlichen Werte der Barmherzigkeit in sich selbst und in jeder ihrer Handlungen zu verkörpern.[19] In einem Vers des Qur'ans teilt Gott den Menschen mit, dass Er sich selbst das Gesetz der Barmherzigkeit auferlegt hat,[20] und fordert die Menschen dazu auf, nicht an seiner Barmherzigkeit zu zweifeln.[21]

Der Qur'an erkennt an, dass der Prophet Muhammad einen erhabenen Charakter[22] und ein vorbildhaftes Verhalten besitzt, wodurch er für die Muslim*innen zum Vorbild wird; so sind sie aufgefordert, nach seinem Vorbild

14 Domsel, Maike Maria: Zwischen Vulnerabilität und Resilienz. Christliche und muslimische Religionslehrer*innen im Umgang mit dem Krisenhaften, in: ÖRF 30(2) (2022), 72–90, hier 77.

15 International Journal of the Malay World and Civilisation (Iman) 4(2), 2016, 103–110. http://dx.doi.org/10.17576/IMAN-2016-0402-10 (abgerufen am 08.03.2023).

16 Dieser Artikel verwendet die Begriffe Rahma/Barmherzigkeit/Mitgefühl/Mitleid synonym mit Compassion.

17 Teile/Kapitel im Qur'an.

18 Sura 7, Vers 156.

19 Vgl. Shah-Kazemi, Reza: My Mercy Encompasses All. The Qur'an's Teachings on Compassion, Peace and Love, Catapult, 2007.

20 Sura 6, Vers 12.

21 Sura 39, Vers 53.

22 Sura 68, Vers 4.

Barmherzigkeit im Umgang mit sich selbst, mit anderen, aber auch mit der gesamten Schöpfung zu zeigen. Dass die Barmherzigkeit allen Menschen gegenüber zu erbringen ist, deutet auch die Sure 80 an.[23] In ihr zögert Gott nicht, Muhammad zu tadeln, als er seine Stirn runzelte und sich von einem blinden Mann, der zu ihm kam, abwandte.[24] Dies weist darauf hin, dass alle Menschen, unabhängig von ihrem Aussehen, ihrer Herkunft, ihrer religiösen Zugehörigkeit oder ihrer Weltanschauung, gleichbehandelt werden sollen.

Die Lebensbeschreibung des Propheten Muhammad – die Sunna – enthält unzählige seiner Aussagen und Handlungen, die über Barmherzigkeit zwischen den Menschen berichten und als Erweiterung anderer ethischer Imperative gelten.[25] Sowohl der Qur'an als auch die Sunna verstehen Barmherzigkeit nicht nur als den Menschen gegenüber anzuwenden, sondern auch gegenüber Tieren und der gesamten Schöpfung. Ein oft zitierter Ausspruch Muhammads lautet: „Seid barmherzig zu den Bewohnern der Erde, und Er, der im Himmel ist, wird barmherzig zu euch sein."[26] Diese und ähnliche Aussagen zeigen, dass die Qur'anische Grundlage der Barmherzigkeit und des Mitgefühls im Charakter Muhammads selbst zu finden ist.

Fünf Säulen und Compassion

Hinsichtlich der fünf Säulen ist Compassion ein zentrales Konzept im Islam, tief in den Lehren und Praktiken der Religion verwurzelt und in verschiedenen Aspekten der islamischen Praxis betont. Durch das Verständnis und die Praxis der Fünf Säulen, in Verbindung mit weiteren ethischen Werten, können Muslim*innen ihre Beziehung zu Gott und ihren Mitmenschen vertiefen und ihr Leben auf eine Weise führen, die Rahma fördert. Die fünf Säulen des Islam basieren auf Barmherzigkeit, in erster Linie auf Barmherzigkeit mit sich selbst (durch das Glaubensbekenntnis und das rituelle Gebet), gefolgt von Barmherzigkeit mit den Menschen und Geschöpfen um sich (durch Zakat,[27] Fasten, Pilgerfahrt oder durch die Entrichtung von Sadaka – Almosen).

Das Glaubensbekenntnis betont die Bedeutung der Einheit und des Friedens und erinnert daran, dass alle Menschen gleich sind, während Gott der einzige

---

23 Mehr dazu in: BADAWIA, Tarik: Gewissheitsparadoxie. Eine antinomische Struktur des Lehrerhandelns im islmischen Religionsunterricht, in: SARIKAYA, Yaşar / AYGÜN, Adem (Hg.): Islamische Religionspädagogik. Leitfragen aus Theorie, Empirie und Praxis, Münster/New York: Waxman, 2019, 109–125.

24 Qur'an 80:1–10.

25 ḤAMMĀDĪ, ʿAlī Muḥammad al-Shurafāʾ: Message of Islam. Compassion, Justice, Freedom and Peace. Toronto: Scansom Publishers, 2017.

26 MEMIĆ, Jakub: Izbor Poslanikovih hadisa, Sarajevo, 1985, 132.

27 Jährliche Pflichtabgabe, eine der fünf Säulen im Islam.

Herrscher über alle ist. *Das rituelle Gebet* wird fünf Mal am Tag ausgeführt und dient dazu, die Beziehung zwischen dem Menschen und Gott zu stärken, um so sein Bewusstsein für seine Mitmenschen und ihre Bedürfnisse zu erhöhen. Während des Gebets werden die Praktizierenden daran erinnert, dass sie Teil einer größeren Gemeinschaft sind und ihre Handlungen und Entscheidungen Auswirkungen auf andere haben können. Das Gebet kann auch in Gemeinschaft erfolgen. In diesem Rahmen beten Menschen für sich selbst und auch für andere, die in Not oder Leid sind. *Der Fastenmonat Ramadan* ist eine Zeit der Barmherzigkeit, in der die Muslim*innen nicht nur auf Essen und Trinken verzichten, sich auf ihre spirituelle Praxis konzentrieren, Gemeinschaft pflegen und ihre Beziehung zu Gott vertiefen, sondern eine Zeit, in der die Muslim*innen besonders ermutigt werden, barmherzig und großzügig zu sein und ihre Zeit und weitere Ressourcen mit anderen Menschen zu teilen. *Die Zakat* dient dazu, den Armen und Bedürftigen in der Gemeinschaft zu helfen, aber auch Mitgefühl und Barmherzigkeit zu fördern, indem sie die Menschen dazu anspornt, sich um andere zu kümmern, ihre Bedürfnisse zu erkennen und zu erfüllen. *Die Pilgerfahrt nach Mekka (Hadsch)* betont die Bedeutung von Einheit und Geschwisterlichkeit in der Gemeinschaft und kann dazu beitragen, das Verständnis und die Wertschätzung anderer Kulturen und Religionen zu fördern und Barmherzigkeit ihnen gegenüber zu verstärken.

Die Praktiken der fünf Säulen des Islam sowie die Betonung von Mitgefühl und Fürsorge für andere bilden eine wertbeständige Grundlage zur Ausübung von Barmherzigkeit im täglichen Leben. Indem die Muslim*innen die Prinzipien der Barmherzigkeit in ihre religiöse Praktiken (gemeint sind sowohl tägliche als auch die Praktiken die jährlich oder ein Mal im Leben durchgeführt werden) einbeziehen, können sie eine tiefere spirituelle Verbindung herstellen und gleichzeitig dazu beitragen, das Wohl und die Unterstützung von Menschen in Not zu fördern.

Zusammenfassend kann gesagt werden, dass die fünf Säulen des Islam und der Wert von Rahma eng miteinander verbunden sind und zusammen dazu beitragen können, eine Gesellschaft zu schaffen, die auf Frieden, Verständnis, Akzeptanz und Solidarität basiert.

Compassion im Lehrplan für islamischen Religionsunterricht

Wie kann aber die Compassion bei Heranwachsenden unterstützt und gefördert werden? Der Lehrplan für den islamischen Religionsunterricht (IRU) in Österreich sieht vor, das Thema Barmherzigkeit zu erörtern und die Schüler*innen bei der Entwicklung der Barmherzigkeit / Compassion zu unterstützen. Das

Thema zieht sich durch alle Schulstufen und wird sukzessive behandelt, beginnend mit der Barmherzigkeit zu sich selbst, zur Schöpfung – Natur, Tiere, Menschen in der Umgebung, Menschen insgesamt, zu Gott. So lässt sich auch Verantwortung auf die jungen Heranwachsenden übertragen und sie für barmherziges Handeln sensibilisieren.[28]

Als ein wichtiger religiöser Aspekt wird die Barmherzigkeit als zentrales Element der Ethik und Moral im Islam behandelt.[29] Den Schüler*innen wird vermittelt, dass die Barmherzigkeit Gottes keine Grenzen kennt und es immer Hoffnung und Vergebung gibt. Außerdem wird betont, dass Muslim*innen selbst Barmherzigkeit gegenüber anderen Geschöpfen Gottes zu erbringen haben, da dies ein wichtiger Teil des Glaubens ist. Der Lehrplan für IRU bezieht sich unter anderem konkret auf Barmherzigkeit gegenüber den Erziehungsberechtigten, der Schöpfung, den Mitmenschen, im Umgang mit Tieren sowie mit sich selbst. Ferner wird auf die karmische Folge von Barmherzigkeit mit der Aussage von Muhammad hingewiesen: „Wer nicht barmherzig ist, dem wird Barmherzigkeit nicht zuteil."[30]

Für die kindliche Entwicklung und die Stärkung des Selbstbewusstseins ist es wichtig sicherzustellen, dass das Kind geliebt wird – von den Eltern, von Freunden, von Lehrer*innen, aber auch von Gott. So wird bereits in der ersten Schulstufe versucht, den Schüler*innen ein positives und liebevolles Bild von Gott zu vermitteln und auf Gottes Barmherzigkeit hinzuweisen. In weiterer Folge nimmt die zwischenmenschliche Compassion im Lehrplan einen prominenten Platz ein. Hier sind Beziehungen in der Familie, im Freundeskreis und in der Ehe inkludiert.[31] Um das Thema Barmherzigkeit durch verschiedene Schulstufen zu verfolgen und didaktisch aufzubereiten, werden unter anderem auch Verse aus dem Qur'an[32] oder Aussagen des Propheten Muhammad[33] angeführt.

Mittels dieser verschiedenen Ansätze können die Schüler*innen lernen, wie wichtig Barmherzigkeit im Islam ist und wie man sie im Alltag praktiziert. Sie lernen, wie man barmherzig mit anderen umgeht, wie ein barmherziger Umgang mit der gesamten Schöpfung und mit sich selbst aussieht. Letztendlich soll dies dazu beitragen, dass die Schüler*innen positive Werte und Tugenden entwickeln und zu barmherzigen Menschen werden, die sich für eine gerechtere und barmherzigere Welt einsetzen.

---

28 Vgl. Lehrplan für islamischen Religionsunterricht, in: https://bit.ly/3NPBMGn (abgerufen am 09.03.2023).
29 Vgl. Ebd. (abgerufen am 07.03.2023).
30 Ebd., in: 17. (abgerufen am 07.03.2023).
31 Ebd., 75. (abgerufen am 12.03.2023)
32 Vgl. Ebd., 111–130. (abgerufen am 21.03.2023)
33 Vgl. Ebd., 136–138. (abgerufen am 25.03.2023)

Entwicklung von Compassion im islamischen Religionsunterricht

Gegenwärtig wird Compassion auf vielen Ebenen zu einem zentralen Element von Bildung und Schule – als Bildungsziel, als Inhalt evaluierter Curricula, als Grundlage von Schulkultur und Klassenklima, als zentrale sozial-emotionale Kompetenz von Lehrer*innen, als Kern der pädagogischen Beziehung sowie als Kern des didaktischen Prinzips des *contemplative teaching*. Es ist daher nicht übertrieben zu sagen: Mitgefühl ist das Herz der Schule, sowohl im direkten emotionalen als auch im übertragenen strukturellen Sinn. Da der Islam die Werte des Mitgefühls und der Barmherzigkeit vermittelt und eine positive Einstellung gegenüber anderen Menschen fördert, kann der IRU zur Entwicklung von Compassion einen wichtigen Beitrag leisten.

Der IRU betont die Bedeutung von Mitgefühl und Barmherzigkeit als zentrale Werte und Praktiken im Islam und trägt zu ihrer Entwicklung bei, indem er den Schüler*innen ein Verständnis für die Diversität und die verschiedenen Lebensweisen anderer Menschen vermittelt. Ethische Grundsätze wie Respekt, Toleranz, Akzeptanz, Verantwortungsbewusstsein und Verständnis für andere Kulturen und Religionen spielen dabei eine wichtige Rolle.

Der IRU lehrt, wie Barmherzigkeit gegenüber anderen Menschen aussieht, unabhängig von ihrem Glauben, ihrer Herkunft und Nationalität. Dabei entwickeln die Schüler*innen die Kompetenzen, die sie brauchen, um anderen helfen und auf deren Bedürfnisse eingehen zu können. Ein weiterer wichtiger Aspekt, auf den der IRU zurückgreift, ist Barmherzigkeit gegenüber der Umwelt. In diesem Rahmen lernen die Schüler*innen, wie sie die Natur und die Umwelt respektieren und für eine nachhaltige Zukunft arbeiten können.

Der Unterricht zielt darauf ab, die Schüler*innen zu barmherzigen Menschen zu erziehen, die in der Lage sind, im täglichen Leben Handlungen in Rahma zu vollbringen und so ein positives Beispiel für ihre Gemeinschaft zu sein. Die Vermittlung von Barmherzigkeit im IRU erfolgt auf verschiedene Weise und kann je nach Lehrplan und Lehrmethode variieren.

Im Allgemeinen versuchen die Lehrkräfte jedoch, ihre Schüler*innen durch praktische Übungen und Reflexion zum Verständnis und zur Anwendung von

Barmherzigkeit im Alltag zu führen. Hierfür eignen sich Rollenspiele[34] oder Geschichten und Beispiele aus dem Leben früherer Generationen.[35] Vor allem eignen sich Gemeinschaftsprojekte zur Entwicklung von Compassion, wie Compassion-Projekte[36] Barmherzigkeits-Clubs, Barmherzigkeits-Wettbewerbe, Barmherzigkeits-Workshops, Barmherzigkeits-Partnerschaften etc. Die Gemeinschaftsprojekte ermöglichen den Schüler*innen die Teilnahme an Wohltätigkeitsaktionen, um Bedürftigen zu helfen, oder an Umweltprojekten, um die Schöpfung zu schützen. Beispielsweise können Schulprojekte, bei denen die Schüler*innen in Gemeindezentren oder Krankenhäusern mithelfen oder an Spendensammlungen teilnehmen, dazu beitragen, dass sie ein Verständnis dafür entwickeln, wie sie anderen helfen und Mitgefühl und Barmherzigkeit nachhaltig praktizieren können. Der IRU kann Compassion betonen, um den Schüler*innen ein tieferes Verständnis für andere Menschen zu vermitteln, sodass sie ihnen auf eine barmherzige und mitfühlende Weise begegnen.

Die Lehrkräfte nutzen alle diese Methoden, um die Entwicklung der Compassion bei ihren Schüler*innen anzubahnen und sie für die Schöpfung zu sensibilisieren.

Zusammenfassend lässt sich sagen, dass Barmherzigkeit ein wichtiger Bestandteil des IRU ist, indem die Schüler*innen lernen, wie sie barmherzig gegenüber Gott, anderen Menschen und der Umwelt sein können. Dieses Vorgehen kann im Rahmen unterschiedlicher Projekte erfolgen, die sich zur nachhaltigen Entwicklung des Mitgefühls eignen. Darunter können etwa Besuche von Veranstaltungen passenden Charakters, von Blinden- oder Flüchtlingsheimen etc. fallen.

Schulprojekt *Frühstück im Dunkeln*

Um die nachhaltige Entwicklung von Compassion bei Schüler*innen zu fördern, wurde in einem Salzburger Gymnasium mit 11 Schüler*innen der 3A Klasse im Rahmen des IRU ein nahe gelegenes Blindenheim besucht, um sich dort mit dem

---

[34] Die Schüler*innen spielen in Rollenspielen verschiedene Situationen durch, in denen Barmherzigkeit gefragt ist. Sie lernen, wie man barmherzig mit einem kranken oder älteren Familienmitglied umgeht oder wie man einem Mitschüler*innen hilft, der Schwierigkeiten hat und auf die Hilfe seiner Mitmenschen angewiesen ist.

[35] Die Lehrkräfte können Geschichten und Beispiele aus dem Leben des Propheten Muhammad oder anderer muslimischer Persönlichkeiten erzählen, um den Schüler*innen zu zeigen, wie Barmherzigkeit im Leben praktiziert wird. Sie können auch aktuelle Ereignisse oder Nachrichten nutzen, um Beispiele zu geben, wie Barmherzigkeit in der heutigen Welt aussieht.

[36] Vgl. KULD, Lothar / GÖNNHEIMER, Stefan: Compassion – Sozialverpflichtetes Lernen und Handeln, Stuttgart/Berlin/Köln: Kohlhammer, 2000.

Alltag sehbeeinträchtigter und blinder Menschen bekannt zu machen, ihre Herausforderungen wahrzunehmen und mit ihnen gemeinsam im Dunkeln zu frühstücken.

Die Erfahrung hat gezeigt, dass Besuche solcher Einrichtungen und Gespräche mit den Bewohnern das Bewusstsein für die Bedürfnisse betroffener Gruppen bei Schüler*innen schärfen und sie zugleich eine andere Perspektive auf das Leben bekommen: Wie Menschen mit Einschränkungen leben und welche Herausforderungen sie haben. Dies kann zu einem tieferen Verständnis für Inklusion, Respekt und Akzeptanz führen, was wiederum eine nachhaltige Wirkung auf die Schüler*innen haben kann.

Dieser Besuch hat ihnen einen Raum eröffnet, in dem sie begannen, ihre Verhaltensweisen und Einstellungen zu überdenken und mehr Mitgefühl in ihr tägliches Leben zu integrieren. Darüber hinaus führte dieser Besuch dazu, dass die Schüler*innen sich für soziale Projekte und Aktivitäten engagierten, die dazu beitrugen, künftig das Leben von Menschen mit besonderen Bedürfnissen zu verbessern. Das betrifft nicht nur den schulischen Kontext, sondern auch ihre private Umgebung.

Im Rahmen des Besuchs wurden alle Schüler*innen von einer blinden Person durch das Haus geführt und begleitet. Ihnen wurden Videos vorgespielt, die Räume und Geräte erklärt sowie Herausforderungen erläutert, denen sie in ihrem Alltag begegnen. Als besonders herausfordernd erwies sich für alle Schüler*innen die Aufgabe, die Straße mit einer Binde vor den Augen und einem Blindenstock in der Hand zu überqueren. Anschließend wurde für alle Anwesenden das Frühstück in einem dunklen Raum vorbereitet, um ihnen einen weiteren Einblick in den Alltag blinder Menschen anzubieten. Während des Frühstücks wurden die Teilnehmer*innen fotografiert. Nach der Ausarbeitung der Fotos stellte sich heraus, wie machtlos und ungeschickt Menschen in für sie herausfordernden und unbekannten Situationen sind.

Im Nachhinein berichteten die Schüler*innen über unterschiedliche Erkenntnisse, Gedanken und Erfahrungen, die dieser Besuch bei ihnen ausgelöst hat. In den folgenden Unterrichtsstunden stand unverändert das Thema Menschen mit Beeinträchtigung im Mittelpunkt. Der Besuch hat mannigfache Fragen der Schüler*innen ausgelöst, die sie im Unterricht weiter erörtern wollten. Unter anderem kam Folgendes zur Sprache: die Fähigkeit, die gleichen Socken anzuziehen, Nägel schneiden, Bügeln, Kochen, Lebensmittel beim Einkauf unterscheiden und Reisen. Ferner beschäftigten sie sich mit Fragen wie: Wie stellen sie sich das Meer vor? Haben sie ein Gefühl für Farben? Was würden sie sich wünschen, wenn sie sehen könnten? Können sie träumen? usw. Es lässt sich festhalten, dass der Besuch bei ihnen etwas bewegt hat, was sie weiterhin beschäftigen wird.

Einführung ins Gespräch und Erkenntnisgewinn aus der Gruppendiskussion

Um herauszufinden, ob der Besuch den Schüler*innen in Erinnerung geblieben ist und sie nachhaltig beeinflusst hat, wurde ein Treffen organisiert. Da viele Schüler*innen nach dem Schulabschluss neue Wege eingeschlagen haben und in anderen Städten leben, trifft sich die Gruppe in einem kleineren Rahmen. Dabei sind Aliyah, Ilena, Leyan, Sara und Shirin.[37]

Die Annäherung an das Thema erfolgte mittels einer Gruppendiskussion. Ein Video eröffnete das Gespräch. Da es sich um junge Menschen handelt, die soziale Plattformen nutzen, wurde das Thema durch einen kurzen biographischen Film von blinden TikTokern[38] eingeleitet.

Schon die ersten Sekunden des Videos wurden von der Aussage Leyans „den kenne ich! Habe das Video schon gesehen" unterbrochen. Das Video habe sie „an den Besuch des Blindenheimes, im Rahmen des Religionsunterrichts, voll erinnert."

Die Gesprächsanalyse ergab, dass der Besuch des Blindenheims bei den Befragten vordergründig positiv konnotiert ist und sie das Projekt als interessant in Erinnerung behalten haben. Grundsätzlich tragen Projekte solcher Art mannigfache Potenziale in sich, was sich in den Aussagen der Teilnehmerinnen widerspiegelt. Im Folgenden wird auf einige Erkenntnisse aus der Gruppendiskussion eingegangen.

Der Besuch ist uns schwergefallen

Während des Abspielens des Videos erinnerte sich Aliyah an ihre Schulzeit, die „echt schön" gewesen sei; sie erinnere „sich gerne an diese." Ilena zufolge habe ihr der Religionsunterricht „immer Spaß bereitet", da sie nicht nur in „einem vertrauten Rahmen war, sondern vieles durch verschiedene Projekte gelernt hat" und das habe „sie im Prozess Erwachsenwerden stark geprägt." Dass das Thema bei ihnen noch aktuell ist, lässt sich aus Shirins Aussage folgern, denn sie erinnere sich „sehr gerne an den Besuch des Blindenheimes im Rahmen des IRU und an das Gesicht ihrer Schulfreundin nach dem Frühstück." Letztens habe sie „das Foto gefunden und in die Gruppe gepostet", worüber alle lachen mussten.

Laut Sara erfolgte das Projekt „vor langer Zeit und ich erinnere mich nicht so wirklich an alles, aber was in meiner Erinnerung geblieben ist, ist, dass wir

---

37 Hierbei handelt es sich um Pseudonyme – die Namen der Schülerinnen wurden anonymisiert.

38 Nikolaos zeigt das Leben eines blinden Menschen: https://www.youtube.com/watch?v=lShFO-1V8VU (abgerufen am 07.03.2023).

mit den Menschen dort gegessen haben, in der Dunkelheit, und das ist uns sehr schwergefallen." Der Wechsel vom Singular zum Plural deutet darauf hin, dass Sara sich nicht an alles erinnern kann, aber zugleich berichtet sie weiter über die Situation, jedoch die ganze Gruppe betreffend. *Schwergefallen* ist in dieser Aussage nicht klar definiert; es ist zu vermuten, dass ihnen das Essen in der Dunkelheit schwergefallen oder die Situation, in der sich Menschen befinden, nicht leichtgefallen ist sowie, dass sie damit überfordert waren. Diese Behauptung lässt sich aus Saras weiterem Bericht ableiten, denn in dieser Situation und „in diesem Raum stellte ich meine eigene Beeinträchtigung fest und wie machtlos ich gerade bin!" Hier ist festzuhalten, dass der besagte Besuch die Schüler*innen zum Nachdenken über das Leben in der Dunkelheit anspornte. Er konfrontierte sie mit ihrer Machtlosigkeit und Unsicherheit, wodurch bei ihnen Mitgefühl und Mitleid an die Oberfläche kamen. Möglicherweise hat dieses Ereignis auch die Entwicklung von Compassion bei Schüler*innen, deren Gefühl nicht gerade stark ausgeprägt ist, ausgelöst.

Wir fanden Blindenschrift faszinierend

Im Rahmen des Projekts ist auch über den Wissenszuwachs der Schüler*innen zu sprechen. Dies bezieht sich vornehmlich auf jene Informationen, die sie im Rahmen der Führung durch das Blindenheim erhielten. Dazu berichtet Sara, „da bei den Medikamenten, bei diesen Verpackungen, es gibt auch eine Blindenschrift und wir wussten früher nicht, was es ist, und das fanden wir halt damals auch voll faszinierend, dass sie dann selber erkennen können durch diese Blindenschrift auf den Verpackungen, welche Medikamente es sind. Also, selber erkennen ohne fremde Hilfe."

Diese Aussage macht deutlich, dass Begegnungen, in denen alle Teilnehmer*innen bereit und offen für die Welt des Gegenübers sind, gewinnbringend und lehrreich sein können. Sara ist *fasziniert* davon, dass die blinden Menschen selbstständig ihre Medikamente erkennen können, aber gleichzeitig auch davon, dass sie jetzt selber weiß, wofür die „Punkte auf den Verpackungen sind." Auf die Hilfe anderer angewiesen zu sein, deutet auf eine Art von Machtlosigkeit und Abhängigkeit hin. Alleine die Schrift zu erkennen und lesen zu können, verleiht ein gewisses Maß von Selbstständigkeit, was Sara *faszinierend* findet.

Saras Wortwahl deutet darauf hin, dass sie mit den blinden Menschen mitfühlt und ihnen gegenüber Mitleid empfindet. Auch wenn der Besuch schon lange her ist, schildert Sara bemerkenswerte Erinnerungen. Sie beschreibt verschiedene Situationen so emotional und deutlich, als ob sie sich erst gestern abgespielt haben, was schlussfolgern lässt, dass sich Sara mit dem Besuch lange danach auseinandergesetzt hat. Daher ist an dieser Stelle die Wichtigkeit der Gewährleistung einer angemessenen Planung und Vorbereitung der Schüler*innen und des Umgang damit im Nachhinein hervorzuheben. Wichtig ist nicht nur, die Schüler*innen auf den Besuch vorzubereiten, sondern auch auf die Erfahrung danach. Die Beeinträchtigungen anderer können für sie emotional belastend sein, daher ist es wertvoll, sich im Unterricht damit auseinanderzusetzen und die Schüler*innen auf die Begegnung adäquat vorzubereiten.

Meine Eltern achten seitdem darauf, wo sie ihr Auto parken

Das Prinzip des Mitgefühls liegt im Zentrum aller religiösen, ethischen und spirituellen Traditionen und ruft die Menschen dazu auf, alle anderen immer so zu behandeln, wie sie selbst behandelt werden möchten. Mitgefühl drängt uns dazu, unermüdlich daran zu arbeiten, das Leiden unserer Mitgeschöpfe zu lindern, uns nicht als Zentrum der Welt zu verstehen und dort etwas anderes zu platzieren, die unantastbare Heiligkeit jedes einzelnen Menschen zu ehren und jeden ausnahmslos mit absoluter Gerechtigkeit, Gleichheit und Respekt zu behandeln.

Durch das Erleben von Dingen aus der Perspektive von Menschen mit Sehbehinderungen haben die Schüler*innen auch ein besseres Verständnis für die Bedürfnisse und Einschränkungen betroffener Menschen entwickelt. Sie haben gelernt, wie sie helfen können, Hindernisse und Barrieren für Menschen mit Behinderungen abzubauen und somit einen Beitrag zu einer inklusiven Gesellschaft zu leisten. So habe der Besuch Shirin

> „mitgenommen, und ich habe meinen Eltern darüber berichtet. Sie haben auch all das, was wir im Blindenheim erfahren haben, nicht gewusst. Bei unserem nächsten Spaziergang habe ich sie halt auf einen Punkt aufmerksam gemacht; Darauf bin ich echt stolz. Ich habe ihnen beigebracht, was es für einen blinden Menschen heißt, wenn die Linie[39] auf dem Gehsteig unterbrochen wird; dass sie nämlich mit ihrem Blindenstock nicht mehr tasten können und nicht genau wissen, in welche Richtung sollen sie weitergehen. Sie waren echt sprachlos, als ich ihnen dies erzählte. Seitdem achten sie selber darauf, wo sie ihr Auto abstellen, und voll lustig, sie machen auch die anderen darauf aufmerksam. Das finde ich echt klasse."

Wie aus dieser Aussage ersichtlich ist, hat der Besuch des Blindenheims bei den Schüler*innen auf ihren Alltag eingewirkt und ihn beeinflusst, wenn auch nicht verändert. Anhand ihrer Berichte ist wahrzunehmen, wie sorgfältig sie darauf achten, dass der für beeinträchtigte Menschen vorgesehene Platz an den Bushaltestellen freibleibt. Leyan, die täglich die Straßenbahn nutzt, ist ebenfalls darauf sensibilisiert. Das geht so weit, dass sie ihre „Bekannten, aber auch andere Menschen" ermahne, wenn sie am Gehsteig etwas abstellen und somit die Blindenstocklinie unterbrechen. Mit der Frage „Wie soll der arme Mensch den Weg

---

39 Gemeint sind Leitstreifen bzw. Bodenleitsysteme, die blinden und sehbeeinträchtigten Menschen helfen, sich mithilfe des Blindenstocks selbstständig in unterschiedlichen Kontexten zu bewegen.

finden, wenn alles zugeparkt ist?" drückt sie ihr Unverständnis für solche Aktionen aus.

Projekte solcher Natur ermöglichen es unter anderem, Schüler*innen zu Multiplikator*innen zu machen, die Menschen ihrer unmittelbaren Umgebung beeinflussen können und sie bei einer Fehlhandlung darauf aufmerksam machen. Die Aussagen Shirins und Leyans verdeutlichen das und bestätigen somit die nachhaltige Wirkung des Projekts in Form der Rolle der beiden als Multiplikatorinnen. Die Sprachlosigkeit von Shirins Eltern stützt die Annahme, sie hätten in diesem Moment Mitleid empfunden, waren aber zugleich von den eigenen Handlungen (falsches Parken) enttäuscht.

Ilena habe ebenfalls ein „schlechtes Gewissen, wenn sie unbewusst an der Bushaltestelle auf der Markierung für beeinträchtigte Menschen" stehenbleibt. Da fühle sie sich, als hätte „sie von jemandem etwas gestohlen." Das schlechte Gewissen in manchen Situationen lässt vermuten, dass sich bei Ilena das Mitgefühl für ihre Mitmenschen verstärkt hat, was sie mit den Worten ausdrückt, „auch im Bus ist es nicht anders. Ich traue mich nicht auf den Platz für beeinträchtige Menschen hinzusetzen, auch wenn der Bus mal fast leer fährt."

Vorurteile und Stereotype

Der Besuch des Blindenheims hat außerdem dazu beigetragen, Vorurteile und Stereotypen gegenüber Menschen mit Beeinträchtigungen abzubauen und die Sensibilität für die Vielfalt von Menschen und Lebensweisen zu erhöhen. Dies kann zu einem besseren Verständnis der Bedürfnisse und Perspektiven von Menschen mit Beeinträchtigung und somit zur Förderung von Empathie, (die lediglich die Fähigkeit zu Einnahme der Perspektive des Anderen beschreibt) und Mitgefühl (beinhaltet darüber hinaus die Bereitschaft sich für den Anderen zu engagieren und ihm zu helfen)[40] führen.

Dass Vorurteile in diesem Zusammenhang vorhanden sind, lässt sich Leyans Aussage entnehmen. Für sie sei der Besuch „eine schöne Erfahrung, weil wir vieles nicht wussten und ich glaube, das hat uns auch gezeigt, dass die Menschen dort mutig sind und eigentlich viel selber machen können, und ich glaube, wir haben sie unterschätzt." *Wir haben sie unterschätzt* deutet darauf hin, dass Leyan im Vorfeld die Einstellung hatte, Menschen mit Sehbeeinträchtigung seien nicht imstande, manchen Tätigkeiten selbstständig nachzugehen, sie seien sich selbst

---

40 Unterscheidung nach Nussbaum, in: NEULINGER, Michaela: Von der Verwundbarkeit zum Mitgefühl, in: DATTERL, Monika / GUGGENBERGER, Wilhelm / PAGANINI, Claudia (Hg): Glaube und Politik in einer pluralen Welt. theologische trends 27, innsbruck university press, 2017, 85.

überlassen und unfähig, die notwendigen Aufgaben ohne fremde Hilfe durchzuführen. Der Besuch hat ihre Einstellung verändert, was sie mit den Worten *die Menschen dort sind mutig* artikuliert.

Sind Vorurteile und Stereotype vorhanden, lässt sich Mitgefühl schwer entwickeln. Nicht selten verfällt der Mensch in die Rolle eines Helfers, was auf beiden Seiten zu Irritationen und zugleich zu einer Art von Unsicherheit führen kann. Aliyah bemerkte: „Wir Menschen urteilen viel zu schnell", was sich negativ auf das Zusammenleben auswirkt. Dass der Besuch des Blindenheims bei ihr Änderungen hervorgerufen hat und sie darauf aufmerksam geworden ist, drückt ihre Aussage aus, sie merke, „mittlerweile gibt es überall Blindenschrift, im Lift, Hotels, auf Verpackungen von einigen Lebensmittel. Sogar Lego hat eine Serie Legosteine mit Blindenschrift produziert."

Conclusio

Ein Besuch in einem Blindenheim kann als ein Projekt betrachtet werden, das die Entwicklung von Mitgefühl bei Schüler*innen nachhaltig fördert. Die Sensibilisierung, die sie im Rahmen des Besuchs erlangen, ermöglicht es ihnen, ihr Leben und ihre Fähigkeiten neu zu entdecken und zu schätzen. Hierbei handelt es sich um Gelegenheiten, die den Schüler*innen zeigen, wie sie durch ihre Handlungen und ihr Verhalten anderen Menschen Freude bereiten, ihnen helfen und somit einen positiven Beitrag zur gesellschaftlichen Entwicklung leisten.

Projekte dieser Art können für die Schüler*innen eine wertvolle Erfahrung sein, die ihnen die Gelegenheit gibt, Menschen kennenzulernen, die anders sind als sie selbst, und Einblicke in das Leben von Menschen mit Beeinträchtigungen zu gewinnen. Sie können ferner eine Gelegenheit sein, Empathie und Mitgefühl zu entwickeln und ein Verständnis dafür zu bekommen, wie Menschen mit Beeinträchtigungen leben und wie sie unterstützt werden können. Darüber hinaus können sie dazu beitragen, Vorurteile und Stereotype abzubauen und zu einem besseren Verständnis der Bedürfnisse und Herausforderungen bedürftiger Menschen zu gelangen.

Derartige Projekte haben weitere Potenziale, beispielsweise, dass die Schüler*innen lernen, Menschen mit oder ohne Beeinträchtigung zu achten und zu respektieren. Sie entwickeln Empathie und Mitgefühl. Durch die Teilnahme an solchen Projekten erfahren die Schüler*innen ein Gefühl der Gemeinschaft und Zusammenarbeit, das es ihnen erlaubt, ihre sozialen und emotionalen Fähigkeiten zu verbessern, indem sie lernen, wie man anderen hilft und miteinander interagiert. Während des Besuchs lernen die Schüler*innen etwas über die Lebensbedingungen von Menschen mit Beeinträchtigungen und wie sie sie mit ihren Fähigkeiten und Ressourcen unterstützen können.

Insgesamt kann der Besuch eines Blindenheims oder einer ähnlichen Institution ein sinnvolles Projekt sein, um die Entwicklung von Barmherzigkeit bei Schüler*innen zu fördern. Hierbei müssen aber im Vorfeld eine angemessene Planung und Vorbereitung gewährleistet sein, um sicherzustellen, dass die Begegnung und der Besuch für alle Beteiligten positiv und respektvoll verlaufen. Wichtig ist es, dass der Besuch in einer sensiblen und respektvollen Weise erfolgt und die Bewohner*innen der Einrichtung ihre Einwilligung geben, die Schüler*innen eine angemessene Vorbereitung erhalten, um sicherzustellen, dass sie sich respektvoll und einfühlsam verhalten und die Privatsphäre und Würde der Bewohner*innen respektieren.

Wichtig bei der Organisation solcher Projekte ist es, die Schüler*innen nicht nur auf den Besuch vorzubereiten, sondern auch auf die Erfahrung danach. Die Beeinträchtigung der Menschen kann sie womöglich emotional belasten, daher ist es bedeutsam, auch diesen Aspekt mit ihnen im Unterricht zu behandeln und sie darauf vorbereiten.

Solche Projekte erlauben es, statt eines einmaligen Besuchs eine langfristige Partnerschaft zwischen der Schule und dem Blindenheim aufzubauen. Dies bedeutet, dass die Schüler*innen regelmäßige Besuche abstatten und sich an Aktivitäten beteiligen, die den Bewohner*innen des Blindenheims zugutekommen. Die Schüler*innen können helfen, diese Aktivitäten und Projekte zu planen und durchzuführen, und dabei lernen, wie man Barmherzigkeit in die Tat umsetzt. Indem die Schüler*innen auf diese Weise in ein Projekt eingebunden werden, können sie Barmherzigkeit nachhaltig entwickeln und lernen, wie sie Verantwortung für ihr Handeln übernehmen und einen positiven Beitrag zur Gesellschaft leisten. Dies würde nicht nur zur Nachhaltigkeit der Entwicklung von Barmherzigkeit beitragen, sondern auch zur Entwicklung einer aktiven Bürger*innenbeteiligung und sozialen Verantwortung.

Literaturangaben

BADAWIA, Tarik: Gewissheitsparadoxie. Eine antinomische Struktur des Lehrerhandelns im islamischen Religionsunterricht, in: SARIKAYA, Yaşar / AYGÜN, Adem (Hg.): Islamische Religionspädagogik. Leitfragen aus Theorie, Empirie und Praxis Münster/New York: Waxman, 2019. 109–125.

BOWLBY, John: Über das Wesen der Mutter-Kind-Bindung, in: Psyche 13 (1958), 415–456.

BUBENHEIM, Abdullāh aṣ-Ṣāmit Frank / ELYAS, Nadeem Ata: Der edle Qur'ān und die Übersetzung seiner Bedeutungen in die deutsche Sprache. al-Madīna al-Munauwara, König-Fahd-Kom-plex zum Druck vom Qurʾān, [2]2004.

DOMSEL, Maike Maria: Zwischen Vulnerabilität und Resilienz. Christliche und muslimische Religionslehrer*innen im Umgang mit dem Krisenhaften, in: ÖRF 30(2), 2022, 72–90. DOI: 10.25364/10.30:2022.2.5.

EMMERICH, Marcus: Differenz und Differenzierung im Bildungssystem. Schulische Grammatik der Inklusion/Exklusion, in: Zeitschrift für Pädagogik 62 (2016), 42–57.

GILBERT, Paul / CHODEN: Achtsames Mitgefühl. Ein kraftvoller Weg, das Leben zu verwandeln, Freiburg in Breisgau: Arbor Verlag, 2014.

ḤAMMĀDĪ, ʿAlī Muḥammad al-Shurafāʾ: Message of Islam: Compassion, Justice, Freedom and Peace, Toronto: Scansom Publishers, 2017.

INTERNATIONAL JOURNAL OF THE MALAY WORLD AND CIVILISATION (Iman) 4(2), 2016, 103–110. http://dx.doi.org/10.17576/IMAN-2016-0402-10 [abgerufen am 08.03.2023].

KULD, Lothar / GÖNNHEIMER, Stefan: Compassion – Sozialverpflichtetes Lernen und Handeln, Stuttgart/Berlin/Köln: Kohlhammer, 2000.

MAAYAN, Davidov / ZAHN-WAXLER, Carolyn / ROTH-HANANIA, Ronit / KNAFO, Ariel: Concern for Others in the First Year of Life. Theory, Evidence, and Avenues for Research. The Society for Research in Child Development 7(2), 2013: 126–131.

MCMURTRY, David: Compassion in Education, in: Pädagogik der Achtsamkeit. Abrufbar unter: https://bit.ly/3ZHb3jW [abgerufen am 07.03.2023].

MEMIĆ, Jakub / HADŽIĆ, Mehmedalija (Hg.): Izbor Poslanikovih hadisa. Starješinstvo islamske zajednice Bosne i Hercegovine, Hrvatske i Slovenije, Sarajevo, 1985.

MIERZWA, Roland: Compassion – Zwischen Mit-Leid, Mitgefühl und Barmherzigkeit, Hamburg: Verlag Dr. Kovač, 2014.

MÜLLER, Rabeya: Behinderung und Integration im Islam, in: PITHAN, Annabele / ADAM, Gottfried / KOLLMANN, Roland et al. (Hg.): Handbuch integrative Religionspädagogik – Reflexionen und Impulse für Gesellschaft, Schule und Gemeinde (Veröffentlichung des Comenius-Instituts), Gütersloh 2002, 184–188.

NEULINGER, Michaela: Von der Verwundbarkeit zum Mitgefühl, in: DATTERL, Monika / GUGGENBERGER, Wilhelm / PAGANINI, Claudia (Hg): Glaube und Politik in einer pluralen Welt. theologische trends 27, innsbruck university press 2017, 73–91.

NIKO - Der blinde Tiktoker erobert Internet, in: https://www.youtube.com/watch?v=lShFO-1V8VU [abgerufen am 11.03.2023].

OLK, Matthias: Inklusion und islamischer Religionsunterricht, in: SARIKAYA, Yasar / ERMERT, Dorothea / ÖGER-TUNC, Esma (Hg.): Islamische Religionspädagoghik. didaktische Ansätze für die Praxis, Münster/New York: Waxman, 2019.

ORGANISATION FÜR WIRTSCHAFTLICHE ZUSAMMENARBEIT UND ENTWICKLUNG (OECD): Skills for Social Progress. The Power of Social and Emotional Skills, Paris, 2015. Veröffentlicht in der OECD I Library. Abrufbar unter: http://dx.doi.org/ 10.1787/9789264226159-en [abgerufen am 07.03.2023].

SCHLOßBERGER, Matthias: Das Mitgefühl als Gefühl, in: BERMES, Christian / HENCKMANN, Wolfhart / LEONARDY, Heinz (Hg.): Vernunft und Gefühl. Schelers Phänomenologie des emotionalen Lebens, Würzburg: Königshausen & Neumann, 2003, 39–51.

SHAH-KAZEMI, Reza: My Mercy Encompasses All. The Qur'an's Teachings on Compassion, Peace and Love, Berkely: Catapult, 2007.

SINGER, Tania / BOLZ, Matthias (Hg.): Mitgefühl, in Alltag und Forschung, München: Max-Planck-Gesellschaft. Online unter: www.compassion-training.org/?lang=de [abgerufen am 07.03.2023].

ULRICH, Dieter / KIENBAUM, Jutta / VOLLAND, Cordelia: Empathie mit anderen entwickeln. Wie entwickelt sich Mitgefühl, in: VON SALISCH, Maria (Hg.): Emotionale Kompetenz entwickeln. Grundlagen in Kindheit und Jugend, Stuttgart: Kohlhammer, 2002, 111–135.

World Health Organization: A Snapshot of the Health of Young People in Europe. Brussels, 2009. A report prepared for the European Commission Conference on Youth Health. Brussels, Belgium 9-10 July 2009.

Autor*innen

Prof.in Dr.in Janieta Bartz, Professorin für Behindertenpädagogik / Disability Studies an der Hochschule Düsseldorf.

Apl. Prof.in Kathleen M. Clark, Außerordentliche Professorin für Krankenpflege und Geschäftsführerin der Augsburg Health Commons, Augsburg University, Minneapolis, USA.

PD. Dr.in Maike Maria Domsel, Privatdozentin für Religionspädagogik an der Universität Bonn und Lehrerin für Katholische Religionslehre und Französisch am Ernst-Moritz-Arndt-Gymnasium Bonn.

Mag. DDr. Christian Feichtinger M.A. M.A., Senior Lecturer und Universitätsassistent am Institut für Katechetik und Religionspädagogik an der Karl-Franzens-Universität Graz.

Dr.in Nina Frenzel, Schulrätin für Gymnasien und theologische Grundsatzfragen der Schulabteilung des Erzbistums Köln.

Jennifer Jakob M.A. M.Sc., Hochschullehrende für Evangelische Religionspädagogik an der Kirchlichen Pädagogischen Hochschule Wien/Krems.

Dr.in Annika Krahn, Lektorin für Religionspädagogik am Institut für Evangelische Theologie der Universität zu Köln.

Prof. Dr. Lothar Kuld, Professor für Katholische Theologie und Religions-pädagogik an der Pädagogischen Hochschule Weingarten.

Dr.in Mevlida Mešanović Mag. Phil. PhD, Postdoc im Bereich Religionspädagogik an der Katholisch-Theologischen Fakultät der Universität Graz, mit dem Arbeitsschwerpunkt der islamischen Religionspädagogik.

Prof. Dr. Peter Rahmers, 2001-2019 Professor für Religionswissenschaft und Philosophie an der Phil.-Theol. Hochschule SVD St. Augustin, 2004–2019 Prorektor und Rektor der Fakultät. Seit 2021 Honorarprofessor für Religionswissenschaft und Interkulturelle Philosophie an der Vinzenz Pallotti University, Vallendar.

Prof. Dr. Bert Roebben, Professor für Religionspädagogik und Leiter des Seminars für Religionspädagogik der Katholisch-Theologischen Fakultät der Rheinischen Friedrich-Wilhelms-Universität Bonn.

Prof. Dr. Martin Rothgangel, Professor für Religionspädagogik an der Evangelisch-Theologischen Fakultät sowie des Zentrums für Lehrer*innenbildung der Universität Wien.

Prof. Alexander Rödlach PhD SVD, Professor für medizinische Anthropologie, Creighton University, Omaha, USA.

Prof. Dr. Willem Marie Speelmann OFS, Professor für franziskanische Spiritualität, Theologie und Geschichte an der Universität Tilburg (NL) und Direktor des Franciscaans Studiecentrum (Franziskanisches Studienzentrum).

Christina Steffens M.Ed., Lehrerin an der Bischöflichen Maria-Montessori-Gesamtschule Krefeld für die Fächer Katholische Theologie und Deutsch, Fachkraft für Montessorikpädagogik in der Sekundarstufe der DMV.

Maurice Steffens, geb. Andree M.Ed., Lehrer an der Bischöflichen Maria-Montessori-Gesamtschule Krefeld für die Fächer Katholische Theologie, Geschichte und Pädagogik, Doktorand am Seminar für Religionspädagogik (Prof. Roebben)

Lukas Wiesenhütter Mag. Theol. M.A., Wissenschaftlicher Mitarbeiter am Lehrstuhl für Systematische Theologie unter besonderer Berücksichtigung gesellschaftlicher Herausforderungen der Universität Bonn.

Prof. Dr. Asfa Widiyanto, Professor für islamisches Denken an der State Islamic University (UIN) Salatiga, Indonesien.

Daniela Zahneisen M.Ed., Doktorandin und wissenschaftliche Mitarbeiterin am Institut für Evangelische Theologie an der Rheinland-Pfälzischen Technischen Universität Kaiserslautern-Landau/Standort Landau mit dem Schwerpunkt Religionspädagogik; Stipendiatin der Barbara-Schadeberg-Stiftung e.V.